Mortal Wounds

Mortal Wounds

The Human Skeleton as Evidence for Conflict in the Past

Martin Smith

Pen & Sword
MILITARY

First published in Great Britain in 2017 by
PEN & SWORD MILITARY
An imprint of
Pen & Sword Books Ltd
47 Church Street
Barnsley
South Yorkshire
S70 2AS

ISBN 978-1-47382-318-1

Typeset by Concept, Huddersfield HD4 5JL.
Printed and bound in England by CPI Group (UK) Ltd, Croydon, CR0 4YY.

Pen & Sword Books Ltd incorporates the imprints of Pen & Sword Archaeology, Atlas, Aviation, Battleground, Discovery, Family History, History, Maritime, Military, Naval, Politics, Railways, Select, Social History, Transport, True Crime, and Claymore Press, Frontline Books, Leo Cooper, Praetorian Press, Remember When, Seaforth Publishing and Wharncliffe.

For a complete list of Pen & Sword titles please contact
PEN & SWORD BOOKS LIMITED
47 Church Street, Barnsley, South Yorkshire, S70 2AS, England
E-mail: enquiries@pen-and-sword.co.uk
Website: www.pen-and-sword.co.uk

Contents

Acknowledgements vi

Introduction viii

1. 'I See Dead People': The Human Body as Archaeology 1

2. The Fragile Body: Recognizing Injuries to the Skeleton 12

3. The Earliest Times: Violence in the Deep Past 31

4. Rolling Back the Temporal Frontier: Modern Humans and the
   Origins of War? 50

5. Out from the Cold: Mesolithic Hostilities? 69

6. 'The Children of Cain': Conflict in the Neolithic 85

7. Cutting-Edge Technology: Violence in Bronze Age Europe 105

8. Out of the Shadows: The End of Prehistory 129

9. Imperial Anger: Violence under Roman Rule 157

10. 'The Judgement of God': Violence in Early Medieval England . . . 184

11. 'The True Son of Gentle Blood': The High Middle Ages to the
    Renaissance 201

12. The Shock of the New: The Changing Face of Violence 221

Conclusion 244

Notes 249

Bibliography 269

Index 286

Acknowledgements

I am indebted to a range of people who have kindly shared their time, expertise and enthusiasm, including academic and professional colleagues as well as a number of my students. Firstly, I would like to thank John Gale for sharing his expert knowledge of prehistoric arrowheads. Thanks also to John Stewart for his comments on the Palaeolithic. I am very grateful to Martin Green for allowing access and providing insights regarding the skeleton from Sovell Down and for allowing the use of the respective photographs and drawings. I would also like to thank Jackie McKinley for kindly sending her original report on the Sovell Down skeleton and for details and references regarding recently examined and forthcoming Bronze Age burials. I greatly appreciate the ever-dependable Iain Hewitt giving up his time to help with image scanning. Many thanks to Stephany Leach for giving permission to use the image of the Feizor Nick skeleton and to Rebecca Redfern for kindly sharing her images of the Tormarton remains. I am grateful to Jonathan Baines for demographic observations of the Winterbourne Kingston skeleton (10053/52) and to Miles Russell for supplying the photographs of the Chesil mirror. Many thanks to Mike Bishop for sharing his opinions on the embedded spearhead (previously regarded as a ballista bolt) from Maiden Castle. I am very grateful to Niomi Edwards for permitting use of her images of human remains from Danebury. Thanks also to Stephen Macaulay, Oxford Archaeology East, for permission to use the image showing the excavated areas at War Ditches, Cambridge and to Sharon Gerber-Parfitt and the Royal Archaeological Institute for kindly permitting reproduction of images from the Sutton Walls excavation. I am very grateful to Ejvind Hertz, Museum Inspektor, Skanderborg Museum, Denmark, for providing photos of the Alken Enge mass grave excavation. Many thanks to Richard Breward, Dorset County Museum, for giving up yet more of his time in caring for the collections and facilitating access to Skeleton Q1 from Maiden Castle. I would also like to thank Claire Pinder, Dorset County Council, for supplying the aerial photograph of Maiden Castle. Many thanks to Mary Lewis for kindly sharing the images of the man from Hulton Abbey, and to Henry Chapman for granting permission to use images from St Martin's in the Bull Ring on behalf of Birmingham Archaeology. I would also like to thank Tim Clarke of the National Museum of Health and Medicine, Springfield, Maryland, for granting permission to use images of human remains from the American Civil War. Thanks also to Nicholas Hall of the Royal Armouries, Fort Nelson, for lending his technical knowledge and practical help assisting with experimental firing of artillery. Finally, I am very grateful to Philip Sidnell at Pen & Sword for his support and enthusiasm and particularly for his unending patience.

Much of this book and the ideas presented in it rest firmly on the achievements of others who are masters of specific periods or particular kinds of analysis and without whose published insights I would have struggled considerably. Having said this, any errors in the text are entirely my own.

Introduction:
'The Best Available Evidence'

Human remains, most frequently reduced just to preserved bones, are among the most common categories of buried evidence that survives from the past. It is impossible to spend much time undertaking archaeological excavation without encountering human burials. But at the same time human skeletons enjoy a special status that makes them distinct from other kinds of material which might be excavated. Whilst archaeologists commonly reconstruct the past from studying the objects people used, the structures they lived in or the landscapes they moved around on, these are all essentially 'secondary' evidence from which the experiences and actions of the respective people are inferred. Human skeletons are different in that they *are* the people of the past, or at least what remains of them, and so constitute a much more direct form of evidence that in many ways is less ambiguous and often more poignant. Whilst we are alive bone is not a static, 'dead' material that simply maintains its form and gives our bodies leverage and underlying rigidity, rather it is a dynamic, living tissue that undergoes a range of continuous changes. The events and experiences that human beings go through during their lives become encoded in the skeleton in a variety of ways that leave the bones as a sort of document waiting to tell the story of an individual's life to anyone with the skills and patience to read it. In this respect human remains are not only one of the most common forms of archaeological evidence, but also arguably the richest in terms of the amount they can tell us. Whatever measure is applied (physical volume, number of bones, number of individuals and so on) more information about the past can be extracted from a given quantity of human bone than from a comparable amount of any other type of archaeological material.

This quality of human remains is particularly relevant to investigations of past violence and conflict, where several lines of evidence exist but each is fraught with problems. Whilst historical sources in the form of the written documents that survive from a given period might seem the most reliable form of evidence, these are limited by the biases of the people who wrote them and are frequently incomplete. On top of this come problems of interpretation, with scholars commonly disagreeing as to what ancient or Medieval authors actually meant. Furthermore, for most of the time human beings have existed there simply are no written records. If the principal form of evidence used to try to understand violence and conflict in earlier times is written documents, then such voices from the past inevitably fall silent before the invention of writing. Such silence has until quite recently lead people to assume that wars did not exist before recorded history. In the absence of written sources, past events and behaviours can only be detected by the physical traces they have left. As regards human conflict there are three types of physical evidence that can provide signs of violence[1] in the past, weapons, defences and injuries apparent in human remains. On one hand the discovery of objects with clear use as weapons might seem an obvious indicator of violent times during a given period. However, such interpretations are complicated by the issue that such items may have been as much symbols of wealth and status as items intended for actual fighting, leaving questions open as to how much use they might have actually seen. Fortifications might seem to be clearer signs of conflict, on the basis that if people were building defences they must have been expecting to be attacked. However, these too have been challenged on the basis of similarly being 'built to impress'. As with weapons and armour, such structures may have functioned as statements of power and authority on an even bigger scale, whether they are Iron Age forts or Medieval castles, and therefore fail to resolve the question of how much actual conflict there might have been in a given period. Here the quality of bone to 'record' events comes to the fore as human skeletons bearing signs of injury consistent with deliberate assaults are arguably the only unmistakeable indicator of the existence of hostilities between people in the past.

Recent years have seen considerable improvements in our understanding of the ways bone breaks in different circumstances and in the recognition of traumatic injuries that occurred around the time of an individual's death. These developments have enabled Biological Anthropology (the field specializing in the study of skeletal remains) to make a major contribution to the relatively new but growing field of Conflict Archaeology. This area of study concentrates on the physical traces left by human hostilities to address questions that often cannot be answered using historical accounts. Such traces commonly include the landscapes people fought over as well as the objects and structures they used, but increasingly also the actual remains of those involved in the fighting. Old collections of human bone have been re-examined whilst new ones have been uncovered, with both strands revealing a wealth (if that is the right word) of evidence for an often violent past. This book therefore comes at an exciting time as it is able to draw upon an important range of cutting-edge research and often high-profile discoveries in this rapidly-advancing field which deserves to be drawn together and presented in a form that is accessible to the general reader. In fact, far too much evidence for past conflict is now apparent to do justice to, or even mention all of, in a single volume and so instead attention has been given throughout to particular case studies of individuals or groups of human remains that exemplify the time and place in which they lived/died and the nature of the conflict they might have been involved in. However, whilst the majority of such evidence takes the form of wounds inflicted upon the skeleton, this book is not intended to simply form a somewhat depressing list of terrible injuries. Instead it explores what this important category of evidence can tell us about the changing face of violence and conflict on one hand, but also of change in human societies in general over thousands of years. Particular issues that are highlighted and explored include the evidence for ritualized violence, the treatment of defeated enemies and non-combatants, the role of war in social change and the demography of conflict, i.e. who was involved – aristocratic 'heroes' or the common person? In addition to such questions the ability to recognize signs of violence in archaeological human remains also raises more fundamental questions including how old is human violence? When can we first recognize 'war' as opposed to violent disputes fought between individuals? The answers to such questions then lead on to the even more significant question of what the relationship is between violence, warfare and human nature.

In terms of coverage some parts of the world and some periods are better represented in this book than others. Perhaps unsurprisingly, examples of skeletal trauma from Europe are known from the archaeological record for nearly all periods. This is more an effect of an issue commonly seen in archaeology than a real phenomenon. Rather than signifying that Europeans have been any more unpleasant and warlike than anyone else, what this really illustrates is where there has previously been the greatest concentration of archaeologists and anthropologists with an interest in such issues. In further reflection of this issue and also my own background, a great many of the examples given are from Britain, but again this shouldn't be taken to indicate that I regard the British Isles as in any way special or different in this respect and an author from elsewhere would be similarly free to cite examples from their own experience. For various reasons, cultural, political and practical, the archaeological and anthropological records of many other regions have been less well explored and less comprehensively published but this is not to suggest that ultimately these areas are likely to contain any less evidence for past hostilities (or any more for that matter) when they come to be more fully investigated in the future.

A criticism that is sometimes levelled at archaeology is that it tends to concentrate on the small things – pots, pits, post holes and so on, individual cuts into the ground and bits of debris left by individual people on a given spot one day sometime around the year 'X'. At the level of each excavated site this view actually has a fair degree of truth to it. However, just as with the study of history, the individual building blocks of archaeological evidence have equal power to reveal a bigger picture when considered together and viewed on a wider level. Returning to the question of the relationship between violence and human nature, this is an example of just such a 'big question', in fact arguably one of the biggest questions we can ask about ourselves and one that has run throughout archaeological studies of conflict in recent years. This debate has often been characterized as swinging between polarized views, commonly associated respectively with the (allegedly) sentimental Swiss-born philosopher Jean-Jacques Rousseau (1712–78) and the rather dour English political thinker Thomas Hobbes (1588–1679). Such views hinge on taking a position on whether we have 'fallen from grace' and things have got progressively worse over time, as Rousseau would have it, or whether we have emerged from a barbaric and chaotic past to a more peaceful era of civilization and security, which is the way Hobbes saw things. Those in the 'Rousseauian' camp operate from the basic assumption that humans are by nature closer to 'Noble Savages'[2] being essentially peaceful and only recently corrupted by wealth and civilization. The opposing viewpoint accords with Hobbes' notion that we have we come out of a prehistoric past where life was 'nasty, brutish and short'[3] to a situation where things have improved and we can look forward to a less violent future. In reality the answer is likely to sit somewhere in between these two positions, and one of the objectives of this book is to explore where that point should lie.

As a growing number of human skeletal specialists have become interested in exploring what human remains can contribute to our views of past hostilities, an expanding body of literature has appeared in recent years, written by and for those with expertise in this field. As is so often the case with academic literature, many of these works present difficult and sometimes rather dry reading for the non-specialist, despite often being high-quality publications on their own terms. By contrast the current book has been written with the intention of providing an introduction to this field and an overview of the current state of the subject that is accessible to a varied range of general readers. In particular it is hoped that this book will be of interest to military history enthusiasts of a range of periods as well as the reader of popular archaeology by presenting a category of evidence that is rarely published in a form accessible to general readers. This volume may also be of use to undergraduate university students as an introduction to the study of conflict through the medium of the human skeleton and I have provided notes to further references throughout for the benefit of those who wish to pursue the issues discussed on a more scholarly basis. Where possible I have cited sources that exist in print as there are no guarantees as to how long material published on the Web will be available.

Archaeologists, historians, palaeoanthropologists or anyone else for that matter cannot look directly into the past. The past is gone, we cannot see it, we cannot visit it, ultimately the only thing we can do is imagine it. However, by 'imagine' I do not simply mean 'make it up', but rather that our views of the past are mental models which we build on the basis of the evidence available. We do this guided by the principle that if it isn't in keeping with the evidence we have, then our model (or aspects of it) must be wrong and therefore needs to be revised. As mentioned previously, when constructing such models of the human past one of the most consistent and frequently occurring categories of evidence is what remains of past people themselves. Most categories of evidence for past human activity are a rather hit-and-miss affair. There are by definition times when any given technology hadn't yet been developed, periods and places for which documentary sources are lacking and times when particular types of social organization were absent. The only truly consistent and unbroken strand of evidence running from before the first appearance of humans to our own time is the remains of the people about whose lives we might be inquiring. Often such skeletal remains may be incomplete, fragmentary and poorly preserved, but no more so and often a lot less than for any other type of evidence.

Whilst some readers may be very familiar with human bones and what they can tell us, as stated previously this group is not the main audience for which this book is intended. Consequently, Chapters 1 and 2 function to present the 'nuts and bolts' from which the material covered in the rest of the book is constructed, in order to make it more accessible and to clarify how anthropologists are able to make the claims they do regarding human remains. Chapter 1 provides an introduction to the human skeleton and what we can learn from it, whilst Chapter 2 gives an explanation of the principles and properties which govern the way bones break and how we can interpret signs of past injuries. To borrow a phrase from the geneticist Matt Ridley, in a way these two chapters are a bit like needing to eat one's greens before moving on to dessert in the (hopefully) more enjoyable parts of the book. Those who have already 'eaten their veg' and have prior knowledge of the human skeleton in archaeology and more precisely how past injuries might be recognized, may well therefore choose to skip these chapters and head directly to Chapter 3 and beyond where the evidence for human hostilities over time as told by the remains of past people is considered.

In attempting to tell the 'story' of violence in a broad sweep, various approaches are possible. The evidence presented here could be grouped together in all manner of ways according to a wide variety of possible themes, such as types of weapons involved, different parts of the skeleton affected, the status of those inflicting or receiving injuries (warriors, civilians, slaves, children etc.) or the circumstances in which such acts took place (tribal raiding, formal battles between armies, state punishments/executions, domestic violence and so on). Whilst any of these options could work equally well on their own terms, such approaches of grouping the evidence from different times and places by category would have the drawback of making the overall thread of different developments over time very difficult to pick out. Consequently, I have opted for a straightforward chronological approach in order to make the elements of continuity and contrast more clear during the progression from our earliest human ancestors to the threshold of the modern world. The sort of terms then used throughout the book to denote particular periods 'Mesolithic, Neolithic, Bronze Age' and so on, originated in the attempts of nineteenth-century archaeologists to make sense of what were then unknown periods of time stretching back before written history. With the modern benefit of a raft of scientific dating methods and the recognition of a much wider range of material evidence of past ways of life than was available to early archaeologists, such terms are arguably no longer necessary. Moreover, we now regard all manner of things as more important in defining the ways human societies have developed than simply what sort of tools people were using. However, these terms do remain useful, even among archaeologists, as a kind of shorthand for broad time periods. Just as no one in the later Middle Ages woke up one day saying 'Good Lord, it's the Renaissance!' similarly nobody ever went to bed in the Bronze Age only to find that the Iron Age had begun the next morning. Archaeological periods overlap each other both in time and space and are essentially nothing more than artificial constructs that help archaeologists to think and communicate with each other and so have been retained here on the basis that however unfashionable, they will be equally helpful to the reader (especially those less familiar with prehistory).[4]

A casual reader new to osteoarchaeological literature or someone coming to the subject through television documentaries could be forgiven for thinking that the past was populated by animated skeletons. Here I have tried to keep the focus on the once-living people these now dry bones represent and to consider the human experience of such injuries by emphasizing their effects on living individuals. I have tried to strike a balance between selecting particular examples that convey the types of injuries and violent acts we are able to recognize, and taking a wider perspective to look at the bigger picture in any given period. In some places and times larger samples are available and more of a 'hard' statistical approach is possible. For other times and regions sufficient numbers of burials have yet to be excavated, or sufficient statistical research has yet to be conducted to pull all the numbers of examples together. In such cases a more cautious approach is necessary but this needn't mean that nothing meaningful can be said. We should also bear in mind that whilst injuries to the skeleton can identify the victims of violence, they do not tell us so much about the perpetrators. Throughout human history the majority of acts of violence are likely to have been carried out by men, and younger men in particular. There are well-considered evolutionary explanations for this pattern and in general we can reasonably assume that this was the case far back into our ancestral past. However, this need not mean that violent actions should be viewed as an exclusively male domain. Examples are known from a range of historical sources and observations of living societies in which women have taken various roles in warfare ranging from the exhortation and encouragement of men to take part in fighting, to the torture of prisoners and to active combat roles as warriors themselves, although this latter has tended to be the exception rather than the rule in most societies.[5]

Lastly, there is in fact so much evidence for past violence now available to us that it might be easy to become desensitized to the reality of the events such evidence derives from, or to overlook the actual people now represented by dry bones and even drier statistics when discussing numbers of examples. In this respect it is worth stating clearly that every individual case mentioned in this book represents a fellow human being who suffered at the hands of another, whether they were a Bronze Age 'hero' fighting his last challenger, a Mesolithic hunter who had strayed into the wrong territory, or a frightened Iron Age child huddled with her mother behind the walls of a hillfort, and this is a point that we should never lose sight of.

Chapter 1

'I See Dead People': The Human Body as Archaeology

Whilst in most circumstances the majority of the body is doomed to decompose and effectively disappear relatively soon after death, if the conditions are right the hard tissues of the body (bones and teeth) can survive in a recognizable state for hundreds or thousands of years. Consequently, the skeletal remains of humans and animals are among the most common forms of material evidence encountered by archaeologists. The current chapter is intended to give an overview and general introduction to the ways in which skeletal remains are investigated and the kinds of information that can be gleaned from them. In reality this is a vast subject, with a huge and ever-growing array of published literature. For those wishing to take further interest in the wider subject of biological anthropology a range of suggested texts is given in the Bibliography at the end of this book.

The Nature of Bone

As mentioned in the preceding chapter, bone is not an unchanging, immutable material that stays as it first forms in the body until (and after) death. Rather it is a living tissue supplied by blood vessels and nerves and continually serviced by an army of specialized cells that build additional bone where it is needed and remove or reabsorb it to use the respective minerals elsewhere in the body where it is not. Like other body systems the skeleton is therefore subject to 'tissue turnover', a process where just like skin or muscle, bone is continually renewed and remodelled to suit the demands placed on it. This process is the basis of a key principle in human osteology known as 'Wolff's Law of Transformation',[1] after Julius Wolff (1836–1902) a German orthopaedic surgeon, attributed with first formally describing it in 1892. This observation states that bone will respond to the biological and mechanical stresses that are placed upon it over time, with the body investing resources in preserving and strengthening parts of the skeleton that are subject to the greatest stress. Consequently it is possible to distinguish the skeleton of a committed bodybuilder from that of a habitual couch potato in terms of differing bone density and in the size and ruggedness of points of muscle

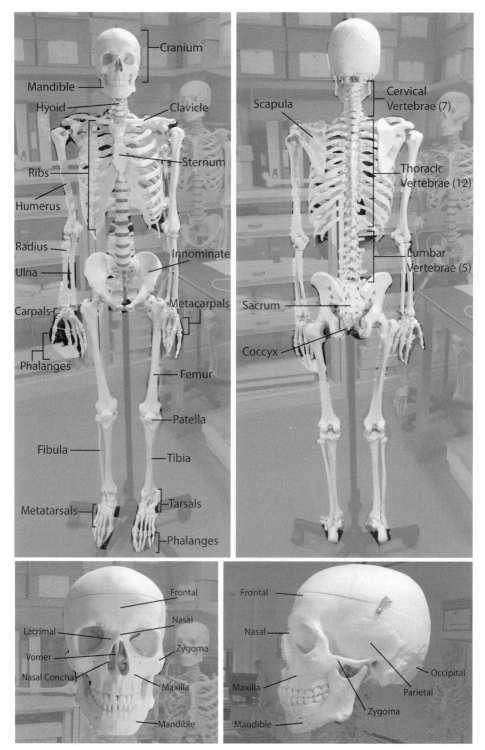

Figure 1.1. The principal bones of the human skeleton.

attachment where additional bone will have incrementally built up in the former but not the latter.

Whilst bone appears to be a solid, off-white, homogeneous material when viewed with the naked eye (Fig. 1.1), at a microscopic level it is in fact a composite material with a fairly complex structure. This is formed of a combination of mineral (mainly calcium) crystals and organic (protein) fibres interwoven in a mutually supporting structure. Twisted fibres of the protein collagen (approx. 5μm or 0.005mm thick) are interlinked in this structure to form a sort of scaffolding into which crystals of a specific form of calcium (called hydoxyapatite) are embedded (Fig. 1.2). These two elements of bone each lend different qualities which combine to give skeletal tissues the important and special properties of being very strong in relation to weight whilst also being resistant to breakage. The calcium crystals confer hardness and rigidity to the bone whilst the collagen fibrils lend it lightness and also

Figure 1.2. Human bone shown at various levels from the whole skeletal system (a) and whole bones (b) to the complex microstructure of bone (c–e) down to the level of individual fibres of protein (collagen) that give resilience and a degree of flexibility, interlaced with regular-shaped calcium crystals which give bone its hardness and rigidity (f and g).

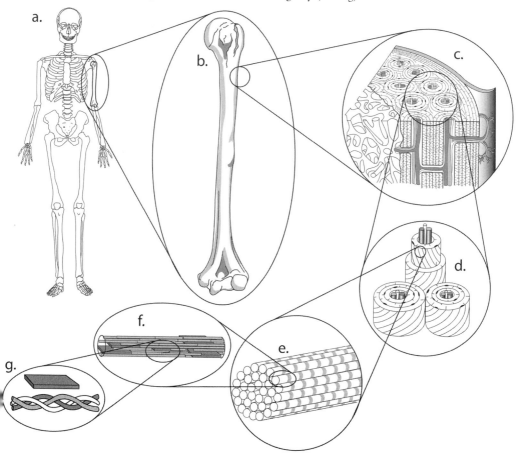

resistance to breakage by allowing bone to deform and bend slightly rather than being an entirely brittle material that would simply snap too easily to have been useful to our evolutionary ancestors. It has been noted before that the human skeleton is about as strong as steel but is in fact five times lighter as a consequence of this composite structure.[2]

Bone Survival

As mentioned in the opening lines of this book human burials are one of the most common forms of evidence encountered in archaeological excavations, but this is not to say that bones are always preserved equally well. Survival of bone over time in the ground is dependent on a range of conditions and is in fact very variable. After death bone is subject to attack from a range of environmental sources, which can include dehydration, cracking and disintegration of surfaces caused by the sun's radiation and erosion by wind and rain if exposed above ground. Bone also attracts the attentions of various living organisms ranging from scavenging by animals, to mechanical and chemical destruction by plant roots, and digestion at a microscopic level by bacteria. Further to this, bone can be subject to chemical destruction in the form of being gradually eroded and dissolved by ground water percolating through it in addition to dissolution by contact with the surrounding earth in areas where the soil is acidic. This last factor is arguably of greatest consequence in effectively removing all but the faintest traces of bone, sometimes in just a couple of centuries. In 'acidic' areas where the soil pH level is hostile to preservation, excavators may find a clearly discernible grave cut containing items buried with the deceased (pottery, metalwork and so on) surviving to be recovered, but nothing remaining of the body except perhaps a smear of discoloured soil. In areas where the geology is more alkaline, bone preservation can often be extremely good over hundreds or thousands of years, but even then the portion of the bone that survives is generally the mineral part with the organic (protein) component decomposing in the ground relatively soon after burial. This latter issue has important implications for the recognition of injuries to the skeleton which are discussed in the following chapter. In rare circumstances other body tissues may also preserve over long periods. Such preservation of soft (as opposed to hard) tissues or 'natural mummification' usually involves some sort of extreme environment. This can be extreme cold as in the glacier that preserved the famous Neolithic 'Ice man',[3] heat and aridity as in the desert-edge burials of Predynastic Egypt or wetness as in the bodies recovered from peat bogs in Northern Europe preserved by this dark and oxygen-starved environment which inhibits the bacteria that would normally cause the body to decay.

Other issues affecting bone survival relate to the conscious actions of the living rather than natural processes. The way in which a society treats its dead can have considerable impact on the extent to which their remains have potential to survive to later be discovered, either accidentally or through deliberate excavation. For example, deeper burials tend to survive better than shallower ones as they are less susceptible to damage by erosion and ploughing, also soil tends to contain less bacteria and invertebrate activity as depth increases. Cremation is obviously unhelpful to the anthropologist but not to the extent popularly believed. Rather than reducing the body to 'ashes' as is often thought, burning a body either on a pyre or in a modern crematorium oven produces skeletal remains that are discoloured and fragmented but nonetheless recognizable to an anthropologist and it is often possible to extract a considerable amount of information from them. Furthermore, the process of burning at high temperatures causes the calcium crystals in bone to fuse together, similar to the way clay in a pottery kiln 'vitrifies' at higher temperatures. This has the effect of making the surviving bone largely impervious to chemical attacks in acid soils and often the only buried bone that will survive in such regions is where the body has been cremated.[4]

It is often said that the way we treat our dead in the twenty-first century is rather uninteresting compared to the great variety of practices that existed in the past. There were undoubtedly many past treatments of the dead that are 'archaeologically invisible' in leaving no traces that can now be identified. For much of prehistory it is likely that many people were disposed of after death by 'excarnation', that is 'burial' by exposure either on platforms, in trees or just on the ground surface with scavengers and the elements soon leaving nothing of the body for a future archaeologist to find. Other prehistoric treatments involve long and drawn-out processes where the remains of a number of individuals might eventually be deposited together as 'disarticulated' bone – i.e. a jumble of separate bones rather than complete bodies placed in individual graves soon after death. An example of such a context is the long barrow assemblages of Neolithic Britain (mostly dating from the centuries either side of 3600 BC) where elongated earth or stone mounds with timber or stone chambers contain the mixed and disarticulated remains of sometimes dozens of individuals. Such practices present obvious challenges for the anthropologist in that any signs of disease or injury can only be discerned on individual bones and it is often simply not possible to look at the distribution of such evidence throughout the skeleton. So for example such an assemblage might contain a skull with an unhealed depressed fracture, a rib fragment with a partially-healed fracture and a vertebra with an arrowhead embedded in it. In this case it may be impossible to say whether these bones represent a single unfortunate individual who had sustained three injuries or three different people each with one injury. Lastly some societies perfected various means of mummifying their dead, deliberately preserving soft tissues. On the one hand such practices offer excellent opportunities to learn more about the individual than is possible from bones alone, but on the other hand, mummified bodies tend to offer a rather biased sample in that only certain sections of society (generally the upper classes) might be selected for such special treatment.

Who Were They? Profiling the Dead

Once issues of bone survival have been taken into account, the first objective in making sense of any skeletal assemblage is to establish the demography of the sample – i.e. 'whose' bones are present? Whether looking at a single individual or a cemetery containing hundreds or even thousands of burials, the same initial questions need to be addressed before any other interpretations can be made. Perhaps obviously, the two most important characteristics to assess are the sex and the age-at-death of the people represented. These two key factors are crucial when trying to make sense of any further areas of inquiry such as health, diet, movement/migration during people's lifetimes and in the case of this book violence and conflict. Rather than either sex possessing any specific features which the other doesn't have, male and female skeletons can be told apart by differences in the precise shape and to an extent the size of particular structures throughout the body. The bones that make up the pelvis[5] unsurprisingly differ to the largest extent with the broad bowl-shaped female pelvis differing from the taller, more compact male version. Similarly, various features seen on the skull are generally more strongly and ruggedly expressed in men than women. However, neither region of the skeleton is infallible and many people exhibit a mix of features with more or less masculine and feminine expression throughout their skeletons. As a consequence, determining sex in this way (visual assessment) can never be 100 per cent accurate, although blind tests have shown that it often comes fairly close. Where skeletons are complete and well-preserved sex determinations are usually correct around 95 per cent of the time.[6] However, as remains become less well preserved, levels of accuracy drop accordingly. The pelvis alone gives a reported accuracy of 90 per cent, followed by the skull (approximately 85 per cent) and mandible 70 per cent. Where assessments are made from the size of particular features such as measurements of the long bones of the limbs, accuracy rates fall to between 70 per cent and 80 per cent.

Various parts of the skeleton can offer indications as to how old an individual was when they died. For the most part such estimations rest on the principle that the skeleton goes through a prolonged sequence of development lasting from before birth until early adulthood. Rather than simply being 'mini-adults' the skeletons of children differ from those of mature people in several ways. In particular the juvenile skeleton has different numbers of elements as parts of different bones appear at different times during a person's early years, for example the ends of the long bones of the limbs do not fuse to the main shaft of the bone until the respective bone stops growing. This process (known as epiphyseal fusion) occurs in a predictable sequence which allows for judgements regarding the age of individuals up to their mid-20s which are fairly accurate (i.e. within two–three years either side). The development of the teeth follows a similar sequence and is an even more precise indicator up to the age of around 21 by which time the third molars (wisdom teeth) are normally in place with no further new teeth to follow. However, once an individual reaches their mid-30s a different principle comes into play as the skeleton begins a gradual process of degeneration which continues until death. In general this presents more of a challenge to the osteologist, as just like other parts of the body, different people's skeletons deteriorate at different rates. We have all known people who look older than their years and can all name celebrities who look younger than they really should. Such variation is determined largely by our genes although diet and lifestyle certainly also have a strong part to play. Consequently, age estimations for adult individuals tend to become wider and less accurate with increasing age. As with sex determination these issues are also made more difficult when the skeleton is incomplete or badly preserved and consequently it is common for ages simply to be estimated within broad ranges i.e. 'Young adult' (20–35 years), 'Middle adult' (35–50 years) and 'Old adult' (50 years and older).[7] The open-ended nature of this last category illustrates a further problem in that establishing upper limits for the age of people in later life is really quite difficult and is a problem anthropologists have yet to resolve. So, whilst it may be clear that a person was over 50 it may be difficult to distinguish the bones of a 60-year-old from those of an 85-year-old.

Once these initial observations determining sex and age have been established the osteologist may wish to investigate any number of other variables to help characterize the individual or group being studied. Such variables commonly include standing height (stature), ancestry,[8] the effects of strenuous activity and dietary habits. There are in fact so many ways to study the human skeleton that it is rare to find all or even most of them applied in any single study. Instead the aspects of skeletal remains studied are largely determined by the questions a particular researcher is trying to answer.

'I Told You I Was Ill': Disease in the Skeleton

At the level of reconstructing individuals the questions anthropologists tend to ask regarding human skeletons fall into two broad areas, 'who was this person?' and 'what happened to them during their lifetime?' Whilst the former is addressed by the biological profiling described above, the latter can be detected in relation to various events and processes including signs of disease. A large proportion of the illnesses that affect human beings leave no signs on bone. Many pathological conditions simply do not affect bone whilst others take effect too quickly to cause discernible changes in the skeleton. For example, in the case of acute infections (those with rapid onset) the sufferer tends to either recover or die before any noticeable bony response can occur. Such a lack of skeletal changes is therefore unrelated to the seriousness of the condition. Whilst the common cold is not detectable in bone, largely because people get better within a few days or weeks, more serious infections such as typhus or bubonic plague tend to kill the patient within a similarly short time. By definition then diseases that do leave signs on the skeleton are 'chronic' conditions, those that take effect slowly and persist for an extended period. In fact this category encompasses a very wide range of ailments including conditions as diverse as joint diseases such as arthritis, dietary deficiencies such as scurvy and infectious diseases like tuberculosis or venereal syphilis.[9]

Accurately recognizing medical conditions is not always an easy endeavour for doctors treating living patients with the benefit of modern diagnostic techniques and the added bonus that the patient can say how she or he feels. Most of us have at some time had friends or relatives who have suffered with an ailment for a considerable time before its cause was finally identified. It is not surprising therefore that attempting to diagnose medical conditions in the dry bones of 'patients' who are no longer able to talk to us is considerably harder. This issue is compounded by the fact that changes to bone caused by disease processes often look very similar to each other. Bone can in fact only respond to disease in two ways, either by building more bone or by losing bone in a given area. This means that individual lesions (abnormalities) caused by different disease conditions can often look very similar to each other. Where specific pathological conditions can be identified it is commonly the patterning of such lesions across the skeleton that is distinctive rather than the appearance of any single change to bone. Once again the issue of how much of the skeleton is preserved is therefore very important. For example, leprosy can produce very distinctive changes in the bones of the extremities and the central part of the face. However, in a case where the small bones of the hands and feet and the delicate facial bones do not survive it would be impossible to recognize the condition no matter how well preserved the rest of the skeleton was. Such issues of bone survival are similarly important in recognizing injuries.

Things don't Equal People: From Hobbes to Rousseau

Whilst the earliest archaeological work in the eighteenth and nineteenth centuries commonly investigated human burials, the deceased individuals

The Importance of Populations: Power and Paradox

Whilst the specific unit of analysis that makes up osteoarchaeological studies will always be the individual human skeleton, the principal aim of such work as carried out today is not usually to inquire about the lives of individuals but rather to produce a more general view of 'the lived experience' in a given region or period. In earlier years many of the articles published on archaeological human remains were case studies with titles such as 'a case of hydrocephalus in an Egyptian of the Roman period'.[10] Whilst such studies had clear value at the time in establishing how a particular disease or injury might look in archaeological bone they tell us little in themselves about life in the past, other than the observation that 'someone (i.e. one individual) was ill'. To find out about the general conditions experienced by the majority of people in a given time or place we need to consider larger numbers. Consequently, more recent works tend to consider the remains of as many individuals as possible from an assemblage or region in order to reconstruct the activities and experiences of the population in general. So we now think in terms of the prevalence of a given disease (i.e. how many people did it effect) in the past and the overall impact it likely had relative to the experiences of other populations.

Ironically, this more mature approach to studying past disease brings problems of its own. The aforementioned issue of only chronic, long-standing conditions leaving marks on the skeleton means that a great proportion of the disease load that past people were subject to is effectively invisible to us and currently beyond our reach. This issue leads to a curious and somewhat counter-intuitive effect in that the fittest and most resistant individuals would live the longest and in so doing would have the greatest opportunity to acquire changes in their bones from any chronic illnesses they might have. Conversely, the least fit individuals, with the lowest resistance to disease, would be more likely to die at an earlier age with their deaths caused by fast-acting conditions (usually infections) that leave no signs on the skeleton. So in fact if an anthropologist encounters a skeletal population characterized by many decrepit and debilitated individuals in middle and old age with copious signs of disease, it can be said to be a 'successful' group of people, essentially because they have lived long enough to acquire such evidence in their bones. If the reverse was true, i.e. an excavated population was found to be dominated by young people whose skeletons appeared disease-free, this in fact indicates a less successful group who despite this apparent absence of maladies are in fact displaying the ultimate expression of ill-health in that they are dead(!) having failed to make it past the first flush of youth. This is a powerful issue commonly known amongst anthropologists as 'the Osteological Paradox'[11] and those studying skeletal remains ignore it at their peril.

themselves (or at least their bones) were generally afforded little attention, with the interests of excavators focused instead on the things people had been buried with (pots, metalwork and so on). In this respect such excavations constituted little more than treasure hunts or mining expeditions seeking interesting or valuable objects. Human remains were rarely commented upon directly and were seldom retained other than as objects of general curiosity (and even then it was usually just the skulls that were kept). By the middle of the nineteenth century this began to change, however, as individuals with knowledge of anatomy and medicine began to take an interest in the bodies of past people found in archaeological graves. British examples include men like John Thurnam (1810–73) who was the medical director of Wiltshire County Asylum. Along with his associate Joseph Barnard Davis (1801–81), a Staffordshire GP, Thurnam made detailed studies of hundreds of skulls he collected from archaeological sites in southern England with a view to classifying them into 'races'.[12] This obsession with what is now known to be a misconceived idea of the physical variation seen in all human populations is also very telling of the overall approach taken towards explaining change over time as it appeared from archaeological evidence. Prior to the mid-twentieth century a high proportion of the interpretations produced by archaeologists for the appearance or disappearance of particular types of object or ways of living hinged upon movements of 'peoples' in waves of invasion and migration. Particular sets of artefacts or styles of manufacture were assumed to relate to particular cultures, so the presence of a given kind of pottery or artistic style of decoration would be taken to indicate the presence of a particular people it was held to be associated with. Therefore the presence of 'Celtic' metalwork was seen to demonstrate the arrival of the 'Celts' in a given area, the appearance of Roman pottery indicated the presence of 'Romans' and so on. Again this rather simplistic notion has long since been realized to be untenable as there are a great manner of ways in which objects, materials and ideas can be circulated and transported across sometimes great distances (trade, diplomatic gifts, copying of styles etc.) that needn't involve the wholesale displacement or genocidal eradication of people by invading newcomers.

This realization that 'things don't equal people' had a number of far-reaching effects on how the past is viewed including a revision of the degree to which the past was conceived as being violent. When all cultural change was regarded to be the result of new people invading a given area and pushing out, subjugating or simply exterminating the incumbent population, a logical conclusion was that the history of human development must by definition have been driven and shaped by wars and aggression. Whilst ideas were already changing slowly, the events of the 1930s and 1940s in Europe had a tremendous impact on such notions as it was realized that ideologies that divided people into different groups by equating biology (i.e. race) with culture had ultimately led to death camps and gas chambers. After 1945 researchers in the human sciences rightly rejected such ideas, bringing a need to then re-evaluate the story of the human past as it was thought to be told by archaeological evidence. This rejection of these old explanations for the ways ideas and objects had spread meant that the wars and invasions that were assumed to have been instrumental disintegrated overnight. As ideas in archaeology moved forward over the following decades, notions of the prehistoric past in particular came to be characterized by a distinct absence of warfare, with a view now taking hold that war was a relatively recent invention afflicting developed societies and conducted by nation states. Prehistory in particular was now seen as a largely idyllic time when people lived in peaceful co-operation, expending their energies in building ritual monuments such as barrows, henges and ceremonial enclosures. Simultaneously the study of history came to focus more on long-term processes and large-scale events rather than the by then outmoded view of changes being driven by wars, pivotal battles, and 'great' leaders.

Returning to the issue of human remains, this sea-change in the way the past was viewed also relegated many previous suggestions relating to damage seen on human skeletons to the status of misguided suggestions based on ill-founded assumptions. Nineteenth and early twentieth-century claims of prehistoric skeletons displaying weapon injuries were now dismissed as being entirely mistaken. The prevailing view had swung from one closely aligned with Thomas Hobbes' 'Nasty, brutish and short' vision of the past to a conception more in keeping with Rousseau and the 'Noble savage' concept of human nature as basically peace-loving and co-operative. The problem with all of these shifts in position, however, was that none of them was being led by the actual evidence. Instead the evidence as people saw it was being shoe-horned into an accepted theoretical position decided in advance, rather than used as the starting point to ask questions as to what had really happened. In the mid-1990s this view was given a name by Lawrence Keeley[13] who referred to such positions as 'the Pacified Past' and argued that slow, peaceful processes of change had been overemphasized at the expense of anything unpleasant or hostile to produce a rose tinted version of the past. If only the bones could tell their own story ...

Chapter 2

The Fragile Body: Recognizing Injuries to the Skeleton

A recurrent issue in the previous chapter was the extent to which the professional and social backgrounds surrounding those investigating archaeological burials had effects on the kind of interpretations they produced. A further aspect of the earlier development of human osteoarchaeology again relates to the kind of individuals who first took up the study of archaeological skeletons. Prior to the 1960s such studies were commonly undertaken by medical doctors essentially as a kind of hobby during their spare time or retirement. It is not entirely surprising that in producing such work these individuals tended to play to their strengths and to give most attention to the areas where their prior expertise could make the greatest contribution. As mentioned previously, a great many earlier published articles on archaeological skeletons focused on diagnosing diseases the respective individuals might have suffered from. Whilst such work was perfectly valid in itself and served to establish a new specialism – Palaeopathology, the study of disease in the past – this is now seen as just one of several areas into which biological anthropologists routinely inquire when analysing archaeological bone. One area that has received growing interest in recent years is the recognition and interpretation of injuries to the skeleton, generally referred to under the term 'trauma'. It was not uncommon for early studies that tried to make sense of breakage to bones excavated from archaeological settings to produce conclusions that were wildly inaccurate. Such errors arose largely from a lack of understanding of the mechanisms by which bone breaks, coupled with the authors failing to realize that bones that have been in the ground for extended periods tend to break in ways that are quite different from the way fractures occur in living people. In consequence many early investigators mistook breakage that had occurred in the ground many years after burial for evidence of dramatic events such as weapon injuries or even human sacrifice or cannibalism. Equally often, the reverse was also true where what would now be readily identified as traumatic injuries occurring around the time of death were dismissed as natural breakage or simply not noticed at all.

Bone is bound by the same mechanical principles as any other material and in this respect the way bone responds to external forces is now relatively well understood. This area of study is a branch of a wider field applying general engineering principles to biological structures known as biomechanics, which also considers questions such as the energy used in walking on two legs (bipedalism) or the bite forces exerted by our ancestors' jaws. With regard to its ability to withstand physical forces without failing (breaking), bone is a relatively strong material in relation to its weight. This property essentially derives from the structure of bone at a microscopic level, as a composite material made up of hard calcium crystals set in a softer protein matrix (see previous chapter). Whereas the mineral (calcium etc.) component of bone allows it to withstand compressive forces, the organic (protein) structure provides resilience and a degree of elasticity or springiness which gives resistance to breaking under tension. When describing the properties of a material in terms of its ability to withstand such forces two key concepts which are often a cause for confusion are 'stress' and 'strain'. Stress can be simply defined as the amount of force exerted over a specific area of a material, so for example pounds per square inch. Strain is a quite different concept that refers to the extent to which an object is deformed – i.e. bent out of its original shape as a result of the stress placed on it. Materials that can withstand a high degree of deformation without breaking are said to be 'plastic' or 'ductile' whilst materials that fail after only a small amount of deformation are referred to as 'brittle'. Brittle materials may in themselves be very strong, in that it takes a great deal of force to induce them to bend, but are characterized by only being able to withstand small amounts of strain before breaking once such bending begins. This is essentially the way bone behaves under physical loads as a material that can take a lot of stress but only a small amount of strain. If the strain placed on an area of bone results in the bone changing shape to an extent less than around three per cent then it will normally resist breaking and will return to its normal shape afterwards. Where force is placed on bone that causes it to change shape by more than this amount the bone will normally fail, causing it to fracture.[1]

Understanding Fractures

The term 'fracture' is often assumed to be a technical term referring to a particular kind of damage to bone, but is in fact a very general term that covers any breakage in the overall form of the bone from a hairline crack to a crushing break into many pieces. Attempts to make sense of injuries to the skeleton are considerably helped by the fact that bones do not break in random ways but rather fracture in patterns that are broadly predictable. There are several factors at play in determining the precise way a bone will fracture if it is subjected to sufficient force. Arguably the most important of these relates to the arrangement of the different components of bone at a microscopic level. The hardness of the mineral fraction means that the overall structure can withstand a high level of compressive (crushing) force. However, when bone is subject to forces that pull in different directions (tension) the issue is not of whether any of the individual calcium crystals will break, but rather how much force can be withstood by the collagen (protein) matrix that is holding them together. When bone fails under tension it is this scaffolding of collagen fibrils that tears, which has important implications for the way fractures form. This combination of properties whereby bone is stronger in compression than it is in tension means that when a break occurs it is the part of the bone that is under tension that will fail first, with the resultant fracture spreading out from that point. Different kinds of loads on the bone will exert tension and compression forces in different combinations and so result in different types of fracture once the load becomes too much for the bone to withstand. For example, a load that causes a bone to bend at the centre will place the bone in compression on the side the load is coming from and tension on the opposite side. Other types of force such as shearing (forces that act in opposite directions) or torsion (twisting) will place the bone under tension and compression in different planes according to the precise angle the load is exerted from (Fig. 2.1).

Other factors that influence the way bones break include the particular shape and thickness of bone at the point where force is applied. Obviously some parts of the skeleton have evolved specifically to withstand a high load, such as the femur, which not only has to take the weight of most of the body

Figure 2.1. Different forms of directional loading forces that can act on bone.

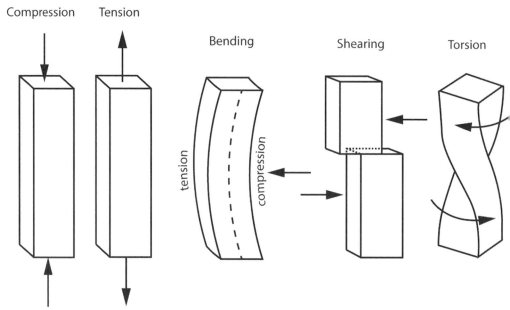

when standing normally, but transfers around three times a person's body-weight through the hip joint each time they take a step and even more when a person runs or jumps.[2] By contrast, parts of the skeleton that are not required to withstand such forces are correspondingly thinner and more lightly built, such as the thin bones at the bridge of the nose which only need to be strong enough to support their own weight and retain their structure without bearing any additional load. As a consequence of this issue it is possible to study the bones of people from different parts of the world who lived at different times and to compare the varying kinds of physical demands their lifestyles exerted on them by comparing the thickness of particular bones in cross section (usually using CT scanning). For example, highly mobile hunter-gatherers display different patterns of cross-sectional thickness in the bones of their limbs from sedentary (settled) farmers. There is also variation in mechanical strength within bones where particular parts of a given bone may be more built up to withstand greater forces in a specific area. This kind of variation in local bone 'architecture' is known as buttressing and has a strong influence on the course a fracture will take as it forms. Fractures will run towards the point of least resistance and so as a bone breaks the split will tend to deviate away from buttressed areas and towards the weaker parts of the bone. Examples of buttressing are particularly evident in the skull where they exert strong effects on the way fractures occur (Fig. 2.2a). For example, facial fractures due to heavy impacts (such as a person's head colliding with a steering wheel in a road traffic collision) tend to form in several predictable patterns known as Le Fort fractures (Fig. 2.2b). Finally the course of fractures is further influenced at a microscopic level by the fact that bone is arranged in fibres that lie along the same direction as each other. This has an effect similar to the way wood behaves when it is cut or struck. Anyone who has sawn or chopped wood will know that it is a great deal easier to persuade the wood to cut or split along the grain rather than across it and the same is true of bone. Again, at a microscopic level fractures will follow the path of least resistance and so will deviate along their course to follow the orientation of local bone fibres (Fig. 2.3).

All the above points in combination are very important from the viewpoint of the anthropologist as they mean that bone tends to break in patterns that are broadly predictable. This then means that examination of the form of fractures can reveal the general mechanism by which an injury occurred. For example, fractures caused by direct trauma – where a force is delivered at the point where the bone breaks – will differ in form from those caused by indirect trauma – where a force delivered elsewhere on the bone causes it to break. So a fracture to a limb caused by a blow from a blunt weapon such as a police baton (known as a parry fracture) will differ from a fracture caused in

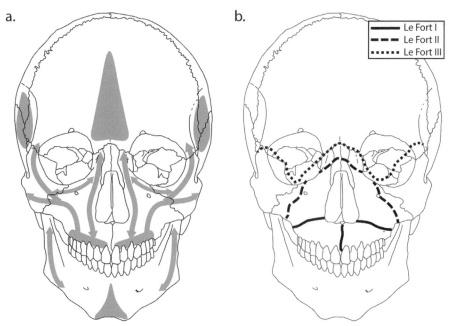

Figure 2.2 (a) Areas of buttressing in the skull, the location of these thicker and denser portions of bone has a predictable effect on the way skull fractures form.[3] (b) Common fractures to the mid portion of the face, these patterns were first described by the French surgeon René Le Fort[4] in 1901 who noted three common types.[5]

Figure 2.3. Common types of fractures in long bones. The nature and direction of forces acting on the bone determine the pattern of fracture when it fails and so can give a general indication as to how an injury might have been sustained.

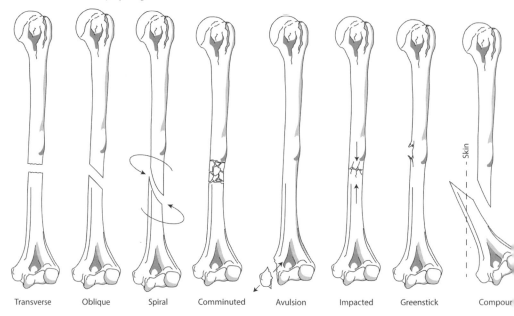

Transverse   Oblique   Spiral   Comminuted   Avulsion   Impacted   Greenstick   Compour

an industrial accident where the limb has been twisted due to being caught in machinery.

Recognizing Violence

The vast majority of injuries in the past, just as today, will have been the results of accidents. Where injuries are apparent in skeletal remains it is often only possible to make fairly general suggestions as to how they were most likely caused. As mentioned previously, bones fracture according to a set of principles that is relatively well understood and for most bony trauma broad statements can be made regarding the overall mechanism through which the injury was incurred. Observations of injured patients presenting for modern hospital treatment make us aware of the most common ways particular types of injury tend to be caused in our own society. For example, a fracture that breaks off and displaces the end of the radius closest to the wrist (known as a Colles fracture) is a common result of falling onto a hard surface with an outstretched hand, whilst a fracture where the tip of the fibula is broken where it forms part of the ankle joint occurs most commonly from slips and trips where the ankle is inverted and the foot forcibly bent inwards. Other fracture types are more challenging to interpret as they may be caused in multiple ways. Rib fractures are a good example of such a non-specific injury as they can be incurred in any number of ways including falls, industrial accidents, traffic collisions, being kicked by an animal or being punched in the chest by another human being. So whilst rib fractures can be caused through violence this is only one of any number of possible ways such an injury might be sustained.

Whilst most injuries fall into the above category there are also some types of trauma to the skeleton which are rarely caused by accident and are much more likely to have resulted from a violent assault than any other cause. One example is nasal fractures (a broken nose). The thin bones that form the bridge of the nose project outwards from the face and break relatively easily when subject to a direct impact.[6] However, in most circumstances people avoid breaking their noses through falling over as we reflexively put our hands out to stop ourselves. As a result many injuries caused through falls affect the bones of the hand and forearm instead of the face. Whilst people can simply be unlucky and it is certainly possible to break one's nose through accidental means, the most common cause of this type of injury is through a deliberate blow aimed at the face (Fig. 2.4). Violence-related injuries are also more easily identified in some parts of the skeleton than others. This is particularly true for the skull and specifically the vault (roof) of the cranium which is by far the most common part of the skeleton on which signs of violence are recognized. In part this is a reflection of the fact that the head is a part of the body very

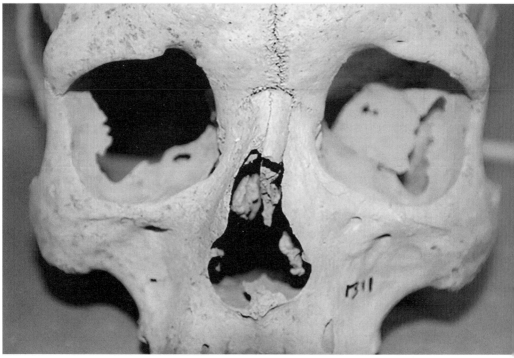

Figure 2.4. An adult male from the Romano-British settlement of Poundbury (Dorset) with a healed nasal fracture. This has caused the nasal bones to deviate to the right and was most probably caused by a deliberate blow from a right-handed assailant striking the left side of the face. (Photograph: Nicola Hancock)

commonly targeted in violent assaults – in modern developed parts of the world head injuries comprise approximately 70–80 per cent of violence-related trauma.[7] However, due to its smooth, rounded form injuries to the cranial vault are also more easily interpreted than on many other bones, as damage caused by impacts with hard objects tends to reflect the shape of the item responsible.

In recent years a great deal of attention has been given towards characterizing and classifying different types of violence-related cranial injuries. Initially much of the impetus for this came from forensic cases.[8] The advantage of such data for anthropologists is that the characteristics of particular types of weapon injury were defined through analysis of modern incidents where the way the respective wounds had been inflicted was reasonably well known. Such work then paved the way for applying such observations to skeletal remains from past periods and has since led to the recognition of large numbers of examples of violence-related injuries on the bones of individuals who lived hundreds or thousands of years in the past. The subsequent realization that violence and conflict may have been much more common than previously accepted is doing much to reshape our views of a range of different periods as later sections of this book will address. Contrary to the impression given by an array of forensic investigation-based TV dramas, it is not always possible to conclusively match a specific item such as a knife or a hammer to a particular traumatic lesion in bone. It is much more commonly the case that the implement responsible for a given skeletal injury can only be identified to a general class of object. These are usually divided into three broad areas; blunt force, sharp force and penetrative trauma.

Blunt-Force Injuries

When bone comes into contact with a hard surface with sufficient force to induce it to fracture, such as in hitting one's head on the ground after falling over, the resultant damage will commonly take the form of one or more linear cracks which travel away from the point of impact. When the object responsible is smaller than the overall portion of bone being struck, such as in the case of a blow with a rounded object (such as a hammer or a baseball bat), this tends to concentrate the force in a small area, causing bone directly at the point of impact to be crushed inwards forming a pond-like depressed area (Fig. 2.5a). Whilst such 'depressed fractures' can be sustained accidentally, when they appear repeatedly within a group of burials or in a particular region or period they are more plausibly interpreted as the result of deliberate blows to the head with blunt objects. In instances where the head is struck with an even greater amount of force, either because the blow has been delivered with a particularly energetic swing or because the implement being used is massive and heavy (such as a Medieval mace) additional fractures can form beyond the area of bone where the blow is struck. These additional fractures tend to take two forms. The first – referred to as radiating or secondary fractures – occur as linear cracks spreading away from the initial point of injury. These may occur singly or several such fractures may form producing a star-shaped pattern, accordingly named stellate fractures. Further to this, in really severe impacts to the head, a third kind of fracture can occur where energy spreads out from the impact to cause ring-shaped fractures around the depressed area, known as concentric or tertiary fractures (Fig. 2.6a).

Sharp-Force Injuries

When a sharp object is driven with enough force to damage bone, the result can be that the bone is cut into rather than fractured. Where such damage doesn't extend through the full thickness of the bone it tends to produce a linear channel which is v-shaped in cross section, simply (and rather unsurprisingly) referred to as a cutmark. There are various other mechanisms that can cause linear features on bone that can easily be mistaken for cutmarks. These can include the bone being trampled or scraped against rough surfaces such as the floor of a cave, channels formed by pressure from blood vessels when the individual was alive, or part of the bone surface being dissolved

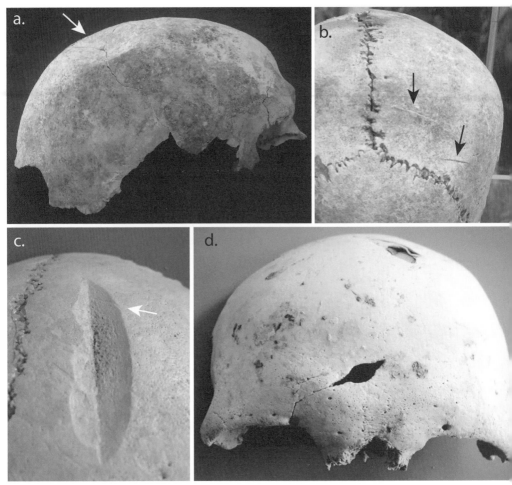

Figure 2.5. Characteristic weapon injuries to bone: (a) Healed depressed fracture from a blunt impact; (b) Incised cutmarks from a thin bladed weapon; (c) Hacking trauma, from a chopping blow with a bladed weapon with striations left in the bone from irregularities in the blade edge indicating the direction of the blow (arrowed); (d) Penetrative injury conforming to the shape of an Iron Age spearhead.[9] (Photographs: (a) Heidi Rasmussen, (c & d) Niomi Edwards)

by contact with plant roots, quite apart from the risks of damage caused by excavators' trowels and other tools when the bone is recovered. However, close examination usually with just a magnifying glass but sometimes a light microscope can usually separate these kinds of 'pseudo-cutmark' from the real thing. Such close examination can also reveal further details such as tiny scratches inside the channel of the cut (known technically as the 'kerf') caused by irregularities in the cutting edge of the item responsible. Such marks, referred to as 'internal striations', can be useful both in determining the kind of implement responsible (for example a smooth metal knife rather than a rough flint blade) and also for indicating the direction in which the cut was produced.

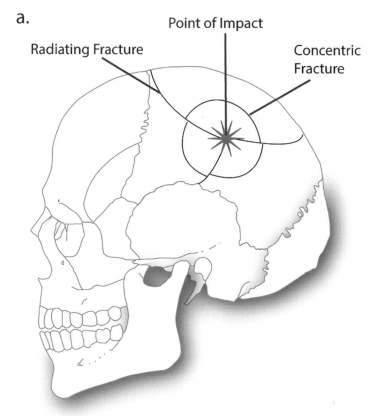

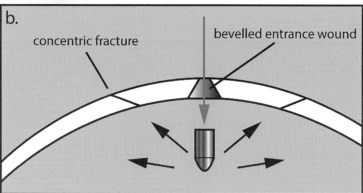

Figure 2.6. (a) Common types of fracture in cases of severe impact to the skull; fractures of this kind may be produced either by a small object moving very fast such as a bullet or a more massive object travelling more slowly such as a club or baseball bat. (b) The same injury seen in cross-section, a cone of bone is punched inwards at the point of impact producing an 'internally bevelled' entrance wound.

When sharp-force trauma (or SFT) produces cutmarks these tend to have been caused by the object responsible being drawn across the bone in a direction roughly parallel to its surface (Fig. 2.5b.). Such cuts will usually be longer than they are deep and are usually referred to as incisions as regards the wounds they cause to overlying soft tissues. When a wound is inflicted by a bladed weapon being swung at the body to strike it in a perpendicular, chopping motion the cutting edge will bite down through the bone and if sufficiently sharp and forceful may even slice through it entirely. The resultant marks in bone (commonly known as 'chopmarks') will often display tiny scratches (striations) across their edges which again indicate the direction the blade was travelling in and so distinguish these from incised cutmarks in which any striations will run along the kerf rather than across it (Fig. 2.5c.).

A further distinction which has been recognized in recent years relates to the observation that some implements that have a cutting edge are also very heavy (such as an axe). When bone is struck by such an object the resulting damage may exhibit aspects of both sharp- and blunt-force trauma simultaneously. Such damage may present in essentially the same way as that from a chopping blow described above, but may then additionally exhibit the kind of secondary and tertiary (radiating and concentric) fractures that occur in cases of severe blunt impacts. More recent writers on this subject have referred to such damage as 'hacking trauma' – succinctly described as 'blunt-force trauma delivered with a sharp object'.

Penetrative Injuries

Whereas incised cuts produced by a linear motion roughly parallel to the body tend to be defined as longer than they are deep, penetrating wounds caused by a more or less pointed object striking the body at a perpendicular angle tend to be the opposite, being deeper than they are long. Weapons that inflict wounds in such a stabbing motion have never gone away, from Palaeolithic spears, to the Roman *pilum*, the Medieval lance and the continuing inclusion of the bayonet in modern infantry equipment. Penetrating injuries can often look less dramatic than the kinds of crushing or slashing wounds described above, but it has long been recognized that such injuries are often more likely to be fatal. When an individual presents at a modern hospital with a stab wound, the most pressing question the examining surgeon will wish to resolve is simply 'how deep is it?' A penetrating wound to the abdomen may be only 2–3cm deep, piercing the skin and superficial muscles underneath, and although certainly painful, may be relatively simple to treat. Conversely, an identical-looking wound might be considerably deeper, piercing sections of bowel, cutting through major blood vessels or damaging organs, and so being much more complex to treat and fatal if not attended to. The switch to light, penetrating weapons such as the rapier or stiletto as the preferred mode of personal 'protection' amongst the upper classes of Early Modern Europe, once armour had been rendered obsolete by firearms, was directly because people understood that such piercing injuries were in fact a much more reliable way to kill an opponent.[10]

Damage to bone caused by penetrating objects to flat areas of bone such as the cranial (skull) vault, or the scapula (shoulder blade) unsurprisingly tends to appear as a hole, usually (but not always) similar in shape to the cross-section of the implement responsible (Fig. 2.5d). For example, various square, rounded and diamond-shaped holes were present in the crania of individuals excavated from the now well-known mass grave of men killed at the fifteenth-century battle of Towton, during the Wars of the Roses (see Chapter 11). Comparison of these defects with various penetrating weapons from the time in the collections of the Royal Armouries allowed the investigating team to make plausible suggestions as to precisely what had caused these wounds.[11] A further defining feature of penetrating trauma to bone relates to the properties of bone fracture, where the respective 'hole' is ultimately produced by the object responsible forcing a section of bone to break away on the opposite surface – for example the interior surface of the cranium. When this occurs the forces responsible tend to radiate outwards from the point of impact and the property of bone to fracture in predictable, linear patterns described earlier in the current chapter comes into play. The section of bone forced away therefore tends to be cone shaped (Fig. 2.6b), giving the effect that the overall defect in the remaining bone will be larger on the side opposite the initial point of injury. This property is referred to as 'bevelling' and is an important distinguishing feature of bony injuries caused in this manner.

Ballistic Injuries

Injuries to bone caused by projectiles – i.e. objects launched through the air – are commonly referred to as ballistic trauma. Whether the respective projectile is propelled by the explosive charge of a firearm, the elasticity of a bow or simply the strength of a person's throwing arm, a similar set of principles operates. For the most part ballistic trauma is essentially no different from the aforementioned categories of injury and the type of damage inflicted to a person struck by such a missile is ultimately governed by its shape. So a pointed projectile such as an arrow will inflict penetrating trauma as discussed above, whilst a blunt missile such as a stone thrown from a sling will inflict crushing damage and may produce a depressed fracture in the same way as any other blunt object. In so far as there are differences in wounds caused by projectiles these relate to the amount of energy involved in launching them and the resultant speed at which such a missile is travelling. The faster an object is moving, the more energy it will impart into a target upon impact. When travelling at slower speeds, a projectile will strike a target with a similar degree of force as if it had been held in the attacker's hand and thrust or swung at an opponent in close contact. For example a bow will propel an arrow at somewhere between 40 and 60 metres per second. However, as the speed of a projectile increases the amount of force required to propel it, and therefore the level of energy it strikes with increases at an exponential rate. This is why a small, light object such as a modern bullet, which travels at hundreds of metres per second, can cause catastrophic injuries on impact as it delivers a huge amount of kinetic energy when it strikes.

As a consequence of this principle, injuries caused by high-velocity projectiles differ from those produced by slower-moving missiles. The latter will cause damage to the tissues they come into direct contact with, for example, an arrow will core out a track through the tissue it strikes, cutting through the respective body area in the same manner as any other penetrating object. On the one hand high-velocity projectiles will cause injury to body tissues in the same way, but on the other, due to the far greater levels of energy involved, such impacts involve additional kinetic energy that travels through the respective body area in a wave, causing further damage by compressing, tearing and stretching areas of tissue which the bullet (etc.) has not even touched. Such waves of energy will often cause a space to open up momentarily, known as a 'temporary cavity' as the surrounding tissues are pushed outwards from the course of the projectile. Such a cavity disappears almost as quickly as it formed as the respective tissues return to their normal position, but with considerable damage and disruption having been inflicted. In cases where such impacts occur in areas of soft tissue there may be minimal damage to the skeleton, other than where the projectile has struck bone directly. However, when such impacts occur in an enclosed space, such as a human skull, there is effectively nowhere for the affected tissues (brain etc.) to expand to as they are constrained by bone. When this occurs the massive levels of energy involved are transferred to the walls of the skull which commonly causes further fractures. Such additional fractures form in similar patterns to those produced in high energy impacts from slow-moving objects (see section on blunt-force trauma above). Initially one or more linear fractures will form which spread outwards from the point of impact (i.e. the bullet entrance wound) known as secondary or radiating fractures (Fig. 3.6). In some cases further fracturing may then occur in a ring around the impact: here such tertiary or concentric fractures appear similar to those produced in blunt impacts. The key factor in the way such patterns of damage are produced is therefore not the nature of the object itself but rather the amount of energy it strikes with. A small, light object (like a 6.5g modern bullet) moving at high speed can impact with a similar overall level of force to a slow moving massive object (such as a 1,000g lump hammer) producing similar effects on bone.

Fracture Healing

The descriptions of injuries given in the current chapter so far all refer to the patterns of breakage that are seen in bone at the time the injury occurs. In fact the majority of injuries observed in archaeological remains tend to be healed fractures which have undergone further distinctive changes as the body recovers. As discussed previously, bone is a dynamic tissue that is continually replenished in response to the stresses placed on it. When such stresses include acute damage to bone caused by external mechanical forces or impacts (i.e. traumatic injuries) the same propensity for bone to remodel itself comes into play in a specialized form. Fractures can often take up to a year to heal fully during which time the process of repair can be divided into four distinct stages. The first of these, the inflammatory stage, begins the moment the fracture occurs and usually lasts for a few days. When bone breaks the blood vessels within the bone will rupture and bleed into the space in and around the fracture. This stimulates localized inflammation – the same basic response of bodily tissues as would be seen in any injury or local irritation such as infection. The area becomes filled and surrounded with fluid in order to protect the damaged tissue and allow immune cells to circulate and deal with any threat such as invading microorganisms. This area of swelling, consisting of fluid and blood which now begins to clot, is referred to as a haematoma. Over subsequent days and weeks osteoclasts (the specialized cells which remove unwanted bone) move in to reabsorb dead (necrotic) bone followed by their counterpart osteoblasts which then arrive to commence bone rebuilding. In concert with another kind of cell – fibroblasts which lay down a kind of scar tissue called granulation tissue – the osteoblasts now begin to construct a 'scaffolding' of initially soft bone matrix which is then mineralized through the addition of calcium crystals to form bridges of new bone between the broken fragments. The haematoma therefore gives way first to what is called a 'soft callus' which then becomes a 'hard callus' as it is converted to bone. The type of bone initially formed at this stage, often simply called 'new bone' (also known as 'woven bone') differs from mature bone in that it is made up of thin strands or spicules of bone similar to the individual spurs of trabecular bone that form the honeycomb structure inside much of the larger parts of the skeleton (see previous chapter). This is a very important point for the palaeopathologist or palaeotraumatologist as it means that bone formed in response to a recent injury or active disease process looks very different from 'normal' bone in the healthy skeleton. The recognition of areas of new

Not Just Broken Bones: The Pathology of Head Injuries

A large proportion of the traumatic damage to bone mentioned in this book is comprised of injuries to the skull. This bias towards head injuries is partly 'real' in that the head is very commonly a target for violent assaults but also a reflection of the fact that injuries are more easily recognized in cranial bone and more easily distinguished as consistent with violence rather than accidents. Many cranial fractures noted in archaeological samples are well healed, indicating that the respective individual lived to tell the tale. However, simply noting the state of healing is as far as many authors tend to comment on such injuries, implying a general approach along the lines of 'so that's alright then'. Obviously, any injury to bone will usually be very painful and cause some degree of temporary or permanent loss of function. However, head injuries often have important and far reaching consequences that may last far beyond the time it takes for the bone to repair itself and so are worth special consideration here.[12]

Head injuries fall into two broad types, 'open' (i.e. where there is a penetrating wound) and 'closed' (where the structures protecting the brain – skin, bone and protective membranes – remain intact). By definition, open head injuries tend to be at least moderately severe, although closed injuries may be equally serious or more so in terms of their consequences. The immediate consequence of any impact to the head is to throw the skull in the direction of the blow, after which the head will snap back in the opposite direction. This movement whipping back and forth throws the contents of the skull against the walls of the cranium, effectively transferring the energy of the impact through the tissues of the brain. In mild instances this may have no discernible effect other than being immediately painful (all of us bump our heads occasionally on door frames, shelves and so on with no adverse consequences). However, more forceful impacts tend to damage or cause destruction of brain tissue and are termed Traumatic Brain Injuries (TBIs). Collision with the walls of the cranium can cause bruising to brain tissue and rupture blood vessels causing bleeding in and around the brain. Such damage tends to occur either close to or opposite the impact and is referred to as 'focal damage', i.e. damage limited to a specific location (Fig. 2.7). The rapid acceleration and deceleration forces the brain undergoes can also damage brain tissue by tearing the thin, threadlike connections between brain cells (axons). This direct damage to the 'wiring' of the brain is known as Diffuse Axonal Injury (DAI), where the term diffuse refers to the fact that such damage tends to be widespread rather than concentrated in a specific area.

Open head injuries involve a penetrating object of some sort (such as a blade or bullet) which by definition will cause focal damage, i.e. disruption of the specific structures (bone, brain etc.) that it comes into contact with. This is not to say that such an injury will not also involve diffuse damage (as above) to other parts of the brain, as the amount of energy needed to penetrate the skull is substantial. Open head injuries also carry the added risk of infection by exposing the affected tissues to the surrounding environment.

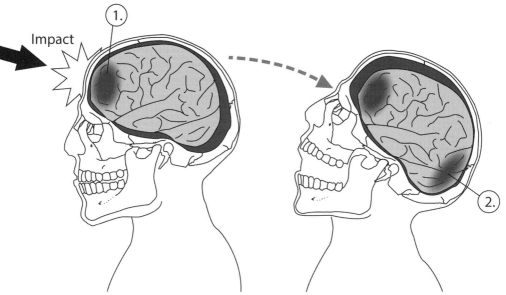

Figure 2.7. Focal traumatic brain injury caused by a blow to the head. (1) The impact throws the head in the direction of the blow, causing the brain to collide with the wall of the cranium and rupturing blood vessels close to the point of impact. (2) Further damage can then occur as the head reaches the end point of this trajectory, when the brain is then thrown against the opposite side of the cranium producing a second focal injury.

The body's responses to any external threat are very broad and tend to be similar whatever the cause, whether to injury, microscopic organisms, large parasites or other triggers. The basic process of 'inflammation' is familiar to all of us where the affected area becomes filled with fluid (swollen) and blood vessels dilate to protect the location from further damage and promote the movement of immune cells to fight any invading organisms. This response is no different in TBIs, where swelling within the brain tissues is a common result. An important effect of such swelling, in conjunction with any bleeding is to increase the pressure within the enclosed space of the skull (known as Intracranial Pressure or ICP). In normal functioning pressure within the cranium is kept within stable limits by various mechanisms. When ICP is raised following a head injury these mechanisms may not be able to reduce it sufficiently and this can cause further problems such as reducing or preventing blood flow to all or part of the brain. This in turn can cause further damage to brain cells due to lack of oxygen. Reducing ICP is therefore an urgent priority in treating cases of TBI.

The Effects of Traumatic Brain Injury

The implications of TBI in terms of how it affects a person's functioning in the immediate and longer terms are very varied depending on the type, location and the severity of the injury. Current clinical practice divides such injuries into mild, moderate and severe categories. Injuries falling within each of these can often be distinguished at the time of treatment by the immediate effects they produce. Mild TBI usually involves loss of consciousness for less than 20–30 minutes and neurological disturbances (i.e. confusion, disorientation, blurred vision) lasting less than 24 hours. Moderate and severe injuries tend to produce longer periods of unconsciousness lasting up to and beyond 24 hours respectively and altered mental states that may go on for up to a week (moderate) and beyond (severe).[13] The precise forms of such impairments are highly varied. Common problems following diffuse TBI include headaches, tiredness, problems with thinking and attention, memory loss, nausea, dizziness, disturbed sleep and mood changes such as depression or irritability. Focal TBI can produce more specific symptoms such as paralysis of particular body parts, abnormal speech, problems using or understanding language or sensory problems (impairment of touch, taste, smell etc.). Both types of injury can result in seizures as well as comatose states and behavioural changes such as impulsiveness or loss of inhibitions.

Returning to the issue of healed head injuries in archaeological remains, the above points are important in that it should always be borne in mind that despite such an injury having 'got better' in terms of bone repair, it may have caused a variety of temporary or ongoing symptoms and changes that affected the life of that individual afterwards. Perhaps of greatest relevance to interpreting archaeological samples is the point that many head injury survivors experience episodes of anger and frustration that lead into aggressive behaviour. Between 11 and 34 per cent of modern patients treated for head injuries have been noted to become aggressive close to the time of the injury, with such behaviour often lingering for some time afterwards.[14] In instances where cranial trauma is common in archaeological remains this may be a further important point. It is often said that 'violence begets more violence' and this may be true in more ways than one. Past victims of violence may themselves have then become violent through such physiological changes even if they were previously placid and even-tempered individuals.

bone is therefore one of the principal ways by which many forms of disease and injury can be recognized in skeletal remains.

Once the broken bone fragments are united and have become fixed, the final stage, known as remodelling, begins. During the hard callus stage, the body tends to build more callus around the break than is needed and once stabilized, the healing fracture is further modified by removal of part of this newly-formed bone to return the fractured area closer to (but usually not exactly like) its original form. During this period the loosely-formed woven bone is also consolidated and strengthened to convert it to a structure essentially the same as uninjured cortical bone. One of the first questions an osteologist will ask on recognizing signs of trauma in skeletal remains is simply 'did the individual survive this injury?' Where signs of healing (referred to by pathologists as 'vital response') are present, the injured person must by definition have survived for a period of weeks, months or years as indicated by the stage of bone remodelling apparent. Where such signs are absent, the fracture must have occurred at least close to the time of death. Such injuries are referred to under the term 'perimortem' trauma as opposed to 'antemortem trauma' for healed/healing injuries, and 'postmortem damage' for breakage to bone that must have occurred after death (the latter is correctly referred to as 'damage' rather than 'trauma' as it is impossible to injure someone who is already dead).

Beaten with Swords or Ploughshares?

An obvious question in response to the find of bones from archaeological contexts with cracks and breaks that might be interpreted as injuries incurred at or around the time of death is 'how do you know the bones didn't just break in the ground?' This is a good point, as such breakage might have occurred centuries after the death of the individual being excavated and as such would tell us nothing about injuries in the past. A very common source of damage to bone is in fact archaeologists themselves, as at times even the most careful excavator may struggle to uncover preserved bone without causing some degree of breakage. This then raises the question how can such 'trowel trauma', as it is commonly called, be distinguished from 'perimortem' injuries (sustained at or close to the time of the individual's death). As mentioned in the preceding chapter, bone is a composite material formed of both organic and inorganic components. Where bone survives in burials that are older than a few decades the organic component is usually severely degraded and it is common in archaeological burials for the surviving bone material to be composed largely of just the mineral (crystalline calcium) part of the bone. Returning to the points made in Chapter 1 regarding the way the composite nature of bone confers flexibility and resilience, this deterioration in the ground has important implications for the mechanical strength of archaeological bone. Anyone who has handled excavated bone will have noticed that it is commonly very light in comparison to bones from the recently deceased, as for example animal bones from a butcher. Excavated bone is also often very brittle and delicate and prone to breakage if not handled carefully. The forces needed to induce a fracture in living bone are in fact at least ten times the force required to break dry bone.[15] Quite apart from having further ramifications for the extent to which bone survives in a sufficiently complete state for useful information to be extracted from it, this susceptibility to damage is also highly relevant to studies of injury in the past as this difference in the structure of preserved bone means that bone from archaeological skeletons breaks in ways that are distinct and quite different from the patterns of fracturing seen in living bone.

Whereas living bone tends to fracture in linear patterns that are broadly predictable, archaeological bone breaks in ways that are much more irregular and more difficult to predict. Fractures in living bone commonly run in a smooth, continuous line with sharp edges. Breaks in dry bone that has lost its organic content tend to be jagged and crumbly with edges running directly across the thickness of the bone rather than angulating to form a sharp margin. The course of fractures in dry bone is also much less predictable and so the kinds of recognized patterns discussed earlier in this chapter such as spiral fractures, Le Fort fractures or concentric skull fractures tend not to occur. Instead, many different types of forces can produce similar kinds of crumbling and shattering into irregular pieces that defy anyone to make sense of how the breakage occurred. A handy way of visualizing these differences which always seems to work well for my own students is to say that living bone fractures similarly to chocolate (I always tell them to imagine hitting a chocolate Easter egg with a hammer) whereas 'dry' bone breaks in a manner similar to digestive biscuits (with a similar amount of crumbs produced).

Lastly, a point that should always be borne in mind when considering damage to the skeleton that might have been caused through violence, is that only a proportion of injuries will affect bone. Wounds to the abdomen in particular may only involve bone in very severe instances where a penetrating injury is deep enough to pierce the spine or pelvic bones. However, injuries to this region in the past will have been the most likely to cause death due to either bleeding or infection, as surgeons were unable to effectively operate on the abdomen without killing their patients until the nineteenth century. Stab wounds or projectile injuries to the chest region may miss the ribs and instead damage the tissues in between and any wound to the limbs may affect muscles and other soft tissues without reaching bone. In 1862 US army surgeon Colonel J.H. Bill published an article detailing his experiences treating arrow wounds sustained by US soldiers fighting the Native Americans of the Great Plains.[16] Here only 30 per cent of the arrow injuries Bill encountered affected bone. This is a sobering thought for osteologists attempting to gain an insight into the frequency of past conflict from examples evident in skeletal remains. On the other hand, however, a point that we can rely on in relation to this issue is that any suggestions we do make on such a basis can generally be assumed to underrepresent the actual number of violent injuries sustained by any group in the past. However, much violence an anthropologist says is apparent, this will almost always be an underestimate of the real picture.

Chapter 3

The Earliest Times: Violence in the Deep Past

Perspective is an important thing. What some authors refer to as 'early' pre-history actually came very late in the human story. The point at which we should regard such a narrative as beginning is itself wide open for debate and ultimately depends on subjective and often quite arbitrary opinion as to what it means to be human. Our current situation ultimately has its origins in the slow but steady rise of primates from among their fellow mammals following the demise of the dinosaurs. We could then place the origins of humanity at the point at which the higher primates diverged from lemurs, lorises and tarsiers, or at any point since, for example when the family of apes split from Old World monkeys, when the common ancestor of humans and chimpan-zees split from that of gorillas or at the point when these two lines then diverged further. This last event later resulted in upright-walking apes that would eventually give rise to various species we would recognize as 'people', whilst the chimpanzee line went off on its own trajectory. If we take this split between ourselves and our closest living relatives as a starting point there were in fact around 6 million years of 'prehistory' preceding our own time. For the vast majority of this time the fossil record is sparse and difficult to interpret and many views on the behaviour of past hominins (all the species descended from the human/chimpanzee split onwards) remain very much a matter of opinion. During the last 500,000 or so years things gradually come into better focus with greater numbers of fossils and improved understanding of our relationships with previous species of humans, including our now extinct cousins the Neanderthals and our immediate ancestors commonly known as Archaic *Homo sapiens*.[1]

The question of when and where violence first entered the human story is similarly difficult to navigate and is again fraught with problems concerning the issue of where to start? Whilst a great many species of all kinds are capable of killing other animals either as prey or in self-defence, a point which has only begun to receive the attention it deserves relatively recently is the fact that individuals are not only competing with other species to ensure the sur-vival of their genes but often equally with other members of their own species.

Aggression between individuals competing for territory or access to the opposite sex (usually on the part of males) is common to a great many species and certainly occurs among primates. In this respect we can reasonably argue that violence is far older than humanity wherever one chooses to place the starting point for the appearance of the first 'humans'. A question that is more difficult to answer is at what point to place the origin of collective violence? The question of when 'war' first appeared, even if defined simply as violence conducted by groups of individuals acting together, has been surprisingly difficult to resolve. Once thought to be a category of behaviour only seen in humans, the initiation of group violence against members of the same species does occur among other animals. The technical term for such behaviour is 'intraspecific coalitionary killing' with such group killing of one's own kind occurring notably among wolves, lions, hyenas and most significantly for us, chimpanzees. Whilst very different animals, these species are similar in being both highly sociable (living in defined groups) and territorial (with the territory attached to the group rather than to individuals).

Amongst the carnivores prone to such coalitionary killing of members of their own species such behaviour tends mostly to occur as a reaction to one or more members of one group straying into the territory of another. However, intraspecific killing can also take the form of one group 'raiding' another group's territory, entering deliberately in order to kill members of the other group. This latter behaviour is more common among chimpanzees, which are particularly given to undertaking such raids. When this occurs the males of a troupe will seek out and attack both adult and infant members of a neighbouring group and kill them often quite ferociously, sometimes literally tearing them apart.[2] Such chimpanzee 'warfare', as some like to call it, is potentially highly significant to wider questions of why humans kill each other and particularly why we sometimes attack each other in groups. The central issue in such debates always comes down to the basic question of whether people are basically peaceful, with any aggressive and violent behaviour being a product of their social environment (i.e. their culture and upbringing) or whether aggression and in particular group violence are pre-programmed in humans as a result of our evolutionary history. These opposing viewpoints are essentially revised versions of the now centuries-old positions associated with Hobbes and Rousseau in modern academic guise. On one hand the existence of hostilities between groups of chimpanzees would appear to considerably strengthen the 'hard-wiring' argument that we come designed by evolution for such behaviour. Given that we share 98.7 per cent of our DNA with chimpanzees this might appear to have settled the argument, or at least it would have done were it not for the existence of another closely-related species, the bonobo – sometimes called the pygmy chimpanzee. This latter species of great ape with whom we actually share the same proportion of our DNA as with the common chimpanzee,[3] simply does not engage in the rather nasty kinds of behaviour their cousins the chimpanzees inflict on each other, either as groups or individuals. In fact bonobos are renowned for being particularly friendly and co-operative creatures, more given to resolving difficulties with another member of their own species by having sex with them than by any confrontational behaviour. This latter point throws a rather large spanner into the works of the 'hard-wiring' argument that has yet to be dislodged. The populations of apes that evolved into humans, bonobos and chimpanzees were descended from a common ancestor and it simply isn't known whether that ancestor behaved more like chimps or more like bonobos or even differently from either.

The greatest barrier to assessing the nature or even the existence of aggressive behaviour amongst our earliest ancestors is that there are no formal burials to examine and fossil remains are for the most part single bones rather than articulated skeletons. Such finds are generally fragmented through exposure to the elements, sedimentary pressures and the actions of scavenging animals. Any injuries that might have occurred from the kinds of aggression seen among chimpanzees and perhaps their cousins who were our early ancestors are unlikely to have left marks on bone, whilst any that did would be challenging to separate from injuries incurred through other causes such as accidents or predators. In order to ask questions about the earliest manifestations of violence then we must turn our attention to injuries that are different in that they exhibit evidence for something only found among the human lineage, the use of weapons. Whilst some higher primates, particularly chimpanzees, are known to use simple tools for a variety of purposes, humans and their immediate ancestors are the only species ever to develop tools with the express purpose of inflicting harm.

Getting Tooled Up: The Emergence of Weapons

The earliest forms of violence involving weapons are likely to have been developed as part of hunting strategies. However, direct evidence of the earliest hunting is difficult to come by. Whilst animal bones with cutmarks made by stone tools show that earlier humans were eating meat, they don't in themselves answer the question of whether the respective animals were hunted or whether they had been killed by predators with the hominins only coming in to scavenge the carcass afterwards. A recent study of fossil beds in southwestern Kenya by Thomas Plummer and colleagues has identified stone tools in association with butchered animal bones dating from around 2 million years ago.[4] Here the prey animals, goat-sized gazelles, are represented by bones from across the skeleton and must have been brought to the site whole, rather than being the scavenged remains left behind by carnivores and so must be the results of hunting. The earliest clear evidence for hafted spears, i.e. where a stone tip is fixed to a wooden shaft, dates from around 500,000 years ago[5] in Southern Africa and the question of how prey were killed in earlier hunting activities remains open to debate. Prior to this, sharpened wooden spears may have been used without stone tips as evidenced by a circular puncture wound noted on the scapula (shoulder blade) of a horse recovered from the British Palaeolithic site of Boxgrove in Sussex. The respective wound is internally bevelled as commonly seen in penetrating injuries to flat bones (see previous chapter), with no signs of healing.

In fact the earliest direct evidence currently available for acts of violence carried out by early humans is found on the bones of another species of primate. The gelada is a species of monkey, similar in appearance to baboons (they are sometimes called gelada baboons) currently limited to the highlands of Ethiopia but once very widespread across Africa, parts of Mediterranean Europe and Asia.[6] They live almost entirely on the ground and are the only primate to exist primarily by eating grass (Fig. 3.1). Geladas commonly live in groups of around sixty, but sometimes as large as 100–200 referred to specifically as herds. Whilst modern geladas are large and robust as monkeys go (the males can be up to 74cm high and weigh around 40lbs), several extinct species known only from fossils were even larger, weighing around 100kg, the same as a small gorilla. At the site of Olorgesaillie in Kenya, dating from between

Figure 3.1. Modern gelada 'baboons': the individuals shown here are both adult males. The frightening appearance of the individual on the right is misleading as he is in fact yawning, but at the same time reveals his formidable canines. (Photographs: L. Maimone; BluesyPete)

400,000 and 700,000 years ago, a curious accumulation of nearly 900 extinct giant gelada bones was excavated in the 1970s at the edge of what had once been a lake. Primate bones are unusual in the fossil record and the accumulation of so many from a single species in one place required a special explanation. The age and sex distribution of the geladas didn't fit with a single dramatic event wiping out a large group in a single instance such as an epidemic, whilst the representation of body parts (comprising bones from throughout the skeleton) wasn't consistent with the bones being carried there and deposited by a river channel which would naturally sort different bones by size. The assemblage also exhibited a consistent pattern of breakage, with the same bones being broken in the same way throughout. This combination of features can only plausibly be explained as the result of these animals being hunted and systematically butchered at the site, with the bones probably accumulating over an extended period rather than in a single episode. Interestingly there were very few skull fragments at Olorgesaillie, but at the earlier site of Olduvai, also in Kenya, a gelada skull dating from more than a million years ago exhibits an unhealed depressed fracture of the kind that would be produced by a deliberate blow with a club-like object and it is reasonable to assume those at Olorgesaillie were killed in a similar way.[7]

Giant geladas are likely to have been formidable creatures and attempting to kill one in this manner could not be taken lightly. Having said that, however, geladas were by no means the largest or the most fearsome prey early hominins were in the habit of successfully hunting: I would still rather take on a gelada than a rhinoceros. In studying the fossil assemblage from Olorgesaillie, Pat Shipman and colleagues noted that modern-day hunter-gatherers in Tanzania (the Hadza) hunt baboons. They do this by surrounding small groups of them and clubbing them to death when they try to break out of the circle. *Homo erectus'* strategies for killing giant geladas may well have involved similar tactics which would certainly be a safer bet than taking on one of these creatures alone. It would appear, then, that practices involving group co-operation and co-ordination in order to inflict violent injuries with weapons go back at least a million years. If the ancestors of modern humans were prepared to engage in such co-ordinated violence against members of another primate species, this then raises the question of at what point such behaviours were first turned against their own kind?

Violence Amongst Early Homo

The oldest example of lethal violence in early humans so far identified was part of a larger bone assemblage recovered from within a vertical shaft inside a cave in Atapuerca, northern Spain known as *La Sima de Los Huesos* (the Pit of the Bones). This context contained over 6,700 fossil bone fragments from a minimum of twenty-eight individuals dating from around 430,000 years ago.[8] Fossil number Cr17 is a well-preserved cranium which has two interconnecting punctures just left of the centre of the frontal bone. These are internally bevelled and show no signs of healing. The team assessing the cranium (led by Nohemi Sala[9]) have argued the two injuries to have been caused by blows from a single implement. Their position on the left side is consistent with a face-to-face assault from a right-handed assailant. Either blow would have been sufficient to cause death and the presence of repeated blows has been argued to be evidence of intention to kill. Whilst the *Los Huesos* cranium is the earliest instance of an unhealed violence-related injury so far recognized, it is by no means the only example of violence in the Palaeolithic. Possibly the earliest healed example so far identified dates from around 1.5 million years ago and was found in Java in 1980. The *Homo erectus* cranium known as Sangiran 38 has at least three rounded depressions which appear to me to be depressed fractures, although not necessarily to other researchers who have made what I find to be a rather tenuous case for these lesions being the result of unusual pathological conditions.[10] Whilst these latter interpretations are certainly possible, the former is considerably more likely.

For much of the period known as the Pleistocene epoch (the time of recent glaciations or Ice Ages, spanning the period between approximately 2.5 million and 11,000 years ago) early human fossils remain hard to come by. However, for the latter part of this period, actually known as the Middle Pleistocene (around 780,000 to 126,000 years ago), things gradually improve, with greater numbers of fossils occurring as their dates become more recent. Close to two dozen examples of healed depressed skull fractures have been identified from this period, representing a considerable portion of the total fossil sample. There is no obvious pattern in terms of how these are spread out geographically with examples known from what is now China, Java, Zambia, Israel, France, Germany, Spain, and Britain.[11] It is a commonly accepted principle among palaeontologists that the fossil record constitutes a sample of past life that can reasonably be regarded as representative of the whole. If this is correct then we should regard the sample of healed blunt head injuries so far recognized from this period as a reliable indication that violent assaults between individuals were a recurrent feature of life among our recent forebears. A further question that currently remains unanswered is of whether such injuries relate to individuals within groups competing for dominance amongst each other, or whether these assaults represent violence between groups more along the 'chimpanzee warfare'/coalitionary violence model – or perhaps more likely, a mixture of both.

Last of the Noble Savages? Violence among Neanderthals

Since they were first recognized in 1856[12] the classic Neanderthals that inhabited Europe and western Asia from 250,000–230,000 years ago until they became extinct at around 39,000 years ago[13] have become the most widely-known species of fossil human. These solidly-built, stocky people were highly successful in that they survived for longer than our own species has so far and colonized a large part of two continents.[14] Neanderthals made and used a wide range of tools, used fire, constructed shelters and wore clothes. They also engaged at least sometimes in activities that don't have a direct practical function in that they made and wore ornamental objects[15] and buried their dead. Although Neanderthals ate some plant foods they were principally successful hunters of a wide range of animals including deer, wild boar, ibex and aurochs (wild cattle) as well as occasionally going after larger and more challenging prey in bringing down now extinct species of elephant, rhinoceros and mammoth. The Neanderthals' robust physique has long been argued to be well adapted to living a mobile life inhabiting a rugged environment fraught with risks and at times enduring extremes of cold.[16] A particular source of such risk is that unlike modern humans, Neanderthal hunting strategies do not appear to have included the use of thrown projectiles. Instead their heavy spears had to be used at close quarters, making hunting a particularly dangerous activity especially when tackling larger prey.

The inherent hazards of the Neanderthal lifestyle are reflected in their physical remains in that practically every reasonably complete Neanderthal skeleton has at least one healed injury. During recent decades the accepted explanation for such injuries is that they were most likely sustained accidentally in the course of hunting and other daily activities moving over rough terrain and to a large extent this view remains plausible. The best-known study of Neanderthal injuries, published by Thomas Berger and Erik Trinkaus in 1995,[17] considered the patterning of such trauma in comparison both to several archaeological samples of modern humans and also the distribution of injuries in nineteenth and twentieth-century hospital patients. None of these resembled the pattern of Neanderthal injuries, which was dominated in particular by upper body, head and neck injuries with a surprising lack of trauma to the lower body given the presumed high risk of falls due to running over uneven ground. However, the Neanderthal pattern was found to provide a convincing match to a further modern sample, American rodeo riders. These specialized athletes collectively display a particular pattern of upper body injuries deriving from a very specific activity which repeatedly places them in close proximity to large, angry animals. The parallel with Neanderthals' close-quarter hunting strategies was seemingly obvious and so the origin of their distinctive trauma pattern would appear to have been found. Berger and Trinkaus' study remains useful and probably explains a large proportion of Neanderthal injuries. However, recent reconsideration of several prominent Neanderthal assemblages has since led to the recognition of a growing number of injuries consistent with violent assaults that arguably call for a reassessment of how this period in human development should be viewed.

The Krapina rockshelter site in Croatia was excavated between 1899 and 1905 with more than 800 Neanderthal bones and bone fragments recovered from 8m of accumulated deposits dating from around 130,000 years ago. These were separate, disarticulated bones rather than articulated skeletons and however these remains arrived there, the site does not seem to have been a place of formal primary burial.[18] The broken and mixed-up nature of the assemblage presented challenges in assessing how many people were represented and estimates for the minimum number of individuals that could be present have varied from as low as fourteen to as many as eighty-two. Victoria Hutton Estabrook and David Frayer have recently re-examined the collection and concluded that the bones more likely represent 'a few pieces from [each of] many individuals rather than many pieces from a few individuals'.[19] The original excavators noted signs of injury in some of the bones and this has been confirmed by Hutton Estabrook and Frayer who identified healed depressed fractures in five pieces of cranial vault (skull), one of which has two such injuries. These were all small rounded or elliptical depressions consistent with these individuals having survived substantial blows from blunt objects. All had smooth, rounded edges meaning that they were well healed although one had additional new bone formation around the injury consistent with the respective wound having become infected. Further trauma at Krapina consisted of a fractured clavicle (collar bone) and two fractures of the ulna. Both the ulnar fractures are located at the distal end (the end closest to the hand) and whilst either could have been sustained accidentally they are also consistent with 'parry fractures'. This is an injury commonly sustained when an individual attempts to ward off a blow with a weapon by bringing up their forearm in defence (see previous chapter). One of these is well healed with the distal end no longer attached. There are two possibilities as to how this occurred: one is that the fracture failed to unite as it healed and so the two bone ends formed a false joint surface and the individual would have suffered at least partial loss of function in the affected hand/wrist. Alternatively Hutton Estabrook and Frayer have suggested the rounded bone end may represent a healed amputation, presumably following an injury that wouldn't heal and had become necrotic (i.e. the tissue had died) or infected. If the latter then this would represent the earliest known example of such an operation.

Early interpretations of Neanderthal injuries viewed them as evidence of Palaeolithic 'homicides'.[20] Obviously this is incorrect or the injuries would not show any signs of healing, but later suggestions that such wounds represent accidents[21] are less convincing when applied to skull fractures. Certainly, it is right to take a conservative approach to interpreting archaeological evidence rather than rushing to the most exciting or dramatic conclusion simply because it might seem more interesting. However, a tendency to effectively do the opposite and opt for mundane explanations in the face of mounting indications that something more is in evidence is arguably just as unhelpful. As will be seen in later sections of this book, rounded or oval blunt-force head injuries have been observed to occur throughout a variety of periods and regions, particularly during prehistory, with considerable consistency. In the context of mentioning a single example of such in an excavation report, putting it down as most likely the result of an accident seems a reasoned and sensible approach. But taken collectively such interpretations paint a picture of prehistoric people as being prone to accidents at a level that simply isn't credible. Moreover, such views also raise the question of exactly what kind of object or surface prehistoric people are assumed to have been repeatedly banging their heads on? The roof of caves is a common suggestion, although one which doesn't explain why such injuries persisted long after the fashion for living in caves and rock shelters had ended. To sustain such fractures accidentally people would need to fall hard against objects with rounded, knob-like projections, although suggestions as to what these might be have not been forthcoming.

Another sticking point of this explanation comes in the location of such injuries. Cranial fractures that result from accidental falls tend to occur more frequently below the crown of the head – a term commonly used is 'below the hat brim line' with head wounds inflicted through deliberate violence tending to occur above this level.[22] In the case of four out of the five examples at Krapina the depressed skull fractures fall above the brim of any hats the Neanderthals might have worn (again this is frequently true of such injuries throughout prehistory) and so are less plausibly interpreted as resulting from accidents. Furthermore four out of the five's injuries are located on the left side of the head in positions consistent with attack from the front by a right-handed assailant and again are less plausibly seen as random accidents. Ultimately, when an explanation needs this amount of special pleading to make it work, the chances are that it is simply wrong. When assessing the plausibility of possible explanations for a particular kind of evidence evolutionary scientists look for what is referred to as the most 'parsimonious' solution. This works on the principle that where there are competing explanations to a problem the simplest is likely to be the most correct. In the case of the Krapina Neanderthals and prehistoric head injuries in general, the simplest explanation for the abundance of rounded, blunt-force skull fractures is that they were the result of being struck on the head by other individuals holding rounded, blunt objects.

Skeletal remains that date back tens or even hundreds of millennia tend not be in the best of conditions and even relatively recently excavated finds of Middle Palaeolithic bone can often benefit from re-analysis as new methods become available. The Neanderthal individual found in 1979 at La Roche à Pierrot near the village of St Césaire (Charente Maritime, France) after which he has become known is an example of such. This young adult, probably male, individual has been dated by associated stone tools to close to the time of the last Neanderthals' disappearance. Twenty years after the excavation a new initiative to reconstruct this individual from numerous eroded bone fragments had become possible in the form of computerised tomography (CT scanning), led by Christoph Zollikoffer of Zürich University.[23] By combining images produced in a series of incremental X-ray 'slices' through each piece of bone, a three-dimensional digital model of each fragment was produced (Fig. 3.2). These could then be refitted to each other to produce a more complete virtual version of the respective bone. When the skull was reconstructed in this way it became apparent that this young man had suffered and survived a significant injury.

The edge of one of the fragments of the frontal bone was smooth and rounded, indicating that rather than having broken in the ground the relative break must have occurred while the individual was alive, with the fractured edge subsequently undergoing remodelling as the wound healed. This linear injury ran in a roughly vertical direction down the middle of the frontal bone although its original extent could only be estimated as the respective bone fragment incorporated only part of the wound. Comparison with a CT scanned reconstruction of a Medieval skull displaying a healed bladed weapon injury showed the two to have remodelled in a very similar manner, where the margin of the wound had folded under slightly and a slight space had opened up where the inner table of the cranium had come away from the adjacent trabecular bone. Zollikoffer and colleagues therefore concluded this lesion to be a sharp-force weapon injury and noted that the orientation of the wound was consistent with an attacker positioned directly in front of the victim. To achieve sufficient force to inflict such an injury with the kind of stone blades in use at this time the implement responsible would need to have been hafted to a wooden shaft to form a spear (hafted axes were not yet in use at this time), although it isn't possible to say whether the weapon was thrown or held in the hands and used in a stabbing motion.

A further sharp-force weapon injury is apparent in the ribcage of one of nine Neanderthals excavated at Shanidar Cave in north-eastern Iraq in the

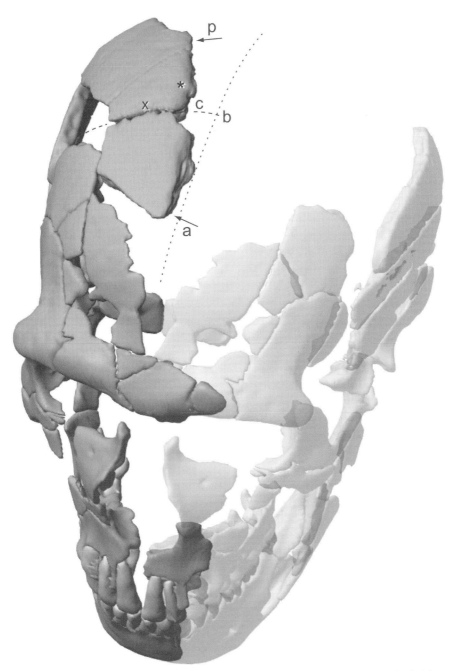

Figure 3.2. Three-dimensional reconstruction of the skull of the St Cesaire Neanderthal from CT scan data showing the course of a healed sharp-force injury (a–b) evident in the form of rounded edges and new bone formation. (Image from Zollikoffer *et al.*, 2002 reproduced with permission from the National Academy of Sciences)

late 1950s. The individual known as Shanidar 3, excavated from levels dating from between 50,000 and 75,000 years ago, aged between 40 and 50 when he died (relatively old for a Neanderthal), has a groove-shaped injury to his left 9th rib. This incised wound must have been made with a sharp blade-like object, most likely a hafted spear point and has also affected the rib above, although this damage to the 8th rib was not noticed until more recently when the bones were re-analysed microscopically by Stephen Churchill and colleagues.[24] The edges of the wound show signs of healing, although the interior of the groove hadn't begun to remodel. This has been taken to indicate that the tip of a stone point which had caused the injury must have stayed lodged in the bone after the event but that this fragment wasn't recovered at excavation.

In penetrating the chest cavity the stone point that injured this man's ribs is likely to have perforated the pleura, the membranes that line the space containing the lung. Such an injury has significant implications in that air may then be drawn into the chest cavity through this puncture every time the individual draws breath. The technical term for this kind of complication is a pneumothorax. A situation where there is air in the chest space outside the lung can be very grave as this unwanted air then exerts pressure which acts to stop the lung from fully inflating. In the worst scenario sufficient air may be drawn into the chest cavity to result in the lung collapsing entirely with the rising pressure then causing further problems by pushing against the heart and associated major blood vessels.[25] Even if this extreme outcome (known as a tension pneumothorax) doesn't occur, there are still risks of other complications such as if there is bleeding into the chest space (a haemothorax) or if collections of fluid and pus accumulate should the wound become infected (known as a pyothorax). Shanidar 3 survived his injury for several weeks and although it isn't possible to say what caused his death it is reasonable to suggest that this wound with its potential complications was probably a significant contributing factor.

In order to investigate how such a wound might have been inflicted, Churchill and colleagues conducted a set of carefully-designed experiments where the chests of pig carcasses were impacted with hafted spear points of the type in use at the time of Shanidar 3.[26] In particular this project focused on the questions of the direction in which the wound was inflicted and the amount of force it was likely delivered with. This latter point is of interest in that it relates to the question of whether the spear that struck Shanidar 3 was held as a stabbing weapon or launched through the air as a thrown projectile. Neanderthals are generally thought not to have used thrown spears,[27] but their evolutionary cousins, modern humans like ourselves, certainly did. The results resembled Shanidar 3's injury very closely and provided some important insights regarding the forces involved. When the spear was propelled with a high amount of energy as would be consistent with a long-range thrown projectile it produced complex patterns of fracturing similar to those discussed in Chapter 2 of the current book with additional (secondary) fractures and spalling or hinging of bone fragments. Shanidar 3's injury lacks these features and instead resembles the results of lower-energy impacts produced by Churchill and colleagues very closely. It was concluded that the wound could have been produced by a hand-held thrust but was more likely the result of a short-range throw with a relatively lightweight weapon. If the latter is true this would introduce the possibility that this individual was a victim not just of violence by a member of another community as is often suggested for lethal assaults but of being attacked by a member of another species, one of our own ancestors.

One of the other Shanidar Neanderthals (Shanidar 1), again a male aged 35–50 at death, exhibits a range of healed injuries. These affect various parts of the skeleton and it is impossible to tell whether they represent a single catastrophic incident such as a rock fall or a number of different events. For the most part it isn't possible to tell how these injuries were sustained, with the exception of a crushing impact to the left side of this man's face that would be consistent with a right-handed attacker striking Shanidar 1 with a blunt object. Here the frontal and zygomatic bones were both crushed in towards the midline, permanently deforming the left side of the face (Fig. 3.3). The structures within the orbit (eye socket) are likely to have suffered damage which may have caused blindness in the left eye. Of even greater significance, however, is a stark difference in size and overall robustness between the left and right arms. Whereas the left arm has the solid form and dimensions normal to all Neanderthals, the right arm bones are thin and withered consistent with a long period of disuse. This loss of bone mass (atrophy) could have resulted from a nerve injury that led to a loss of use of the limb in early life, but Erik Trinkaus and Michael Zimmermann,[28] who comprehensively studied the assemblage in the 1980s, have argued that this is unlikely as the pattern of bone loss would be much more uneven if it occurred whilst the individual was still growing. Instead the pattern of bone thinning in a limb of otherwise normal dimensions is consistent with a sudden loss of use during adulthood. In this regard the fact that the facial injury is on the opposite side of the body may well be significant. If this blow caused damage to the left hemisphere of the brain, either directly or through a subsequent brain haemorrhage this could have resulted in loss of use of the opposing side of the body, effectively as seen in a stroke. On a more positive note, Shanidar 1 is commonly cited as probable evidence for care and support among Neanderthals. As with later periods, evidence for individuals surviving for long periods with debilitating injuries, whatever their cause, gives us an insight into an altogether different sphere of

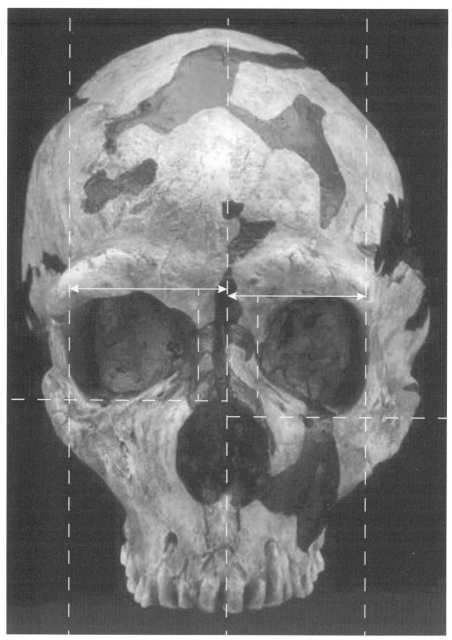

Figure 3.3. The face of the Neanderthal known as Shanidar 1 showing signs of a healed blunt injury earlier in life which has caused the face to develop unevenly. The left eye socket in particular is lower and narrower than the right. (Photograph: James Gordon)

human interaction and raises equally important questions regarding the nature of such apparent compassion.

The notion that research never operates in a vacuum has arguably more relevance to the study of human evolution than any other area of scientific inquiry. Having been the first species of extinct human to be identified, the history of Neanderthal studies and the history of Palaeoanthropology are largely one and the same.[29] Changing views regarding the nature of Neanderthals and the extent to which they have been seen as closer or more distant from ourselves have been constantly influenced by developments in thoughts and attitudes that have occurred in wider society since the sixteen bone fragments of the original Neander Valley find were first recognized in 1856. Early conceptions of the Neanderthals varied from outright refusal to accept their existence, with the initial find argued to be a diseased modern human, through images of brutal ape-like savages to gentle but pitiable and slow-witted figures doomed to become extinct as soon as superior versions of humans showed up on the scene. These ideas were developed against a backdrop of European imperialism and an approach to anthropology often referred to as 'scientific racism' where it was held that certain 'races' were superior and therefore destined to supersede and out-compete their supposed inferiors. With explanations of change throughout the archaeological record dominated by invasions and conflict, it isn't really surprising that such thinking was also implicit in attitudes to the Neanderthals.

By the 1930s a different view was beginning to emerge as it was noticed (sometimes incorrectly) that Neanderthals had buried their dead. This prompted a change in attitudes that gathered momentum over subsequent decades where the position of Neanderthals shifted from being seen effectively as members of the animal kingdom to being 'humanized' and to have exhibited behaviours that come under definitions of 'culture'. The apparent discovery of flowers laid on one of the Shanidar burials in the 1960s (prompting the title 'the First Flower People') and more recent discoveries of built structures and personal ornaments (jewellery) has since moved the Neanderthals into a position where their behaviour doesn't look radically different from that of modern humans in the Palaeolithic. This has led Julia Drell to characterize recent views of Neanderthals as effectively modern people 'trapped in archaic [and by implication inferior] bodies'. She further argues that in a way throughout the last century and a half Neanderthal studies can often be criticized for not really being about Neanderthals. Rather Neanderthals have been used as a yardstick to define and measure ourselves by showing what we are not.

Throughout the last 80 or so years, as the range of recognized Neanderthal activities has progressively been extended, the one aspect of behaviour that has become less and less prominent until it had effectively disappeared from accounts of these people's lives is violence. One of the defining changes in social attitudes in general during the same period has been a growing acceptance of difference and diversity in society, which is of course very welcome. Among palaeoanthropologists this kind of increasingly sympathetic approach to 'others' has arguably been extended back into the past, with earlier views of the Neanderthals now regarded essentially as a kind of racism. Modern writers are therefore now very careful not to write anything that could be seen as derogatory or defamatory to the Neanderthals' character (such as suggesting they wielded clubs and behaved aggressively). Over the last 150 years then prevailing ideas have swung from an image that was so 'solitary, poor, nasty, brutish and short' it could have been written by Thomas Hobbes himself to a version where Neanderthals have more recently become effectively the 'last of the Noble Savages' (Fig. 3.4). Rousseau would surely approve.

As mentioned earlier, almost every reasonably complete Neanderthal has at least one healed injury. The predominant explanation for these injuries has been that they mostly represent accidents, particularly during hunting. Something that has always struck me as strange about this view is the relative lack of injuries to the legs. As Berger and Trinkaus'[30] famous study noted, most Neanderthal trauma is located on the upper body. If Neanderthals were at constant risk of falls when running over uneven ground we should surely see a higher proportion of knee and ankle injuries. Whilst the 'rodeo rider' hypothesis of Neanderthals being injured by getting too close to the food they were hunting makes good sense and probably does explain a proportion of their distinctive injury pattern, there are now a good number of recognized injuries that simply don't fit this explanation. In particular, the blunt injuries at Krapina and Shanidar are much more convincingly interpreted as resulting from deliberate blows delivered by other people with blunt objects, whilst the spear injuries suffered by the St. Cesaire and Shanidar 3 individuals are more plausibly seen as attempts to kill them than clumsiness on the part of their friends. A further point of note regarding the 'rodeo rider' study was that the

Figure 3.4. The changing face of the Neanderthals: (top left) František Kupka's savage, bestial 1909 conception of the La Chapelle-aux-Saints Neanderthal based on the opinions of Marcelin Boule; (top right) Charles R. Knight's 1915 reconstruction of Neanderthals as docile, dim-witted creatures based on information supplied by Sir Arthur Keith; (bottom left) the rather sprightly 2006 reconstruction of an older Neanderthal at the Neanderthal Museum (Germany); (bottom right) 'El Neandertal Emplumado' (the Feathered Neanderthal) Fabio Fogliazza's imaginative 2014 reconstruction, again based on the La Chapelle Neanderthal, has more than a hint of *Last of the Mohicans* to it; taken together all these reconstructions demonstrate the difficulties of separating 'scientific' reconstructions of the past from notions and ideas that are in vogue in wider society at the time. (Images by permission of © Illustrated London News Ltd/ Mary Evans; das Neanderthal Museum, Mettman; Getty Images)

question it addressed was largely based on a view that patterns of trauma among Neanderthals differed from those seen among modern humans and so therefore required explaining. In fact, as will be shown in later sections of this book, the frequency of head and upper body injuries in modern *Homo sapiens* both during the Palaeolithic and throughout later periods of prehistory is much higher than was previously realized. Depressed cranial fractures and other kinds of violence-related injury have since been identified in far greater numbers due to a combination of new research on recognizing such injuries and a greater willingness to look for them. These issues have in fact prompted Erik Trinkaus to publish an article[31] updating the views stated in his 1995 'rodeo rider' study where he suggests that whilst the original hypothesis remains useful, other causes of injury should also be considered, with violence a key candidate.

One question raised by the signs of assault apparent among these now extinct people is of who was responsible for inflicting such injuries? Given that they predate the appearance of modern humans in Europe,[32] the blunt injuries at Krapina can only represent violence between Neanderthals. However, it is interesting that the two individuals with apparent spear injuries at St Césaire and Shanidar are both relatively late and occur at a time when modern humans and Neanderthals occupied the same parts of the world. The observation that Shanidar 3's injury seems to have been caused by a thrown spear – the hallmark of modern *Homo sapiens* – would appear to indicate violence occurring between these two species of human. Given that modern humans were clearly prepared to use such implements both against hunted animals and members of their own species it seems unlikely that they would not be at least equally prepared to use them against a different kind of human, especially if as Stephen Churchill[33] has suggested, the ability to kill at a distance with thrown weapons might have tipped the balance in their favour. John Shea of Stonybrook University, New York, has also commented on the subject and argues that 'Upper Palaeolithic humans were not fools, nor were they necessarily nice people. If they perceived Neanderthals as ecological rivals and had the ability to displace them by coalitionary killing, they probably did so.'[34]

It has long been thought that modern humans could have out-competed and marginalized the Neanderthals entirely by gradual encroachment without any need to invoke direct hostilities between the two to explain the latter's disappearance. In fact just a decade ago there was no indisputable evidence that modern *Homo sapiens* and Neanderthals ever came into direct contact. This situation has now changed, however, with the publication of some quite astounding genetic research which reveals that Neanderthals and modern humans must have interbred. According to this study between 1 per cent and

4 per cent of the genomes of modern humans of non-African origin consists of Neanderthal DNA.[35] The circumstances in which such interbreeding took place are very much open to speculation. Whilst such unions may have taken place in entirely peaceful circumstances, they may equally have involved hostilities. It is possible to invent polarized scenarios of either peaceful inter-action or violent rapes committed by one species against the other, but the reality could also have lain somewhere in between. For example, as observed in more recent hunter-gather societies (see the following three chapters), raids between groups of either species could have involved the abduction of individuals who then remained with and became part of the attacking group. Such abductions most commonly involve women or children and in a Palaeo-lithic setting where social groups were small this would be a way to increase group size that could increase the long-term survival chances of the group as a whole. A Neanderthal child growing up in a Modern group or a young *Homo sapiens* growing up in a Neanderthal band might then later breed within their new community. These latter issues are likely to be a subject of debate for some time to come and perhaps the most important point is simply that the genetic data on this issue mean that the two species definitely came into direct contact. Certainly, it can be argued that the once-dismissed notion that conflict between the two species may have played at least a partial role in the demise of the Neanderthals is now worth reconsidering.

Lastly, a major influence on people's willingness to see evidence for violence among Neanderthals has been an underlying assumption that if Neanderthals engaged in aggression and savagery that this would distance them from ourselves and reinforce ideas that these people were primitive and inferior in comparison to modern humans. A century ago such notions fitted the overarching Western world view very well. However, such a concept is itself based on a view that modern *Homo sapiens* were not given to behaving violently towards each other, at least during the Palaeolithic. In fact the following chapter and those that follow demonstrate that such notions of a peaceful prehistory are no longer tenable. Wherever prehistoric skeletal assemblages have been assessed in recent years, signs of physical assaults are apparent as an aspect of life. Human prehistory was often a violent place and one of the greatest risks to the lives and well-being of our prehistoric ancestors appears to have been other people. In fact then, we can now say that if the Neanderthals were in the habit of behaving violently this doesn't render them distinct and distant from our own species but is rather just another example where the Neanderthals' behaviour would seem to mirror that of modern humans. If we want to think of the Neanderthals as being close to ourselves we should also think of them as capable of the full range of human actions, one of which is aggression.

Chapter 4

Rolling Back the Temporal Frontier: Modern Humans and the Origins of War?

The last 39,000 or so years have been a very unusual chapter in the human story. On one hand this point is true for obvious reasons regarding the huge technological and social developments that modern humans have achieved over recent millennia and particularly the last few centuries. But apart from the unique and dramatic innovations that make our world 'modern', the era in which we live is peculiar in that this period is the first time for millions of years that only one species of hominin has been alive on the planet.[1] Following (and perhaps because of) the appearance and spread of anatomically modern humans (*Homo sapiens sapiens* – HSS) out of Africa and into Europe, Asia and beyond, at least two other species of humans – the Neanderthals and the newly-discovered Denisovans[2] became extinct, leaving our recent ancestors as the sole surviving members of the hominin line. When modern humans first appeared somewhere between 200,000 and 150,000 years ago[3] they were distinguished more by their anatomy than their behaviour. In comparison to earlier forms of human these new people were tall, lightly-built and big-brained but initially employed tool technologies, hunting strategies and social organization that were essentially the same as those of their immediate ancestors. However, around 50,000 years before the present, things began to change quite dramatically, with the appearance of a variety of complex new behaviours not seen before.[4] HSS campsites became more formally organized than in previous times, new technologies were developed such as sewn clothing, fishing equipment, more complex structures to shelter from the elements and improved hunting technologies. Even more striking, however, is the appearance of something that in strict terms has no practical use – the creation of works of art. Both carved and painted rock art and portable art in the form of sculpture survive from throughout this period (the Upper Palaeolithic) in sometimes exquisite forms. The appearance of complex formal burials at this time further underlines a new propensity for behaviour based in something other than immediate practical concerns.

This sudden flowering of new ideas and behaviours seems to have happened very quickly, to the extent that it is generally referred to as the 'Upper Palaeolithic Revolution' (UPR) and is plausibly regarded as one of the most important changes to have ever taken place in human societies, at least on an equal footing with the birth of agriculture or the Industrial Revolution. Quite why this happened when it did is unknown, but as for how all these changes might have come about there is strong support for the idea that some sort of 'rewiring' of the human brain occurred at this time which permitted people to make connections and think laterally in ways their ancestors had simply not been capable of. This change is held to have conferred a range of advantages including greater capacity to think in abstract terms, with consequent advances in the ability of forward planning and probably simultaneous increases in the complexity and versatility of language. The technological advances seen at this time are united in that they generally hinge upon combining materials or qualities of things that people already had access to but which had never been used in such ways before. Bone carved into needles and combined with sinew and skins could produce sewn clothing. Flint could be knapped more efficiently to make smaller points for hafting to wooden shafts which could then be launched through the air with one of the new spear-throwers carved from bone or ivory to kill prey at a distance with less risk to the hunter. Bone carved into a specific shape and combined with fibres allowed fish to be caught with hook and line, whilst the variety of stone artefacts in use now proliferated into a diverse kit with a tool for every occasion. Possibly the most convincing explanation for these changes offered to date are the thoughts of Stephen Mithen[5] who suggests that whilst previous species of humans possessed discrete bodies of knowledge and intelligence for application to specific needs and problems (finding food, attracting a mate, making tools etc.) these areas had been mutually inaccessible. That is to say that one body of 'knowledge' had no bearing or connection with another and early humans therefore only used one such mental module at a time (one analogy Mithen uses is of a Swiss Army knife with multiple tools that can only be used independently). What seems to have changed at the time of the UPR is people's ability to think laterally and make connections between the different categories of knowledge and understanding they possessed, which could explain the new-found ability to combine the properties of materials into efficient new technologies.

A change like that proposed by Mithen where people developed a new capacity to make linkages and produce new combinations of ideas would certainly explain the differences between modern human and Neanderthal technologies as the latter had access to all the same 'things' as the former (stone, bone, wood, antler etc.). But it simply appears the Neanderthals didn't exploit these available materials in the same way – 'they just didn't get it', to quote my old lecturer Simon Buteux. Whilst the new ways of hunting, keeping warm and sheltering from the elements conferred considerable survival advantages, the apparent mental changes that made these innovations possible also appear to have had what might be called 'side effects'. If humans now possessed an improved ability for symbolic and abstract thinking this would appear to explain the emergence of art at this time, some of which involves the clear mixing-up of different aspects of the real world such as both sculpted and painted representations of 'hybrid' figures with mixtures of human and animal features. Mithen further suggests this enhanced tendency to mix things up in the mind to have resulted in what can broadly be called religion, where aspects of the natural world (animals, trees, the sun, moon, earth etc.) became imbued with characteristics and personalities that exist among people and were imagined to have relationships both with humans and each other as sentient entities capable of conscious actions.

Whilst worshipping astronomical objects or conversing with trees may not in reality provide any tangible benefits, such behaviour doesn't in itself cause people any harm either, which might explain why religious activity has survived over time rather than succumbing to natural selection as conferring disadvantages. However, an aspect of human behaviour which has received relatively little consideration in relation to the apparent changes in mental functioning that took place during the Upper Palaeolithic is the propensity for people to behave unpleasantly towards each other. We know from the examples discussed in the preceding chapter that aggression and violence were certainly not new at the time of the UPR, but this then raises the question of whether the form taken by human hostilities was any different afterwards? Whilst clearly worth pursuing, efforts to resolve this question remain dogged by the perennial issue of Stone Age archaeology – that of small numbers of samples and poor preservation. During this period burials seem to have been fairly unusual events, with most people dealt with after death in some other way that isn't recoverable archaeologically, perhaps most likely just being left exposed to scavengers and the elements. However, this doesn't mean that we shouldn't try and there are certainly some intriguing aspects to the evidence that we have.

Plus ça Change? Business as Usual or New Ways of Doing Things?

Where injuries resulting from violence have been recognized among the remains of Upper Palaeolithic humans they commonly take forms that are essentially similar to those discussed in the previous chapter. The Mladeč Caves in Moravia (Czech Republic) were the site of the discovery of what is currently the earliest dated assemblage of early modern humans from Europe for which a significant range of different parts of the skeleton and multiple individuals of differing age are represented. Originally excavated in 1882, this assemblage is now known to date from 31,000 years ago.[6] When the bones were reassessed at the beginning of the current century by a team from the University of Vienna led by Maria Teschler-Nicola[7] an adult male individual was noted to have a healed depressed skull fracture. This was located on the frontal bone above the man's left eye, consistent with the now familiar pattern of assault from a right-handed opponent with a blunt object. Also in Moravia is a site that takes its name from the nearby village of Dolní Věstonice. Here parts of more than thirty individuals have been recovered. Although these are mostly scattered fragments, three better-preserved adults each had a healed cranial injury.[8] Looking beyond Europe, the caves of Qafzeh and Skhul in Israel are among the best-known Palaeolithic sites. Dating from 80,000–100,000 years ago, human remains from these caves are likely to represent some of the earliest movements of modern humans out of Africa.[9] Again an adult male from Qafzeh has a depressed fracture to his frontal bone, whilst a particularly large and robust skull from Skhul (individual IX)[10] has an injury interpreted as being caused by a blow from the rear to the left side of the head.[11]

As with the preceding period the healed blows recognized from this time are also accompanied by lethal injuries. The burials discovered at the site of Sunghir in northern European Russia, excavated between the 1950s and 1970s are the most elaborate and best known from the Upper Palaeolithic. The burial of an adult male in his late 50s or early 60s was particularly impressive, with the powdered mineral pigment red ochre scattered around his head and covered by around 3,000 mammoth ivory beads that were either strung together or more likely sewn to clothing[12] (Fig. 4.1). Having first been reported on in 1965, a further discovery was made in 2009 when the skeleton was re-examined by Erik Trinkaus and Alexandra Buzhilova.[13] After an adherent layer of sediment was cleaned from the bones these new analysts noticed a slit-like defect in the body of the first thoracic vertebra (the highest vertebra to articulate with a pair of ribs). This lesion measured 10mm in length and was wedge-shaped, tapering from 2.2mm at one end to 1.2mm at the other, and was concluded to have been made with a sharp object that could only be a human-made artefact. Microscopic analysis showed no signs of healing indicating the man did not survive this event. The position of the wound meant that the object must have entered at the level of the junction between the upper chest and neck, just above the clavicle on the left side, narrowly missing the oesophagus but cutting through various layered muscles in this region. Crucially the object would have cut into one of two major

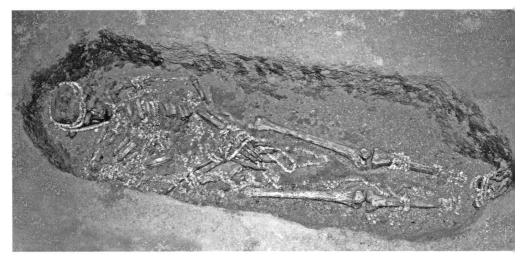

Figure 4.1. The elaborate Upper Palaeolithic burial of Sunghir 1 (northern Russia) covered in thousands of mammoth ivory beads probably originally fixed to clothing. It is now apparent that this man died from a penetrating injury to his neck, probably from a thrown or thrust spear. (Photograph: José-Manuel Benito Álvarez).

blood vessels, the jugular vein or the carotid artery. Damage to either of these would result in loss of blood flow to the brain causing loss of consciousness followed shortly by death. The bow and arrow had not yet been developed and so this injury is likely to have been caused by a spear tip either thrown, or thrust at close quarters.[14] As mentioned previously, formal burials are very rare from this period and do not appear to have been the standard way of dealing with the dead. The recognition of this injury raises the question of whether the fact that the Sunghir 1 male died through violence may have been the reason he was singled out for this special treatment.

At Montfort-sur-Lizier in southern France[15] a single vertebra from a younger adult individual with a quartzite projectile point embedded deeply in its body was recovered in 1894 (Fig. 4.2). The point may have been either an arrow or spear head and entered from the front and about 30 degrees to the individual's right. The projectile pierced the full thickness of the vertebral body (the solid cylindrical section that supports weight through the spine) and protruded 2–3mm into the neural canal. The point would therefore have caused some damage to the spinal cord although this was the least of the individual's problems as to enter at this level (the 5th to 7th thoracic vertebrae) it would have pierced the right lung and heart and so was immediately fatal. This site dates from the very end of the Palaeolithic, spanning the junction with the subsequent Mesolithic (13,000–8,000 BC). Also at the close of the Late Upper Palaeolithic an adult individual excavated from the cemetery site of Voloshkoe in Ukraine had a flint point embedded in the first cervical vertebra (the top of the neck which articulates with the base of the skull) whilst a further adult male had a projectile point embedded in his sternum.[16] The ubiquitous objection that has been raised for decades on end whenever a

Figure 4.2. A mid-thoracic vertebra recovered from deposits dated to the very end of the Palaeolithic at Montfort-sur-Lizier (southern France). The quartzite point piercing the vertebral body entered at the level of the heart causing death instantly. (Photograph: Didier Descouens)

lethal weapon injury is noted from early prehistory in particular is that it could have been a 'hunting accident'. Like the other catch-all explanation of prehistoric people banging their heads on the roofs of caves, this is indeed entirely possible for any one individual but surely cannot wash for all four examples from Sunghir, Montfort-sur-Lizier and Voloshkoe (not to mention other examples noted below). Again, if we accept the commonly-held principle that what survives in the fossil record is a reasonable sample of the whole, this notion would require us to also accept that Palaeolithic people were so clumsy that they were in the habit of accidentally killing their friends as a regular occurrence. We have no reason to think that the mental qualities and aptitudes of Upper Palaeolithic people differed in any significant way from our own and so such a view is really not credible. Given that they survived at all in this environment whatever these people were, they certainly weren't incompetent.

Who Gets Hit? Sharing Violence Around

As noted, violence-related injuries recognized among early modern humans do not differ substantively from signs of violence observed among Neanderthals. However, an interesting observation that is apparent during the Upper Palaeolithic but not for the preceding periods relates not to how these kinds of injuries were inflicted, but rather which members of society were the victims of such assaults. It is in this period that signs of violence inflicted on women and children first become apparent. Notably, one of the three intact burials with head injuries mentioned previously from Dolní Věstonice was in fact female. Returning to Qafzeh cave, one of the younger individuals excavated (Qafzeh 11, dating from 90,000–100,000 years ago) had a well-healed depressed skull fracture to his or her frontal bone.[17] Whilst this was noted at the time of excavation, further insights have more recently been provided when the skull was re-examined using CT scanning by Hélène Coqueugniot of the University of Bordeaux.[18] Capturing data in three dimensions in a digital form like this allows features to be accurately measured as well as just examined visually and measurement of the volume of Qafzeh 11's cranium revealed it to be markedly under-sized given the individual's age at death (12–13 years). Coqueugniot and colleagues argue that this deficit must have resulted from delayed growth of the brain apparently resulting from the head injury. This is a clear example then of the sort of issues discussed in Chapter 2 regarding the long-term consequences of trauma to the head. Qafzeh 11 will have experienced learning difficulties relating to this retardation of brain development as well as a range of other possible deficits such as problems with speech, controlling movements or performing tasks. He or she may also have undergone behavioural or personality-related changes from what would clearly be classed in modern clinical terms as at least a moderate brain injury (see Chapter 2). When it was first published in 1981 the original description of this injury was that it had ultimately been 'benign'[19] on the basis that it was well healed and had involved no significant repercussions. Of course this assessment was of its time and is understandable without the benefit of CT scans and digital reconstructions. However, this example does underline the issue of osteologists viewing healed injuries as having been overcome with no lasting effects once the bone had remodelled. Even in this case the extent of the brain injury was only apparent because it had occurred whilst this individual was still growing. With regard to questions surrounding the nature of violence among early modern humans this point is of further significance in this sense as in order for the injury to have taken effect in this way it must have occurred when the individual was several years younger. Even taking into account the point that people would probably have been regarded as 'adults' at a much younger age in the prehistoric past there is no doubt that this significant injury was inflicted on a child.[20] A further child from the caves at Es Skhul, close to Qafzeh on the slopes of Mount Carmel in Israel[21] also has a depressed area in the middle of the frontal bone, although due to issues of preservation it is difficult to distinguish whether this relates to an injury before death or to taphonomic (post-mortem) damage after.

If the violent trauma noted on women and children from this period was limited to blunt injuries these assaults might be explainable as examples of what would now be called child abuse or domestic violence – essentially violence within communities. However, two further examples of assaults with deadly weapons are much more likely indicators that at least some hostilities at this time occurred between groups. Excavated in 1942, San Teodoro cave at Messina, Sicily was found to contain an adult burial dated to the latter stages of the Upper Palaeolithic. As with other examples, more recent re-analysis in 1993 provided new information regarding this individual including the conclusion that she was female.[22] A further observation noted was the presence of a flint projectile tip, suggested to be from an arrowhead, lodged in the woman's right pelvis.[23] It is difficult to reconstruct the trajectory of projectiles without knowing the position the individual was in when the injury occurred, although if we assume the woman to have been standing upright, the position of the flint fragment is consistent with an attack coming from behind on the right side. She had survived this incident, evidenced by signs of healing in the surrounding bone, although the injury continued to trouble her as there are also signs of ongoing infection causing an abscess to form with drainage channels in the bone through which pus and fluids would have continued to discharge through a persistent wound to the surface. A stone point was also found lodged in one of the thoracic vertebrae of one of two children aged between four and six in the cave that became known as the *Grotte dei Fanciuli* (Cave of the Children) at Balzi Rossi in in northern Italy.[24]

In the case of the above examples of weapon injuries noted in females the question is raised of whether this is more an artefact of the form of the modern human skeleton being more familiar to us, so it is simply easier to determine the sex of remains from the Upper Palaeolithic than for earlier periods. Additionally as we move forward in time we have better preserved and more complete skeletons to examine than the sparse, disarticulated fragments that generally survive from the Middle and Lower Palaeolithic, all of which might shed doubt on whether there was a genuine shift in terms of who was being targeted, or whether things simply come into better focus over time. The rarity of child burials from earlier during human evolution again makes comparisons difficult, but on the face of the evidence available it is certainly tempting to suggest that a change had occurred and acts of violence might now have taken on more complexity than just males competing with each other.

Long Hawks versus Short Doves

Attempts to make sense of weapon injuries among Upper Palaeolithic people usually fall somewhere between two opposing positions (other than the aforementioned tendency to explain them away as accidents). In the first view such assaults are seen as evidence of conflict between groups and so essentially

Co-operation and Conflict: A Deadly Combination?

The question of both why and how modern humans radiated out from Africa to colonize the rest of the Old World when they did has been debated among palaeo-anthropologists for decades. The time when this event occurred (some time after 70,000 years ago) is not characterized by any particular environmental change which might have provided more favourable conditions than were previously prevalent for humans to spread out into other continents. Nor were there any developments in the human body to alter people's physical capabilities at this time. Curtis Marean of Arizona State University has argued that in order to account for this rapid expansion 'after thousands of years of confinement to the continent of their origin'[25] any suggested explanation needs to do two things. First it must explain why the process began when it did, and secondly it must demonstrate a mechanism by which such expansion could have taken place. Marean offers some interesting thoughts of his own on this subject. Rather than resulting from a single change, he suggests modern humans' unique propensity for spreading into and conquering new environments to be the result of two important and apparently contradictory factors. He suggests that new traits appeared in humans at this time, which at once made them both excellent collaborators and ruthless competitors. Essentially this notion involves humans taking behaviours that are common to all species at the level of individuals and developing an ability to apply these at the level of larger groups. Our everyday lives see us co-operating to a unique degree in often highly complex activities with others who are not closely related to us. Marean argues that rather than something people learn as they grow up, this is instead a genetically determined trait specific to modern humans which he terms 'hyperprosociality'. In principle this sounds like an entirely innocuous thing that could only lead to a more harmonious and presumably less stressful kind of living. However, the other side of the 'hyperprosocial' coin is that one of the things humans are then prone to doing is engaging in conflict with other groups who are perceived as competitors. In fact the acquisition of hyperprosocial tendencies may have been a self-accelerating process – an evolutionary one-way street. Over time groups that work together more effectively will be at an advantage over those that don't and the former will outcompete (if not simply annihilate) the latter, then being in a position to pass their genes for such behaviour on to the next generation.

A further component of Marean's argument draws on research conducted in the 1960s investigating aggressiveness in birds.[26] This work found that aggressive behaviour was selected when it was essentially worth doing, such as in defending food resources. In situations where food cannot be defended or is simply too costly to patrol, aggressive behaviour simply doesn't pay off. When such principles are applied to early humans they predict that resource defence would make sense where one or more crucial or high-quality resources are both abundant and predictable. In Africa land-based wild resources are often neither plentiful nor predictable, but around 160,000 years ago modern humans began exploiting a new environment where the opposite was true – the coastline. Once people learned how to exploit the rich and previously untouched shellfish beds that lay in southern African coastal areas they gained access to a high-quality source of calories and protein requiring relatively minimal effort to exploit it (shellfish are neither difficult nor dangerous to catch). As such these predictable and also static resources may have been the trigger that favoured co-operative defence from which the development of hyperprosocial behaviour followed. When this newly-acquired propensity for co-operation was employed in combination with the novel technology of thrown projectiles that appeared later during the Upper Palaeolithic, groups of modern humans moving into an area then had a considerable advantage over any existing groups already living there. Marean suggests that this is what allowed our ancestors to spread so rapidly and successfully into the rest of the world, eliminating Neanderthals and other forms of human along the way until these earlier populations of Europe and Asia had dwindled to nothing. If these suggestions are correct, the human propensity to engage in genocide, viewing 'different' people as enemies to be exterminated, may be very deep rooted. Although, on a positive note such tendencies can be overcome, just like any other biological instinct and so need never come into play, as the ability of modern people to reason is arguably far more powerful.

some form of what might be called 'war' – albeit possibly involving only small numbers of people.[27] In the second view these wounds are regarded more minimally as only constituting definite evidence for the involvement of two people – an assailant and a victim, and therefore better characterized simply as 'homicide'.[28] At the heart of this debate lies a familiar dichotomy: ultimately this question rests on the issue of whether 'war' is a recent, sociocultural invention or whether it is a 'hard-wired', essentially innate behaviour that existed long before complex societies. The former view therefore holds that whilst humans had always been capable of violence on an individual level, the practice of collaborating in groups in order to inflict death or injury on other groups was simply absent from the world until really quite late in the development of human societies. These polarized positions have recently been described by Mark Allen as the 'long versus the short chronology of war' characterizing proponents of these views as 'hawks and doves' respectively.[29]

On one hand it is entirely possible that prehistoric weapon injuries could indeed represent nothing more than disputes between individuals. Where we have healed injuries delivered with some form of bludgeoning weapon such a view may be plausible in that it is possible (although certainly not advisable) to strike someone in anger with a blunt object without intending to kill them. However, such a statement does not hold for sharp objects. Attempting to shoot someone with an arrow or stab them with a spear implies a definite desire to kill them. At a time when human groups were small and survival was highly dependent on the success of the group as a whole, killing members of one's own group would seem a very ill-conceived thing to do. Over time groups that were in the habit of killing their own members would be at an 'adaptive disadvantage' in relation to those that didn't. Put into plain speech this rather dry technical term actually refers to issues as serious as the difference between survival and death for the overall group. Furthermore, even accepting the possibility that individuals may kill each other in relation to personal disputes, and that such disputes need not be confined to arguments between two men, the presence of young children with severe or fatal injuries as at Qafzeh, Skhul or the *Grotte dei Fanciuli* is difficult to fit into this picture.

Humans are a highly social species that tends to behave territorially. Putting the temptation to invoke the kind of raids conducted by chimpanzee troupes against neighbouring groups to one side, as that debate is fraught with even more unresolved problems, it may be more productive to look forward to times after the Palaeolithic than to look for answers in the rather foggy and indistinct periods that went before. Upper Palaeolithic people were mobile hunters and foragers, possessed of the same biological and mental capacities as ourselves. As such it would seem reasonable to look to observations of mobile hunting and foraging people over recent centuries and to ask the question of whether such peoples engage in conflict between groups and if so what form do such hostilities take? Accounts of conflict among hunter-gatherer peoples usually fall into one of two categories. Such reports tend either to have been produced by recent social anthropologists (ethnographic accounts) or by European explorers and colonists writing at times of initial contact in colonial times (referred to as ethnohistorical accounts). Each of these categories has drawn its share of criticism. Accounts written centuries ago at times of early contact tend to be accused of bias, particularly on the grounds of serving vested interests by presenting indigenous peoples as 'savages' in need of civilizing (and usually Christianizing) with such a process simultaneously resulting in them being dispossessed from the land they occupied. Modern observations are generally credited with more academic objectivity, but tend instead to be criticized on the grounds that the few hunter-gatherer peoples now left in the world have been pushed out into difficult environments where survival is much harder. Any conflict they engage in therefore results either from this newly-imposed scarcity of resources or from contact with the 'corrupting' influence of developed societies. On one hand, neither of these criticisms is completely unfounded and both views have a good degree of validity (although I am less convinced by claims that such peoples were Noble Savages to whom conflict was unknown before 1492 etc.). But on the other hand, both categories of report repeatedly refer to particular patterns of behaviour that show considerable consistency between different world regions and over time. It seems very unlikely that different sources of error and bias in either type of report should always produce the same kind of 'inaccurate' result, in fact such a consistent error would itself need a lot of explaining. Therefore it is much more plausible to take the view that the reason the same issues keep occurring in accounts written in different times and places is because those issues are real.

In particular, the acknowledgement and maintenance of territorial boundaries is a key feature of hunter-gatherer warfare, with the killing of strangers trespassing without permission occurring as standard. A further frequent occurrence is simply the killing of vulnerable strangers on sight wherever they might be.[30] What archaeologists would call the 'material culture of warfare' has also been present as a standard feature among foraging peoples until all but the most recent times. What this term refers to is simply 'things' that people have constructed that make warfare possible. In this case examples include specialized weapons for killing people rather than just for hunting animals, defensive strategies such as shields for personal protection, fortifications for settlements and modes of transport such as boats or canoes designed for ferrying raiding parties rather than just fishing expeditions. This latter point is particularly important as war among hunter-gatherers frequently involves a selected group (usually of young men) entering the territory of another group in order to ambush and kill vulnerable individuals, to abduct people (most commonly women) or to take resources. This 'hit and run' style of attacking enemies is therefore by definition very unequal, with raiding parties generally preferring to ambush a single individual at a time rather than take on larger numbers, unless through some additional advantage such as the common favourite of mounting a surprise attack on a sleeping community at dawn. Warfare among such peoples rarely involves formal battles where two groups of a similar size meet at a mutually-acceptable location to 'fight it out' on roughly equal terms. In summarizing what is known from accounts written by the earliest Europeans to visit New Guinea, Paul Roscoe[31] notes warfare among the varied groups inhabiting the island to be characterized by the notion that any member of an opposing group could be attacked – this is an important point which I will return to later. Groups in New Guinea were until very recently given to raiding other communities with objectives including the taking of food resources, abducting women or sometimes to take trophies in the form of headhunting. The earliest days of European contact in Australia produced frequent accounts of weapons designed specifically for use against people (including 10-foot long barbed spears known as 'death spears') and of deadly warfare occurring amongst aborigines.[32] Australia is of particular interest in this respect as its indigenous people had been living continuously in effective isolation before 1788. Here such ethnohistoric accounts are complemented by archaeological evidence extending back thousands of years including skeletal remains with embedded stone points and blunt cranial injuries that would not look out of place in the Middle or Upper Palaeolithic (or the Mesolithic or Neolithic for that matter) of Europe or Western Asia.[33]

Of course there is more than one type of situation in which human beings will sometimes engage in violence. Although having said this violent acts themselves tend to fall into a relatively small number of categories. As shown in Chapter 2 most assaults can be listed under a fairly short number of broad classifications (attacks with projectiles versus close-quarters assaults, striking a victim with a blunt rather than a sharp object etc.). If this was the only level at which such acts were worth considering the current book could be really quite short. A common observation amongst anthropologists (both biological and social) and also archaeologists is that the way to understand human activity is not to look simply at the behaviour itself but to consider its 'social context' – i.e. how was it understood by the individuals actually involved, what did they think they were doing? Debates concerning whether we can recognize war in the past, or even determine whether it existed, commonly hinge upon differing ways of defining war. An obvious pitfall in such an approach is that if one adopts a definition of war that excludes a particular kind of behaviour or social group then it is possible to neatly 'prove' that war did not occur in a given time or place. For example, a definition that says war can only exist between nation states would automatically lead to the conclusion that before such forms of government appeared war did not exist. Similarly a definition that describes war as armed conflict between large groups of people (hundreds or thousands) would automatically exclude conflicts between small groups. This is all very well for a theorist writing in relative security in a modern developed country, but would provide little comfort to an individual in a society composed of small groups being ambushed by a raiding party from another village intent upon killing them. In the case of peoples who live by hunting and foraging it is arguably a more useful approach to consider what such people themselves actually think and how they regard the operation of war.

The motivations stated by people involved in violence are varied, although a common recurrence is the claim that acts of violence are prompted and justified by a desire for revenge against some injury or insult. Where such revenge is acted out solely against the individual perceived as the perpetrator, it seems quite reasonable to categorize this as a personal dispute. Even if the respective individual was then ambushed and killed by a dozen members of the injured person's family, such a dispute would remain a personal matter and neither those involved nor any anthropological observers I know of would be inclined to say this group was 'at war' with the individual they are attacking. In fact to call such a situation war would make the term rather meaningless. This then raises the question that if the acts of violence (clubbing, spearing etc.) do not in themselves differ between war and other situations then what is it that makes war stand out as a distinct state of affairs at all? The key to understanding this issue may lie in the question of who is targeted rather than how they are assaulted. A point noted above was the notion that in a state of war anyone who is a member of the opposing group can be 'legitimately' attacked. In this state of affairs such thinking is brought into play regardless of whatever issue a given group may cite as justification for going to war. So, for example the killing of one individual by one or more outsiders may provoke a desire to take revenge against the community those outsiders belong to in general rather than simply to exact justice against the killer(s) specifically. The most influential writer to explore such issues in recent years is the social anthropologist Raymond Kelly[34] who refers to this specific way of thinking during times of war as the 'Principle of Social Substitutability'. This very specific kind of logic hinges on the idea that an attack on any member of one's own group is regarded as an attack on the community as a whole. Similarly, the entire community to which the attackers belong is regarded as responsible and therefore all or any members of that group are considered appropriate targets for revenge. In such instances raiding parties (usually composed of young males) will tend to attack any vulnerable individuals they encounter from the opposing group whether lone females or even children. Returning to the Upper Palaeolithic examples noted in the current chapter, again it is perfectly possible that any one of these represents an individual 'homicide' resulting from a dispute between two people, but the finds of adult females and particularly children with lethal spear or arrow injuries would appear to fit the model of 'war' as defined by Kelly's 'Social Substitutability' much more convincingly.

The majority of examples of violence-related injuries from earlier prehistory crop up in ones and twos and it is therefore again understandable why some writers have argued these to be examples of nothing more than individual homicides. However, Site 117 at Jebel Sahaba on the East bank of the Nile in northern Sudan cannot be so easily explained. Excavated in 1965–6 as a rescue project in advance of the building of the Aswan High Dam and dating from *c.*12,000 to 14,000 years ago, during the period often referred to as the 'Epipalaeolithic', the site constitutes the earliest full example of a formal cemetery currently known. Containing at least fifty-nine individuals (forty-six adults and thirteen children), systematically laid out flexed on the left side with their heads to the east, this pattern differs from groups of burials elsewhere, which at most comprise just a few individuals buried in proximity to each other. Whilst the site was significant for this reason alone, it is perhaps better known as the earliest example of another phenomenon. At least twenty-six individuals (45 per cent) had met a violent death, indicated by chert arrowhead tips located in close proximity to or embedded in bone. The excavator Fred Wendorff[35] found a total of 110 stone point fragments in close association with the skeletons and in positions consistent with having penetrated the body. Many were located in the chest cavity or the spine. Eight individuals had cutmarks on bones with no signs of healing. Further work by an international team is ongoing at the time of writing this book to re-examine the assemblage using modern techniques including electron micros-copy which has revealed even more examples of embedded arrow tips and impact marks.[36] Repeated examples of healed violence-related injuries also indicate that these people had experienced hostilities before.

A question all this might leave is whether these people were the victims of one or more raids or massacres involving multiple deaths in a single episode, or whether these individuals were killed perhaps singly, in repeated small-scale attacks? Either way it would appear that the people of Jebel Sahaba were subject to aggression from beyond their own community as this number of violent deaths in a single cemetery cannot be conveniently explained away as the result of clumsy hunters and arguments between individuals. Adding to the unpleasantness of this picture is the presence of six people with frac-tures to the ulna – or 'parry fractures' as mentioned in Chapter 2, apparently sustained while putting their hands up to defend themselves. Perhaps most shocking is the observation of two individuals with stone points embedded in their sphenoids. This is an irregularly-shaped bone that sits in the middle of the skull and is difficult to access except from underneath. For these stone weapons to have penetrated at this point these people must have been shot, or perhaps more likely speared from underneath their chins or even through their open mouths. This implies the killing of people lying on the ground rather than standing upright and fighting. Furthermore, these two injuries in such an unlikely location imply a degree of systematic behaviour on the part of the assailants. Taken together then, the evidence from Jebel Sahaba would seem more consistent with a massacre than with a battle or repeated attacks on individuals. To put it another way – if evidence of a massacre from this period were found, what would it look like? Recent analysis of the physical type of the Jebel Sahaba people has shown them to be most similar in physical proportions to sub-Saharan people from further south and to be distinct from other North African groups at that time.[37] This could be taken to suggest these people to be relatively new arrivals in the area, which may have rele-vance to the fact that others in the region chose to attack them. It would appear then that this site constitutes the earliest undeniable evidence for war in which the logic of aggression directed apparently at all members of another group is clearly in play. It is a sobering thought that evidence of human groups attempting to annihilate each other is found in the very earliest human cemetery to which we have access.

Rolling Back the Temporal Frontier – When did War Begin?

Of all the issues considered by researchers who have attempted to make sense of conflict in prehistory, each bringing to bear the bodies of theory offered by their respective academic backgrounds (archaeology, evolutionary psychology, social anthropology, human osteology etc.), the most strongly contested is simply the question of the antiquity of war – when did humans first engage in this very specific form of group behaviour? In recent decades a degree of consensus on this issue that had its origins in the decades after 1945 has been steadily eroded. First the idea that war appeared only with states and civilization, having been absent to any important degree in prehistory, gave way to a view that war probably appeared in the Bronze Age with the development of the first specialized weapons and personal wealth. This notion has since fallen away with the more recent recognition of evidence for conflict in the Neolithic and then the Mesolithic (see Chapters 5 and 6). Effectively there has been a kind of 'Temporal Frontier' that has been progressively rolled back as more cumulative effort has gone into considering the question of war in prehistory over the last 20 years in particular, although the issue of where the 'frontier' should finally stop remains an open question.

This brings us back to the opposing viewpoints of those who favour the Long versus the Short Chronology of War and which we should regard as being more correct? I would argue that actually this isn't a useful way to frame the question. In fact as Mark Allen has observed,[38] proponents of the 'Long' and 'Short' chronologies disagree principally because they are talking at cross purposes. They are arguing about the time of the first appearance of different things and referring to both as 'war'. Coalitionary violence may well have a long chronology, stretching back millions of years to the time of our last common ancestor with chimpanzees. Having said this, war in the terms understood today may be a more recent development but not as recent as some would like to claim. Rather than emerging fully formed at some specific point in time (whether recent or distant from our own), it is more likely that war developed over time in a series of incremental steps with long periods in between when relatively little changed (Fig. 4.3). The next major step beyond collective forays into the territories of other groups as observed among our close relatives is likely to have been the development of co-operative hunting and in particular hunting of big game. Groups capable of working together

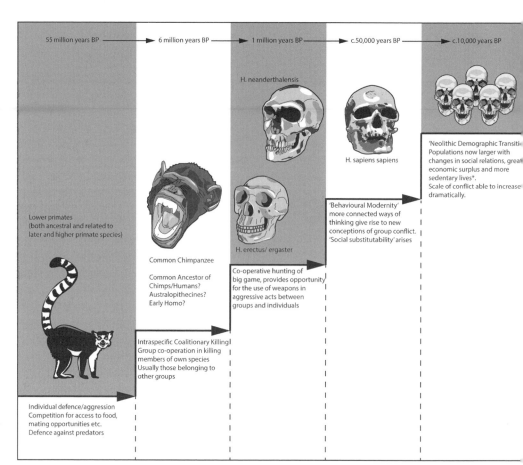

H. neanderthalensis

H. sapiens sapiens

'Neolithic Demographic Transiti
Populations now larger with
changes in social relations, grea
economic surplus and more
sedentary lives*.
Scale of conflict able to increase
dramatically.

'Behavioural Modernity'
more connected ways of
thinking give rise to new
conceptions of group conflict.
'Social substitutability' arises

Lower primates
(both ancestral and related to
later and higher primate species)

Common Chimpanzee

Common Ancestor of
Chimps/Humans?
Australopithecines?
Early Homo?

H. erectus/ ergaster

Co-operative hunting of
big game, provides opportunity
for the use of weapons in
aggressive acts between
groups and individuals

Intraspecific Coalitionary Killing
Group co-operation in killing
members of own species
Usually those belonging to
other groups

Individual defence/aggression
Competition for access to food,
mating opportunities etc.
Defence against predators

Figure 4.3. The debate over when war first appeared as a human behaviour is often character-ized as a polarised argument between a 'long' versus a 'short' chronology: war is seen either as having existed continuously since at least the time of the split between humans and chimpan-zees; or it is regarded as essentially absent until the last few thousand years. The above sche-matic proposes an alternative view; 'war' as it is understood today did not appear fully formed at any single point in the human past, but rather developed incrementally, as a range of important changes each contributing to make such behaviour possible. In this alternative model – 'the Stepped Trajectory' – war in its 'modern' form relies on a combination of biological drives, technological innovations and refinements in mental capacities before finally becoming more practicable following changes in population sizes and social relations (see also Chapter 6).

to kill large prey with specialized equipment will have been at an imme-diate advantage over those that did not if these new innovations were then employed in the kind of raiding behaviour that by this time may already have existed for millions of years. A million or so years later the appearance of 'behavioural modernity' at the time of the UPR then brought more than just further technological innovations. This time is regarded as unlike any previ-ous period because of the rapid advances that came in people's abilities to think in abstract terms, make forward plans and also to make mental con-nections in ways that had never occurred before. The concept of 'Social

Substitution' as the defining psychological aspect of war as opposed to other situations in which violence may occur raises a further question in itself of exactly when this very specific and quite unusual mode of thinking first appeared. In looking for the most likely period for its emergence I would suggest the time of the UPR, with its explosion of lateral thinking bringing new ways of looking at old situations and behaviours, is probably the surest bet. The notion of social substitution in conflict by its very definition involves a fairly advanced degree of abstract reasoning. Evidence for human behaviour from before the UPR shows only very minimal development over the preceding hundreds of thousands of years with no signs of the new mental connectedness that seems to have led to other uniquely modern behaviours at this time such as art and religion. On the other hand, we have no reason to think that Upper Palaeolithic people had mental capacities that differed from those of people today and there is therefore no compelling reason provided by evolutionary psychology for arguing that social substitution (and therefore war as it is now understood) should only have appeared after the Upper Palaeolithic.

If this 'stepped trajectory' model is correct then the complex, developed and uniquely modern version of coalitionary violence which we call war has neither a long nor a short chronology but is, like any other aspect of human behaviour, the result of a series of step changes, each made possible by what had gone before. Whilst Neanderthals or earlier species of Homo may well have engaged in violence against other groups, such behaviour is likely to have been something undertaken periodically and opportunistically rather than planned in advance in response to an understanding that a state of 'war' had come into play. As to why such behaviour may have developed at all during the human story, for any strategy to be retained in the long term it generally needs to convey an adaptive advantage, i.e. it must improve the survival chances of a given group or individual. In considering hunter-gatherer warfare Steven Le Blanc notes that even if raiding only kills one or two people at a time, if such a process is sufficiently frequent and one group gets the upper hand, the other group will either be annihilated or forced to disperse in the long run.[39] If such behaviour has a selective and therefore a genetic aspect we would expect to see consistent patterns over long periods and between regions, which is precisely the case for hunter-gatherer societies. Le Blanc has further pointed out that as patterns such as killing strangers on sight or a desire for revenge appear to be almost universal, they are therefore likely to have existed for a very long time. In response to the question of why human beings adopted co-operative violence against other groups as part of the range of survival strategies they practised, the short answer then is simply 'because it works'. If I am correct and war as it is now understood has a beginning that lies in the genetic changes that made the UPR possible, then it would seem to have entered the world at the same time that a whole package of other modern behaviours were born. Perhaps I will be proved wrong and in the future repeated examples of female *Homo erectus* or Neanderthal children will be discovered with lethal weapon injuries, or an equivalent assemblage to Jebel Sahaba with a whole community targeted for violence will be found from a time predating modern humans, but for now it would seem such behaviour in its most developed form is a social strategy exclusive to ourselves.

Chapter 5

Out from the Cold: Mesolithic Hostilities?

The retreat of the great ice sheets that had covered much of the northern hemisphere during the most recent glaciation opened up new habitats for all manner of plant and animal life and brought new opportunities that humans were quick to exploit. Over the millennia since the last Ice Age reached its coldest and greatest extent at about 20,000 years ago (known as the Last Glacial Maximum or LGM[1]) a way of life reliant on hunting mammoth, rhinoceros and reindeer had slowly given way to one based on a wider range of prey, particularly horse, red deer and bison, with a simultaneous growth in the amount and variety of gathered plant foods that made up people's diets. By around 9600 BC the climate had assumed a pattern that we would largely recognize today. The range of plants and animals exploited by humans could then widen further, along with a great expansion of the landscapes in which such resources were found. Rather than being restricted to small pockets of the continent where conditions were barely favourable to permit human survival (known as refugia), the inheritors of this new Eden had the whole European land mass at their disposal. The period spanning this time between the melting of the ice, and the adoption of farming, that took place in an expanding wave moving northwards and westwards across Europe during later millennia, is generally referred to as the Mesolithic (Middle Stone Age).[2] Where reference is made in the current chapter to 'Mesolithic' peoples this term is used simply to denote peoples living in the environments that became available after this change, subsisting by hunting and gathering, rather than any strict reference to particular dates.

The sample of burials from the European Mesolithic that are accessible to us is rather patchy. In some regions fairly large cemeteries have been excavated from the period containing clear cross sections of society, from newborn infants through to the elderly. In other parts of the continent burials are more sparse, cropping up in single figures, whilst in many areas Mesolithic human remains are all but unknown. The principal example of the latter is Britain where very few human bones of Mesolithic date have been encountered, possibly because the dead were being dealt with differently from other parts of the continent. One suggestion, based on the preference for living near to the coast, is that burial at sea may have been a favoured option.[3] Where formal cemeteries are known, these often coincide with coastal areas where people seem to have lived a relatively settled life in larger groups, such as at a range of sites in southern Scandinavia. Such burials commonly contain elaborate arrangements of grave goods and show a great deal of care being taken with the dead. Examples include two women buried together on the island of Téviec, Brittany,[4] accompanied by flints and boar bones, wearing jewellery made from sea shells and covered by a roof of deer antlers (Fig. 5.1), or the burial of a newborn infant laid on a swan's wing at Vedbaek Boggebakken, Denmark, next to a woman who may have been her/his mother.[5] It may be that inland areas with fewer formal burials indicate a more mobile way of life. A common feature of human remains that are known from many areas without formal cemeteries is what has been referred to as the 'loose bone phenomenon'.[6] Rather than complete skeletons, what human bones there are in such regions often occur simply as single bones or scatters of a few skeletal parts. This latter category probably derives from funerary practices where the dead were left exposed to the elements (or excarnated) rather than dealt with by burial.

The limitations of the burial record of Mesolithic Europe are further compounded by the fact that large areas where the dead might have been buried

Figure 5.1 The 'Ladies of Téviec' this double burial of two women accompanied by a range of placed objects and covered by a 'roof' of deer antlers is here shown as reconstructed for display in the Museum of Toulouse.[7] (Photograph: Didier Descouens)

are effectively no longer accessible. The environmental changes that ended the last glaciation did not stop with the melting of the ice sheets, as the newly-exposed regions continued to alter over the following millennia. Much of the landscape once occupied by people in north-west Europe has since become what we now call the North Sea and so is effectively lost to us for the time being.[8] This now-drowned region, known to archaeologists as 'Doggerland', is thought to have been among the richest landscapes in Europe, with abundant hunting and fishing opportunities and diverse plant life.[9] Through a combination of events in the northern hemisphere including release of water from a glacial lake in North America and an undersea land slippage causing a tsunami, Doggerland was completely submerged by 6500–6200 BC. Consequently, as time wore on great swathes of previously rich and well-stocked landscapes began to disappear before people's eyes. It is tempting to suggest that this reduction in viable hunting, gathering and fishing territories may have put sufficient pressure on resources to cause people to compete for access to them in a way not previously necessary. Given that archaeology is by definition the study of the material traces of the past it is perhaps unsurprising that archaeologists often produce these kind of 'materialist' explanations for past conflict which focus on access to resources and environmental conditions. The extent to which such issues really took effect during the Mesolithic is difficult to say. Certainly, scarcity of resources can lead people to fight and kill each other over access to them. However, in our own time where such a phenomenon has been observed it tends to take effect in areas where human survival is very marginal and where environmental changes have tipped the balance in an already tenuous situation. Given the small and scattered nature of human groups during the Mesolithic and the still considerable expanses of available land even after the inundation of what is now the North Sea, the circumstances in this instance don't really fit the picture of conflict arising from economic scarcity except perhaps on a very localized level. If we want to find the causes of Mesolithic violence it seems we must look elsewhere.

The question of how much violence occurred during the Mesolithic and whether it was mostly confined within groups or ever broke out between communities has tended to produce starkly differing opinions. As with other periods in prehistory, views expressed on the subject have rarely sat on the fence and those who have offered their thoughts have tended to swing towards one of two opposite poles. Whilst a few writers, such as Nick Thorpe of Winchester University,[10] have suggested that violence was likely a very common occurrence, many more have taken the opposite view on the basis that the small, scattered populations occupying Europe at this time would rarely have bumped into each other and had little to fight over if they did. Further-more, in these times of mobile populations, the opportunities to opt out of conflict by simply moving away from anyone 'problematic' were such that warfare is again argued to have been an infrequent occurrence, simply because it would have been so easy to avoid. Of course this latter view rests firstly on an assumption that people choose whether to engage in conflict for entirely practical reasons, which is a point of debate in itself that I will return to later. Secondly, although the idea of hunter-gatherers being able to simply walk away from trouble makes sense in itself, this too is based on an assumption. Such a notion assumes that people who don't live a settled way of life wouldn't regard the places they visit as 'their' territory. In fact, as explored in the previous chapter, there is a wealth of evidence gathered by a wide range of observers from early European explorers to recent social anthropologists that people who subsist by hunting and gathering are often both extremely terri-torial and highly sensitive to trespass. For example, in discussing life among Native Americans in California David E. Jones comments that: 'Every child was drilled in recognizing the particular boulder or stream that marked the boundaries of his or her people's territory. To cross the boundary invited death.'[11]

It might be assumed that the existence of violence in Mesolithic Europe (or the lack of it) could be established relatively easily on the grounds of whether or not human skeletons from the period tend to display weapon-related injuries. On one hand this is true, but a problem that arises in the Mesolithic which didn't affect earlier periods is the fact that towards the end of the period not everyone was pursuing 'Mesolithic' ways of life at the same time. New ways of doing things which rested upon the uptake of agriculture and herding domestic animals spread into Europe from the west of Asia in a pro-cess which took around 6,000 years to run its course. Consequently, for much of the European Mesolithic a gradually expanding 'frontier' existed between regions where life relied upon hunting and gathering as it always had and the new Neolithic ways of life characterized by reliance on domesticated plants and animals along with a range of other social and technological innova-tions.[12] The existence of such a frontier zone poses a problem for interpreting signs of Mesolithic violence in that it raises the further question of whether such evidence relates to conflict among 'Mesolithic' people or whether it in fact represents fighting between hunter-gatherers and farmers as the latter gradually encroached upon the former. Given the wide range of historically-documented instances of conflict occurring during periods of contact between peoples pursuing very different ways of life known from recent centuries, it is easy to see why such a prehistoric version of the Wild West might seem an entirely plausible idea. The question of whether such frontier zones actually existed at this time is a separate debate in itself, but returning to the initial question regarding violence and warfare confined among hunter-gatherers, any evidence for such therefore needs to pass the further test of clearly predating the arrival of farming in a given region or areas adjacent.

In fact violence-related injuries which preceded the appearance of Neolithic ways of life have been recognized from a diverse range of European locations. In Franchthi Cave in southern Greece two out of seventeen Mesolithic skeletons had depressed cranial fractures.[13] Both individuals were male, one of whom had three head injuries, one healed and two unhealed. The unhealed fractures had been caused by severe impacts that were heavy enough to produce radiating and concentric fractures (see Chapter 2) and to have penetrated the inner table of the skull. In the absence of soft tissues it isn't usually possible to be certain about what caused an individual's death, although either of these perimortal wounds would have been sufficient to do so. The picture is similar in other parts of Europe where individuals with the common prehistoric ailment of depressed skull fractures crop up in ones and twos in regions throughout the continent. An adult male with a healed fracture to his right parietal bone consistent with a blow from a club-like implement was excavated at Hardinxveld-De-Bruin in the Netherlands.[14] Across the sea to the west of this region land that had been part of a larger north-western extremity of the continent at the time when the ice had receded, had since been inundated leaving two large islands, known to us as Ireland and mainland Britain. Directly across the water from what is now the Netherlands the skeleton known as Tilbury Man was discovered during the construction of Tilbury Docks in Essex in 1883. The bones were those of an older adult and were originally assumed to date from the Palaeolithic simply due to the considerable depth at which they were discovered. Later reassessments took the view that the burial more likely dated from the Mesolithic on the basis of the stratigraphic layers he had been situated in. This has recently been confirmed as the skeleton has been re-examined and radiocarbon dated by Rick Schulting of the University of Oxford,[15] placing Tilbury Man in the late Mesolithic (6065–5912 cal BC). By the time of this man's death he had acquired (and survived) two significant head injuries, visible as depressed fractures on his frontal bone, one of which lay across his left orbit (eye socket) which distorted its shape and may have affected his vision.

Returning to the little island of Téviec off the coast of southern Brittany, an adult male with two arrow points lodged in his spine was uncovered in excavations carried out in the 1930s.[16] More recently further victims of violence from the site were recognized when the two adult females, buried in a single grave mentioned earlier, were re-examined as part of a project to remount the skeletons for display to the public by the Museum of Toulouse. Visual inspection accompanied by CT scanning of the skeletons revealed both women to have skull fractures from around the time of their deaths.[17] Several sites along the Muge river estuary in Portugal consist of large shell middens, elongated mounds of shellfish and other occupation debris built up over multiple generations of human habitation in the same place. Among over 200 burials excavated from these sites were three individuals with fractures to their lower ulna of a kind commonly produced when people attempt to ward off a blow with a blunt object. A further three adult individuals had depressed skull fractures whilst one man had a stone arrowhead tip embedded in his right calcaneus – the bone that forms the heel of the foot.[18]

Further examples of deliberate bodily harm have been recognized at several sites on or near the coast in southern Scandinavia. At the southern Swedish site of Skateholm four individuals were found with fractured skulls consistent with blows from blunt implements. One of these, a young adult female, had been apparently killed by a blow to the temple and then laid next to an older man in a single grave. Steven Mithen[19] has suggested the woman might have been ritually killed to join her partner. Whilst this is certainly plausible, that fact that such suggestions are impossible to test once again illustrates the difficulty of interpreting individual acts of prehistoric violence. Two men at the site appear to have been killed by arrows. One man, buried as a collection of disarticulated bones rather than an intact body, had an arrowhead embedded in his pelvis, whilst another had been laid on his front with several arrowheads in the grave fill. The excavator originally suggested that the mourners had shot arrows into the grave after depositing the body.[20] Whilst this is possible, it also seems rather unlikely and this view probably tells us more about the extent to which until very recently people would rather construct slightly odd interpretations, commonly invoking ritual, rather than accept signs of prehistoric violence for what they were, even when the latter offered a far simpler explanation. Here it is arguably more plausible that the man had been shot repeatedly in the back with the arrowshafts remaining sticking out of his back when he was buried, obliging those burying him to place him on his front. A similar arrangement to the double burials at Téviec and Skateholm was found at the Danish site of Henriksholm/Bøgebakken where an adult male with a bone projectile point lodged between his 6th and 7th cervical vertebrae was buried along with two other individuals. Whilst the first man was clearly killed by this weapon, David Frayer of the University of Kansas[21] has suggested that despite lacking signs of injury on their skeletons the other two individuals in the grave may well have also been victims of violence. It seems unlikely that three adult individuals in a small-scale society would all happen to die at precisely the same time, two of natural causes.

Further examples of violent injuries to women and children are again apparent in an adult woman with a large depressed skull fracture from Gongehusvej in Denmark[22] and a child aged around 10 from Tågerup, Sweden,[23] with an arrowhead embedded in her or his pelvis. Rather than being an exhaustive list of all the instances of violence recognized from Mesolithic Europe, what the above examples illustrate is the general spread of such injuries, which occur throughout the time between the receding of the ice sheets and the adoption of agriculture and across Europe wherever human remains have been found from this period, as well as affecting both sexes and people of differing ages (see Fig. 5.2 for the locations of these and other examples).

An area that offers particular opportunities to ask questions regarding the extent to which violence among 'Mesolithic' people was driven, either directly or indirectly, by the appearance of 'Neolithic' neighbours is the Iron Gates Gorge. This region spans a section either side of the Danube where the river forms the modern border between Serbia and Romania. Here a series of excavated sites span a period of about 1,500 years (7000–5500 BC) during which the transition to farming occurred in the region. Through a combination of archaeological stratigraphy (observation of the layers in which human remains were discovered), chemical analysis of bones and teeth and radiocarbon dating it is possible here to attribute the human burials to either the period before or after the arrival of Neolithic ways of living in the area.[24] In terms evocative of those used in relation to European colonization of the New World these periods are referred to by researchers working in the region as 'pre-contact' and 'post-contact' respectively. The region is also unusual for Mesolithic Europe in that burials have been excavated in relatively large numbers compared to other regions. Here the sites of Lepenski Vir, Vlasac, Padina, and Hajdučka Vodenica have produced human remains from a minimum of 418 individuals between them.[25]

The skeletal assemblages from Vlasac and Lepenski Vir have been studied by Mirjana Roksandic of the University of Toronto, and colleagues who note a number of injuries consistent with violence at both sites. Here four individuals were found to have healed depressed skull fractures, all on their frontal bones and all of whom were male. One of the individuals had two such injuries, whilst another also had an unhealed cranial fracture that may have caused the man's death. A further male aged approximately 18 had a projectile point, most probably an arrowhead, embedded in his left ilium (the upper part of the pelvis). Interestingly the point was made of bone rather than flint which raises the question of how widespread such technology might have been at this time, not to mention whether other examples have gone unnoticed as being arrowheads. The projectile had penetrated the gluteal muscles and made its way through the full thickness of the bone, protruding into the peritoneum

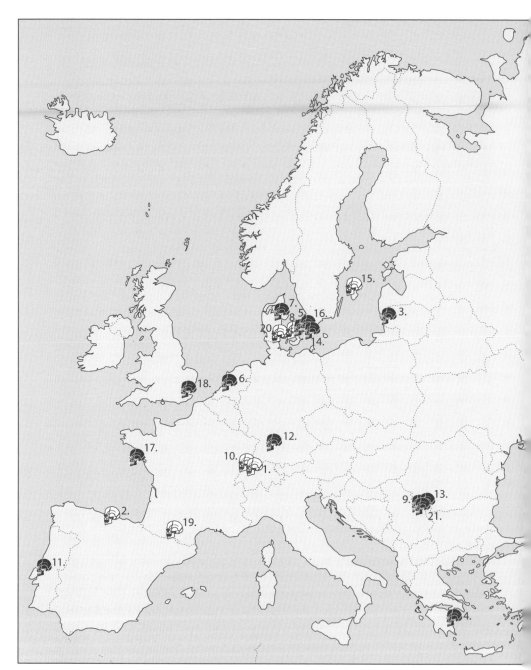

Figure 5.2. Map showing the distribution of violence related injuries recognized in Mesolithic human remains from Europe (shaded skulls = sites mentioned in the text),[26] (1) Birsmatten Basisgrotte, (2) Colombres, (3) Donkalnis, (4) Franchthi Cave, (5) Gonghusvej Vedbaek, (6) Hardinxveld-De-Bruin, (7) Henriksholm/Bøgebakken, (8) Korsor Nor, (9) Lepinski Vir, (10) Mannlefelsen 1, (11) Muge Valley, (12) Groser Ofnet Cave, (13) Schela Cladovei, (14) Skateholm, (15) Stora Bjers, (16) Tågerup, (17) Teviec, (18) Tilbury, (19) Le Trou Violet, (20) Tybrind Vig, (21) Vlasac. (See chapter notes for sources[27])

(the abdominal cavity). Whilst this would not cause death immediately it would have produced internal bleeding and introduced a considerable likelihood of infection in the abdomen (peritonitis) which is commonly fatal. The lack of bone remodelling shows that the young man did not survive for an extended period after this injury. Lastly an adult female displayed a fracture of the lower third of her right ulna. Although this injury was fully healed the ends of the bones had failed to knit together, so the broken end of the bone was no longer connected to the rest of the shaft. This type of healing occurs when broken bones are not properly immobilized (splinted) during the healing process. Whilst the woman could still have functioning in this limb, as the forearm is made up of two bones and the accompanying radius was uninjured, she would have experienced a reduction in strength and could no longer have engaged in strenuous tasks with this arm. Fractures of the ulna can occur through falls, although such injuries tend to affect the radius much more commonly and would also tend to occur closer to the tip of the bone nearer the wrist as people commonly fall onto their outstretched hand. Breaks of the distal third at the point where this woman's ulna was injured are more commonly caused by a direct impact and this injury is most plausibly interpreted as a 'parry fracture' (rather ominously known as a 'nightstick fracture' in the US)[28] – a defensive injury incurred in fending off a blow.

Farming first appeared in the Danube region at around 6500 BC. Of the six individuals noted above, four are dated firmly during the pre-contact period, predating farming by several centuries. Of the remaining two, one is not well dated but was eating a pre-contact (Mesolithic) diet, whilst the other might be from either before or after the appearance of farming. An objection that is sometimes raised in relation to observations of numbers of weapon injuries from periods in which burials are relatively sparse is that people dying violently might be specially selected for being buried as opposed to being disposed of after death in some other way such as cremation or exposure. This is a fair point as if true it would mean that the sample of human remains available to modern investigators is skewed and gives an impression of violence being more common than it really was. However, the respective injuries from the Iron Gates region are predominantly healed, meaning that we have no reason to think that these individuals actually died violent deaths. The frequency of injuries can therefore be taken to be at least reasonably reflective of the general population. From the above sites, on the right bank of the Danube, this frequency works out at 2.3 per cent of the total sample (6 out of 263). However, this crude figure doesn't take account of preservation – i.e. the fact that most skeletons are far from complete and so simply counting individuals gives a figure that may be unreliable. If just the five head injuries are considered and these are expressed as a percentage of the total number of skeletons with sufficiently preserved crania, the figure changes to 4 out of 109, and when only male skulls are considered it becomes 4 out of 42, just under one in ten males.

A distance of 60km away on the opposite side of the Danube a further fifty-seven burials of people eating pre-contact diets have been excavated at the site of Schela Cladovei. Of these, five individuals had projectile wounds whilst a further fourteen had evidence of further violent injuries, giving a total preva-lence of nineteen out of fifty-seven (33 per cent). Here some of the radio-carbon dates overlap with the appearance of farming, but again others predate the arrival of agriculture and herding. Clearly then, the people of the Iron Gates region were indeed given to engaging in violence before the Neolithic and most if not all of these injuries cannot be ascribed to hunters fighting with farmers along a frontier zone. Nor can these assaults be explained away as symptoms of hunter-gatherers being put under pressure by encroaching farmers to the extent that 'Mesolithic' people began fighting for the remain-ing territory amongst each other, as in most cases the arrival of farmers and herders was still centuries away.

One potential criticism of any view of how much Mesolithic people might generally have been at risk from their fellow human beings is that many of the sites where signs of violence are apparent are relatively large and involved people who had stopped roaming around the landscape, opting instead to settle in one place. This is particularly true for the Muge estuary, the Iron Gates region and the Scandinavian sites mentioned earlier such as Skateholm and Tågerup, where the inhabitants were more hunter-fishers than hunter-gatherers. Such sites fit the picture mentioned in the previous chapter (see feature p. 58) where access to predictable, abundant resources such as rich coastal regions makes such places worth defending, so fighting and territori-ality become much more likely. Once such a settlement has become estab-lished, the inhabitants may choose a specific area to bury their dead and over time sizeable cemeteries may appear, therefore leaving higher numbers of bodies, some complete with terrible injuries, for archaeologists to find thousands of years later. The obvious objection here then, is that Mesolithic people living further inland probably lived in smaller, more mobile groups, didn't produce large cemeteries and would be less likely to fight each other as they could simply walk away from contested resources that weren't worth the trouble anyway, as any other location might be equally good. A further prob-lem in interpreting all this is that, as with earlier prehistoric periods, it is gen-erally difficult to assess whether people who were clearly deliberately killed during the Mesolithic met their demise as single victims in 'one-off' killings or whether they died as part of larger actions in which groups of people were attacked together. Furthermore, whilst tribal warfare can certainly involve the killing of single individuals (see previous chapter), this may be difficult to differentiate from 'homicides' involving just two people, an attacker and a victim, if the evidence consists simply of a single fractured skull or an arrow point lodged in bone.

An instance that appears much less ambiguous and also flies in the face of the suggestion that inland hunter-gatherers would have had less reason to fight, was provided by excavations in a cave in Bavaria in 1908 (Grosser Ofnet), which remains arguably the most striking (or just plain shocking) example of evidence for Mesolithic violence. Here two shallow pits were found dug into the floor of a low chamber that was too small for human habitation. Each pit contained a number of human skulls, arranged 'like eggs in a basket'[29] with the faces mostly pointing west. The Ofnet skulls have been examined and debated by various scholars during the last century with opinions regarding their likely date ranging from the Palaeolithic to the Neolithic. This issue was eventually settled through radiocarbon analysis which dated the skulls to the late Mesolithic,[30] although disagreement persists over exactly how many skulls were present due to some being more damaged and fragmented than others. David Frayer assessed there to be thirty-one individuals in the larger of the pits with a further six skulls in the second.[31] Of these twenty-three were children (aged under 15), all but one of whom were under 11 years with just over half of these aged under 6. Among the adults, which includes individuals aged over 15 who were probably classed as adults at the time when they lived, there were five males and ten females.

At a time when infant and child mortality will have been high and women frequently died in childbirth, the overall profile of this group could easily be explained as consistent with the accumulation of natural deaths in a small community over time. However, two aspects of the Ofnet skulls suggest that something else was going on. Firstly, these individuals were indeed represented by skulls – that is to say the cranium and mandible (lower jaw) together, rather than just the cranium alone. Of further significance was the fact that the skulls were also accompanied by cervical vertebrae – the bones of the neck. This means that each must have been placed in the pit as a severed head, rather than simply a dry skull separated from the rest of the skeleton after the flesh had decayed, and indicates that the heads must have been removed at least relatively soon after death. The heads of the females were accompanied by pierced red deer teeth and shells which appear to have been strung together as necklaces they had been wearing. The second shocking aspect of the Ofnet 'skull nest' is the presence of unhealed injuries, which are clearly present on six individuals and likely on two others.[32] All the injuries were consistent in size and shape with having been inflicted with stone axes.

Of these, two individuals were adult males who had multiple injuries positioned consistently with having been struck by a face-to-face attacker. The remainder all consisted of a single blow to the back of the head which would have been fatal, including two observed on young infants. The most recent examination of the Ofnet bones by Jörg Orschiedt of the Freie University, Berlin, also noted cutmarks made with stone blades on the neck vertebrae of nine individuals. These are open to interpretation in two ways, either as further strengthening the suggestion that these people were decapitated, rather than just their bones being picked up a long period after they died, or alternatively as evidence that the respective individuals had their throats cut.

All this is grim stuff. The picture at Ofnet would appear, as suggested by David Frayer, to relate to a massacre where the members of a single community were violently and systematically killed, perhaps whilst the majority of men were away from the main group. This butchery was then followed by a ritual component where the heads of the slain individuals were removed and deposited in the ground apparently in a single act, rather than in a series of gradual additions to the pits.[33] The heads had been sprinkled with red ochre, a natural earth pigment containing iron oxide, commonly used in prehistoric burials. Effectively it would appear that the severed heads formed a 'votive offering', the ritual placement of items or substances in the ground in order to thank or appease some form of supernatural entity who it was believed would appreciate such a submission. Of course it is possible, as is usually the case with prehistoric remains, to suggest other interpretations. For example, the Ofnet heads might represent ritual killings or sacrifices carried out within a single community rather than conflict between two groups. However, given the likely small overall size of Mesolithic communities, to deliberately kill so many of the most productive and potentially useful members of a group in this way, the young people and women of childbearing age, would be very ill-advised just on a practical level, without considering the distressing nature of such an extreme act. As with other examples cited previously (such as explaining fatal injuries as hunting accidents) whilst such an explanation can't be disproved it also takes far more 'special pleading' to make it work and I would agree with David Frayer that viewing Ofnet as representing a Mesolithic massacre is much more plausible. Here the killing of children and infants again suggests the principle of 'social substitution' to be in effect (see previous chapter) where any member of an 'enemy' community is regarded as representative of the whole and a viable target for hostile action. This latter facet of the evidence is effectively then the signature of 'war' in the Mesolithic rather than simply 'homicide' committed between quarrelling individuals.

Most recently, at the time of writing a newly-published find from Kenya has indicated that violence between groups of hunter-gatherers at this time

'Senseless Violence': War among the Huron

In recent times war has generally been seen as a largely functional endeavour involving the practical application of force in an organized and strategic manner to attain specific goals. Aside from differences in technology and in the way societies are organized, variations in the way warfare is conducted are largely determined by the objectives those involved are trying to achieve. If this statement is true then it should be possible to draw some broad conclusions regarding the likely nature of conflict in a particular region or period by considering the probable goals of the people doing the fighting. This sort of 'common sense' approach may work reasonably well with regard to nation states during the last few centuries but tends to encounter problems when applied to less developed societies and particularly for prehistoric periods. In fact one of the reasons underlying the common assumption that war did not effectively exist during most of prehistory was the lack of recognizable strategic objectives to fight over. This is certainly the case for the Mesolithic as what property existed was essentially evenly distributed, social groups were small with only simple levels of organization and strategic territorial objectives would seem very difficult to define.

As mentioned in the preceding chapter, a line of evidence that is often helpful in trying to understand prehistoric societies is the observation of modern (or at least relatively recent) societies still living in ways that are broadly similar to those of past peoples. Attempts to understand prehistoric hunter-gatherers or foragers are therefore often informed by observations of modern forager groups or historical accounts of such, usually by colonial European observers in recent centuries. Such thinking is sometimes criticized on the basis that just because one group of people is observed to engage in a particular behaviour today this doesn't prove that people definitely acted the same in the past. However, this is not what such arguments are saying. Instead the point of such 'ethnographic' (or ethnohistorical' accounts) is that they show that a particular behaviour *can* occur in a given set of circumstances and so they do provide evidence by showing what is possible. This is an important point in the case of warfare as pre-industrial, tribal peoples have indeed been observed to engage in organized hostilities despite a lack of obvious strategic objectives, as they might be understood in the modern sense.

An example of a tribal people engaging in warfare with little in the way of strategic organization or support from social hierarchy can be seen in accounts written by French explorers who observed and recorded conflict among Native American peoples in what is now Eastern Canada in the early seventeenth century. In particular Samuel de Champlain (1574–1635) wrote about the way war was conducted by the Huron of the Great Lakes region against their enemies the Iroquois. Amongst the Huron, participating in warfare was very significant to male status and provided an important opportunity for young men to demonstrate bravery and leadership. Such activities usually took the form of small-scale raids that would typically result in the deaths of a few 'enemy' individuals (commonly in single figures and possibly as low as just one victim) in order to satisfactorily demonstrate such personal qualities. These incursions would commonly lead to counter-attacks in revenge by the opposing group in a self-perpetuating cycle of raiding and scalping, whilst a further objective was the capture of prisoners, a particular source of prestige for the individual claiming credit for the capture. In considering Huron warfare John Robb[34] of Cambridge University has pointed out that rather than a means to achieve some wider objective such as taking resources or territory, war among the Huron was in fact an aim in itself. Young men would participate in warfare effectively for its own sake because of the opportunities for personal advancement within their own community it offered, rather than to achieve any further 'practical' goal. Rather than being directed by more senior figures in society, who in fact would often advise against it, raiding activity therefore tended to be driven by young men who had still to attain high status. Consequently, Champlain was rather perplexed when having travelled a considerable distance accompanying a Huron war party in 1609, with a view to providing assistance from his musket-armed soldiers, the Huron were content to conduct brief raids on a few villages and then to return home without achieving anything recognizable to him as a strategic objective (Fig. 5.3). Later in the century this lack of strategic organization in warfare would in fact lead to the Huron's downfall when they were defeated by a large and well-organized army of Iroquois in 1649. The Huron's lack of organization resulted in them being overwhelmed in the face of the Iroquois' co-ordinated assaults on well–defined tactical objectives.[35]

Figure 5.3. Depiction of a battle between Huron and Iroquois warriors in 1609; having accompanied them on a raiding expedition, the French explorer Samuel de Champlain and his companions assisted the Huron by using their firearms to inflict surprise and fear. The Iroquois had not previously seen Europeans or the new technology they brought with them.[36]

Just over a century later the same region saw events that mirrored those of 1609 in reverse. In 1757, when the French and British were fighting each other for possession of North America, the siege of the British Fort William Henry ended when the British surrendered and were granted generous terms by the French General Montcalm allowing them to leave the territory unmolested carrying their arms but no ammunition.[37] Montcalm's army had been considerably bolstered by large numbers of Native American allies who had arrived from all over the Great Lakes region to join the fight. Having travelled sometimes considerable distances to take scalps, prisoners and plunder, many of these young warriors were as exasperated at this apparent failure to act upon victory as Champlain had been with their ancestors a hundred years earlier. Against the wishes of their French allies the Indians pursued and fell upon the retreating British column. The subsequent massacre was later made famous in James Fenimore Cooper's *Last of the Mohicans*[38] although it is now recognized that this attack resulted from the two cultures' inability to comprehend each other's values rather than treachery on the part of Montcalm as has been popularly believed.[39]

was not confined to Europe. At Nataruk on the edge of what was once a lagoon, the bones of at least twenty-seven individuals were discovered eroding out of the ground by a team led by Marta Lahr of Cambridge University.[40] None had been buried in graves, with the bodies either having fallen into the water or been left on the shore. Twelve were articulated skeletons, of which ten had lethal weapon injuries. Of these five (or possibly six) had penetrating wounds to the head and neck consistent with arrow injuries. Five had blunt head injuries and three had stone points embedded in bone or in the chest or abdominal cavity. Of sixteen adults in whom sex could be determined there were eight females and eight males, with six children also represented by fragmented bones.[41] Here it would appear again that a small community had been massacred, with the bodies in the water perhaps being those of people attempting to escape. Unlike some of the European groups mentioned previously, who were becoming increasingly settled, this was not the case with the Nataruk people who were fully mobile hunter-gatherers.

The previous chapters have shown that violence has been a feature of life in human societies since before modern humans existed. Whilst hostilities within and between groups were clearly not a new development during the Mesolithic, a question the examples given in the current chapter does raise is of whether such behaviour increased or declined at this time (or whether it didn't significantly change at all). Virginia Hutton Estabrook of the University of California, Riverside[42] has considered this question in a study where she listed all the known European examples of violence-related injuries in the Palaeolithic and compared them with all those identified from the Mesolithic. This was not as simple an endeavour as it might sound, as the nature of the evidence available from these two periods is actually quite different, so it is not just a straightforward case of counting them. On the one hand there are many more Mesolithic examples of human skeletons showing signs of violence. However, there are a great deal more Mesolithic skeletons available to examine, and these are generally much more complete than the poorly-preserved and fragmented examples that survive from earlier periods. The greatest area of difference Hutton Estabrook found was in the proportions of perimortem injuries (i.e. injuries occurring around the time of death which may or may not have been the cause of death) of which many more were apparent from the Mesolithic. However, such injuries are commonly the most difficult to spot in archaeological samples partly because they are the most susceptible to postmortem damage. In particular, the outer surfaces of bones that have spent thousands of years in the ground can often become so eroded that the distinctions between the smooth, regular margins of perimortem fractures and the rough, irregular edges of postmortem damage can be effectively lost. As a consequence of the extreme age and incompleteness of many Palaeolithic samples it wasn't possible to say with certainty whether the greater levels of perimortem trauma apparent among Mesolithic remains is 'real' or simply a product of better preservation. On one hand the examples discussed in the current chapter leave no doubt that violence was a feature of Mesolithic life. Such hostilities affected both sexes and all ages and occurred between different communities at least some, if not most of the time. However, with regard to how frequent such behaviour was, for now the jury remains out on the question.

Chapter 6

'The Children of Cain': Conflict in the Neolithic

The period generally referred to as the Neolithic (New Stone Age) is one of the most interesting phases of human development as well as arguably one of the most important, and has continued to generate excitement and disagreement in equal measure since the term was first suggested by archaeologist John Lubbock in 1865.[1] Current definitions of the period have widened their focus from the sort of tools people were using in favour of more rounded views that consider how people were making a living generally. The Neolithic is commonly described as the time when humans stopped living in small mobile bands subsisting by hunting and gathering, and instead settled down to a sedentary lifestyle, making a living by herding newly-domesticated animals and farming crops of novel modified strains of the wild grains that had previously formed only a modest part of their ancestors' diets. In reality, however, the situation was much more complicated than this simple picture, with a wide range of new behaviours and technologies appearing at around the same time (although in different orders in different regions) but as a rather patchy process rather than a sudden shift, that appears rapid only because we are so distant in time from these events. In so far as the Neolithic can be defined it began as early as 9500 BC in some regions of Western Asia and gradually spread to Europe by means that are a continued subject of debate, reaching Greece by around 6500 BC and Britain and Ireland by *c.*4000 BC. The extent to which these new ways of living depended upon agriculture or pastoral semi-mobile herding also varied over time and space and in some regions such as Britain, the earlier Neolithic appears initially to have been based largely on herding, with agriculture taking a more secondary role. So rather than a sudden shift from a life of mobile woodland foraging to one of cleared arable fields and permanent settlements, the Neolithic is perhaps better seen as a process, a time of change during which the shift from one to the other was made over 1,500 years or more, only leaving a settled landscape that would be more familiar to us by the beginning of the Bronze Age.

This period also brought changes to other aspects of people's behaviour. Whilst there is likely to have been no shortage of ritual beliefs and religious actions in the preceding periods, the Neolithic was different in that people now began inscribing such ideas on to the landscape they occupied in a variety of collectively-built structures and spaces. The Neolithic stands out particularly as a time when monumental architecture first appeared in the form of burial structures (commonly stone or earthen mounds containing timber or stone burial chambers) enclosures, stone circles and processional avenues which appear for the most part to have had ritual or ceremonial functions. It is arguably the appearance of such collectively built edifices – often involving tens of thousands of hours to construct – that really sets the Neolithic apart from earlier times in that the way society was organized and how people related to each other must have undergone significant changes for these new endeavours to be possible. Each of these constructions required people to organize themselves in larger numbers and in ways that were more complex and co-ordinated than ever before. Such organization also implies that some people were in a position to marshal the labour of others on a scale previously unseen.

You Only See What You Look For

If the current chapter were being written 20 years ago or more it would probably have been very short. This is because up to that time only limited evidence for conflict occurring during the Neolithic was recognized with little appetite to look for any more. Of all the prehistoric periods that came under the spell of what Lawrence Keeley[2] called 'the pacified past' (see Chapter 1) the Neolithic was most greatly affected. Between the late 1960s and the mid-1990s various conceptions of the prehistoric past prevailed but all were characterized by the notion that prehistory had been relatively peaceful with any significant unpleasantness beyond the odd dispute between individuals, occurring later rather than earlier. Prior to the development of metalworking, humans were presumed not to have made any objects exclusively for killing other humans and hence there were no items specifically manufactured as weapons. The Neolithic dead were often found buried collectively with little in the way of grave goods to indicate differences in wealth and no obvious ranking in terms of importance. Taking a broader, systems-level view it was clear that at a societal level things were good in Neolithic Europe. In order to free up the time it must have taken to build all manner of monuments from stone tombs in Greece to the thousands of megaliths erected in rows at Carnac in Brittany and great earthwork enclosures in Britain, society as a whole must have been generating a considerable surplus. Not only were the builders of such being taken out of any economically-useful activity, but also the efforts of others would be needed to feed them while they were engaged in such construction. The Neolithic therefore came to be seen as a largely egalitarian time when people came together to expend their economic surplus collectively on ritual monuments, blissfully unaware of the carnage and group hostilities their descendants would one day engage in.

Of course this is an oversimplification of how the Neolithic was viewed and the blanket denunciation of the views of the 1960s and 1970s as the 'pacified past' – essentially projecting the hippy vibes of the time onto prehistory – has been questioned by John Carman[3] who notes that not everyone thought this way. However, such views were certainly commonly expressed, in terms that were often quite unambiguous. In an otherwise very useful book *The Stonehenge People* Rodney Castleden described the European Neolithic as 'a land without war', characterized by 'a very long and uninterrupted period of peace, never since attained anywhere in Europe'.[4]

Hindsight is a wonderful thing and it is easy to see why such views were prevalent given the information available to archaeologists at the time. On the one hand the skeletal remains of this new breed of herders and farmers have been excavated in considerably greater numbers than those of their Mesolithic forebears, but regardless of this, the Neolithic burials that are available to examine are still sparse and poorly preserved in comparison to more recent periods. For most of the Neolithic, as for much of prehistory in general, people were disposing of their dead in ways that are archaeologically invisible, probably excarnating them (exposing them to the elements) or perhaps cremating them and scattering rather than collecting and burying the burned remains. Later Neolithic burials are relatively rare whilst those of the earlier Neolithic (mostly mid-fourth millennium BC) tend to be poorly preserved, highly fragmented and disarticulated so the bones of multiple people are mixed up, making it often impossible to reconstruct individuals. Injuries on skeletal remains are often difficult to recognize in the best of circumstances. Given the general state of Neolithic remains coupled with a lack of effort to look for any signs of violence that might be present it is arguably unsurprising that no one spotted any beyond the most obvious.

Signs of the Times?

Whilst Neolithic sites and monuments have always received a lot of attention, human remains from the period had until recently become rather neglected. However, the last few years have seen a renewal of interest in the remains of Neolithic people as a broad range of previously-excavated burials, some uncovered as long ago as the mid-nineteenth century, have been re-examined after languishing unloved in dusty museum collections often for many decades. This fresh attention has led to a variety of new insights including the realization that in fact signs of violence during this period are startlingly

common. Now that the appearance of past injuries on bone is well documented and the mechanisms by which bone breaks are better understood than
they once were (see Chapter 2), three categories of injury have repeatedly
been noticed on Neolithic skeletal remains. The first two consist of injuries
inflicted at close quarters, probably with a mixture of blunt instruments and
edged stone artefacts (axes etc.). These can be divided into healed and
unhealed injuries which have mostly been identified on the skull. In the case
of the former, the blow was sufficient to damage the bone, resulting in
depressed areas of the skull vault, usually rounded in form with smoothed
edges where the bone has later remodelled over time (Fig. 6.1). Such cases are
generally those where the impact failed to penetrate through the inner table
of the cranium and produce a potentially fatal route for infection to get in or
to cause events inside the head later leading to death. For unhealed injuries
the opposite is true, where the offending object has penetrated the cranial
vault fully, either causing direct damage to the brain or indirect damage due
to subsequent bleeding or swelling within or around it. Such injuries are
apparent through the lack of bone remodelling indicating the individual to
have died either immediately or shortly afterwards (Fig. 6.2). The third category of injury involves assaults at a distance using projectiles, generally in the
form of arrows. Here the use of such weapons is apparent either through projectile points (arrowheads) being found lodged in bone, or suspiciously located
in relation to the body, for example lying within the chest or abdominal region
consistent with being embedded in soft tissues which have long since decayed.
Lastly, projectile injuries may be recognized where damage to bone is consistent with being punctured by pointed objects and so identified even when
the 'murder weapon' is missing, although this last category is much less commonly noticed.

   Archaeologists are very fond of producing maps that show the distribution
of particular types of site or artefact in order to look for patterns and concentrations, and how these change over time. When the occurrence of Neolithic
human remains with signs of violence is plotted on a map the results are rather
striking. For Britain, rather than showing some zones where violence and conflict were more prevalent with other areas appearing more peaceful, the distribution of Neolithic injuries essentially mirrors the distribution of surviving

Figure 6.1. British Neolithic individuals with head injuries who 'lived to tell the tale'. (Top) The
skull of an adult male from Clachaig on the Isle of Arran (Scotland), imaginatively displayed in
front of an array of Neolithic and Bronze Age spears and axes at the Hunterian Museum,
Glasgow. This man has a healed depressed fracture to his right frontal bone (arrowed) consistent with a blow from a rounded blunt object.[5] (Middle) An individual from Orkney with a
similar healed pond-like depressed fracture. (Bottom) the cranium of an adult female from
Dinnington long barrow (S. Yorks); this woman survived two such blows to the head.

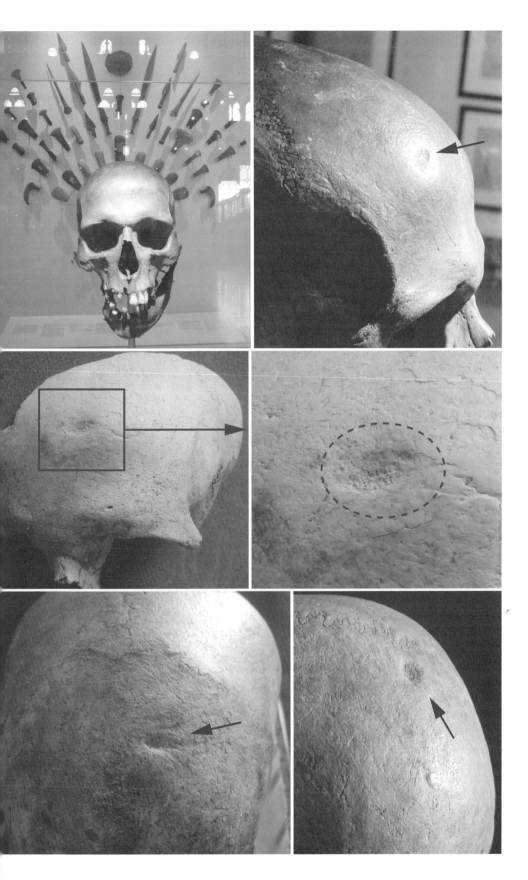

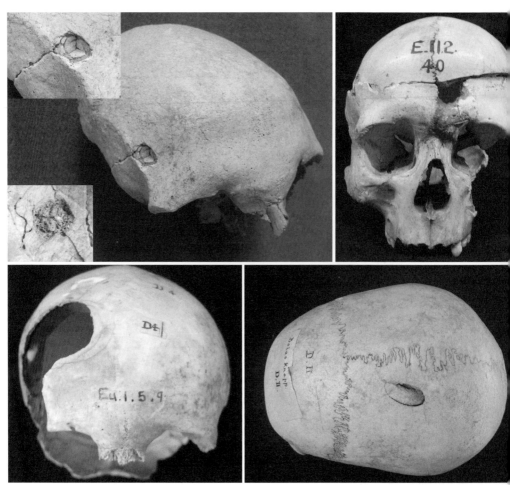

Figure 6.2. Unhealed head injuries consistent with violent assaults. (Top left) Individual from Orkney with a crushed-in area of bone (a comminuted fracture) possibly caused by a sling stone, with a punched-out 'bevelled' area on the inner surface of the skull. (Top right) Adult male from Rodmarton (Gloucestershire) with a linear fracture radiating from left to right consistent with a severe impact. (Bottom right) Cranium of a child from Belas Knap (Gloucs) displaying the result of a savage blow to the head with a rounded club-like object. (Bottom left) Adult from the same burial monument with an axe-shaped defect penetrating the skull vault.

Getting to the Point: Prehistoric Archery in the Lab

Whilst arrowheads embedded in bone are a pretty obvious and indisputable sign of deliberate violence, their presence in close proximity to the body is more open to interpretation. In the past such objects might have been interpreted as 'grave goods', even despite a lack of any other items for the deceased to take with them into the afterlife. On more recent consideration it may in fact be more likely that these stone points arrived 'in' rather than 'with' the body, possibly being responsible for the deaths of the individuals concerned. In cases where arrows damaged bone but where the arrowhead didn't remain lodged where it struck, this will only be recognized if the person examining it knows what to look for. Several years ago, I noticed holes in several Neolithic skulls that looked suspiciously like the kind seen in modern gunshot wounds in having a 'bevelled' form (see Chapter 2) where the hole is larger on the inside than on the outside of the skull (Fig. 6.3). It occurred to me that these might well be arrow wounds but on looking for published examples of 'known' arrow wounds to the skull it became apparent that in fact there were none. Essentially when people had interpreted similar holes (usually in Medieval crania) as arrow wounds this was purely on the basis of suggestion, rather than comparison with any kind of documented example. Essentially such interpretations were saying 'this is probably an arrow wound because this is what an arrow wound probably looks like'. Anyone involved in academic research occasionally stumbles across situations like this, where the only option is to either admit that nobody

Figure 6.3. External (left) and internal (right) views of unhealed penetrating head injuries. These wounds are similar in form to modern gunshot wounds with the exception of being elliptical in shape consistent with having been caused by similar-shaped objects, most likely flint arrowheads. (Top) Littleton Drew, (bottom) West Tump (both sites in Gloucestershire).

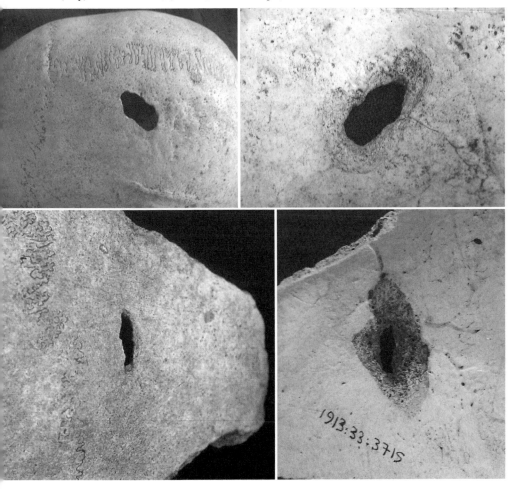

knows the answer or try to find it out for yourself, so I decided to conduct some experiments of my own.

Will Lord is a master flint knapper who kindly agreed to make a selection of Neolithic arrows for me. With flint points set into hardwood shafts using beeswax and fletched (anachronistically) with pheasant's feathers, these were real things of beauty. Deciding what sort of experimental samples to shoot them at presented more of a problem. Whilst the bones of other animals are essentially very similar to humans in terms of their composition they obviously differ in shape and particularly so for the skull. With our large brains nothing has a skull quite like our own and so results obtained from shooting animal crania just couldn't be relied upon. Instead a more workable option was found by looking at the overall type of bone required. The human cranial vault (the dome of the skull) consists of two layers of cortical (solid) bone with a layer of spongy, trabecular bone in between. In this respect areas of flat bone within animal skeletons are actually very similar and a portion of the skeleton in quadrupedal animals that offers a particularly useful example is the scapula (shoulder blade). The scapulae of a cows and pigs are triangular pieces of flat bone of about the same thickness as a human skull and formed of a similar 'sandwich' of cortical (solid) and trabecular (spongy) bone. Cattle scapulae are also quite large (about 12 in in length) and so presented a helpful-sized target for shooting at (Fig. 6.4).

The results were of interest from several points of view. Firstly, where arrows penetrated all the way through the scapulae the resulting 'wounds' in the bone tended to be elliptical in shape with a punched-out or bevelled area on the side opposite to where the arrow struck. These holes were therefore essentially the same

Figure 6.4. Experimentation with Neolithic arrows. Repeated shots through cattle and pig scapulae produced elliptical, bevelled holes, similar to those seen in some Neolithic people's heads.

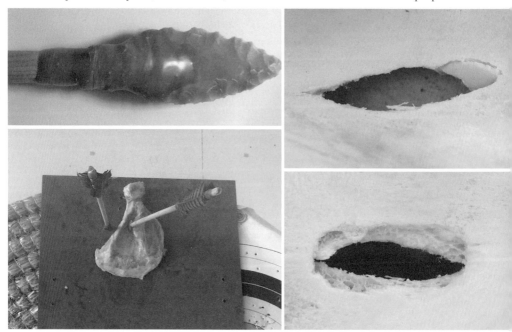

as those recurrently seen in Neolithic people's heads. Further experiments with a replica stone axe generated similarly interesting results which again look very similar to examples of cranial trauma seen in bone from the period. Secondly, where the arrows didn't puncture all the way through, small fragments of flint were visible embedded in the bone approximately 50 per cent of the time. Lastly, where no embedded flint was visible examination of the bone at high magnification using an electron microscope revealed distinctive signs in the form of numerous parallel grooves scraped into the bone by the many tiny irregularities in the flint. Similar grooves were later identified in a suspicious looking slit-like hole in one of the vertebrae of a human skeleton from Feizor Nick cave in Yorkshire (see Chapter 7). These marks not only showed that this individual had probably died from an arrow wound to the abdomen, but also proved that the marks identified in the experiments can survive to be recognized thousands of years later.

burials (Fig. 6.5). Wherever there are human skeletons to study there are individuals with injuries caused either by blunt objects, axe-like implements or arrows. In terms of numbers, people with injuries are never in the majority, but they do make up a significant percentage of the overall population available for study. My own most recent assessment is that of 431 British Neolithic crania available for study, 52 (or 12 per cent and so 1 in every 8.3 people!) had one or more healed or unhealed injuries. Given that this figure doesn't include the rest of the body[6] plus the fact that not all injuries affect bone, it is likely that the real numbers were actually higher, painting a picture of the Neolithic as a really quite stressed and violent time to be alive (compare this to the modern UK murder rate of less than 1 per 100,000 per year),[7] Of course, this need not be the case as it may be that the sample of the population that has survived to be investigated is in fact 'biased'. Most of the Neolithic burials that have been excavated from Britain come from long barrows and it is certainly the case that only a minority of people will have been buried in these special structures. We don't know how people were selected for such special treatment after death but one possibility is that dying violently might earn you such a burial.

Whilst the above point should not be dismissed, there are also reasons to think that the Neolithic was indeed a violent time compared to more recent periods. Where individuals do not have perimortem injuries we have no reason to think that these people died a violent death, that had then qualified them for special burial in a monument. However, these individuals frequently display healed injuries consistent with violence, sometimes with two or even three depressed injuries to the skull in the same person. It would appear then that even for those who (as far as we can tell) didn't die at the hands of others, violence was a genuine and recurrent aspect of life. Furthermore, the

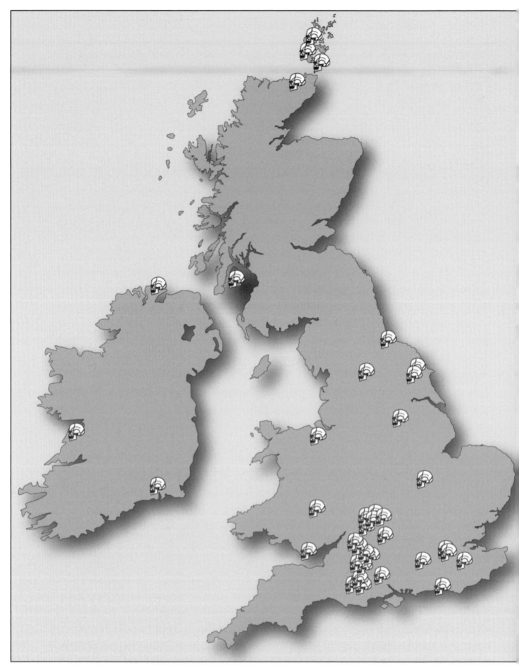

Figure 6.5. Neolithic sites in Britain and Ireland where human remains with violence-related head injuries have been excavated. The sites marked comprise fifty-two injured individuals representing 12 per cent of the wider sample of Neolithic individuals available for study.

investigation of growing numbers of Neolithic burials from beyond Britain is now combining to tell a very consistent story across a very broad region. From Ireland to Romania and Sweden to Turkey, a remarkably similar picture is emerging, where the appearance of farming and signs of weapon-based assaults go hand in hand.[8] Whilst other parts of Atlantic Europe such as Brittany or northern Germany might be subject to the same 'long barrow' bias as British material, elsewhere this is not the case. Areas with widely different styles of burial show similar signs of hostility and it would appear that the idea of a violent Neolithic can no longer be easily dismissed.

A further aspect of Neolithic violence that is hinted at but remains unproven relates not to what is present but what is absent from some bone assemblages. It is not unusual for human remains in collective tombs to exhibit unusual patterns in terms of which bones are present, with prominent and robust parts of the skeleton sometimes curiously missing. In particular some long barrow assemblages don't have as many crania as they should, prompting the question of whether the skulls of venerated ancestors were sometimes removed from tomb chambers at some point after the bodies had decomposed. In two instances however this may not have been the case. At the chambered monuments of West Tump and Nether Swell[9] (both in Gloucestershire) similar series of cutmarks were noted on two human clavicles (the collar bone). These marks are located at the attachment point of one of the neck muscles, with the other end of the muscle attaching to the skull. In explaining why these muscles were cut through it seems most likely that this relates to removal of the head. If someone wanted to decapitate a body using stone tools this couldn't be done by simply cutting straight through the neck as might be done with a sword or similar weapon in later periods, and so individual muscles and other structures would have to be severed one by one using a flint blade. As to why this was done, it could still be the case that the head of a venerated ancestor was being removed for use in some sort of ritual and presumably those taking it didn't wish to wait for the body to decompose. Alternatively, the fact that the heads had been removed so soon after death might imply a different scenario, in which the heads might have been taken as trophies rather than representing the actions of grieving mourners. An intriguing find at the site of Bergheim in western France is even more suggestive of Neolithic trophy-taking. Here a circular pit was found to contain the articulated skeletons of seven individuals, three adults – two males, one female – and four children, piled unceremoniously on top of each other. One of the adult males had multiple unhealed head injuries, whilst his left upper arm had been amputated through the humerus. Beneath this group were seven amputated left arms piled together at the centre of the pit.[10] This arrangement is odd even by Neolithic standards. It would appear that all seven individuals were deposited at the same time and, given the violent death of one of the adults and the multiple disembodied limbs, it seems reasonable to argue that this deposit represents something other than bereaved relatives sending their deceased kin on their way following natural deaths. A more plausible interpretation is that all seven articulated bodies, plus the arms, represent deliberate killings. It is tempting to construct a scenario where the severed limbs represent trophies taken from enemies slain in conflict whilst the articulated bodies represent prisoners then executed and deposited in the pit as part of an offering or sacrifice, similar to the trophy heads from Ofnet Cave (see Chapter 5). Of course this is speculation, but given the nature of the evidence this certainly seems a plausible explanation. Certainly, such removal of body parts here and at the British sites mentioned above raises the question of how many 'loose finds' of human bone from prehistoric sites might actually represent similar activities?

'We Know Where You Live': Enclosures and Settlements

In terms of the types of implements available for use as weapons and the specific nature of violent acts between individuals the Neolithic did not differ significantly from the times that preceded it. As with their Mesolithic ancestors, the weapons that were accessible to Neolithic people consisted of blunt club-like objects, stone-edged tools primarily designed for woodworking (axes and adzes) and equipment otherwise used for hunting (spears and arrows), with the possible addition of sling stones. Certainly there are no obvious differences between the types of violent injury that have been identified on Neolithic bones and those recognized in Mesolithic skeletons. However, this is not to say there were not other kinds of difference between the ways warfare was practised during the two periods. An important area where there is a clear divergence is in the issue of scale. The excavation of an early Neolithic enclosure at Asparn Schletz in Austria began as an essentially routine investigation intended to answer fairly standard questions in pre-historic archaeology such as the date and length of occupation, the range of uses of the enclosure, the subsistence choices of the inhabitants and so on. The excavators were therefore surprised to find large quantities of human remains in the enclosure ditch which didn't conform even to the strange treatments of the dead sometimes seen in Neolithic burials. The ditch contained the skeletons of sixty-seven individuals, including men, women and children, the bodies having apparently been thrown into the ditch with no signs of care and left to be gnawed and scattered by scavenging animals. Continuing excavation along the ditch circumference would later raise this number to over 100, leading the excavators to estimate that perhaps up to 200 people may have been deposited there altogether.[11] When the bones were examined in detail they were found to show repeated signs of fatal injury, particularly in the form of club or axe wounds to the head.[12] A similar sight was encountered at Talheim in Germany where again a Neolithic enclosure ditch was found to contain the mass burial of thirty-four individuals of varied ages and both sexes.[13] Again there was no sign of any care or respect being taken in the way the bodies were placed and the skeletons displayed violent injuries throughout, similar to those at Asparn–Schletz. In the case of each of these assemblages it would appear that a whole community had been massacred. Unlike Schletz, at Talheim the ditch was filled in and the bodies covered over, with the site then re-occupied, presumably by the attacking group.

Whilst once is an incident and two could be coincidence, three indicates a pattern. The chance discovery of a third early Neolithic mass grave at Schöneck-Kilianstädten near Frankfurt, has since provided further evidence of inter-community conflict during this period.[14] Here a long v-shaped pit, that may be part of a longer boundary ditch, near a settlement, was found to contain the jumbled and broken bones of at least twenty-six people. Of these thirteen were adults, nine of whom were males with two assessed as being females aged over 40. Of the remainder, ten were children under 6, with two children aged between 6 and 8 and one adolescent. Once again repeated unhealed head injuries consistent with blows from axes and blunt objects were found throughout the assemblage in addition to two bone arrowheads in close proximity to the remains which were probably lodged inside the respective bodies when they were placed in the ditch. A further observation that has not previously been seen from this period was a curious repeated pattern of breakage to the tibia and fibula, consistent with deliberate systematic smashing of these people's lower legs close to the time of death. This behaviour could be interpreted in several ways. On one hand the excavators suggested it may be evidence of torture, painting a grim picture of terrified people obliged to watch as their kin were treated in this way one by one. No less unpleasant is the possibility that this was a practical measure intended to stop people escaping so they could then be killed with certainty. A third alternative is that this was a ritual act carried out after the people had died intended to disable them in the afterlife. If this latter possibility is correct this would give an insight into a spiritual dimension of conflict at this time which is not usually accessible to us. In analysing these remains Christian Meyer and colleagues from Mainz University, point out that whatever the reason, this behaviour suggests hatred and contempt for this 'enemy' group, as does the careless dumping of their bodies in a pit afterwards. Certainly however, the systematic nature of the Schöneck-Kilianstädten massacre indicates planning and organization and again suggests early Neolithic warfare as having stepped up in terms of becoming both more complex and more intense.

Several sites in the British Isles also show signs of co-ordinated assaults by apparently large groups. Crickley Hill in Gloucestershire has been discussed in numerous publications for the striking find of hundreds of arrowheads scattered around a defensive palisade trench and several entranceways that indicate a concerted attack by archers. Hambledon Hill in Dorset is equally well-known as a Neolithic causewayed enclosure that had been made defensible and which was also attacked and the defences burned down on two separate occasions. Two adult male skeletons were found beneath a collapsed section of the surrounding palisade, with arrowheads situated in their chest cavities. Several other British enclosures of this period show similar signs of attack including Carn Brea in Cornwall and Maiden Castle in Dorset.[15] Although these British sites have not produced evidence of massacres in the form of mass burials as at Asparn-Scheltz or the two sites in Germany mentioned previously, the point remains as noted by Rick Schulting that 'whoever was attacking these sites was trying to get in there to do something and whatever it was it wasn't going to be very nice'.[16] Taking a wider view of the nature of such intergroup raiding, such behaviour would be categorized by evolutionary scientists under a class of survival strategies referred to as 'free riding'. Free riding can take many different forms and includes strategies as varied as the multiplication of malarial parasites in the human bloodstream, the infestation of the gut by a tapeworm or the way a cuckoo substitutes its own eggs in the nest of another unsuspecting bird. In their book presenting recent thinking on the evolution of the human mind *Thinking Big*, Clive Gamble, John Gowlett and Robin Dunbar point out that as a means of gaining at someone else's expense, raiding is just such a strategy – 'Why work, when for a very modest expenditure of energy and a small risk you can acquire all your needs from the products of another's toil.'[17]

A Brave New World?

Together these rather unsettling sites present us with the earliest evidence certainly for Europe and possibly in the world, of large, co-ordinated groups of individuals acting collectively to attack similar-sized groups within substantial defended structures. The fact that those under attack went to the trouble of constructing defences, again a considerable collective undertaking, makes it clear that the possibility of such group assaults was envisioned in advance as a very real threat. Essentially this appears to be the point at which 'war' in the sense that it is understood in modern developed societies made its first appearance. This is not to say that I take the view espoused by some social scientists[18] that 'lethal hostilities' between small groups of people as outlined in the preceding chapters should not be seen as war. On the contrary I would argue that the mindset of the participants is the same (regarding any member of an opposing group as representative of the whole and therefore a legitimate target) and essentially the behaviour exhibited by groups of Mesolithic people raiding and feuding is unlikely to have been much different from their Neolithic successors. But what had changed is the scale at which such hostilities were conducted. As in many other spheres of life something was different about the Neolithic that brought mechanisms into place that permitted people to call upon and organize much larger groups of participants in collective endeavours than ever before (whether building a 300-foot long barrow or annihilating the people who live in the next valley). This is an important point, firstly because the advent of this new highly-organized form of conflict represents a departure that set human social development on a unique trajectory that is still being played out today. Secondly, however, the appearance of co-ordinated attacks of the kind seen at Talheim, Schletz, Crickley Hill and their like is important in that it begs the questions of why this new behaviour should appear at all and why at this time? Anatomically modern people whose brains and thinking capabilities were no different from our own (or at least we have no reason to think so) had existed for tens of thousands of years by this point. What was so different about the Neolithic that people should suddenly decide to make this step change towards more organized warfare?

The answer probably lies in the economic base on which these new societies rested. In a society where the status of men derives from success at hunting, even the most skilled hunter is unable to guarantee to find and kill game every time, with such endeavours always involving a strong element of luck. The meat obtained from successful hunting expeditions tends to be shared out with others, which both cements relationships and ensures that each individual can count on receiving meat from others next time, should he fail to achieve a kill himself. By its nature such a system serves to keep group sizes small (you can share a deer with half a dozen friends but not with forty or fifty) and also prevents any one individual from rising above the group in any substantial way. It is also the case that a given area of land has a set 'carrying capacity' in terms of the number of people it can support in this way before available game animals and edible plants are exhausted. Certainly the accumulation of surplus is difficult for foraging peoples and so there is limited opportunity for economic differences to develop between individuals. Should conflict arise in a society consisting of scattered bands of mobile hunters, the opportunities to bring others in to join your cause are few and the rewards for joining such a fight would be correspondingly limited. Consequently, whilst there is certainly evidence for hostility between groups during the Mesolithic, with the potential for brutal massacres of one band by another, as seems apparent at Ofnet cave (see previous chapter), we have no reason to think that this ever went beyond the scale of a few dozen participants on either side.

The switch to reliance on domesticated plants and animals had implications that went far beyond a change in diet. In considering the wider basis of human sexual relationships the geneticist Matt Ridley[19] has previously noted that this shift opened new opportunities for personal advancement of a kind that had not previously existed. Unlike hunting, making a living as a farmer or herder offers considerable rewards for those who have the greatest aptitude. The best herder who breeds more cattle and the most adept farmer who grows more crops are in a position to generate substantial surplus with which they can buy the labour of others less successful than themselves. In this respect not only did the Neolithic see the appearance of economic inequalities but also the first instances of the fact familiar to us, that wealth generates more wealth. Furthermore, the new economy also had social implications in that such successful and wealthier individuals were in a position to support more than one spouse. Observations of pastoralists (societies based on herding) all over the world concur in noting that in such societies, wealth (in the form of cattle) is owned and inherited down the male line, marriages are exogamous and patrilocal (the wife leaves her family to join the family of her husband) and also polygamous, with the most powerful and successful men having the greatest number of wives. This latter point in particular serves to further increase inequality in such societies. Firstly, given that the ratio of men to women will normally be roughly equal, in a society practicing polygamy some men will never be able to marry. Secondly, such inequality is further heightened within a generation or two when polygamous men generate large numbers of descendants. This will further put some individuals in a position to command the allegiance of many more individuals than they could have done as a member of a small-scale band of foragers and creates wider groups of related individuals who by being less mobile will also become more territorial regarding the smaller area they now range over. Rather than the stable, egalitarian society imagined a generation ago, the Neolithic might in fact be more accurately characterized as an unequal and inherently unstable society, and perhaps this is what we are seeing manifested in the skeletons preserved from this time.

The existence of larger groups sharing a community bond and the greater need to stake claims to territory would be consistent with both the construction and the fairly even distribution within the landscape of many Earlier Neolithic monuments, particularly the long 'burial' mounds of Atlantic Europe which occupy far more space than is necessary simply to house the dead. Instead these seem to be built as statements on the landscape with the 'ancestors' they contained being used to legitimize such claims by providing undeniable proof that 'we have always been here'. Together all these changes were a recipe for a new and different manifestation of conflict of the kind in evidence at Schletz, Hambledon Hill and so on. Firstly, there was now more to fight over in terms of livestock and harvested crops to steal, grazing and cleared arable land to move into and, arguably most unsettling to modern sensibilities, a particularly attractive resource to take control of is likely to have been other people. In a situation where wealth, property rights and the opportunity to marry were now unevenly distributed, those with the most to gain also had the least to lose. Hence, in addition to the greater number of social ties now giving rise to larger and better networked groups than had existed before, it could also at least at times have been relatively easy to persuade those young men with the least to go to war and take what they felt they had been denied. Examples that support this view are again in evidence in the three massacre assemblages identified in Austria and Germany[20] all of which exhibit an unusual demographic make-up. The mass burial at Talheim is comprised of adult men and women of all ages plus older children but there are no young children present which raises the question of what happened to them in a society where the birth rate is likely to have been high. The burial group at Schletz is even more suspicious, here there were adult males, children of all ages, older adult females but no women of child-bearing age. A similar pattern is in evidence at Schöneck-Kilianstädten, where the only two women present were over 40. This absence of young women is made to appear even more sinister by the presence of young children at both sites. In the latter example half the assemblage were children, begging the question 'where are their mothers?' In each case it is possible that the missing group were buried elsewhere and have not been found yet, alternatively they might have been spared by the attackers. In the case of the Talheim children, this would hardly have been merciful, as being simply left to fend for themselves would leave slim chances of survival anyway. However, it is arguably more likely that the 'missing' individuals in each case were taken away and subsumed within the community of the attacking group. In a society where marriage was distributed unequally such raiding may have been the only option available for some men to acquire a wife.

Where evidence of warfare has been identified from an archaeological source in the last couple of decades it has been commonly assumed that such conflict must have resulted from scarcity of resources. On this basis there has been a tendency among archaeologists to look to the environmental evidence for signs of some natural downturn in local conditions that might have caused lands to flood, rivers to dry up or crops to fail. In some instances such events are very much in evidence, a well-researched example is a period of drought that lasted for several decades beginning around AD 1100 in the south-western region of North America. Here the archaeological record shows a shift from burgeoning complex societies probably in the early stages of civilization/state formation with settled agriculture and thriving trade to a landscape character-ized by defensive structures, abandoned settlements and human burials show-ing signs of violence, trophy taking and even cannibalism.[21] However, this is an unusually clear example and for the vast majority of instances such environ-mental 'smoking guns' are simply not in evidence. This is so for the European Neolithic, when if anything environmental conditions were very favourable.[22] This means we must look elsewhere for the causes of conflict. The concept of war being brought on by scarcity of resources is still perfectly viable but we have no reason to blame that scarcity on what the weather was doing. In all but the most marginal of situations people in the past generally had access to as many natural resources as they could ever want. Lack of access to resources is likely to have been a very real experience for people living through much of the last few thousand years but more often than not the blame for such scarcity is more plausibly laid at the feet of other human beings.

Returning to the point that there were no drastic differences between Mesolithic and Neolithic 'weapons' an area where this may not quite be true is in regard to projectiles. The Neolithic saw the appearance of larger leaf-shaped arrowheads (Fig. 6.4) replacing the composite points of the Mesolithic which consisted of multiple small (microlithic) flint points fixed in wooden or bone settings. The reason for this change remains open to debate, although Roger Mercer[23] has suggested the answer may lie in the choice of targets Neolithic archers were shooting at. The microlithic arrows of the Mesolithic were intended primarily for hunting, Mercer argues that this was not the case for the cattle-dominated landscapes of the Earlier Neolithic when evidence for hunting of wild animals is comparatively sparse. Instead he suggests that the new doubled-edged Neolithic arrowheads were designed specifically for shooting at people. Whether the Mesolithic versions had simply represented a desire to use more limited supplies of flint in an economic manner remains a sticking point in this argument, although there is certainly ample evidence for people targeting other human beings with these new 'weapons of mass destruction'.

Essentially, much of the conflict that took place certainly during the Earlier Neolithic may not have differed significantly from the small-scale raid and ambush-type warfare that had already been prevalent for millennia, and is likely to have resembled the warfare witnessed by Champlain in the north-eastern part of North America (see previous chapter), both in conduct and objectives. It is tempting to see large-scale engagements of the kind apparent at the enclosure sites mentioned as the 'normal' expression of Neolithic war-fare. However, given the frequency of finds of individuals among burial assemblages with bashed-in skulls or arrows in their backs turning up in ones and twos, it seems more likely that for the most part Neolithic warfare was conducted at the scale of tit-for-tat raiding. In such raids perhaps only a couple of individuals might be killed, with the raiding party responsible then going home satisfied. Large-scale attacks aimed at annihilating whole communities as in evidence at some Neolithic enclosures may have been a much less common occurrence, although the overall number of people that might be killed in conflict during small-scale raids and ambushes was still high. Teasing out the nuances of causes and effects of changes in the way people lived in the past is rarely simple, particularly in the case of prehistoric periods separated from us by thousands of years. In the case of the larger communities people began living in during the Neolithic, such a change can be satisfactorily explained in purely economic terms on one hand, but an additional driver pointed out by Clive Gamble and colleagues[24] may have been the threat of warfare from other groups which drove people to live in ever larger communities. A group choosing to remain smaller than the average was at risk of annihilation unless they were lucky enough to have friendly neighbours.

Whilst much of what we know about the Neolithic has been refined and clarified through continued study over recent decades the concept of this period as one of tranquil co-operation has been largely overturned. In discussing what we would now see as horrendous assaults and brutal murders of people of all ages and both sexes and the abduction of people as an objective in such conflict, many of these events may be rather uncomfortable both for the general reader and for scholars of prehistory. The massacre of whole communities and the abduction of women is really not very 'PC' and essentially the sort of thing that prehistoric archaeologists had spent many years trying to get away from, but seems undeniable from the wealth of evidence now apparent. This brings us back then to the likelihood that the peaceful Neolithic was indeed a modern construction that tells us more about the course of the twentieth century AD than the thirty-seventh century BC (the time of many British long barrow burials). In fact it may be that faint echoes of such events in prehistory have always been with us in the form of various origin myths and so in a way had never been forgotten. It is interesting to note that Homer's *Iliad*, the founding work of Western literature, is centred upon the abduction of a woman. Although many details of the version of this narrative that has survived by being written down rather than passed on orally date from around the eighth century BC,[25] it is likely that much of the overall story was recalling at least the kind of events that had occurred during earlier times further back in prehistory. Whether such folk memories stretched back as far as the Neolithic is rather a moot point, as if the idea of fighting wars over access to women dated from a time closer to that of Homer this rather implies that such behaviours did not simply die out as societies emerged from the period of early domestication covered in the current chapter, but continued into times when societies became more complex. In this regard it is of further interest that the founding myth of Rome, the 'abduction of the Sabine women'[26] essentially describes a raid by young men from one community to take women from another. Again, this may represent a remnant of memory from an earlier time when such events actually took place. One ancient text that may indeed represent a folk memory from the advent of farming is the Old Testament account of Cain (the tiller of the Earth) slaying his brother Abel (the herder) with the jawbone of an ass – interpreted as referring to an early form of sickle.[27] If this early part of the Bible can be taken as containing a mythologised account of the transition from a gathering existence to one of agriculture and pastoralism it is certainly interesting to find the invention of farming specifically associated with the invention of murder.

Returning once more to the (false) dichotomy of the ideas of Hobbes versus Rousseau, the examples discussed in the present chapter might be seen as confirming the latter, i.e. that the advent of farming and settled living was a 'bad thing' that heralded a descent into a new form of endemic tribal conflict from which we have yet to emerge. However, it should also be pointed out that there is as much evidence for care and co-operation amongst Neolithic people as there is for unpleasantness. Such aspects of society are not the main focus of this book but this is not to say they were not equally important and there is as much reason to see the Neolithic as a new dawn that brought a wealth of fresh possibilities, as a fall from grace into inequality, theft and murder. Perhaps the most important point of note in regard to this book, however, is that without the evidence from human skeletal remains none of this would be apparent and the overwhelming picture of the Neolithic might still be one of 'New Age' farmers living idyllic lives and channelling their spare energy into building monuments together, so their afterlife could be as peaceful and egalitarian as this one had been.

Chapter 7

Cutting-Edge Technology: Violence in Bronze Age Europe

The technological and social developments that defined the Neolithic combined to make it a time of change unlike anything that had gone before. When viewed in comparison to earlier times, the Neolithic appears as a period of startling transformation. Certainly the late Mesolithic landscape of mobile hunter-gatherers was very different from the increasingly settled and divided land of farming communities in place by the time the Neolithic gave way to what has traditionally been called the Bronze Age. However, the reality of life for most people living through these times may have been far less dramatic, with processes of change and the introduction of 'Neolithic' innovations actually stretching out over two millennia. For most of this period life would have seemed to be carrying on as it always had for the vast majority of folk, with little if any sense that the times they were a-changing. By comparison, the periods that followed are shown through the material traces people left behind to have been a period where social development carried on accelerating and where communities continued to be transformed at a much faster rate. The importance of farming for subsequent human history is difficult to overstate, but the arrival of metalworking comes a close second in terms of its impact on the development of societies. Here in spite of any 'postmodern' claims that dividing time purely on the basis of the tools people were using is an outmoded way of thinking about the past, it is undeniable that a new technology, the like of which had never been seen before, was in fact driving a whole range of social and economic changes to the extent that metal-using peoples really could be said to have entered a new era, quite different from their stone-reliant ancestors. Meanwhile, at the same time that the societies of northern and western Europe were undergoing the later stages of the Neolithic transition to a settled agricultural economy and experiencing the first effects of new metal technology, peoples at the opposite fringes of Europe had already embarked on a dramatic new trajectory with the rise of civilization. In this respect the eastern Mediterranean areas surrounding the Aegean Sea (Greece, Asia Minor and the Levant) that gave rise to civilizations such as the Minoans, the Myceneans and the Hittites, are best seen as a separate region from the rest of Europe. For the purposes of the current chapter (and the one that follows) the term Europe is best read as 'Barbarian' Europe (as the Greeks would later put it), in this case meaning the remainder of the continent where a more consistent set of general trends is apparent.

As with earlier developments, the appearance and effects of metal technology did not appear everywhere simultaneously,[1] but broadly speaking the Bronze Age in Europe can be said to encompass the period between 2500 and 800 BC.[2] During the earlier part of this period metal objects remained relatively rare and although powerful individuals undoubtedly existed, possession of such items seems to have remained a relatively small part of the overall way they expressed their positions. During the later Bronze Age, after about 1300 BC, the demonstration of social status and therefore relative power appears to have become progressively bound up with the possession, display and control of increasingly elaborate and often intricately-produced metal items. Perhaps the greatest effect of metal, however, was its status as a newly portable and durable form of 'wealth'. When wealth existed largely on four legs as it is likely to have done in the Early Neolithic, and an individual's status might be signified by how many cattle they owned, such assets could only be transported as far as you could persuade them to walk. With the arrival of metal artefacts, accumulated wealth became eminently easier to transfer and networks of exchange sprang up throughout Europe which far surpassed the smaller-scale and short-distance networks of earlier times. The fact that bronze requires the combination of two metals that do not generally occur together further necessitated the establishment of trading networks. As a consequence of such networks, by the later Bronze Age new innovations spread very quickly between regions and over long distances.[3] For the first time something that could realistically be called a 'world economy' had appeared.

Other innovations that spread through much of Europe at the beginning of the Bronze Age include a distinctive new form of pottery known as Beakers. Originating in Spain and spreading northwards and eastwards through France, Britain and Germany, these individual-sized drinking cups, contrasting with the larger vessels they replaced, have been taken in the recent past to be part of a growing emphasis on the individual in society. Often found in graves, Beakers are part of a package of grave goods accompanying a new trend for increasingly elaborate individual burials that appear to signify increasing competition in society to acquire personal wealth and differentiate oneself through prestige items. A further example of the latter is the arrival of horses as prized possessions. Residues of probable alcoholic beverages detected in Beaker pots have led some authors to liken this arrival of alcohol and horses to the appearance of such in the plains region of North America after European contact, and to speculate as to whether they might have had similar effects.[4] The 'Beaker package' also commonly includes bronze daggers and archery equipment. There is an old adage in archaeology that 'the dead don't bury themselves'. This refers to the fact that the way a person is presented in death by the clothes and objects placed on and around them is a kind of constructed picture that tells us how that person (at least in the minds of those burying them) wished to be thought of. If there is a common thread running through the way those buried with Beakers wished to be seen, it would appear to be in the identity of a warrior. Since the nineteenth century, the spread of Beakers across Europe has sparked debate about whether or not these new 'pint pot'-like vessels signified the arrival of invading hordes of a specific people, referred to simply as the Beaker folk. There is good reason to be very sceptical about this as in fact throughout Europe there is as much evidence for things staying the same locally as there is for change and it is much more plausible that this style of pottery spread through trade and exchange than any large movements of people. However, a question this then raises is who in society did these trendy new vessels appeal to? It would seem that a new elite may indeed have appeared, characterizing themselves specifically as warriors, with this concept spreading between regions as the objects associated with such a status were taken on locally. In a way then, as my colleague Christopher Knüsel pointed out whilst I was writing this book, 'the "Beaker People" may have been very real, they just needn't all be related'.

Lords of the Bling? Keeping up with the Neighbours

The appearance for the first time of specialized weapons and apparent defensive gear further sets the Bronze Age apart from the times that went before, as a time when a distinct set of manufactured items concerned specifically, and it would seem undeniably, with violence emerged.[5] By around 1400 BC the bronze daggers of the Beaker period had undergone a process of development first into elongated 'rapiers' and then into fully-recognizable swords, with the simultaneous appearance of helmets, shields and items of armour also made of bronze. The term used amongst scholars of this subject is that a 'material culture of violence' had arisen. This term essentially refers to instances where people's views about aspects of the world or themselves are 'made solid' in that such ideas shape the kind of objects people make and value. Earlier readings of the archaeological record of this time took this evidence quite understandably at face value and assumed that the arrival of swords, shields and suchlike could only signify an increase in hostilities, along with the rise of a newly-distinguished warrior class at the upper end of society. By the mid-twentieth century the Bronze Age had come to be seen as effectively the point at which human conflict became something more than the simple disputes between individuals that were thought to have been the worst things that likely happened in the otherwise peaceful Stone Ages, and instead took on a new pattern of group conflict, effectively therefore being the time at which 'war' first appeared. This notion of the birth of war being bound up with the emergence of individual wealth and elite groups fed perfectly into what were loosely called 'Marxist' readings of the past. 'Class war' had arrived, the new social distinctions and wealth inequalities that accompanied the appearance of metal technology seeming in stark contrast to the peaceful equality of the preceding Neolithic. In light of such unsettling changes, this assumed appearance of hostilities seemed entirely consistent with the evidence. Such opinions were further bolstered by the appearance of rock carvings from various parts of Europe showing helmeted and shield-bearing warriors, often apparently fighting each other with weapons recognizable as swords, halberds and so on.[6]

It would seem then that the existence of a rise in conflict as an obvious consequence of the appearance of metalworking was unquestionable. However, by the closing decades of the twentieth century a different set of approaches had arisen that precisely set out to challenge such straightforward readings of the archaeological record that had been based on supposed 'common sense'. Here it was pointed out that the underlying notion on which such views rested was an assumption that the ways people choose to represent themselves and the world around them are reliable reflections of reality. In questioning this idea John Robb of Cambridge University framed this issue in dry academic terms as the idea that 'symbolism and social action tend to be consistent' before rephrasing this succinctly as equivalent to saying that 'TV violence makes violent kids'.[7] Essentially, this was the idea that if the art and material culture of Bronze Age Europe seemed concerned with fighting it must therefore follow that violence and conflict were very common. But what if this was not the case? A possible suggestion put forward to explain the violent character of life in the Neolithic, as evidenced by the numbers of individuals now known from the time displaying head injuries (see Chapter 6), rests on the notion that human beings (males especially) are naturally driven to compete against each other, with such drives rooted deeply in our evolutionary past. In this respect the novel technologies of the Bronze Age could be seen either in simple terms as functional items that conferred practical new advantages in violent competition against others (it is not surprising that the Bronze Age is sometimes referred to as the time of the first 'arms race'), or alternatively as having had more subtle and complex effects. It is interesting that a large proportion of metal items recovered from this period are objects that would be worn or carried by individuals, rather than being more general household items or ornaments. By providing a new channel to outdo one's neighbours without actually killing them, the opportunities for the accumulation and most importantly the display of wealth and presumably also status, offered by the shiny range of new warrior gear might actually have led to a reduction in violence by providing an alternative, 'bloodless' way to compete.

Whilst this latter idea might at first seem rather far-fetched, it is in fact given a fair degree of support by the fact that many examples of protective gear in the form of bronze shields, helmets and breastplates from this period were actually rather thin and flimsy. In particular a well-known set of experiments conducted by John Coles in 1962, which would be unlikely to pass a modern health and safety risk assessment, demonstrated replicas of bronze shields recovered from excavations to offer little protection from sword cuts.[8] Consequently it is often argued that such items were indeed mainly for display rather than practical use. This notion is further supported by the frequency with which bronze weapons in particular are found deposited in bogs, lakes and rivers as part of a wider tradition of the ritual placement of valuable objects in such locations at this time. Often such weapons have been deliberately put out of use by being bent or snapped, whilst many examples show no signs of use, suggesting they were made solely with the intention of sacrificing them in this way. The ability to further impress one's level of wealth on others by demonstrating the capacity to destroy it and give it away to whatever supernatural recipients people believed were waiting for it beneath the surface of lakes and rivers may again be seen as a channel with which to out-compete one's neighbours and so again the idea that 'more swords equals more fighting' is called into question. So once more we are left with a problem. The wider archaeological record can be read in more than one way and it is not clear to what extent Bronze Age violence is a figment of the modern imagination, an assumed view imposed on people who actually led relatively peaceful lives, or whether signs of violence during this period are in fact staring us in the face and some people just don't want to see them. Once again, it would seem only the remains of Bronze Age people themselves may hold the answer.

Rich, Single and Dead; New Burial Traditions

Until very recently accounts of Bronze Age burials aimed at summarizing the general picture tended to emphasize the Early Bronze Age (c.2500–1500 BC) as differing in character from the sorts of burial practices generally associated with the Neolithic. Whereas the 'classic' version of Neolithic burials, certainly in Britain and much of north-west Europe, centres on numbers of people being buried together in collective tombs and burial mounds, often in a jumbled and disarticulated state; by contrast the burials that appear from around the time of the arrival of bronze tend to differ firstly by consisting usually of a single individual, often sealed by individual burial mounds. Secondly, the placement of grave goods, objects presumably intended to accompany the deceased into an afterlife of some sort, became increasingly common. The classic interpretation of this change has long been to view it as indicating more visible divisions in society, with those possessing greater wealth and presumably status now being marked out as distinctive after death. On one hand, then skeletal remains from this period can be said to be easier to make sense of as we have more articulated individuals to study, commonly in a better preserved state.[9] However, on the other hand the case also remains that the burials that survive from this period are relatively few in number and may well represent only the upper echelons of what seems to be an increasingly divided society. In previous decades archaeology in general was often criticized as simply the study of rich people (and mostly rich men at that) with the majority of the population of any given time remaining largely ignored and invisible. Whilst much has been done in more recent years to correct this,[10] the Bronze Age could still reasonably be said to be the period from which point onwards such issues begin to bite. But, however unrepresentative of society as a whole these burials might be, they are still easier to extract information from than those of the Middle Bronze Age. From around 1500 BC a change occurred across most of Europe where cremation became the favoured means of disposing of the dead. As discussed in Chapter 1, all manner of osteological observations become more difficult when bone has been burned, although this need not mean that we can't say anything and such burials are still worth the effort involved in analysing them. With regard to the question of whether signs of violence are present, these have been observed in both cremated and unburned burials from various points in the Bronze Age.

The Impacts of Technology

In 1977 two stone burial chambers (cists) were discovered in the course of quarrying near Pitdrichie Farm, Aberdeenshire, each containing an adult male, both accompanied with a Beaker pot.[11] Both skeletons were dated by radiocarbon to the eighteenth century BC[12] and could well have been buried at the same time. In this respect it was of further interest that both men had healed skull fractures, whilst one also had a healed broken nose. The excavators speculated that these injuries might have been incurred violently. This is certainly the case for the second individual; having examined this injury first hand I can confirm that rather than simply being a 'fracture' this wound was caused by a sharp implement. Here a thin, straight-bladed object had struck the head at a shallow angle, removing a slice of bone and leaving a roughly triangular hole in the skull vault. As it ran out of energy this blow had forced a section of the skull wall upwards and this portion of the bone had remained in this position as the wound healed, leaving a raised ridge with a rounded edge along one side of the wound (Fig. 7.1). There were no signs of the wound

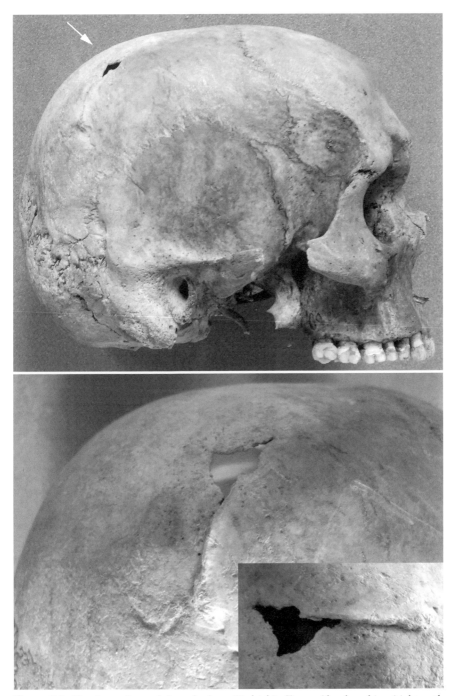

Figure 7.1. Cranium of an adult male from Pitdrichie Farm, Aberdeenshire (eighteenth century BC) with a healed sharp-force injury.

having become infected and this man clearly got off lightly given the potential seriousness of this injury. The margin of this wound was too straight to have been caused by a stone implement and too thin to have been an axe. Swords had not yet been developed at this point, whilst spearheads tended to have triangular rather than blade-like profiles, and so it is more likely that this wound was inflicted with a bronze dagger, of which various types are commonly found in burials from this period. Some of these have blades over 30cm long and would certainly be capable of inflicting such a wound. Even without this insight, the excavators (Ian Shepherd and Margaret Bruce) rightly noted at the time that many of the adult males buried with Beaker-style grave goods exhibit injuries, speculating that these might indicate the 'warrior identity' which these individuals were presented with in death might be more than just symbolic.[13]

The observation noted above in fact makes the man from Pitdrichie the second earliest British individual known to have been injured with a metal bladed weapon. The individual known as Racton Man excavated near Chichester in 1989 was a male, aged at least 45 years, buried with a bronze dagger. A lack of funding at the time meant it was not possible to obtain a radiocarbon date until recently when this man was revealed to have died some time between 2300 and 2150 BC.[14] This date range was surprisingly early as it places the dagger as being one of the earliest bronze artefacts known from Britain. The dagger is implied to have seen a good degree of use, having been sharpened repeatedly, whilst recent re-examination of the skeleton has revealed an unhealed blade wound to his right humerus, close to the elbow consistent with a defence wound where the arm was raised to block a blow to the head. A second possible blade cut to his scapula may indicate a second strike which then hit the man beneath the armpit. Neither injury would have caused death immediately, although could have done so in time due to blood loss, so it may well be that a further injury not affecting bone was responsible for his demise. Racton Man's visible injuries therefore grant him the dubious honour of being the earliest British individual known to have suffered trauma from a metal-bladed weapon. To have possessed a bronze weapon at this early date this man must have been a very prominent and presumably powerful individual. In this respect it is of further interest that Racton Man was particularly tall, standing at more than 6ft. This is quite remarkable for an individual of this date[15] when the average stature was around 5ft 7in. Several other richly-furnished burials from the Early Bronze Age were those of very tall individuals including the well-preserved Gristhorpe Man, originally discovered in 1834 near Scarborough in a coffin formed from a hollowed-out oak log. This individual was placed with a range of grave goods including a bronze dagger with a whalebone pommel. Recent analysis shows that he had suffered two rib fractures earlier in life and stood between 5ft 10in and 6ft tall. Measurements of various portions of the skeleton show him to have had a muscular build in his prime, with a healthy body mass index by modern standards. Chemical analysis of his bones (stable isotope analysis) also reveals him to have eaten a diet high in animal protein.[16] More recently, an adult male of Bronze Age date excavated at West Ridge near Amesbury, Wiltshire was found to have stood 6ft 2in tall in life, making him the tallest known prehistoric person. This man too had a healed injury having suffered a blunt blow to the head, which had subsequently become infected.[17]

It would seem then that there may be a link between the section of society afforded rich burials, the acquisition of violence-related injuries and the achievement of tall stature during life. In the main the height one reaches by adulthood is largely determined by our genes, but if you want to grow tall being well fed certainly helps.[18] Leaders and chieftains in various tribal cultures have often been titled simply as 'big men'. Often this designation makes no reference to such individuals' physical size but rather simply their position as a prominent figure in their society. However, it would seem that during the British Bronze Age at least, those in powerful positions commonly were larger individuals. This raises the question of whether such rank was to an extent hereditary with the sons (and possibly daughters) of chiefs enjoying a better diet than the average person and so growing taller during their lives, or whether individuals who were already large and at a physical advantage were simply better at assuming such positions presumably through being more effective warriors (or perhaps a combination of the two). Either way, it would seem an elite class of people had indeed come into being, perhaps similar to the mentions in later written accounts we have for 'heroic' societies[19] appearing from the Bronze Age onwards where Homeric-style elites enjoyed a privileged position of relative wealth and feasting, supposedly justified by their role as protectors of those beneath them.

'The Whites of their Eyes': Bronze Age Arrow Injuries

Whilst there is no shortage of examples of hostile actions that were 'up close and personal' in this period, weapons that kill at a distance remained popular and there is certainly clear evidence for the continuing use of arrows as weapons of war. A well-known Beaker burial excavated at Barrow Hills, Radley (Oxfordshire) was that of an adult male who had a flint arrowhead situated within his thoracic cavity close to his spine. The tip of the arrowhead was broken in a manner consistent with an impact leading to the suggestion that it had in fact caused the man's death.[20] As mentioned in the previous chapter, arrowheads stuck in bone are a rather obvious indicator of such an injury, but in cases where the 'murder weapon' hasn't lodged in part of the skeleton, any signs left on bone may be much less obvious. Feizor Nick Cave in the Yorkshire Dales contained the skeleton of an adult female, placed without grave goods and initially of unknown date (Fig. 7.2). When this skeleton was examined by Stephany Leach, the leading UK expert on cave burials, she noticed a small slit like defect in the front of the woman's 12th thoracic vertebra (the point where the ribcage meets the lower back). This slender area of damage had straight, well-defined edges quite unlike the rough, crumbly breakage normally seen when bones are damaged long after death and therefore looked suspiciously like an unhealed injury. The most likely candidate was a pointed object such as a sword or spear tip and it seemed likely that the woman might date perhaps from Romano-British or Anglo-Saxon times. Stephany and I later analysed the vertebra by scanning electron microscope in order to get a detailed view of the edges of the wound. This led to a small 'eureka' moment when it became clear that the edges of the slit in the bone had tiny striations – microscopic scrape marks running in the same direction as the overall wound that must have been made by the object causing the injury.[21] Such striations are inconsistent with the smooth edges of metal weapons and are a tell-tale sign that a mark on bone has been produced by stone implements, in the case of Britain most probably flint. Rather than an Anglo-Saxon then, it seemed more likely that this was a prehistoric individual but when during prehistory had she lived? On radiocarbon dating the skeleton the result of 2210–2030 BC was obtained, revealing the woman to have in fact lived and died in the Early Bronze Age. The wound was therefore most likely to have been caused by an arrow rather than a spear tip, as the latter had been replaced by bronze at this date. The woman had been shot in the abdomen at a fatal point. In order to penetrate the spine at this level the arrow would have to first pierce the aorta, causing rapid death from internal bleeding. Given her lack of grave goods the question of whether the woman had been formally buried in the cave by grieving relatives or simply placed there by whoever killed her, remains open. For example, whilst the woman might

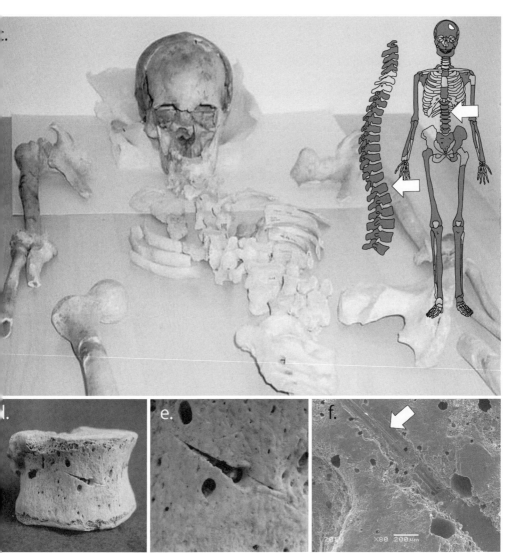

Figure 7.2. The woman from Feizor Nick Cave, Yorkshire (a and b) with an unhealed penetrating wound to her 12th thoracic vertebra (c–e), revealed by scanning electron microscope to have been caused by a flint arrow point (f).

have died in a conflict between communities, she might equally be a Bronze Age murder victim with the cave acting as a convenient place to conceal the body.

The frozen mummified body of a man discovered high in the Alps in 1991, now universally known as 'Öetzi the Ice Man', has been the subject of a great many books, articles and TV programmes and now forms the centrepiece of a dedicated museum in Northern Italy, where he enjoys pride of place as undoubtedly the most famous prehistoric person from Europe. Although commonly referred to as a 'Neolithic' man, Öetzi should more properly be classed as having lived during the Copper Age or Chalcolithic, with a copper-headed axe among the many possessions he was found with. Ten years after his initial discovery, careful X-ray analysis of the body by a team of clinical radiologists led to the discovery of a flint arrowhead embedded in the Ice Man's chest cavity.[22] He had been shot from behind with the arrow piercing his left scapula and lodging between the scapula and ribs in his shoulder area. The arrow's trajectory passes through the vicinity of the brachial artery, the major vessel that supplies the arm with blood and although only one of several injuries he is now known to have suffered it is likely that this is what caused Öetzi's death, through loss of blood.

Recent re-examination of cremated bone material dating from the time of the first local appearance of metal, excavated in Navarre, Spain during the 1980s has revealed the tip of an arrowhead lodged in a human cuneiform bone (one of the bones of the central part of the foot). Despite the bone having been burned it was also possible to discern signs of healing, indicating the respective individual to have walked around for some time with the arrowhead tip embedded in their foot.[23] During my own experiments, mentioned in the previous chapter, I noted that flint fragments very commonly became embedded in bone. The arrowhead tips broke on impact about 50 per cent of the time, meaning attempts to pull one out would be highly likely to leave a piece stuck in the bone. Anyone surviving being struck by an arrow of this type might well therefore carry a piece of the offending article permanently lodged in part of their skeleton from that point onwards.

Saints or Sinners? Ritual Killings

Where injuries incurred at the time of an individual's death have involved damage to bone it is sometimes possible to give fairly detailed assessments of the manner of their demise (as shown variously throughout this book). However, as with the woman from Feizor Nick, judgements about the actual circumstances in which such injuries were inflicted are often much less certain with multiple possibilities apparent. The burial that has come to be known as 'The Stonehenge Archer' is a further example. Discovered by chance during an excavation investigating the nature of the local environment in the past, this young adult male (aged 25–30) had been placed formally on his left side in a pit which cut through an earlier ditch at Stonehenge. The man wore an archer's stone wristguard, designed to protect the forearm from being hurt by the bowstring when shooting an arrow.[24] He was also accompanied by several arrowheads, initially interpreted as further grave offerings, until closer analysis of the man's bones identified the tips of flint arrowheads embedded in his left fourth rib and in the back of his sternum.[25] His 11th and 9th ribs both had v-shaped cuts at their margins where arrows had cut into them, passing through into the chest and abdomen. The shot that penetrated the sternum had been delivered from behind, having pierced the heart before becoming embedded in this bone, which would certainly have killed him, unless he was already dead when this arrow struck.

The most straightforward explanation for this man's death is simply that he was killed in conflict. This might explain firstly the fact that this otherwise formal 'Beaker' burial lacked the rest of the usual set of grave goods found accompanying such individuals, with a Beaker drinking vessel most conspicuous by its absence, the wristguard therefore being present simply because the man was wearing it when he died. He might also then be seen as having received a 'hero's burial' which is what selected him for placement at such a prestigious and impressive location. However, the fact that he had been shot so many times raises further questions as to whether the man was simply unlucky, or whether there were other reasons why his body was impacted several more times than is strictly necessary to kill someone. It might be that the arrows were shot into the man's body after death as a purely ritual or symbolic act, in which case he might not have been involved in violence at all, although this wouldn't explain the lack of grave goods. Alternatively, this individual may be an example of a practice observed ethnographically among tribal societies in recent centuries, known among social anthropologists as 'overkill'. This is where multiple attackers each inflict an injury on an often already dead opponent. In some cases such behaviour simply related to the level of feeling borne towards a hated enemy, but in other cases it had more formal social meaning.[26] For example, each person striking a blow or shooting an arrow may then be seen as receiving some of the prestige and enhanced social status conferred by 'killing' an enemy, even though in strict medical terms as we would now see it, only one person present might have actually caused their death. A further possible interpretation is that his death didn't occur during fighting but was instead an entirely ritual affair. In such a scenario the Stonehenge Archer becomes a prehistoric 'St Sebastian'. The latter was purportedly a member of the Roman elite Praetorian Guard who converted to Christianity at a time when doing so was bad for your health[27] and was sentenced to death by being tied to a post and repeatedly shot with arrows. If this was the case a further question arising would be whether the Archer's death represents the execution of a criminal or social deviant or in fact a human sacrifice? Given that all the arrows striking bone have penetrated from behind, it seems most likely to me that he simply fell forwards after being struck by whichever arrow hit him first and was then shot repeatedly in the back as he lay on the ground. If this was the case, the evidence as it presents is plausibly interpreted simply as a 'straightforward' conflict-related death with no specific need to invoke ritual killings or odd treatments of the dead, although these latter possibilities cannot be ultimately ruled out.

An example of deliberate killing that appears more clearly to have been carried out for ritual reasons was uncovered in advance of building development at Cliff's End Farm at the Isle of Thanet in Kent. Here a range of features were present concerned with domestic occupation, ceremonial activities and the placement of the dead. In particular a large pit dating from the early tenth century BC contained the remains of several humans and animals in a carefully-placed arrangement. This group appears to be centred on the body of an elderly female who has several sword cuts to the back of her head. These were clearly fatal and are placed consistently with the woman having been struck whilst kneeling down, leading the excavators (Jackie McKinley and colleagues) to suggest she may have been a willing victim. The possibility of her death representing an execution seems unlikely in light of the amount of care with which she was then placed in the pit. Laid on her side, with her left hand holding a piece of chalk up to her face and her right hand positioned so that her index finger was extended to point to the centre of the overall site, the woman also had a pair of new-born lambs resting in her lap. Also present were two children and a teenage girl. The body of the teenager was laid across the feet of the old woman, with her head resting on the head and neck of a cow. At least a year before the woman died another pair of lambs had been placed further down in the pit along with a deposit of cremated human bone, whilst a further group of partially disarticulated bones from an adult male had been placed in a bag or bundle on the opposite side of the pit, level with the woman's line of sight (had she been alive). This complex arrangement led the excavators to suggest the woman's death to have been a sacrifice, which given the deliberate killing of the animals present then raises the likelihood that at least some of the other individuals in the pit, the teenager in particular, had also been killed in order to form part of this larger offering. In terms of how we might view the woman, they have further suggested that whilst on one hand she could be seen rather callously as a 'disposable old lady' on the other hand her status might rather have been that of a 'wise matriarch' and therefore both a greater loss to the community and of more presumed value to whatever powers this sacrifice was intended to appeal to.[28]

Safety in Numbers? The Changing Scale of Conflict

On one hand then, where acts of violence are apparent, the Bronze Age looks essentially pretty similar to the periods that went before it in terms of the occurrence of single individuals, predominantly (but by no means all) adult males, with weapon injuries. The principal differences apparent at this time are firstly changes in technology as evidenced by injuries that must have been

Another Hole in the Head: Interpreting Trepanations

The practice of trepanation – cutting holes in the skulls of living people by drilling or scraping until a piece of bone was removed leaving an opening in the skull vault – was widespread throughout a variety of world regions in prehistoric times. Examples of individuals who had undergone this procedure are known from all over Europe during the Neolithic and Bronze Age.[29] Examples with no signs of healing are difficult to interpret in so far as it isn't possible to say whether the 'patient' was alive at the start of the procedure and died during or shortly after the operation, or whether the skull was cut into after death to produce an 'amulet' – a piece of cranial bone that might then be kept for having some kind of perceived magic/ritual power. However, a large proportion of excavated examples are well healed with rounded edges, with writers on the subject often expressing surprise at the high proportion of people who survived the operation.

On occasion, healed (and sometimes unhealed) head injuries have been mistaken for trepanations.[30] This has tended to occur partly where people had failed to notice features that would be seen in skull fractures which are not caused by trepanations, such as depression of an area of the cranial vault or bevelled internal margins (see Chapter 2). Another reason that is actually more pervasive, however, is simply that trepanation has often been the default interpretation that people have opted for when faced with a hole in the head that otherwise requires explaining. This tendency can in turn be argued to stem once again from the wider trend noted in previous chapters, either not to look for signs of violence in prehistory or to seek alternative (non-violent) interpretations to explain it away when such evidence is un-missable.

In speculating on the possible reasons why such procedures might have been carried out a further issue that has received less attention than it might have done, probably for the same reasons as cited above, is the extent to which trepanations might have been conducted in order to treat head injuries.[31] As discussed in Chapter 1, one of the most pressing problems in attempts to treat significant trauma to the head is the issue of raised pressure inside the skull (ICP) caused by bleeding and swelling in or around the brain. One way to relieve such pressure, and thereby to reduce or avoid damage to brain tissues is to make an opening in the skull by cutting into it. Such an operation, which would now be called a craniotomy, would therefore have been in continuous use since prehistory.[32] A further issue in relation to depressed fractures is the effect of sharp edged fragments of broken bone being driven into the brain and causing further damage and bleeding. It is likely that people learned over time that injured individuals tended to survive better if the wound was 'tidied up' and these broken fragments were removed. Figure 7.3 shows some early Bronze Age examples from Brittany of individuals who had undergone trepanations and survived. Healed prehistoric trepanations have been observed from a variety of world regions with a surprisingly low incidence of evidence for infection. It is likely that such operations were regarded as a form of magic and I have often wondered whether knapping a fresh flint blade might have been part of the prescribed ritual. If this was the case such practice would provide

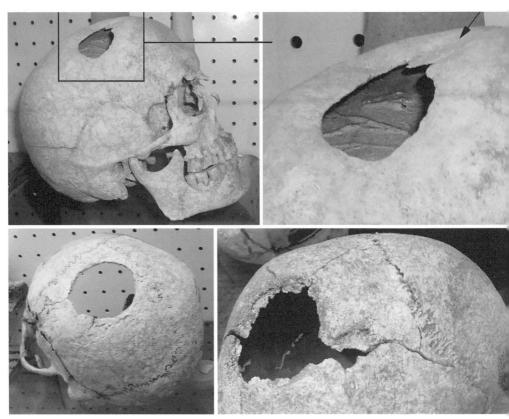

Figure 7.3. Prehistoric trauma surgery? Late Neolithic and Bronze Age skulls from Brittany displaying large healed trepanations. The example shown in a. and b. clearly overlies a depressed cranial fracture (arrowed), whilst the other two examples occupy large areas of the cranial vault above the hat brim line and may also have been carried out to treat head injuries. (Examples from the Musée de la Préhistoire Finistérienne)

the 'surgeon' with an effectively sterile instrument, which may go some way towards explaining the apparent success rates.

In this respect many (but obviously not all) trepanations may therefore act as a kind of secondary or proxy indicator for trauma to the head. Studies of the subject commonly note the most frequent locations of trepanations to be the parietal bones followed by the frontal bone, with the left parietal being the most common.[33] This would be consistent with the treatment of head wounds, as injuries inflicted in assaults from a face-to face, right-handed opponent occur most commonly on the left side of the head. Additionally, applying the 'hat-brim line' rule mentioned in Chapter 3, whereby injuries below this line are more commonly the results of falls whilst those above are more commonly due to violence is also consistent with a high proportion of prehistoric trepanations relating to assaults rather than accidental head injuries. The very tall Beaker individual from West Ridge, Wiltshire, mentioned earlier as having a healed blunt head injury had in fact received treatment with his wound being trepanned. In this case there were signs of subsequent infection, whilst the wound was located on the left parietal bone.[34]

inflicted by metal weapons, secondly the fact that these individuals appear wealthy and well-fed and thirdly in the appearance of some individuals who appear to have been ritually killed. Whether the latter was a new type of custom that came to prominence in the Early Bronze Age, or whether the way such people were placed in burials simply makes such practices more recognizable to archaeologists, remains open to debate. This point is where the current chapter might end with such a picture derived from what might be called the 'standard' burial record of the Bronze Age. However, a number of examples have also come to light in recent years where human remains have been encountered in both larger numbers and more varied circumstances than is generally the norm, either grouped in formal cemeteries or dealt with in ways that suggest less respectful treatment. Single skeletons with weapon injuries only provide concrete evidence for the involvement of two people – an attacker and a victim. Where greater numbers of individuals are present more complex situations come into view, particularly with regard to the question of a whether a class of people identifying themselves on the basis of being warriors had come into existence.

La Motilla del Azuer is an impressive site situated on the plain of La Mancha in what is now central Spain. Construction at this location consisted of an artificial mound on top of which a central stone fortress was built containing a rainwater reservoir and set within three walled enclosures, with a small village surrounding this arrangement. The site was occupied from 2200–1350 BC with some inevitable rebuilding during this time, and may have functioned not dissimilarly to a Medieval castle in controlling and protecting the surrounding farmland. Over a hundred burials have been excavated since the site was first investigated in 1976, of which sixty-four have recently been analysed by a team from the University of Granada led by Silvia Alejandra Jiménez-Brobeil.[35] The twenty-nine children present among these burials showed no signs of injury, as did all but one of the eleven women, the exception having a Colles' fracture, a break to the tip of the radius usually sustained by falling on to an outstretched hand. However, the twelve adult males present exhibited a different picture, with seven head and neck injuries and six injuries to the remainder of the body between them. Several of the injuries below the neck may well have been accidental, but those to the head and face were highly consistent with violence, including two broken noses (see Chapter 2), eight blunt force cranial injuries and eight injuries caused by bladed implements. All of these wounds were healed with the exception of two of the blunt head injuries which must therefore have been received at or close to the time these men died.

A further individual buried at this site suffered a particularly violent death. Burial 60 contained an adult male, aged around 19 or 20, lying flexed on his side and accompanied by a pottery vessel. Dating from earlier during the site's use (2040–1870 BC), this man's bones exhibit more than two dozen weapon injuries. These include eight incised cuts to the vault of the skull in addition to a penetrating wound near the top of his head on the right side made with an object with a triangular profile (perhaps a spear point). The injuries were followed by a massive blow with a club-like object which forced a section of the skull vault inward leaving a large hole (42 × 37mm). Below the neck the man had sustained further sharp force injuries to his left arm and hand consistent with defence wounds, whilst he also had two cuts to his right femur. In addition his ribs, spine and left hip (ilium) displayed signs that he had been stabbed from behind at least a dozen times. It is not possible to determine exactly which order these injuries occurred in and several different sequences are possible. If we disregard the fact that any further injuries that didn't affect bone cannot now be detected, it is likely that the stab wounds to this man's chest were the cause of death, either through the lungs failing due to being punctured or filling with blood (or a combination of the two) or simply dying through blood loss. The blow to the head must have come after the blade wounds as secondary fractures that radiate from the point of impact stop at some of the latter, which means the cuts must have occurred first. Whilst not causing death immediately this horrendous blunt injury would have rendered the man unconscious, if he wasn't already.

The team from Granada have interpreted the man from Burial 60 to have been the victim of a murder. Whilst we certainly can't disprove this, it seems to me to be at least equally plausible, if not more so that he had died in conflict. Situated at a defended site which incorporated a water reservoir and was therefore set up to withstand a siege, with the male population exhibiting a range of both healed and unhealed weapon injuries, it seems more likely that this man was one of a group of individuals specifically involved in its defence. The sharp-force injuries on his skeleton have been assessed to have been produced by at least two different implements, possibly an axe and a dagger (swords had not yet been invented), whilst the presence of a third weapon evidenced by the puncture wound to his skull would suggest at least three assailants, i.e. people fighting together in a group. The man was formally buried with the same care as that given to the others buried at the site which would argue against him being either a slain enemy or a social deviant singled out for punishment. Going back to the principle of parsimony mentioned in Chapter 3, i.e. the idea that the simplest solution to a problem is likely to be the most correct, one has to work a lot harder to explain this man as anything other than someone who had died in an attack on the fortress.

At the site of Sund in Norway a large collection of human bones was excavated in 1968, dating from some time between what was the Early and

Middle Bronze Age locally (1500–1100 BC).[36] These remains were difficult to analyse due to poor preservation but were assessed to be from between twenty to thirty people with about half being adolescents and children. Among the adults present a range of injuries was apparent, several of which were un-healed cuts most likely inflicted with swords. Rather than being explainable as 'normal' burial practice for the area this deposit actually differs starkly from other burials of the same date at the nearby site of Toldnes. The Toldnes burials were formally laid out, with people buried in individual chambers (cists) under stone mounds and accompanied with a rich and impressive array of objects. By contrast the Sund assemblage with its collective mix of adults and children, buried with little formality, lacking grave goods and displaying unhealed weapon injuries looks suspiciously like the results of a massacre. In addition to these wounds from the time of their deaths, five of the adults, all either male or where sex couldn't be determined, also had healed injuries. Whilst three of these could have been sustained accidentally two had healed blade injuries again consistent with sword cuts, leading the osteologist who later analysed them (Hilde Fyllingen) to suggest that perhaps these were mem-bers of a warrior class as they had 'seen action' before. Several of the children showed signs of malnutrition in their bones and teeth,[37] further leading to the suggestion that this community was under stress at the time these events took place. Such a conclusion was not hinted at by other types of evidence from this period and region, where the accepted view had previously been of a peaceful Bronze Age, along the lines that weapons etc. were prestige items for display, rather than practical use.

Both the best known and the most striking example of violence from Bronze Age Britain was uncovered initially in 1968 when a gas pipeline was laid across farmland at Tormarton in Gloucestershire.[38] Here the skeletal remains of three adult males were disturbed, two of whom showed clear signs of violence at the time of their deaths (Fig. 7.4). The men were aged between their mid-20s and late 30s. One exhibited three injuries, two of which were obvious without specialist opinion as the weapons responsible remained embedded in the man's bones in the form of bronze spear tips. The first of these was lodged between two of his lumbar vertebrae and would have pene-trated the man's spinal cord, rendering him paralysed below the waist. The second spear tip was embedded in his right pelvis (ischium) having been thrust in deeply from behind. In both cases it would appear the spear tips snapped when attempts were made to remove them, whilst the presence of two weapons implies there to have been at least two assailants. This individual also had an oval-shaped perforation in his skull vault, on the left parietal bone towards the back of his head. This wound may have been inflicted following the two spear thrusts with the man lying prone on his front and so would

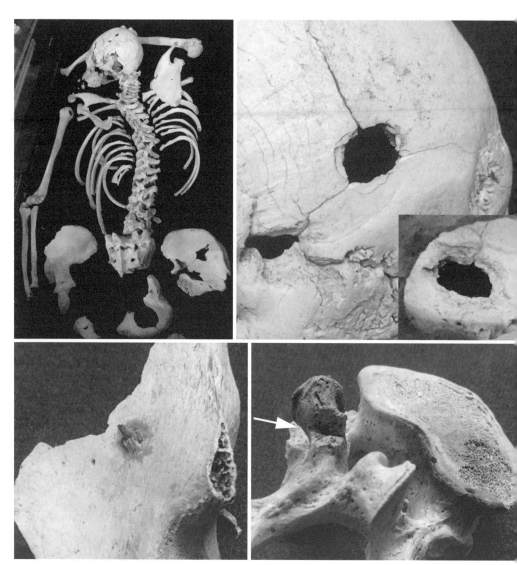

Figure 7.4. One of three young adult males deposited in a Middle Bronze Age boundary ditch at Tormarton (Gloucestershire). This man has an oval-shaped perforation at the back his skull which may have been the wound that killed him (interior view inset), after he had been incapacitated by spear thrusts to his pelvis and spine. (Photographs by Rebecca Redfern)

represent the '*coup de grâce*' that ultimately killed him. Another of the men had a lozenge-shaped perforation in his left pelvic bone (ilium) consistent with the profile of a spear of the same type, which again must have been thrust in from behind with considerable force. This second individual showed no other signs of injury, whilst no injuries were apparent on either the third man or on the bones of two other males recovered when the site was later re-excavated in 1999–2000 by Richard Osgood (a leading expert on Bronze Age warfare). With five adult males in their prime[39] all buried together, two with terrible injuries, it seems unlikely that any of these latter three died naturally and so it is reasonable to assume that other wounds these men suffered didn't damage bone.

In addition to the fact that these men were interred together as a group, having apparently fought with multiple opponents, the feature they were buried in may reveal further detail about the circumstances of their deaths. Osgood's re-investigation of the burial location revealed that in fact the men's bodies had been deposited in a substantial linear ditch 3m wide and 70m long, of a type that became common in Britain from the Middle Bronze Age onward, usually interpreted as marking the boundaries of territories. The men had been placed in the ditch with no signs of formality and without any kind of grave goods. Rather than being left open the ditch had then been filled in. As Richard Osgood has suggested it seems quite reasonable to view the ditch as holding some significance for the presumed dispute in relation to which these men were killed. Boundaries of this kind exist to stake claims to land. In this case environmental samples from the excavated feature reveal that the surrounding landscape was one of recently cleared woodland. The ditch itself contained no plant remains, meaning it could not have remained open for long before it was backfilled. Consequently, it seems most likely that the ditch represents an attempt to stake a new claim to territory which had then been challenged by others who regarded the area as being already theirs. It is unlikely that those who had gone to the effort of digging such a large feature would be prepared to then fill it back in and so it would therefore seem most likely that the bodies in the ditch represent the incoming group who had been unsuccessful in establishing rights to the land. The Tormarton group have been radiocarbon dated to the later Bronze Age (1315–1050 BC) which broadly coincides with the date of the only other example of such an injury from this period in Britain. The pelvis of a man excavated at Dorchester on Thames, Oxfordshire, about 50 miles west of Tormarton, had a spearhead tip similarly embedded and was dated to 1260–990 BC.[40]

A further example of evidence for multiple individuals involved in conflict is provided by an interesting set of finds from the Tollense river valley in north-eastern Germany. Human bones had been repeatedly found for many years along a 2km stretch of the valley, although their date remained a mystery until 1996 when a well-preserved humerus was discovered with a flint arrowhead embedded in it. The arrowhead was of a type in use in the Middle Bronze Age of the region and since this find over 9,000 further human bones have been recovered from the river and its banks. The bones generally occurred singly in isolation with very few articulated with any other bone. These remains have been calculated to be from at least 124 people, although this is only a minimum estimate, the true number of people represented remains unknown and may be much higher. The most plausible explanation for these finds would be that somewhere at a point upriver as yet unidentified, a prehistoric cemetery, once well away from the water, was now being cut into by the river having changed its course. If this was the case the 'demographic profile' – the general composition of the population represented by the bones – should reflect the pattern that would be expected in a normal cemetery population. So the numbers of males and females should be roughly equal and the adult population should contain more people over 40 than under (life expectancy in the past was actually greater than is popularly believed[41]). The question of children being present is dependent on whether they were treated the same way in death as adults, but assuming they were, the youngest in society should also be well represented as child and infant mortality will have been high. Lastly, assuming the cemetery had filled up slowly over generations, which is what would be expected unless it related to some sort of catastrophic event such as an epidemic, the dates of the individuals present should be spread out over an extended period.

However, this was not the case. The Tollense valley assemblage differed considerably from these expectations, firstly in that radiocarbon dates obtained from the bones are narrowly clustered around a single point in time, 1200 BC. Secondly, the bones for which age and sex could be determined (mainly the cranium, pelvis and femur) were almost exclusively those of young adult males. To add to this emerging picture, the humerus with the embedded arrowhead was joined by repeated examples of other unhealed trauma including both bladed-weapon injuries and blunt-force impacts. It would appear then that these were the dead of a battle who had been thrown into the river. This may have been done simply as a practical measure to dispose of large numbers of (presumably) enemy corpses, although given the propensity of Bronze Age people to place offerings in rivers and lakes the possibility should also be considered that the bodies had been deposited in the water as ritual offerings by the winning side. The team analysing these remains led by Jörg Orschiedt of Berlin University[42] have also suggested that not all of these individuals might have been killed in action and that some might represent prisoners who were executed (or perhaps sacrificed) after the event. Similar practices may be apparent in Britain where during the last couple of centuries hundreds of human crania have been recovered from the River Thames, mostly through dredging. A recent study by Rick Schulting and Richard Bradley of Oxford and Reading Universities demonstrated many of these to date from the Middle Bronze Age through to the Iron Age, with some displaying blunt injuries and sword cuts.[43] Some of these finds may simply relate to burials eroded by the river and washed downstream or bodies placed in the water as a form of burial practice. However, the possibility must also be considered, especially regarding those with weapon injuries, that a proportion of these 'river skulls' represent trophies placed in the water as offerings.

Once again, the examples given in this chapter are far from exhaustive and have rather been selected to illustrate the overall range of evidence. Despite all the instances discussed above, the question posed earlier in this chapter of whether the proliferation of weapons and armour once bronze had become widespread, relates to greater levels of violence or instead represents an alternative way for people to outdo each other without actually fighting, remains difficult to answer. Violence-related injuries certainly appear frequent among the burials that are known from this time, although as mentioned earlier, the usual issue afflicting prehistoric burials is in play where we only have access to a sample of society and can't really say how representative this was. My gut feeling on the subject is that violence or the threat of it must have been at least a relatively frequent aspect of life not least because of the long-distance trading networks that now spanned Europe. Anyone controlling such a network who wasn't prepared to defend it vigorously would soon find they had lost that control to someone who was. But regardless of this point, whilst the burials we have can't specifically tell us how frequent violence was, they do have several things to say about the character of violent acts during this time. A suggestion sometimes put forward in discussions of this period is that conflict between groups may have commonly been resolved by fights between champions – single individuals selected to represent the whole community. Rock art images from this time commonly depict just two figures fighting, rather than groups of individuals, whilst the existence of such a custom at least in some times and places is verified by later written sources. The biblical story of David and Goliath is perhaps the best known example of a written account often interpreted as recounting a fight between two champions (in this case of the early Iron Age[44]). On one hand perhaps many of the Beaker period individuals buried singly with weapon injuries could represent such a tradition of single combat. However, the existence of repeated examples of groups of people with weapon injuries buried together and also single individuals with injuries apparently caused by multiple assailants, are just not consistent with a picture of conflicts being resolved by single champions. Perhaps then what is in evidence is a situation similar to what we have for the Medieval period where written and artistic sources tell one story but the remains of the dead tell another. The idea of chivalry is one of the strongest themes throughout Medieval literature and art, but human skeletons with weapon injuries from this time indicate vanquished opponents to have been treated in a very different manner (see Chapter 11). Lastly, the use of violence against human beings in an entirely ritualized manner comes into clearer focus at this time. In this respect many Bronze Age examples of violence suggest something more sophisticated than people simply lashing out in anger against each other. Whether such practices were new or are simply more visible to us because of the way the respective victims were buried remains unclear. What such instances do reveal, however, is that people had realized the 'performance value' of acts of violence. The deaths of individuals such as the Stonehenge Archer, the old woman from the Isle of Thanet or the men buried at Tormarton, all have a common theme. They clearly represent theatrical acts designed to convey a strong message to those watching or hearing about them. Whether such a message was 'We serve the gods'; 'Crime doesn't pay'; or simply 'Don't mess with us!', what these burials demonstrate is something uniquely human – the use of violence as a means of communication. In these times before writing, such messages would have been as clear and as bold to those 'reading' them as anything the written word could ever have conveyed.

Chapter 8

Out of the Shadows: The End of Prehistory

Between the Renaissance and the nineteenth century the only sources of information recognized by Europeans regarding events that happened before the birth of Christ were accounts given by Greek and Roman authors from classical times, coupled with the Bible. During the formative years of what we now know as archaeology, when upper-class individuals collected interesting objects they had dug out of the ground from in and around the enigmatic mounds and stone monuments that dotted much of the continent, such writings from classical times provided the only framework by which this confusing array of odd structures, puzzling objects and mysterious human burials might be understood. At a time when the Old Testament account of the Creation was taken at face value and the Earth was understood to be less than 6,000 years old,[1] far-flung areas such as Britain were assumed only to have been populated for a few centuries before the arrival of the Romans in the first century AD.[2] It therefore followed quite logically that the standing stones, burial mounds and other earthworks scattered throughout the European landscape must have been built by the barbarian peoples discussed by Greek and Roman writers. In central and western Europe such peoples were therefore held to be the warlike Celts cited by a broad range of ancient authors, with northern parts of the continent having been inhabited by Germanic tribes as described by writers such as Julius Caesar and Tacitus. As peoples about whom written accounts exist, but who wrote nothing themselves, such groups have often been referred to as 'proto-historic' rather than prehistoric people, commonly perceived as elusive, romantic figures almost visible but still shrouded in the mists of time.

As archaeology developed from an upper-class leisure activity to an academic discipline during the nineteenth and twentieth centuries, the writings of classical authors continued to form the backbone of the way the period that had now come to be known as the Iron Age was understood.[3] In particular the notion of the Celts as a distinct people with a common language, who had spread across the continent in a series of invasions and migrations, was never questioned until very recently. Until the latter half of the twentieth century the idea that specific types of objects signified the presence of particular groups of people formed the bedrock on which all other archaeological interpretations were built. It was therefore assumed that arte-facts dating from the Iron Age in what was thought of as the Celtic home-land in central Europe, must represent the material culture of the 'Keltoi' or 'Celtae' as the Greeks and Romans referred to them respectively. Further-more, studying the distribution of such objects throughout other regions could then allow the spread of Celtic peoples as they marauded across the con-tinent to be traced. Consequently, when a distinctive style of metalwork char-acterized by flowing curved designs was identified as appearing in central Europe at around 500 BC, now known as the La Téne style, this was naturally assumed to be the handiwork of Celtic craftsmen. The appearance of such styles of artefact at later dates in other parts of the continent was therefore held to indicate the Celts on the move as they spread out to occupy other regions. This distribution both fitted in with and further reinforced the emerging idea of a kind of pre-Roman Celtic commonwealth stretching from Turkey to Ireland and from Scotland down to Spain. Furthermore, the related group of languages spoken by modern peoples living on the western fringes of Europe (Welsh, Scottish/Irish Gaelic, Breton etc.) were taken to be surviving dialects of the original Celtic language once spoken across the continent. It therefore followed that the people of these regions must represent the last remnants of this once-great people, keeping the last flames of Celtic culture alive through their music, their oral histories and their free, independent spirits.

This image has occupied the popular imagination for nearly three centuries and continues to form the dominant view taken by the greater portion of the general public, not least in the parts of Atlantic Europe where people identify their heritage and ancestry as being 'Celtic'. According to such a view, the current populations who trace their heritage to these regions are regarded essentially as the direct descendants of groups who arrived during the Iron Age, also being popularly assumed to be genetically distinct from the later arrivals who came after them, such as the predominantly 'Anglo-Saxon' pop-ulation of England. However, widespread reconsideration of the available evidence over recent decades has led to a general rejection of this view amongst several disciplines. The great edifice of the 'Celtic World' as it was previously seen has more recently come tumbling down as archaeologists and historians, aided by linguists and geneticists, have realized this notion to be derived more from the eighteenth and nineteenth-century imagination than from reality. In fact no ancient author referred to Britain, Ireland or any other part of Atlantic Europe as being Celtic, and as pointed out by Simon James 'no one in Britain or Ireland called themselves "Celtic" or a "Celt" (and no one applied such names to them either) until after 1700".[4] Whilst a people calling themselves Celts (or at least referred to as such by others), originating north of the Alps and moving downwards into northern Italy and the Balkans after 400 BC, may have been very real, we no longer have reason to believe that such people spread their language, culture or indeed their genes very much further. The styles of finely-decorated metalwork that have come to be designated as 'Celtic' did indeed find their way further afield, spreading outwards from this central zone across the continent. However, as noted in Chapter 1, objects and ideas can be transferred across large distances through any number of social interactions between people, including commercial trade, the exchange of gifts or simply the copying of new and exotic styles by local craftspeople. Transfer by these kind of means is what appears to have happened in the case of La Téne artefacts, where the peripheral regions of Europe actually display more evidence for continuity from the preceding Bronze Age than for change, as seen in persistent local styles of houses, pottery and burials. Additionally the 'La Téne' objects that do occur in such regions are in fact made in local versions of the style and are more consistent with adaptation by existing populations, rather than intrusive objects brought along by invaders forcing the locals out (Fig. 8.1).

The matter would then seem to have been settled by careful attention to the archaeology, except for the question of the presumed Celtic languages. If the westward migration of Celts that supposedly brought them as far as Ireland, Wales, Scotland, Cornwall and Brittany never happened, then what accounts for the shared language group that persists today in these regions having apparently survived from a time before modern English and French (etc.)

Figure 8.1. The Chesil Mirror, a southern British example of an object decorated in a local adaptation of the Continental La Téne style. (Photograph by Miles Russell)

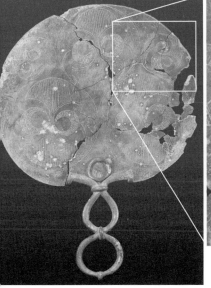
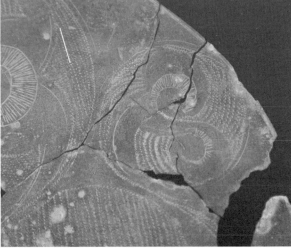

existed? Barry Cunliffe, now Emeritus Professor at Oxford University, has recently offered an interesting alternative suggestion based on a series of modern linguistic studies.[5] These studies are in broad agreement that the language now known as Celtic diverged from other Indo-European languages sometime between 4000 and 2500 BC. Cunliffe notes that all modern European languages are spoken in the areas where they first developed, rather than having mysteriously disappeared at their point of origin but survived elsewhere. Given then that both Celtic place names and people speaking modern Celtic languages are distributed across the Atlantic edge of Europe, it seems more sensible to suggest that this is where the original version of the language first developed. To get away from the cultural baggage associated with the term Celtic, Cunliffe suggests the alternative term of 'Atlantean' and queries whether this language may in fact have first appeared in Spain and was then spread northwards into France, Britain and later Germany, along with Beaker pottery and metalworking. This rather neat suggestion not only explains the distribution of these languages today but also fits well with the archaeological evidence, unlike earlier theories.[6] If this is correct the modern 'Atlantean' languages spoken in Ireland, Wales etc. are indeed remnant dialects of a prehistoric language once widespread across western Europe, but it just wasn't 'Celtic'.

So what has all this got to do with violence and conflict in the past? The answer is that when the accepted view of 'Barbarian' Europe rested on Greek and Roman accounts, the picture this generated was of a society dominated by a bellicose warrior aristocracy who liked nothing more than fighting and existed in a permanent state of inter-tribal warfare. For example, a well-known line from the Roman author Strabo describes the Gauls as 'war-mad and both high spirited and quick for battle'.[7] Archaeological finds of swords, shields and helmets coupled with elaborate defended sites in the form of the many hundreds of hillforts that dot much of Europe served to bolster this view and the notion of a warlike Iron Age seemed indisputable. Of course, when the 'Celtic world' came crashing down as the hard evidence was reassessed and the supposed Celtic invasions evaporated, the notion of the warlike Celtic aristocrat dissolved along with it, as new conceptions were put forward to explain the archaeological record. Items of warrior gear such as the famous Battersea shield recovered from the Thames or the fittings for a decorated scabbard found at Standlake in Oxfordshire[8] were now seen as prestige goods indicative of nothing more than friendly trading contacts. Defended sites were now seen through fresh eyes simply as high-status structures built to impress, rather than as evidence that much fighting ever took place. This explanation was also rather self-fulfilling as the larger, more elaborate and more staunchly defended a site appeared to be, the more it was then argued to function as an expression of prestige and display rather than as a practical fortification. Once again therefore we have the notion of apparent evidence for conflict actually representing little more than a means of competing to out-do the neighbours. By the early 1990s views of the European Iron Age had undergone a thorough pacification, having metamorphosed from being seen as the most warlike part of prehistory to now being regarded as one of the least.

A New World Order

The transition from bronze to iron as the principal metal from which every-day items were made, must have had profound effects at a continental level as the complex networks of trading contacts built up over the previous thousand years on the basis of copper and tin now disintegrated. The advantage of manufacturing from a single ore which occurs widely meant that metal production became a more localized affair and in this respect communities became more self-sufficient and less interdependent on other groups else-where. Over time populations appear to have grown, as evidenced by large numbers of settlements and signs of widespread land divisions across much of Europe. Distinct regional groups emerged with their own material cultures evident in pottery and art styles, with distributions that suggest well-defined territorial boundaries. Elite groups holding sway over society are increasingly apparent, with new trading networks in evidence, particularly along rivers and seaways. The emerging aristocrats of Iron Age Europe had a clear liking for high-quality metalwork, including a new range of often-elaborate warrior gear in addition to marking themselves out through horse ownership and pro-ducing their own coinage. These 'new money' elites were also the principal actors in a different pattern of exchange where prestige items from the civili-zations of Greece and Rome in particular were acquired by prominent indi-viduals who could then bolster their positions by redistributing them among their followers. My own department has spent the last few years excavating the site of such a local elite at Winterbourne Kingston in Dorset where Roman jewellery, wine amphorae, chickens (a trendy new arrival from the Continent) and other fine items such as a carved ivory knife handle from what is now Turkey have all been uncovered. Here it seems that if the 'Dorset mafia' offered you a 'present you couldn't refuse', you were then in their service and it would be unwise to forget such an obligation. For the first time we also become aware of named groups of people in the descriptions of bar-barian tribes provided particularly by Roman authors. Although such tribal identities should be taken with a healthy dose of scepticism, as some 'tribes' may have been more real than others, with some such identities being little more than Roman creations that made it easier to govern and most importantly tax people once the legions rolled in.

In parts of Europe and for portions of the Iron Age burials were a relatively standardized affair with the dead laid out in single graves, some more richly furnished with objects for the afterlife than others and such burials grouped together in sometimes large cemeteries. In other regions such as France and particularly Britain human remains discovered in Iron Age contexts indicate a very broad range of differing practices where there seems to have been no single way the dead were treated. The most notable point regarding Britain during this period is there simply aren't enough burials to account for the very dense and widespread settlement of the landscape that is apparent. A large proportion of people were most likely dealt with in death by leaving them exposed to decompose and with their bones subsequently weathered and scattered by natural processes, particularly during the earlier part of the period. Such practice would certainly explain the many 'stray bones' which commonly turn up on Iron Age occupation sites with no sign of the rest of the skeleton. In some British regions such as central southern England burials occur in re-used storage pits, particularly during the Middle Iron Age with later burials laid out in specifically-dug graves. Such burials occasionally include individuals furnished with warrior paraphernalia (weapons, helmets, shields etc.) with arguably the most elaborate being in northern England where prominent individuals were buried with dismantled chariots. Where weapons and armour survive from this period they are commonly either found with the dead or in sacrificial deposits often in bodies of water in apparent continuation of such practices stretching back to the Bronze Age. Some such items are highly elaborate and once again raise the question of whether they were manufactured specifically for display or ritual rather than intended for use in conflict. Consequently, it isn't possible to reach a conclusion on the basis of such objects as to whether the image of 'war mad' barbarians claimed by Strabo might actually have any truth in it.

Used in Anger: Weapon Injuries

Whatever wider symbolic functions weapons, shields and their like may have fulfilled in society at this time, there are certainly sufficient examples of weapon-related injuries to indicate that such items were indeed also put to practical use, such as the skull of an adult male with an unhealed sword cut, found in a ritual deposit at Fiskerton, Lincolnshire.[9] Sarah King of Cerro Coso College, California, has produced a useful study of cemeteries in the north and south of England (Yorkshire and Hampshire) which found low overall numbers of weapon injuries,[10] but with the majority of such being sharp force wounds from swords or daggers. One individual, a male aged 30–40 from Acklam in east Yorkshire, had five unhealed sword cuts to his head. There was a predominance of young adult males among this sample, although the find of a female aged around 50 with a healed blade wound to her frontal bone illustrates that women were not exempt from such violence. At Wetwang Slack, also in Yorkshire, an adult female was found to have a spearhead situated in her abdomen with the point close to her spine,[11] three individuals at Burton Fleming were similarly found with spearheads in their abdominal and chest regions,[12] whilst a skeleton with a spearhead embedded in its pelvis was found buried near the Thames at Long Wittenham in 1901.[13] As in earlier periods in prehistory there are also isolated examples of blunt head injuries dotted among Iron Age assemblages, such as the middle-aged man from the ongoing excavation site at Winterbourne Kingston, Dorset (shown earlier in this book in Fig. 2.6a) who has a large healed blunt injury to his right parietal bone consistent with a heavy blow to the head from behind.[14] At least two and possibly three crania with unhealed blunt injuries were found placed in the ditch surrounding a hillfort at Ham Hill in Somerset during recent excavations there.[15] Other blunt head injuries from this period commonly affect smaller areas (just an inch or so in circumference) and have been suggested to have been caused by sling stones, such as the two individuals from Wetwang Slack or the three individuals with such wounds (two women and a man), from Maiden Castle (Dorset).[16]

Getting a Head in Barbarian Europe

An aspect of culture that is repeatedly in evidence across the continent throughout the Iron Age is a preoccupation with the human head. Both in sculpted forms and metalwork, representations of heads are one of the most common motifs in the art of the period. This fascination was not just confined to artistic representation, with finds of both decapitated heads and headless bodies discovered repeatedly in excavations over the last century or so, especially in France.[17] Where the former are noted, these are distinguished from examples where the cranium has simply been removed from an already decayed body in that the mandible (lower jaw) and one or more neck vertebrae are also present, indicating that this was indeed a severed head.[18] The custom of retaining the severed heads of slain enemies as trophies is mentioned by various Greek and Roman authors, particularly in reference to the Gauls. Arguably the best-known of such mentions is by the Greek author Diodorus Siculus, writing in the first century BC, who claimed that: 'When their enemies fall they cut off their heads and fasten them about the necks of their horses ... and these first-fruits of battle they fasten by nails upon their houses, just as men do, in certain kinds of hunting, with the heads of wild beasts they have mastered.'[19] This source goes on to famously cite the Gauls as also keeping the embalmed heads of vanquished foes in chests, in order to show them off to guests and boast of their prowess.

Although such sources make no mention of Britain, a similar custom appears to be in evidence in the British Isles, with examples noted at a number of sites. The aforementioned skull from Fiskerton, Lincs, placed as part of a ritual deposit complete with a sword is clearly a strong candidate for such an interpretation. An adult axis vertebra (the second neck vertebra) from Maiden Castle had been sliced through with a sharp bladed implement, although this find was among a mixed sample of disarticulated bones and was separated from the rest of the skeleton so it isn't possible to say whether the head was removed or buried with the rest of the body.[20] The aforementioned crania with weapon injuries found in the ditch at Ham Hill are also likely candidates for trophy taking. The site of Sculptor's Cave near Covesea in the north of Scotland was investigated between 1928 and 1930, during which time around 1,600 human bones were discovered, although the vast majority of these were not kept and are now lost. Among those that were retained are seven neck vertebrae which have clearly been sliced through, consistent with decapitation. Recent radiocarbon dates obtained from the surviving bones by Ian Armitt (Bradford University) and colleagues[21] have shown these vertebrae to date from around the third century AD, still classed as 'Iron Age' in this region as the Roman advance never penetrated this far north. Despite the other bones recorded being spread throughout the skeleton, only around 1 per cent are bones of the skull. Armitt has suggested that given the impracticality of carrying decapitated bodies to a remote and inaccessible cave it seems more likely that these individuals, along with three more whose bones are now lost, were decapitated in the cave, with their heads then taken away by their killers. Amongst various different types of deposition of human remains excavated at Danebury Hillfort in Hampshire were finds of isolated human skulls in placed in pits.[22] Such placement would fit as part of the wider tradition of placing offerings at the base of storage pits after the pit ceased to be used, apparently to thank or appease some sort of deities with dominion underground. In this case the skulls might be seen simply as belonging to people who had died naturally, having been removed and placed in the ground sometime after the body had decomposed. However, of ten skulls in which sex could be determined, seven were of young adult males, with several exhibiting severe unhealed head injuries. Given this profile and the violent deaths implied, it seems more likely that these were the heads of slain enemies, severed shortly after death rather than the skulls of venerated relatives collected after a longer interval.

The Last Ditch: The Man at Sovell Down

A further example indicating that the weapons of the Iron Age were not just ornaments for wealthy individuals was uncovered in rural Dorset in 1997. Excavations ahead of development at Sovell Down near the modern village of Gussage All Saints revealed a linear ditch dating from the Bronze or Iron Ages, containing the headless skeleton of a man, later dated to around 300 BC. The body had been lying on its back with the left arm bent across the abdomen and the right leg tightly flexed but the left leg relaxed (Fig. 8.2). No grave goods were found and the overall appearance was not of a careful, formal burial but rather that the body had simply been rolled or dropped into the ditch. There are all sorts of reasons why parts of a skeleton may be missing at excavation, such as being damaged by ploughing, moved by burrowing animals or when part of a grave is cut through by further digging in a later period. Consequently, it shouldn't be assumed that any absent body parts relate to events around the time of death. In this case a skeleton without a head shouldn't automatically prompt the dramatic conclusion that this represents an individual who was decapitated. Having said that, it is always good practice in anthropology for analysis to start in the field and a body missing a head understandably prompted the anthropologist involved (Jackie McKinley of Wessex Archaeology[23]) to pay careful attention to the remaining bones of the neck so that this possibility could be assessed. In fact, damage to the top two remaining bones of the spine (the 3rd and 4th cervical vertebrae) was evident which showed the neck to have been cleanly sliced through with a straight and clearly very sharp blade either at the time of death or shortly after (Fig. 8.3).

Figure 8.2. Skeleton of an 18–25 year old male deposited in a boundary ditch at Sovell Down (Dorset) having been violently killed and decapitated. (Photograph by Martin Green)

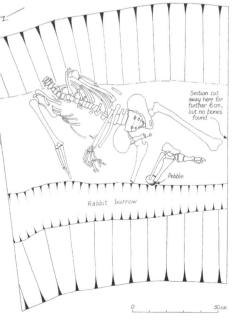

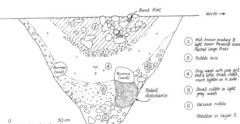

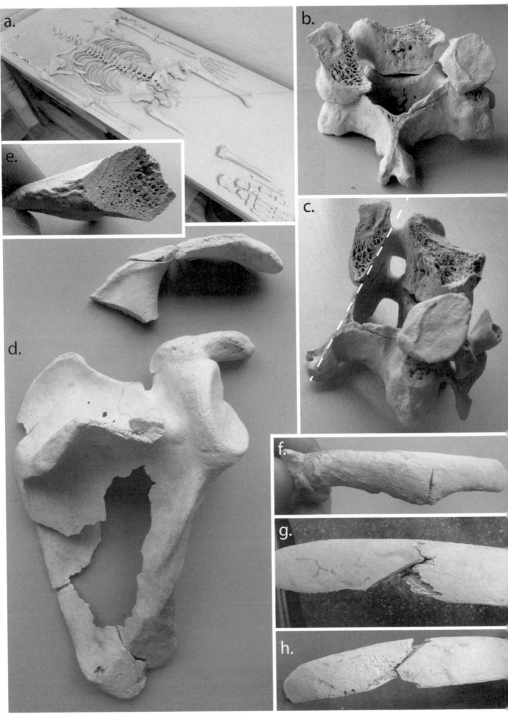

Figure 8.3. Detail of the headless man from Sovell Down: (a) the bones that were present at excavation; (b and c) the third and fourth cervical (neck) vertebrae, positioned to show the plane in which they have been sliced through; (d) the right scapula has been sliced through in four places with detail of one of the fragments; (e) showing linear scrape marks in the bone left by irregularities in the blade edge; (f–h) ribs from the right side with cuts again made by a thin, sharp-bladed implement.

Resolving one archaeological question usually leads to several others, in this case the realization that this man was in fact decapitated then raised questions over the circumstances in which this took place. Execution or death in combat are two obvious possibilities, whilst for prehistoric societies, unusual traumatic deaths always carry the possibility of a ritual killing such as a sacrifice. Lastly, the possibility remains that the head was removed after death as part of some form of burial rite. In this instance further light was shed on the question by other injuries located elsewhere on the skeleton. The man had several further bladed-weapon injuries, again inflicted with a very sharp implement to the right side of his torso, all delivered from behind. His right scapula (shoulder blade) had been cut into in five places, three of which had sliced clean through the bone, cutting it into four separate pieces. The man's ribs displayed similar cuts indicating four further blows from a sharp implement with a narrow blade, some severing the ribs in two and penetrating the chest cavity. These slashing cuts were all positioned consistently with attack by a right-handed assailant striking from behind.

As to the order in which these various cuts were inflicted, as is usually the case several scenarios are possible. It could be that the decapitation took place first with the sword cuts to the body occurring afterwards. In such a case the slashes to the torso would effectively constitute the kind of 'overkill' mentioned in the previous chapter, where individuals continue inflicting 'harm' to an already dead opponent either as an expression of anger or hatred or for specific ritual purposes. Such ritual might be regarded as further harming a slain enemy in the afterlife, or constitute a message as a kind of 'calling card' specific to a given group of people.[24] Whilst such an explanation is possible, it seems less likely in that the sword cuts are all concentrated in a single area, whereas acts of overkill tend to target multiple body parts. Another possibility is that the wounds to the torso were delivered first, which would certainly have severely incapacitated this man if they didn't kill him outright. If the man then fell forwards, the two sword blows that between them severed his head might have been delivered as he lay on the ground or perhaps supported himself on his hands and knees. The steep angle at which the neck was severed is more consistent with a blow from behind with the neck horizontal and the face looking down, rather than a decapitation from the front with the man's body positioned lying on his back. The sword cuts to the scapula are grouped closely together and lie at similar angles suggesting rapid repeated slashes with a great deal of force by a single individual. It seems most likely this was a frenzied attack that left the man unable to escape or defend himself, with the decapitation either finally killing him or taking place shortly after he died.

As to the wider interpretation of the circumstances of this man's death, the frenzied nature of his injuries and lack of care in his burial would seem to rule out the possibility of a controlled, careful, ritualized killing as suggested for the Bronze Age woman from Thanet mentioned in the previous chapter. However, whether this man died defending himself in combat, running away from an attacker or was simply ambushed from behind remains unknown. A further point to remember is that once again we cannot know whether other injuries were present which didn't affect bone, and of course it isn't possible to say if any head injuries played a part in this man's death. A suggestion made by McKinley was that the man might in fact have been felled by a blow to the head. This may have caused him to fall to the ground, exposing his back to the sword blows apparent on other parts of his skeleton. In such a picture these wounds might then have been inflicted by someone standing in front of the stricken man raining blows down from above. The fact that the head was not present in the burial implies it was taken, presumably shortly after death as a trophy, once again suggesting the Continental custom of headhunting was also prevalent in Britain.

Behind the Barricades: Fortified Sites

There can be doubt from the above examples that Iron Age people were not averse to resolving their differences through violent means. Once again, however, the find of small numbers of individuals with weapon injuries sheds no light on whether these examples represent disputes at the level of individuals or perhaps small-scale feuds between families, or whether these people might have received their wounds as part of larger episodes of organized conflict. The modern conception of warfare commonly centres on the notion of battles involving large numbers of participants, as are known to us through countless accounts from historic periods. However, trying to solve the question of whether such large engagements ever took place at any particular time in the past through archaeological means generally presents quite a challenge. Battles are by definition fleeting events which commonly take place over periods of days or even just hours. Whereas archaeology is well suited to uncovering the incremental layers built up by many years of activity in a given place, the sites of battles that may be very well known from historical accounts are often decidedly difficult to locate on the ground, with differences of opinion frequently going unresolved. Such challenges are even greater for prehistoric periods when the character and frequency of any conflicts that might have taken place often remains an open question.

In searching for candidates that might potentially answer the question of scale in past conflict, the most fruitful avenue is likely to be sites with structures interpreted as defences. As specific locations that indicate at least a perception of violent threats, such sites potentially offer the possibility of detecting whether large scale hostilities might have taken place. By considering multiple sites it should then in principle be possible to also make suggestions as to whether attacks on such structures might have been rare or frequent occurrences. All this sounds very straightforward, but the interpretation of fortified sites from Iron Age Britain provides an example that things might not be quite so simple. As constructions particularly associated with the

Iron Age,[25] the thousands of enclosed sites commonly on high ground, collectively known as hillforts, which still dot much of the European, and particularly the British landscape, have been thought of in various ways as opinions have varied over time regarding the character of Iron Age life. Initially thought to have been built by invading Romans or Danes, or embattled Saxons, the first excavations at British hillfort sites in the nineteenth century revealed them to generally date from a few centuries immediately prior to the rise of Rome. During the twentieth century hillforts became an integral part of the invasion-fuelled theories of migrating Celtic peoples, that served to explain changes over time during the period, such as the Belgae who supposedly invaded southern Britain from Gaul. This trend culminated in the work of Sir Mortimer Wheeler who famously interpreted the evidence he found at Maiden Castle in Dorset (Fig. 8.4), in terms of the valiant resistance of the natives to invasion by a highly organized foreign state (Rome), strongly coloured by his military background and the spectre of German invasion in his own time.[26] As with other facets of Iron Age life, during the later twentieth century militaristic conceptions of hillforts gave way to more peaceful interpretations viewing them as social, economic and ritual centres that often weren't even workable as effective defensive structures.[27] Burned gateways were interpreted as the ritual decommissioning of such structures, whilst these sites are generally so big that often only tiny proportions of their overall area beyond the entrances were ever excavated. The vast majority of hillforts have simply never been dug at all, and so the question of whether signs of destruction might be present is largely unanswerable. Many British hillforts occur in regions where human bone does not preserve well, such as much of the north of England or Scotland. Moreover, where human remains with injuries were found, the convenient answer was simply to blame the 'bloody Romans', as the peaceful natives surely wouldn't have behaved so badly.

Such explanations invoking the Roman conquest were generally difficult to disprove in the absence of scientific dating. However, more recent views have gradually shifted back towards an acceptance that these structures may indeed have played a role in conflict among the indigenous population. Now that radiocarbon dating has become standard, a number of key sites where human remains with weapon injuries have been found have been shown to predate the Roman invasions by centuries. Furthermore, recent excavation work at several sites coupled with re-analyses of previously excavated skeletal remains from others is now combining to produce a rather different picture. Fin Cop is the name given locally both to a prominent hill in Derbyshire and the Middle Iron Age fort situated at its top. The hill is surrounded on three sides by steep river valleys meaning the summit can only easily be reached from the

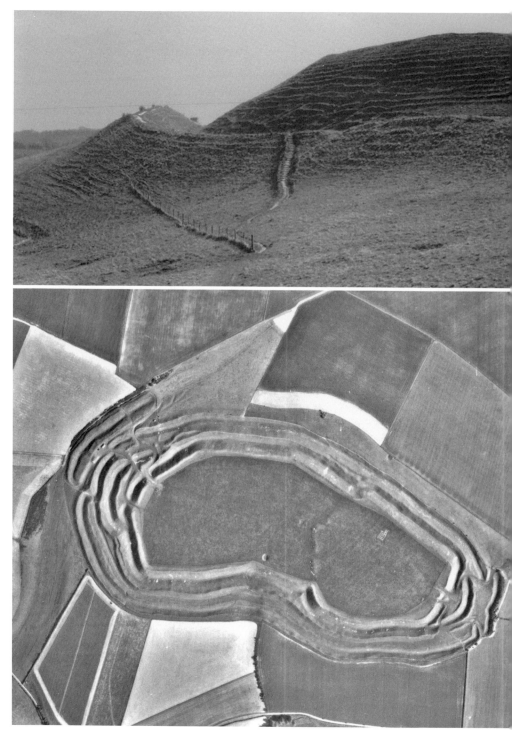

Figure 8.4. Maiden Castle hillfort, Dorset. The immense banks survive to a height of 6m and enclose an area of approx. 47 acres. (Photograph by Chris Downer)

east. Rather than requiring a complete circuit of defences, the hilltop therefore only needed to be fortified across this side in order to make it defensible. Such defended sites known as promontory forts are in fact fairly common throughout the British Middle Iron Age. The defences consisted of a wall built from stone quarried out of a continuous ditch cut through the limestone of the hill. A second line of similar defences outside the first was not quite finished at the time the site went out of use. Rather than simply being abandoned, excavations in 2009 and 2010, led by Clive Waddington of ARS Ltd and benefitting from a large number of volunteers, have shed new light on the last days of the hillfort.[28] A series of trenches across the ramparts revealed the stone walls to have been demolished, apparently in a single episode, whilst the remains of multiple individuals were found intermingled with the demolition rubble. In total the bones of a minimum of fifteen individuals were recovered, comprised of five adults, a teenager, eight young babies and a child around 2 years old. The sex of only two of the adults could be determined, both of whom were women aged 20–25 and 25–35 respectively. The bones were articulated, indicating they must have been deposited as fleshed bodies, and lay in positions suggesting they had simply been dumped into the ditch rather than carefully placed, and none had any grave goods. The wall debris lay over, under and around them and had not been dug through to insert the bodies, indicating they had been placed there at the time the wall was demolished, rather than buried in graves later cut through the rubble. Radiocarbon analysis dated the likely placement of the bodies to between 355 and 300 BC.

Whilst a range of interpretations are possible to explain the presence of the bodies in the ditch, all but one seem implausible. Waddington and colleagues have pointed out that if the site was simply being used as a sacred enclosure to deposit burials this wouldn't explain why they all seemed to have died and been placed there at the same time. If these people had died in an epidemic this would raise the question of why only women and children were affected, whilst both suggestions fail to explain why the defences were demolished when the bodies were placed in the ditch. A more plausible suggestion by far is that these people were killed after the hillfort was attacked and overrun. The fact that a large proportion of these remains were infants whilst the only adults whose sex could be identified were women suggests deliberate selection on this basis. This raises the question of what happened to the men from this community. Were they killed and disposed of at another location nearby or had they already been defeated elsewhere leaving the remainder of the community more vulnerable? Furthermore, the four trenches that were excavated collectively account for only 15m (or 4 per cent) of the total 360m length of the defences. The trenches were also widely spaced which raises the question of how many more bodies are likely to be in the ditch in total? The fact that the outer defences were unfinished also suggests a community hastily trying to react to a perceived threat. How the individuals from the ditch were treated remains ultimately known. No signs of trauma were noted on the bones recovered which may suggest them to have been killed in a systematic and controlled manner such as throat-cutting or strangulation. Two of the adults had patches of new bone on various parts of their skeletons, such as the ribs, limb bones and skull. Such signs are always difficult to interpret as this response can be triggered by various causes, but a rather grim possibility is that these bony reactions may represent areas of bruising from recent blunt injuries. If these women had been kept alive as prisoners for a period before they were killed, these patches of delicate, porous bone may derive from mistreatment during captivity. The hillfort was never re-occupied after the defences were slighted. The excavators have noted intriguingly that the name of an old trackway leading up to the hill –'Pennyunk Lane' – appears to originate in Celtic (or rather 'Atlantean'). This name translates to mean something approximating to 'Hill of the Young' perhaps carrying echoes of the dramatic events that once took place at its summit.

Events of the kind in evidence at Fin Cop were not confined to the north. War Ditches is the name of a defended enclosure, formed by a roughly circular ditch 6m wide and 4m deep, that once occupied a hilltop south of modern Cambridge. Much of the original site has been destroyed by quarrying during the last two centuries, but a series of seven small excavations conducted between 1893 and 2009 combine to produce a consistent overall picture of dramatic events at the site.[29] All seven excavations, which were evenly spread around the enclosure at points across the ditch (Fig. 8.5), produced two results in common. The first was a 'destruction layer' formed of rubble with charcoal mixed in, consistent with earthwork and timber defences on the inner edge of the ditch being demolished in a single swift episode. The second was the repeated find of human skeletons spread throughout the destruction layer at points all around the circumference. The majority of human remains were encountered either in archaeological investigations, or accidentally through quarrying before 1960 and the published assessments of numbers are vague and difficult to evaluate. In total at least twenty-three individual skeletons have been claimed to be present in addition to further unspecified numbers of both 'skeletons' and disarticulated bones. Adults of both sexes were clearly present but the overall make-up of the group of people in the ditch is unclear as the majority were assessed before modern methods of determining sex and age were available. Where descriptions and published photos are available the positions of the bodies are contorted in ways that suggest a degree of decomposition had set in, with joints in positions that are unachievable in life, such as the legs being bent backwards at the hips under the body.

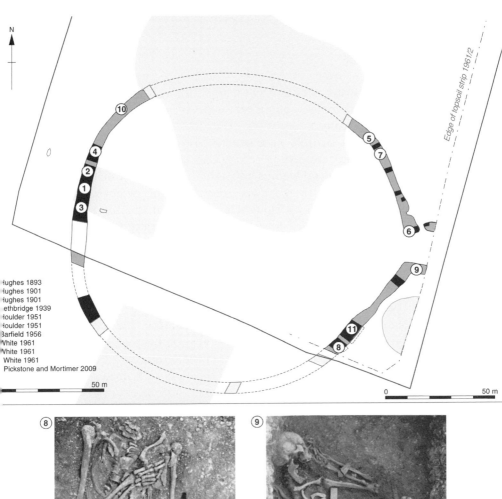

Hughes 1893
Hughes 1901
Hughes 1901
Lethbridge 1939
Houlder 1951
Houlder 1951
Barfield 1956
White 1961
White 1961
White 1961
Pickstone and Mortimer 2009

50 m

0   50 m

Edge of topsoil strip 1961/2

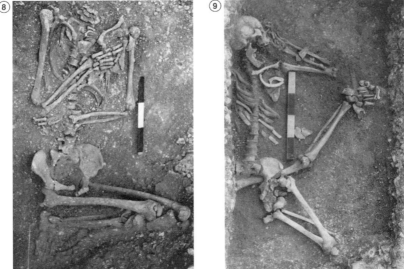

Figure 8.5. Plan of the War Ditches hilltop enclosure near Cambridge, showing the locations of various trenches excavated between 1893 and 2009, with two of the skeletons encountered by the 1961 excavation inset, adult male (left) and female (right) both assessed to be around 30 years old. (Image: Oxford Archaeology East; reproduced with permission, from Pickstone and Mortimer, 2012)

Some bones were noted as having 'cut marks' although no further detail was given to assess whether these might represent weapon injuries or were produced in some other way. One excavation in 1939 recovered a charred torso (as distinct from the scatters of fragments usually found when cremated burials are discovered), suggesting a body that had been partially burned at the time the site was destroyed. This event took place sometime around 380 BC and may have occurred quite soon after the defences were constructed, as suggested both by radiocarbon dates and also the fact that the ditch was not completely finished at the time the defences were demolished. The enclosure was too small to be a settlement and would rather appear to have been a central place constructed specifically for defence (even though it may also have had other uses in less troubled times). As at Fin Cop, the various excavations only covered a small proportion of the total ditch circuit (around 20 per cent) between them, raising the question of how many bodies must originally have been present? Again it would appear that a community of people taking refuge in a defended site had been massacred.

A further example of collective violence in the setting of a British hillfort can be seen to the east in Worcestershire. At 981 ft high, Bredon Hill is an imposing feature in the landscape with the impressive earthwork ramparts of Kemerton Camp hillfort at the summit positioned to allow commanding views over the Severn Valley. Well-known excavations of the site in the 1930s uncovered numerous fragments of human bone from around the entrance, which were interpreted at the time as relating to a massacre having occurred there.[30] Recent re-examination of these remains by Gaynor Western and Derek Hurst has shed further light on this interpretation, including obtaining radiocarbon dates that show the human remains to date from sometime between the middle of the second and first centuries BC, rather than following the Roman invasion as was previously assumed.[31] The excavators described a mixture of partly articulated and disarticulated bone fragments, re-assessed by Western and Hurst as representing at least thirty-six individuals. Of these twenty-nine were adults, with two adolescents and five children aged under 13. Where sex could be determined, fifteen males and six females were apparent, most of the adults present being males aged between 18 and 34. The body parts represented were consistent with the pattern that would be expected if complete bodies were left to decompose naturally, with no suggestion of any selection or manipulation of the remains and so it would seem these were the remnants of bodies simply left in the entrance way after death. The modern re-analysis has noted various unhealed cuts made with bladed implements as well as blunt trauma and chopping marks made by heavier blades. These wounds occur either on the long bones of the limbs or on the face and head with the majority concentrated on the latter. Once again then it would seem members of a community using a defended hilltop enclosure had been attacked and killed. Other excavated features close to the human remains may provide further circumstantial evidence of the way this event unfolded. The presence of an undisturbed pile of sling stones close to the entrance in addition to the find of domestic tools (metalworking hammers and a sickle) among the human remains has led to the suggestion that this was a surprise attack, with a group of those inside the fort rushing to defend the gateway with whatever was to hand. If correct this would then raise the question of what happened to the rest of this community? The original excavators theorised that they must have fled the fort by the 'back door' – in this respect it is certainly an interesting point that hillforts commonly have two entrances. Perhaps this is what happened with those escaping simply never returning, although the fact that the dead were just left in the entrance rather than removed when those who had fled later returned could also be interpreted to indicate that the rest of the community suffered a similar fate elsewhere.

Other examples include the famous site of Danebury in Hampshire, the most intensively investigated hillfort in Europe, excavated by Barry Cunliffe[32] mainly during the 1970s and 1980s. Here one of the entrances was at one point burned down, with many human skeletons discovered at the site from this time bearing weapon injuries, including sword cuts, spear thrusts and small blunt injuries that may be the result of sling stones. Although it may have been costly to the defenders, it would appear that this attack was not successful, with the gates then rebuilt and occupation continuing, whilst the dead were buried formally rather than simply left exposed or slung into the enclosing ditches as at the less fortunate sites mentioned previously. The single ditched hillfort that overlooks the village of Spetisbury in Dorset may also have once been the scene of violent events, although human remains found at the site are now lost. Here it was claimed that eighty to ninety skeletons were discovered 'laid irregularly' together in a rectangular pit by workmen digging a railway cutting in 1857. One of skulls was interpreted as having 'a piece cut out with a sword or some other weapon' on the left side.[33] Whether this interpretation was correct is now impossible to assess but, regardless of this point, the simultaneous burial of so many people requires explaining, particularly as a further forty skeletons were uncovered the following year. Such a mass burial might relate to an epidemic rather than violence, although the find of an embedded spearhead in another skull suggests the latter is more likely. Just 20 miles away from Spetisbury Rings, the best-known British hillfort is Maiden Castle near Dorchester, where Sir Mortimer Wheeler famously interpreted a cemetery at the eastern entrance to contain the victims of a Roman assault on the fort.[34] This interpretation was later called into question as it was claimed that although some violent injuries were certainly apparent, most of the eighty-six individuals buried in this cemetery displayed no signs of any trauma. Niall Sharples,[35] of Cardiff University, also pointed out that those with injuries might have received them elsewhere and simply been brought to this prominent site to bury them. Unlike some of the aforementioned sites the Maiden Castle burials were in individual graves in which people had been formally laid out in the local style. With no other signs of the fort having been attacked, the 'Roman massacre' interpretation was generally dismissed as a product of Wheeler's over-fertile imagination.

More recently the Maiden Castle skeletons have been re-examined by Rebecca Redfern, osteologist at the Museum of London.[36] This new analysis found traumatic injuries among 74 per cent of the overall sample, in contrast with the figure of just 27 per cent when the bones were first examined in the 1940s. This group included burials from several different phases of the Iron Age dotted at various points around the eastern end of the site. When only the skeletons from Wheeler's 'war cemetery' were considered, Redfern's figure went up to 87.5 per cent. These unhealed wounds included bladed-weapon injuries, blunt-force impacts and penetrating injuries consistent with wounds from spears, either thrust or thrown. These injuries were dispersed throughout the body, although head wounds were particularly prevalent and a disarticulated neck vertebra had been sliced through indicating the person to have been decapitated. Unlike at some of the other sites mentioned earlier, all the injured individuals were adults. Both sexes were affected, although the majority of injuries were present on males. Consideration of the overall age profile of the injured group also identified the cemetery as differing from a normal archaeological cemetery in having a greater proportion of young adult males than would normally be expected.[37] This unusual pattern is more consistent with episodes of conflict, rather than what is called an 'attritional profile' – a term which refers to the larger proportions of children and older adults and the balanced sex ratio that normally characterizes cemeteries that have built up over time through natural deaths.

On one hand then this new assessment might be taken to show that Wheeler had got it right in the first place. However, this may still not be the case. The carefully placed graves in this cemetery may in fact have built up over as much as two centuries between 100 BC and AD 100, and there is no reason to think that all the burials were deposited at the same time or in relation to a single event. It is equally plausible that the wounded individuals represent multiple episodes of conflict and Niall Sharples was quite correct to observe that we have no reason to think any of these people necessarily died at Maiden Castle. By the time of the Roman conquest the hillfort had largely gone out of use and the gates and timber palisades on the banks may no longer have been defensible. It might be the case then that this prominent place was used specifically as somewhere to bury those who had died violently and the burials might have come from a much wider area, rather than being the inhabitants of the hillfort. Lastly, the one piece of evidence held up since the time of Wheeler as the 'smoking gun' that proved the Roman army must have been involved is the well-known skeleton of a male with the tip of a pointed iron weapon embedded in his spine (Fig. 8.6). Wheeler described this find as the tip of a 'Roman ballista bolt' and this interpretation has largely stuck ever since. However, recent re-examination by Mike Bishop, a seasoned expert on Roman military equipment, has called this into question. Mike has pointed out that in fact this double-edged weapon point differs in form from known examples of Roman ballista bolts which are all square in profile. The find is therefore simply consistent with a spear or javelin and is neither

Figure 8.6. Double burial of two adult males excavated at Maiden Castle – here reassembled for display in Dorset County Museum (a). The man on the left has a sword cut (arrowed) which has sliced off a sliver of his lower jaw (b), in addition to a weapon point lodged in his spine (c). Rather than the 'ballista bolt' claimed by Sir Mortimer Wheeler, this is in fact a small spear point with nothing to identify it as necessarily Roman. The second man has a wound from a thin bladed weapon slicing his frontal bone in two (d). Both have been buried in the native 'Durotrigian' fashion accompanied by pots made in the local style.

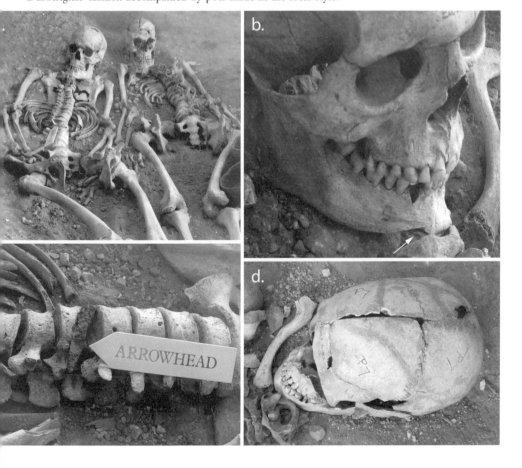

distinctive of Roman nor native manufacture.[38] All that can be said for certain then is that the Maiden Castle 'war cemetery' indicates one or more episodes of violence during the latest part of the Iron Age. In light of this point it is of interest that a number of the excavated individuals also had healed injuries, especially blunt head injuries consistent with having experienced violence before, which further suggests a more complex situation than a single assault by Vespasian's troops.

The British hillfort sites where there is evidence for conflict in the form of human remains are spread out both in geographic terms and in their respective dates. Given the dating of the violent events in evidence at Fin Cop and War Ditches it could be plausibly suggested that where conflict occurred during this period it may have been most prevalent in the Middle Iron Age (generally accepted as *c.*400–100 BC) with the period that followed being more settled. Such a view would fit with the commonly cited idea that such a period of warfare ultimately resulted in the formation of large, settled territories as smaller regional groups were increasingly swallowed up by larger ones. This would fit the pattern that is seen of smaller, simpler hillforts gradually being abandoned with larger, more elaborate versions arising which might actually represent less, rather than more conflict. On one hand this seems a plausible idea, although the violence evident at Kemmerton Camp and Maiden Castle, lasting into the first century BC and possibly beyond, would indicate that a simplistic picture where actual violence went out of fashion as a new order arose clearly isn't the whole story. Of course the majority of hillforts show no signs of such dramatic events. There is an old saying in archaeology that 'absence of evidence' can't necessarily be taken as 'evidence of absence'. On one hand the fact that so many sites of this kind don't appear to have been attacked would fit the notion that they were never seriously built for defence but rather as status symbols etc. One problem with such a view is that it is not really possible to disprove. However, an alternative suggestion is that rather than offering proof of a peaceful society, hillforts without signs of destruction and massacres may simply be those that worked – i.e. the defences did their job. In fact if the majority of such structures were effective at offering protection in the face of very genuine threats, this would explain why people were prepared to expend the considerable time and energy required to build them in the first place. If hillforts were always doomed to fall as soon as a sufficiently determined enemy showed up this would beg the question of why so many were ever constructed? In regard to this point an interesting ethnohistorical observation is provided by the accounts of various European explorers as they first travelled into the North American Mid-West in the seventeenth and eighteenth centuries. Descriptions of these journeys mention numerous large fortified settlements complete with defensive ditches and wooden palisades that bear many similarities to the defended enclosures of Iron Age Europe. In describing such forts in the Missouri River region the French explorer Pierre Gautier de Varennes concluded them to be 'impregnable to Indians' on the basis that the latter lacked artillery.[39] Similarly, in the absence of siege machinery, and without standing armies able to mount prolonged sieges, Iron Age Europeans' only option to attack such sites would be to burn the gates. This would expose attackers to concentrated missile bombardment from above making it a risky tactic at best. If it was known that attacks against such sites were largely bound to fail, this would deter people from trying in the first place, and make the building of such structures a worthwhile investment. Even having made such an investment, the multiple killings at Danebury suggest that where these fortifications were effective the defenders might still pay a high price, whilst the human remains from Fin Cop, War Ditches and Kemmerton Camp all illustrate that the threat of collective violence such defences appear to suggest was in fact very real.[40]

Given to the Gods: Ritual and Violence

As in earlier periods, the treatment of some Iron Age individuals who had clearly been violently killed suggests something more going on than simply people fighting each other. The excavation of a Mid- to Late Iron Age cemetery at Sarliéve-Grande Halle in central France[41] revealed an unusual burial at its centre. This young adult male had been decapitated with a sharp bladed weapon, evidenced by flat plane slices through his first and second cervical (neck) vertebrae and across the base of his skull. The man had been laid on his back with his head put back in its normal anatomical position. His elbows were rotated inwards with his wrists crossed as if they were bound. On one hand this latter observation would appear to suggest an execution, but the careful arrangement of the body and the man's location at the very centre of the cemetery suggests a privileged position rather than the disdainful treatment that might be expected in the case of a criminal or social deviant. It seems more likely then that this man was ritually killed, presumably as some sort of sacrifice, similar to the Bronze Age examples mentioned in Chapter 7.

Returning to the ongoing investigations by my own department at Winterbourne Kingston in Dorset, burials at the site dating from the late Iron Age often occur as carefully-placed bodies in reused storage pits.[42] However, one such individual uncovered in 2010 had been subject to a different kind of treatment. Here an adult female was found lying at the base of a pit, lying on top of the remains of various domesticated animals including cows, horses and dogs. Rather than simply representing domestic rubbish thrown into a convenient hole in the ground, the animal remains had been laid out in a carefully ordered pattern, alternating between horse and cattle bones. When excavating such pits it is common to find such carefully-placed material when reaching the bottom, often consisting of pottery and other artefacts in addition to animal bones and sometimes complete animals apparently placed as offerings (the technical term is a votive deposit) to some perceived entity with dominion underground, perhaps giving thanks for keeping stored material fresh when the pit was in use. Unlike the other burials at this site, which were usually laid on one side in a flexed position and accompanied with individual grave objects such as pots and brooches, the woman in this pit was lying face down with no signs of careful placement (Fig. 8.7). There were no manufactured grave goods present and effectively the woman appeared to have been placed as just one part of the offering in the pit rather than receiving respectful treatment as part of formal funeral practice. On one hand it might be the case that this woman had died in some way perceived as unusual or unnatural and as such was given different treatment in death. On the other, it is equally plausible, if not more so, that she was ritually killed with the specific intent of placing her body in the pit. If this latter possibility is correct this then raises the familiar question of what status this individual might have held, was she a criminal, a war captive or perhaps a slave who had been selected for such

Figure 8.7. The skeleton of a Late Iron Age woman deposited face-down at the bottom of a pit along with the remains of various animals at Winterbourne Kingston (Dorset). Rather than a careful, formal burial this woman appears to have been ritually killed to become part of the same sacrificial deposit formed by the animal remains. This suggestion is further supported by fine cutmarks on her clavicle and neck vertebrae.

treatment at some time regarded as important or auspicious? There are no obvious injuries to her skeleton consistent with any cause of death which then raises the question of whether she might have been killed in some way that doesn't affect bone such as strangulation. One piece of evidence that might hold the key is a small linear cut into one of her clavicles (collar bone) with no signs of healing. This might suggest an attempt to cut her throat with the damage to the clavicle, possibly suggesting the woman struggled. Once again, this example illustrates that not all prehistoric burials should necessarily be seen as the work of bereaved relatives trying to come to terms with a loss beyond their control.

At Danebury three adult males were found placed in a freshly-dug pit at the base of a quarry for a newly reconstructed rampart.[43] The placement of these bodies seems related to the construction work and may represent a 'foundation deposit', a type of offering placed in the ground at the time a new building or other structure was constructed. If this is the case, this again raises the question of who these men might have been and how they might have been related to the newly-built rampart. Iron Age society may have been far from egalitarian and one tentative possibility is that these men were slaves involved in the building work, who had been sacrificed once the work was completed to ensure this new endeavour received the appropriate divine approval. The aforementioned site of Sculptor's Cave where at least seven individuals were decapitated[44] is also suggestive of ritual killings. As noted earlier it would have been fairly impractical to carry multiple decapitated bodies to this inaccessible place and is more plausible that these individuals were brought to the cave, presumably a place regarded as having some special significance, in order to be killed.

Whilst skeletal remains can often be interpreted in several different ways, the reality of ritual killings during this period is confirmed beyond doubt by the most well-known finds of human remains from Iron Age Europe.[45] These are the well-preserved individuals recovered from waterlogged areas across Denmark, north Germany, parts of northern England and Ireland, collectively known as Bog Bodies. The acidic and anaerobic environment of the peat bogs of northern Europe is hostile to the kinds of bacteria responsible for the greater part of decomposition and consequently has the effect of preserving skin, hair and soft tissue, making these among the best-preserved archaeological bodies available to modern researchers. Rather than unfortunate travellers who lost their way and sank into bogs accidentally, such individuals frequently display evidence of being deliberately placed in peat bogs after having been killed. Several examples are bound or, as in the case of an adolescent male from Windeby (north Germany) also blindfolded, whilst some have ligatures around their necks indicating strangulation, a cause of death which usually leaves no trace on the skeleton. The most famous of several bodies found at Lindow Moss in Cheshire has in fact been 'killed' three times by strangulation, a blow to the head and also having his throat cut, further indicating a high degree of symbolism rather than some other circumstance such as the 'mugging' of a traveller crossing the marshes.

In all these cases the question remains open of whether the individuals being killed in such controlled circumstances were chosen from within the respective community or whether they were outsiders. If these were people being killed by their own community, it would raise the question of whether their deaths represent punishments or whether they were sacrifices. If those killed were outsiders this implies them to have been captives taken during conflict. The possibility of such 'prisoner sacrifice' illustrates a common challenge in trying to recognize and make sense of evidence for religious or ritual practices in prehistory. Prehistorians frequently observe that unlike more recent times, ritual practices are likely to have been bound up with everything else people did and so separating particular acts into 'secular' and 'religious' activities just isn't possible. As mentioned in the preceding chapter the practice of depositing human crania in water as evidenced by large numbers of finds from the River Thames spanned a long period across the Bronze and Iron Ages possibly continuing into the Roman period. For much of this time burials on land are relatively rare, whilst the locations of 'Thames crania' correspond with the spots where swords, shields and other sacrificial items were found and so seem more likely to have been also deliberately placed rather than the skulls having eroded out of burials and floated off down the river. Rick Schulting and Richard Bradley's[46] recent study of such crania found 13/150 (8.7 per cent) to have weapon injuries implying that at least some of these crania may represent the heads of slain enemies.

An example which reinforces the idea that such acts may have taken place has recently been provided on a striking scale by a find in Denmark. In the Alken Enge wetlands, an area of bog which was once a small lake near modern Lake Mossø, a team from Skanderborg Museum and Aarhus University has been uncovering waterlogged remains of hundreds of individuals deposited in the lake at around the time of Christ. The area containing these well preserved, disarticulated bones is thought to cover around 3,600m^2 and only a sample of it can currently be excavated (Fig. 8.8). The 240m^2 area excavated by 2012 had yielded bones from 240 individuals, all assessed as male and aged between 13 and 45, with the overall area estimated to contain the remains of as many as a thousand individuals.[47] The bones of these men exhibit varied weapon injuries including blade wounds, blunt trauma and penetrating injuries consistent with spear thrusts, whilst the remains also exhibit signs of gnawing by scavenging animals indicating they were not deposited in the lake

Figure 8.8. Well-preserved human bones from the waterlogged former lake bed at Alken Enge, Denmark. Here the disarticulated remains of hundreds of individuals were deposited in the lake, many displaying weapon injuries as apparent in the bottom right image. (Photographs courtesy of Skanderborg Museum/Ejvind Hertz)

immediately, but left exposed for some months after death. Rather than being simply collected and deposited in the lake, many bones show cutmarks which suggest any remaining soft tissue was manually cut away before they were placed in the water. A particularly unusual find was comprised of four pelvic bones threaded on a wooden stick, further indicating these remains were placed in the lake as individual bones, rather than intact bodies. Given the overall picture this evidence presents it would appear that a battle had taken place with the remains of those killed later collected and brought to the lake and deposited in the water as offerings, possibly in thanks for victory. Whether these bones represent vanquished enemies or valiant heroes from the winning side, or perhaps a mix of both, remains unknown. Something we should bear in mind, however, is that both these concepts stem from relatively recent modes of thinking and prehistoric people may have had a very different mindset. For example during the seventeenth and eighteenth centuries the Iroquois of the north-eastern part of North America regarded death in battle as a terrible fate, with the souls of slain warriors doomed to wander the earth ever seeking revenge.[48] If the Germanic peoples using the Lake Mossø site had a similar belief, their desire to collect and immerse the remains of fallen fighters might stem more from a desire to neutralize or placate the 'angry dead' rather than to honour fallen heroes or sacrifice vanquished enemies. Whatever the reason, to collect, process and transport this many remains from a battlefield that may have been a considerable distance away represents a considerable undertaking and such a task was clearly very important to those involved.

As with other parts of prehistory, human remains dating from the Iron Age fill a crucial gap that simply cannot be addressed by other lines of evidence. Here the remains of the dead provide clear evidence for a range of violent acts both committed by and against single individuals and larger groups. The sheer size of many hillfort sites, coupled with the large numbers of dead implied at several of them, suggest organized conflict to have further escalated in scale by this time. The staggering find of a thousand dead, apparently from a single battle, as revealed at the Danish site near Lake Mossø reinforces this notion, constituting the largest single engagement in prehistoric Europe for which we have clear evidence. Meanwhile, ritualized killings and the incorporation of the respective people's bodies and body parts in sacrificial deposits appear to have been widespread. Coupled with the apparent rise of headhunting as a means of demonstrating one's prowess and status, such practices are suggestive of a deepening power and symbolism being afforded both to violent acts and to the remains of those who suffered them. Of course, just as with any other period it would be easy to be carried away by the kind of dramatic examples presented in the current chapter and to forget that for most of the time the reality of everyday life throughout the period is likely to have been stable and tranquil and governed by the rhythms of seasons, crops and herds, with cycles of raiding and violence perhaps erupting only periodically. However, it would also seem reasonable now to revisit the notion of the warlike 'barbarian' elites alluded to by Greek and Roman authors as being generally accurate at least some of the time. It would appear that Iron Age fortifications, weapons and those who wielded them could reasonably expect to see action at least occasionally (if not frequently) during their lives. Certainly, it would be the case as Rome expanded beyond the Italian peninsula that the conquest of Europe would involve more than just 'symbolic' opposition. The Romans would bring many things with them that were foreign to other parts of the Continent, but war wasn't one of them.

Chapter 9

Imperial Anger: Violence under Roman Rule

For all that changes in past societies might sometimes appear dramatic and rapid from a modern vantage point, in reality social change tends to occur at a slow and incremental rate as far as it is experienced in most people's lives. Even the most sweeping revolutions tend to exert their greatest effects at the top of a given society, leaving the lower orders to continue living on the same land, tilling the same fields, speaking the same language and passing the same essential values on to their children as they did before. This last point is of particular importance as the very fact that societal change is generally gradual means that human societies can benefit from the accumulated knowledge and experience of any number of generations that have gone before. If societies had to completely re-invent themselves once a generation, the vast majority would be doomed to fail. The fact that people can indeed draw upon the ways of doing things laid down by their parents, grandparents and earlier forebears then has the slightly curious effect of giving human cultures a kind of life of their own. Anyone alive at a given time in the past could be reasonably secure in thinking that a hundred years later, when all of their own generation was dead, their descendants were likely to be subsisting, speaking and thinking in ways that were not dramatically different from those they were familiar with in their own lives. In recent decades the process by which such transmission of culture across generations occurs has attracted growing attention among social scientists, and is referred to in academic terms as 'Social Reproduction'.[1] A point that tends to strike all students of archaeology sooner or later as their studies progress is the way the subject commonly borrows all manner of theories and techniques from other subjects in order to then apply them to the past. In an example of such borrowing a great deal of thought has more recently been given to the ways Roman society 'reproduced' itself.

One of the most important means by which the Roman social order ensured its own survival and spread over time was in fact through acts of violence conducted at a range of different levels. Violence was an intrinsic part of the Roman world. One of the largest empires the world has ever seen did not come into existence by being nice to its neighbours (or at least any 'niceness' came in the context of a very clear carrot and stick approach, with a particularly big stick) and there is no question that violence, both real and threatened, played a central role in the establishment and maintenance of Roman power. At the level of individual (male) citizens, anyone wishing to advance themselves in public life could only do so having first pursued a successful military career. At the highest level the definition of such success involved the conquest of new territories and so the expansion of the Empire came to be built into the fabric of the Roman social system. However, violence in Roman society was not just reserved for uncooperative barbarians. Back on the home front acts of violence were also instrumental for controlling slaves, punishing criminals and entertaining the masses, as well as being regarded as an integral part of raising children in the 'correct' manner. To use a modern cliché, violence was 'in the Romans' DNA'. In fairness this is likely to have been true at least to some extent for all pre-modern societies but in the case of Roman society we are able to see this point far more clearly.

The term 'structural violence' refers to a concept that has become popular in some academic circles over recent years which focuses on the idea that whilst violent acts are committed by individuals, simply looking at such actions as unpleasant behaviour carried out by a 'bad' or at least misguided person doesn't always tell us very much. For example, when a soldier inflicts harm on a member of an opposing army this may have little to do with his personal opinions and we are likely to learn little that is useful by considering such events from the point of view of a single individual. The concept of structural violence centres on the notion that some aspects of particular societies involve structures that result in harm being inflicted on groups or individuals at a systematic level. The exact nature of what is classed as 'harm' is open to debate and I personally find some versions of what has been claimed to be structural 'violence' rather unconvincing. For example, a social caste system where the poorest people are more likely to be under-nourished and catch diseases can be argued to be morally wrong but not because these things constitute 'violence'. But aside from this there are clear cases where the basic concept fits really very well and Roman society may be one of the most clear-cut examples. Here violence was carried out in a systematic manner by some members of society against particular groups or individuals on the basis that it was the legitimate thing to do. With the added benefit of copious written sources from the time, we can see that violence was without question a key factor in holding Roman society together and so a question such as 'were the Romans violent?' would be quite redundant. However, something arguably a good deal more interesting such a situation offers is the opportunity to ask more nuanced questions, such as what are the different ways in which violence manifested itself in this increasingly complex society? How was it used? What roles did it play? As Roman influence began to spread after the Punic Wars and the old social order of the Republic finally gave way to continued expansion under the Empire, the extent of its dominion became vast. Whilst its geographical limits might be fairly straightforward at any point in time, deciding where to set the points where Roman history should begin and end are far less clear cut and a chapter in a book of this type can only hope to scratch the surface in any sense. Even more so than with the preceding chapters I am therefore obliged to pick on what I hope are a few useful examples that illustrate the extent to which human remains might also have a story to tell in informing us about some less pleasant aspects of life under Rome, some of which may simply not be accessible through other means. Here I have confined things to the time between the end of the Republic (27 BC) and the point when the Empire split into Eastern and Western halves (AD 285) purely as these are convenient dates, but many other parameters could work equally well.

The Sons of Mars: Skeletal Evidence for Roman Conquest

Large engagements by the Roman army were in fact relatively few and far between during the Imperial period. Part of the reason for this was simply practical, in that in order to provision thousands of men within a given province it was necessary to split them up and avoid large concentrations of troops in one place for long periods, to prevent them exhausting the local economy and capacity of the land to produce food. Furthermore, when large-scale battles were fought in the ancient world, the majority of those killed could probably not expect to be buried. Instead, after any local looters had stripped the corpses of anything of value, the dead would simply be left to the ravages of scavenging animals (ranging in size from flies and beetles to buzzards and wolves) with the defleshed bones then exposed to the elements. Experiments in taphonomy (the science of post-mortem decay), conducted initially to assist with modern forensic cases have demonstrated that the combined actions of such forces upon human remains left exposed would mean there was nothing left to find within 20 years at most[2] and certainly little prospect of such remains ever being recovered archaeologically in our own time. Consequently it is unsurprising that we have relatively few examples of Roman soldiers, or those killed by them with combat injuries to study.

An example that confirms these points is provided by what is arguably the Roman army's best known defeat. The *Clades Variana* or Varian Disaster took place in AD 9 when the Roman commander Publius Quinctilius Varus led three legions on what was expected to be an uneventful journey through a supposedly pacified region from their summer to their winter quarters in southern Germany. The legions never reached their destination, instead falling victim to a carefully-prepared ambush by local Germanic tribespeople under their leader Arminius. The Germans made effective use of the terrain to funnel the long, strung-out Roman column into a narrow area bordered by marshes on one edge and partially forested high ground on the other, rendering defensive manoeuvres extremely difficult.[3] The discovery of what is almost certainly the site of the main ambush as Kalkriese, Lower Saxony, has also shown that Arminius' tribe (the Cherusci) had constructed a wide turf wall with a wooden fence on top, from which to mount their attack. Over 3,000 metal fragments of Roman military equipment recovered in the area were all found in front of rather than behind this rampart. Six years after the disaster the Roman general Germanicus visited the site and found the scattered bones of large a number of the dead, which he ordered to be buried in pits. Excavations by Wolfgang Schlüter, the district archaeologist based at nearby Ösnabrück, revealed five pits in front of the turf wall containing disarticulated human and animal bones. The bones showed signs of weathering consistent with having lain exposed for an extended period before burial. All were from adult males of military age, where it could be determined, and several crania had unhealed sharp-force injuries. However, even these skeletal remains only survived to be found because in this unusual circumstance the site of the battle was later revisited and attempts were made to bury what was left with some dignity. Had Germanicus not done this there would be no material trace of the 18,000 or so men that made up Varus' legions, with only their fragmented equipment left to find.

A further example that in its time may have offered the best opportunity so far known for examining the remains of Roman soldiers killed in action was uncovered during a programme of excavations conducted in the 1930s at the once Roman-held city of Dura Europos in southern Syria. This walled city fell to a determined siege by the Sassanid Persians in c.AD 256 despite concerted efforts to bolster the fortifications by its Roman defenders. In addition to providing a wealth of information about the city in general the excavations, led by the French Academy archaeologist Claude du Mesnil in collaboration with Yale University, revealed striking details about the complex nature of siege warfare in this period.[4] The fortifications ringing the city are studded with projecting towers that allowed the defenders to rain missiles on anyone approaching the walls. One of these, 'Tower 19', along with an adjoining section of wall, had partially collapsed and Du Mesnil's excavations established that this had been caused by the attackers tunnelling beneath the defences to undermine them. However, du Mesnil found not only the Persian tunnel but also a second tunnel dug outwards from within the city – a Roman countermine designed to intercept the attackers and prevent them from collapsing the defences (Fig. 9.1). This astonishing find held further surprises in

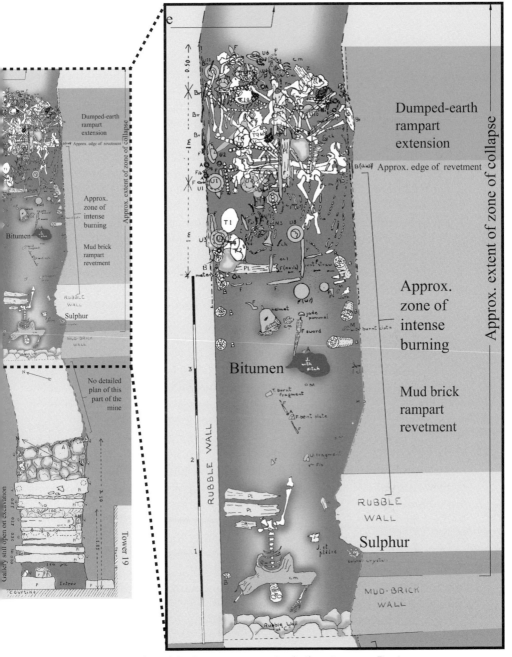

Figure 9.1. Composite plan of the Roman countermine built to intercept Persian attempts to undermine the walls at Dura Europos and the archaeological deposits found within it, with the section containing human remains enlarged on the right. The remains of the Roman defenders and their equipment are at the top of the image, with the skeleton of one of the Persian attackers, found still wearing his chainmail shirt, in the lower part of the image. (Courtesy of Simon James; adapted from various drawings by du Mesnil)

containing the skeletons of at least nineteen Roman defenders, tightly packed together in a section of the tunnel measuring just 2m in length. Amongst this tangled pile of bones were fragments of military equipment including sections of chain mail, parts of swords and a javelin and a particularly large sword with a rock-crystal pommel, as well as the iron bosses and other mountings from Roman shields. There were also preserved fragments of wood, leather, clothing and even hair which had survived in the mine's unique environment, whilst three groups of coins were suggested to have been the last pay the soldiers ever collected.

There were signs of intense burning in the Roman countermine, with residues of bitumen and sulphur found close to the bodies along with fragments of straw and other accelerants indicating a deliberate and apparently successful attempt to thwart the Roman counter-offensive by burning the wooden supports holding the roof up. Perhaps most intriguingly, a few metres away at the Persian end of the Roman tunnel a further male skeleton was found lying on his back with his lower legs heavily burned, wearing a mail shirt and with a sword that had a pommel made of jade from Chinese Turkestan. Close by was a high-domed Persian helmet. Du Mesnil interpreted all these men to have been killed in fighting in the mine, with the Romans coming off worst and the attackers managing to fire the countermine before reinforcements could be sent. Sadly, the human remains were not recovered and were likely reburied where du Mesnil found them and so further skeletal analysis isn't possible. However, Simon James has recently conducted a careful re-analysis of the original records. This new examination has both highlighted problems with the original interpretation and suggested an alternative that is more consistent with the evidence. The tightly-packed jumble of nineteen bodies in just a 2m section of the tunnel raises the question of why these men should all have died in precisely the same spot. In fact it would have been virtually impossible for them even to stand close enough together for this to happen regardless of how they died. Instead James suggests the bodies were moved after death. The combination of bitumen and sulphur in the Persians' possession would have produced a highly noxious and toxic combination of smoke and gases which if released from the Persian mine, approximately one storey lower would have been drawn up into the Roman countermine in the same way a chimney works. This would have had the effect of incapacitating if not killing any Romans in the higher tunnel, with the Persians then free to move in and finish off anyone left alive before piling up the bodies and setting the supports ablaze. James further suggests the well-attired and finely-equipped Persian found by du Mesnil may have been the individual responsible for starting the blaze, perhaps being the officer in charge of the firing party, who was himself overcome by the smoke and accelerants and then also died in the tunnel. This striking incident is particularly unusual in archaeological terms in capturing events that must have taken place in just a few minutes in a unique time capsule. The strategies in play by both sides also reveal a great depth of sophistication in siege warfare at this time on the part of both the Romans and their opponents, as well as providing a unique insight into the last moments of individuals who died in a bravely-fought and desperate action where rather than being iron or steel the weapons that killed them would be classified in modern terms as 'chemical warfare'. Such subterranean efforts to breach enemy defences from below would remain in use up to the First World War.

When dealing with the Roman accounts of a military conquest an obvious question is of the extent to which the level of opposition claimed is accurate, as opposed to containing elements of exaggeration and propaganda. When the Roman general Vespasian made his way across south-western Britain in AD 43 he was claimed to have 'fought thirty battles, subdued two warlike tribes and captured twenty towns'[5] although the precise scale of such battles is not known and it remains unclear whether the 'towns' surrendered peacefully or put up a fight. However, the examples of Iron Age violence on sometimes large scales explored in the previous chapter would certainly fit with Roman accounts of meeting concerted opposition during the conquests of Western Europe undertaken during the times of Julius Caesar, Claudius and other Roman rulers. One probable example of individuals who fell resisting the Roman advance was excavated in the west of England by Kathleen Kenyon[6] during 1948–51. The site of Sutton Walls, a fort running around the contours of a long narrow hill in Herefordshire, sits in the most densely clustered zone of hillfort construction in Europe. Here the defences consisted of a single bank and ditch with two entrances located at the east and west ends. As is common for such large sites, Kenyon was only able to open up trenches that revealed relatively small areas in relation to the overall area of the fort and chose to concentrate on the western entrance. Interestingly, during the last stages of pre-Roman occupation the ditch was recut and the height of the ramparts raised in an apparent effort to renew the defences, shortly before a 'great disaster' befell the fort and its occupants. At the base of the recut ditch Kenyon came across 'a remarkable conglomeration of human skeletons' with no trace of the ditch silting up, indicating these bodies had been deposited close to the time the defences were redug (Fig. 9.2). She described the skeletons as lying 'at all angles and in all positions, obviously thrown in haphazard. Some lie singly, some in a veritable pile.' In total the bones of at least twenty-four individuals were identified, with the exception of two children all were aged between 17 and 50 but mostly younger adults. It was possible to determine the sex of ten individuals, all of whom were male. Weapon injuries,

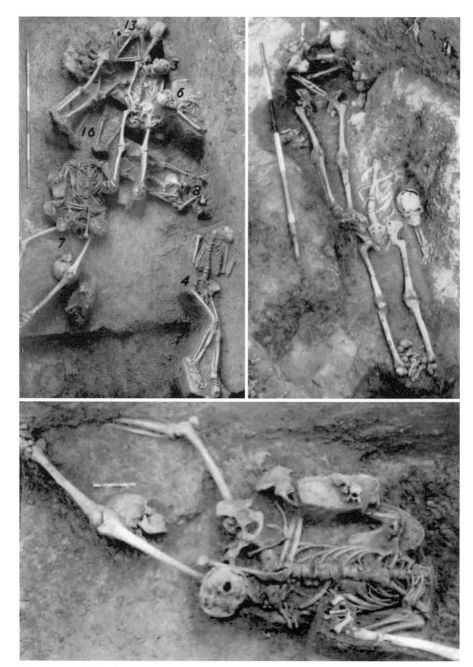

Figure 9.2. Skeletal remains uncovered in the recut defensive ditch at Sutton Walls, Herefordshire, illustrating the haphazard way they were deposited, with several individuals' decapitated heads apparently thrown in with similarly little care. (Photographs by Kathleen Kenyon, reproduced by permission of the Royal Archaeological Institute)

mostly to the skull were noted in five individuals including blade wounds and penetrative trauma from sword or spear thrusts. Eight individuals had been decapitated, either with their heads thrown into the ditch next to them, or in three cases with their heads lying at unnatural angles consistent with partial decapitations where the bones of the neck had been cut through, but the head remained attached by some soft tissue. No objects were associated with any of the bodies, all but one of which occupied a relatively small area in two of the excavated trenches. Kenyon was of the opinion that more bodies likely lay further round to the north in unexcavated parts of the ditch. After this event the defences were either deliberately demolished or allowed to fall into rapid decay, although the lack of scattering of the human remains by scavengers suggests the former is more likely as this would cover the bodies over, whilst the site does not appear to have been reoccupied until much later.

On one hand this traumatic event could be viewed as further evidence that Late Iron Age Britain was far from peaceful, with conflict between groups carrying on right up to the time of the Claudian invasion. Whilst this possibility cannot be ruled out, the perception of a threat specifically during the middle of the first century AD indicated by the redigging of the ditch, in conjunction with the repetitive manner in which the dead were treated rather swing the balance of probability in the direction of Roman involvement. Whilst decapitating one's enemies was clearly a common native practice in Iron Age Britain, the picture at Sutton Walls is different in that the severed heads were still there to be found. Rather than the natives abandoning their fashion of trophy-taking it may be more plausible to view the systematic way these men were decapitated and their heads thrown into the ditch with them as more consistent with the treatment one could expect following defeat by the Roman military machine. Furthermore, where direction could be established the decapitations were interpreted to have been carried out from behind, and so would appear more consistent with the execution of prisoners than with decapitation during combat or after death. There is certainly no shortage of written accounts of defeated enemies being decapitated as 'punishment' for daring to resist the Roman advance,[7] with such methodical treatment forming part of a deliberate policy of reacting ruthlessly to resistance whilst rewarding those who accepted the new regime peacefully. Although this interpretation remains speculative, on balance the evidence at Sutton Walls looks more like the work of foreign invaders than the last gasp of local in-fighting before Britain became a province of empire.

The Hand of the State: Crime and Retribution

There is no doubt that violence was used as a means of social control long before a small town on the Tiber began to rise in importance, eventually to lead a vast empire. Various examples cited in the previous chapters illustrate the use of violent acts to send messages aimed at influencing the future behaviour of those 'reading' them, going back at least as far as the Bronze Age. However, the arrival of Roman civilization in barbarian Europe brought a new aspect to such socially-sanctioned violence. Under Roman rule, retribution for wrongdoing became the domain of the state. This change was significant firstly in that it placed everyone in at least general agreement as to what the rules were through the innovation of written laws displayed in public spaces. Secondly, the impact of state-controlled justice is hard to overestimate in that now judgements and punishment were meted out by an impartial third party against whom revenge was both ill-advised and ultimately pointless. When such punishments involve damage to the body they are effectively a kind of ritualized violence and as such may be difficult to distinguish from the kinds of ritual killings apparent in periods preceding the rise of Rome, however various likely candidates have been suggested. In Britain there is a trend apparent during the later Roman period for some burials to be decapitated. This practice is thought largely to have involved cutting the head off after death, perhaps to stop the deceased from returning to haunt or otherwise trouble the living. But in some cases aspects of such burials make the notion of decapitating the dead seem less likely. For example, the burial of an adult male at Guilden Morden in Cambridgeshire was found lying prone (face down) having been decapitated but with the head replaced in its normal position.[8] This individual also had his arms crossed as if his hands were tied. Other examples have been suggested to have been killed by decapitation rather than being already dead when their heads were severed, based on the angle of the cut. Where this indicates a blow from behind with the head bowed, consistent with the victim in a kneeling position, it seems more likely to be the cause of death, as suggested for two adult males found at the site of Jesus Lane, Cambridge.[9] Whilst it would in theory be possible to prop up a dead body in this position it is hard to see why someone might want to. In these cases the respective individuals were buried within otherwise normal cemeteries and so an interpretation of these killings as the execution of war captives would not be plausible. In a further example, twelve decapitated individuals buried at different times in the Roman cemetery of Durocobrivae (modern Dunstable, Bedfordshire) were located in the cemetery but interestingly their graves were placed in the boundary ditch on the edge of the burial ground, apparently marking them out as distinct from the rest of dead.[10] Again the angle of the cuts indicated these people had been kneeling with their necks bent forward with the blow generally coming from behind and to the right. Here two individuals had also been subject to further mutilation. An adult male had his right lower leg cut off between the knee and ankle, whilst

'A most cruel and disgusting punishment'

The means of execution most strongly associated with the Romans is crucifixion, principally because this was the manner by which Jesus of Nazareth is recorded to have been killed in arguably the best-known execution in history. However, despite this prominent status there is a surprising degree of uncertainty regarding exactly how crucifixion causes death. One reason for this is that (thankfully) there has been no opportunity to observe this practice during recent centuries.[11] Since the nineteenth century a great variety of writers, mostly with medical backgrounds, have made suggestions as to how death occurs in crucifixion, with most aiming specifically to deduce how Christ might have died. However, the ideas of such authors have varied considerably with a broad number of different suggestions as to the precise physiological effect, or combination of effects most likely to have been fatal. Matthew Maslen and Piers Mitchell[12] (the latter now of Cambridge University) produced a study considering a large sample of such publications and found that many fell down because they failed to look at any primary evidence from the time crucifixion was practised. Rather than using sources written in Latin and Greek, most medically-orientated discussions have relied on a small number of sources which exist as English translations. Such studies have also commonly based their assumptions on the classic way Jesus has been depicted on the cross which is based on artistic convention rather than any evidence from the time (Fig. 9.3).

Crucifixion is generally understood to involve hanging an individual by their outstretched arms from a structure with a horizontal crossbeam, with the legs fixed to an upright supporting beam. In fact there was a fair degree of variety in terms of how the Romans crucified people. Whilst some such structures may have been classically cross-shaped, others were T, Y or X shaped and in other cases may have simply involved an upright post to which the victim's hands were fixed above their head, sometimes called a *crux simplex*. The positions people were placed in were also varied, with some people crucified upside down. The manner in which people were fixed to such structures may also have differed in using ropes rather than metal nails. The only convincing archaeological evidence for crucifixion identified to date is in the form of a right calcaneus (the bone that forms the heel) recovered from a tomb dating from the first century AD in Israel (Fig. 9.4). This bone had an iron nail driven through its full thickness from right to left, consistent with the foot having been nailed to the side of a wooden structure. This method of fixing the feet is therefore at odds with classic representations of Jesus' crucifixion which universally depict a single nail driven through the top of both feet, fixing them to the front of the cross. The means of fixing the hands has drawn a degree of debate with observations derived from rather dubious experiments with cadavers[13] revealing that again traditional depictions of Jesus with nails through the palms are inaccurate, as the respective tissues are not strong enough to support the body's weight and would simply tear. In order for this to work the nails would need to pass between the two forearm bones (radius and ulna), although it may be the case that

Figure 9.3. Christ's crucifixion as conventionally depicted with nails passing through the palms and a single nail through the dorsum (top) of both feet. (Detail of illuminated manuscript image c.1500, German, artist unknown; Getty Museum)

such practices were not needed for crucifixion to have its intended effect, which may have worked equally efficiently by simply tying the hands in place.

This particularly cruel way to treat people fulfilled several functions, acting as a means of torture as well as a means of execution, whilst displaying the victim's suffering as a message to others. Crucifixion was generally reserved as a punishment for non-Romans and particularly those who challenged the authority of the state such as the Jews who resisted Roman rule in AD 70[14] or the slaves who took part in Spartacus' famous rebellion in the preceding century.[15] This is perhaps one of the

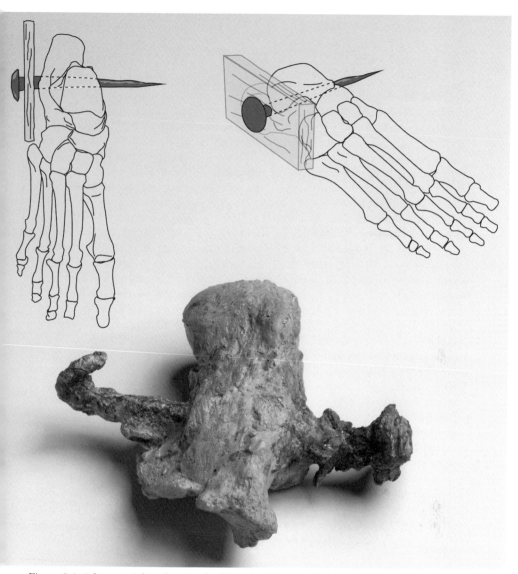

Figure 9.4. A human right calcaneus (heel bone) with a crucifixion nail piercing the full thickness of the bone, from a tomb dating from the first century AD, indicating that nails were hammered through the sides of the feet rather than as shown in conventional art and sculpture. (Collection of Israel Antiquities Authority, photograph © The Israel Museum, Jerusalem, by Meidad Suchowolski)

earliest examples of the commonly-observed phenomenon that 'crimes against the system' usually attract the most severe punishments. Much of the attention given to the medical effects of crucifixion has focused on the fact that the arms are held in a fixed position outstretched or above the head. Over time this would cause considerable strain on the respective muscles as the individual fought to hold themselves up. Eventually the arm muscles would be exhausted and the person would then simply hang by their shoulder joints under gravity. Whilst this may not sound particularly problematic in itself, it is in fact very serious as it means the chest would then be pulled into a permanent position of expansion where it becomes increasingly difficult for the person to breathe out. By fixing the person's feet with nails they are prevented from pushing themselves up with their legs to alleviate the strain on their arms and chest, as it would simply be too painful. Furthermore in the case of the archaeological example noted above, a flat piece of olive wood was situated on the outside of the foot with the nail passing through, apparently to prevent the individual from working their foot free. On other occasions the victim's legs were broken below the knees, which again would prevent them from taking their weight through their legs. By stopping the person from breathing out, death would therefore occur through slow suffocation, although other factors would also be taking effect. During normal activity the action of moving our legs assists our circulation by pumping blood back up to the heart through a series of non-return valves in the veins. By immobilising the legs this effect is compromised and slowly blood and other fluid will pool up in the lower extremities. Both nailing the feet or breaking the legs would further exacerbate this effect due to inflammation and blood loss. In addition both whilst crucified and probably for some time prior to this, the person would become increasingly dehydrated, further lowering blood pressure. All these effects would combine to place growing strain on the already compromised cardiovascular system. Written accounts also agree in that the victim would have been additionally traumatized by being beaten (possibly with a *flagrum*) beforehand, which may have induced various injuries such as rib fractures and possibly internal as well as external bleeding that would further add to the physiological stresses placed upon the body. In summary, this method of execution can be said to have caused death through a combination of factors affecting the heart, lungs and circulatory system simultaneously. There can be no doubt that this would be a slow, painful and particularly unpleasant way to die. Different sources cite death as taking different amounts of time to occur, from a few hours to a few days. Attempts to arrive at a conclusive single estimate, again usually written by medical professionals[16] are equally varied and in fact such variations are likely to result from different ways the punishment was carried out in combination with the relative fitness of the victim. Certainly, it would seem that the Roman author and orator Cicero was well justified when he described crucifixion as: 'A most cruel and disgusting punishment'.[17]

an adult female had both her legs chopped off above the knees. As stated, when archaeologists report parts of skeletons to be missing from graves it is always good to be sceptical as this may relate to disturbance such as ploughing or rabbit burrowing. However, in this case the severed parts had been placed in the grave with the rest of the bodies. The man's severed left lower leg was positioned beneath his right and the woman's severed legs were placed by her torso with the feet by her neck and so there can be no doubt about the deliberate nature of these acts. Other physical punishments practised in Roman society commonly involved beating or whipping. Three groups in particular were subjected to such punishments, the first being soldiers living under the tough regime of army discipline, the second were criminals and the third were slaves, for which there is some skeletal evidence, covered later in this chapter. The most severe version of such punishments, usually reserved for condemned criminals involved implements designed to be particularly painful and damaging, such as the *flagrum*, a multi-tailed whip with bones or lead balls attached to the ends designed to rip the flesh from an individual's back.

Are You Not Entertained? Violence for the Masses

A further export brought to a wider area by Roman civilization was the use of institutionalized violence as a source of entertainment. Gladiatorial combat has conventionally been known about through written sources and artistic representations, with archaeological evidence for the most part consisting of the structures in which such events took place. Perhaps the most important contribution made by the study of such places is simply to reveal how widespread such entertainments must have been, with almost every urban centre throughout the Empire having its own amphitheatre. However, more recently the identification of several cemeteries associated with gladiatorial arenas have shed new light on this aspect of civilized social life. In 1993 excavations at the site of the ancient city of Ephesus in western Turkey uncovered a mass burial area located 300m away from the site of the city's Roman stadium and dating from the late second or early third century AD.[18] Here a 3m thick layer was found to contain the disarticulated of bones of at least sixty-eight individuals buried at different times, with repeated disturbance as subsequent bodies were added, having the effect of separating and mixing the previously buried remains. Where sex and age could be determined all were males aged between 20 and 30 with two exceptions, a male aged 45–55 and a woman buried in the same area with a gravestone indicating a slave. The mixed-up nature of the rest of the assemblage meant that bones had to be analysed individually rather than as complete skeletons, although sufficient crania were complete to permit observation of repeated individuals with head injuries. Analysis by Fabian Kanz and Karl Grosschmidt of the Medical University of Vienna noted eleven individuals who had a total of sixteen healed cranial injuries between them. Of these six had single wounds with the remainder having two each. These were a mix of blunt-force injuries and blade wounds with five penetrating injuries inflicted with pointed implements. None of these healed wounds had penetrated the inner table of the skull, hence the individuals had survived. A further ten individuals had unhealed injuries that must therefore date from around the time of their deaths. Of these three were from blunt impacts with the remainder being penetrating injuries.

Given the proximity of these young men with repeated injuries to the city's stadium (part of which is known to have been converted for gladiatorial shows), it is reasonable to suggest this was likely a burial place of gladiators. This observation is strengthened by the presence of carved tomb reliefs depicting gladiators in addition to some unusual patterns in the injuries seen. Firstly, the presence of healed injuries demonstrate the respective individuals to have seen action before. This might have been in actual fighting or in training as gladiators, although the latter would likely have involved wooden weapons as the owners of gladiator schools would not wish to lose money on their investments by risking the death of a fighter outside the arena. Gladiators tended to be drawn from the ranks of slaves, prisoners of war and condemned criminals, and certainly the second of these groups might well have been involved in fighting prior to entering a gladiatorial school. What is of particular interest, however, is that the only individuals with multiple injuries were those whose wounds had healed: those who died with unhealed injuries each only had one. This is unlike the pattern commonly seen in relation to warfare-related injuries as discussed variously throughout the current book, where often a blow which incapacitates an opponent then allows an assailant to finish them off by inflicting further wounds, as seen in the man from Sovell Down in the previous chapter. The fact that each had only one injury would be consistent with a controlled and highly-regulated form of fighting where once an opponent was brought down, the assailant would step back and await further instructions. All the injuries were to the front or side of the head with none from the rear, consistent with face-to-face combat, running away was not among the options open to gladiatorial contestants who were expected to demonstrate their virtue by accepting death unflinchingly. Lastly two of the injury types present were particularly distinctive. Several individuals had round puncture wounds all of a similar diameter (15mm). In three cases (two healed and one unhealed), these punctures occurred in pairs, each pair spaced around 50mm apart. The two anthropologists involved have suggested these multiple punctures are consistent with a *fuscina*, a trident used by a particular type of gladiator – the *retiarius*, a lightly armoured fighter also armed with a net intended to represent a fisherman. According to written and artistic sources (Fig. 9.5) the *retiarius* was commonly pitted against the *secutor*, a more heavily-armoured opponent representing a sea monster. Given the apparent lack of head protection in the cases at Ephesus this may indicate different pairings between a trident-armed fighter and a less well-armoured adversary. A second unusual injury type noted was that several individuals had unhealed blunt injuries to the side of the head produced by an implement

Figure 9.5. Gladiators depicted in a Roman mosaic from North Africa. The central figure lacking head protection is a *retiarius* (the fisherman) who has dropped his trident after receiving a wound to his leg from his more heavily-armoured opponent. Inset is a cranium from the gladiator cemetery at Ephesus with two healed puncture wounds, suggested to have been caused by a trident. (Photograph courtesy Karl Grosschmidt)

with a rectangular profile. Here it was suggested that this might relate to something that happened after the fight, where dying gladiators were dispatched by an arena servant dressed as *Dis Pater*, the Roman god of death, and wielding a hammer. This tradition went back to the roots of Roman gladiatorial contests in fights held during Etruscan religious festivals.[19] As in other parts of the Iron Age world, religion and ritual remained bound up with other activities just as much for the Romans as for other peoples.

Between 2004 and 2005 York Archaeological Trust excavated an unusual cemetery at Driffield Terrace in the centre of modern York. The burials spanned the Roman period, but dated largely from the late second to the early third century AD.[20] Here, despite being situated on a major road leading out of the city, the group buried in this cemetery did not fit the expected profile for an urban population. Of eighty-two skeletons recovered, all but one were males where sex could be determined, seventy-five were adults younger than 45 and only four were children. Six of the adult males had features of their facial skeleton consistent with some degree of African ancestry, whilst chemical analysis of tooth enamel showed those buried in this cemetery to have more diverse origins than the general population of Roman York. In seven instances men were buried together in pairs, whilst there was also one triple and a possible quadruple burial. As mentioned previously, a feature of late Roman burial practice that may seem peculiar to modern eyes is that people were sometimes decapitated before they were buried. This practice is not well understood and seems largely to have been carried out after death with the head then placed next to the body or in between the knees or feet. Usually less than 10 per cent of Roman burials in Britain involve such decapitations. However, at Driffield Terrace 70.8 per cent of the bodies were decapitated, the majority having been carried out from behind. This feature is more consistent with death by decapitation rather than removing the head from an already dead body which more often occurs from the front with the body laid on its back. This group also displayed extensive evidence for violence-related injuries.

There was a high frequency of healed injuries, particularly to the face and head, in addition to the several individuals whose teeth had been broken by impacts and fractures of the first metacarpal (the bone at the base of the thumb). This latter injury is commonly caused either through punching or in contact sports (see Chapter 12). Nine individuals had healed rib fractures, whilst there were repeated examples of injuries to the legs and ankles consistent with falls in addition to a healed blade wound to the back of one man's right thigh. Unhealed blade wounds were also common, including a cut to the lower end of one man's femur and two individuals with cuts to the backs of their hands. Some of the cuts to these men's necks may also have been combat-related rather than controlled decapitations. Most unusually, one man had a series of circular punctures to both sides of his pelvis. These have been identified as bite marks inflicted by a large carnivore such as a bear or a tiger. Lastly, one man was buried with heavy iron rings encircling both his lower legs. He had ongoing inflammation and probable infection in the adjacent bones indicated by new bone formation, indicating that these painful objects must have been in place for some time before he died.

As far as how the Driffield Terrace cemetery might be interpreted only two suggestions appear to hold water. Given the almost exclusively male profile of this group and the high frequency of violence-related injuries they had suffered, this might be a cemetery reserved specifically for soldiers. However, the repeated incidence of double and even triple burials is not consistent with other Roman soldiers' burials which normally occur singly. The individual who had been attacked and presumably killed by a large carnivorous animal takes some further explaining, whilst the man with iron rings on his legs is simply not consistent with a soldier but rather a treatment more likely to indicate a criminal or a slave. This latter point may be the most telling about this group as a whole as the second possibility, that this was a cemetery for gladiators, would mean these men would have held the status of slaves. The presence of individuals with diverse origins, in addition to a wide range of injuries commonly seen in modern contact sports such as broken noses and fractured metacarpals, is further consistent with these men being gladiators. Gladiatorial pairings commonly involved juxtaposing two very different fighters with different advantages and limitations. The pitting of a fast, lightly-armoured man against a better-protected but slower opponent was a frequent combination and it is tempting to suggest that this was the function intended by the iron rings cruelly placed around the aforementioned man's ankles as these would have the effect of slowing him down. The high number of decapitations may represent a local means of despatching defeated gladiators rather than a blow to the head as used at Ephesus, whilst the presence of a large carnivore would also fit the picture of gladiatorial shows where specialized beast fighters (*bestiarii*) would take on exotic animals to provide a further spectacle. In fact, the overall picture at Driffield Terrace with all these unusual aspects considered together would be a lot harder to explain as anything other than a gladiator cemetery. Lastly the one female individual buried at this site might hint at the possibility of a female gladiator (such individuals are certainly known from written sources), although this point remains speculative. Returning to the issue of decapitation, if this was indeed a means of despatching defeated gladiators practised in Britain, this may explain another unusual group recovered close to the site of London's Roman amphitheatre. Here Rebecca Redfern and Heather Bonney (the latter from the Natural History Museum)[21] have noted this assemblage, which consists only of decapitated crania, to only include males. There were similar patterns of healed frontal and parietal head injuries to those from the gladiator cemetery in Ephesus and Redfern and Bonney suggest these London examples may represent a similar group in that gladiators were excluded from burial with the rest of society. Other suggestions are possible, however, such as executed criminals or trophy-taking by the Roman army, although the first suggestion seems the most likely.

Harnessing Humanity: Roman Slavery

As complex and multi-faceted entities, human societies can be considered from a great variety of different standpoints. For example, Roman civilization can be regarded either as a positive force bringing peace, prosperity, literacy and justice to unenlightened and impoverished societies, or alternatively as an arrogant and oppressive power stamping its authority on others, destroying their cultures and dismantling social networks that had grown up over many centuries. In fact both these points of view are valid on their own terms and the position one might choose to take rests to a large extent on which aspect of the evidence is most strongly focused on.[22] In this respect a view that could be taken on the civilizations of the classical world is that for literally millions of people they were little more than an enormous prisoner of war camp.[23] Whilst over time huge numbers were born into slavery, the principal circumstance in which slaves were initially acquired was in the aftermath of conflict, where captured people were just one of the resources that made conquest a profitable endeavour. Slavery was the engine that drove the ancient world, and wherever civilization appeared slavery flourished with it. In focusing on the achievements of such societies it is easy to forget that all the great architectural edifices of Greek and Roman high culture, from temples to bath houses and aqueducts to theatres, were built by the sweat and toil of enslaved people. The principles of democracy, opportunity and equality under the law, as exemplified by Rome and Athens in particular are often seen as beacons of rationality and fairness that form the foundation of the way we do things today. However, it should also be remembered that such privileges were only ever fully enjoyed by a limited number of (male) citizens with these societies simultaneously denying freedom to many others in order to function. In this respect slavery is arguably one of the most clear examples of 'structural violence' as mentioned at the start of this chapter, firmly underpinning the civilized classical world.

As with other aspects of everyday life, the vast majority of our information on slavery at this time comes from written sources. On one hand such texts might potentially tell us a great deal, although they also come with substantial limitations. A perennial problem in the study of ancient slavery is that whilst a great many contemporary authors mention the subject, none of them were slaves themselves. In trying to reconstruct the experience of slavery we only ever hear from the masters. Consequently it is difficult to construct a picture of what was 'normal' in the life of a slave. Some slaves may have been treated relatively well (excepting the fact that they weren't allowed to hand in their notice). Those who worked within family households in towns and cities might have the best living and working conditions as well as the best relationships with their masters, although this is likely to have varied considerably. Some writers such as the Roman satirist Martial do comment on the mistreatment of slaves, but this is only in the context that those guilty of ('unjustified') cruelty were 'bad masters', not that slavery was in itself bad. The slaves likely to receive the worst treatment and least likely to be viewed as individual human beings were those working in industrial settings such as mines, quarries or large farming estates. These are also the groups that receive the least attention by Roman authors. With regard to archaeology, the most prominent and best-preserved evidence left by any society and the Romans in particular, generally relates to those of wealth and status. Recognizing any signs left by the poorer people in past societies and in particular those at the lowest level in a state of slavery is much more challenging. In recent years a thriving category of study has arisen focusing on skeletal remains known to be those of slaves from the Americas and the Caribbean between the seventeenth and nineteenth centuries. Such studies have repeatedly found these groups to have experienced extremely difficult and stressful living conditions and to exhibit extensive signs of that which anthropologists call 'biological stress'. Skeletal changes associated with poor nutrition and severe physical strain on muscles and joints are strongly evident, leaving no doubt (if there ever was any), that such people were treated appallingly.[24] Whether this tells us anything about ancient slavery however, remains rather frustratingly unanswered, as we simply can't know how closely the two compare, although such studies do at least illustrate that a 'bioarchaeology of slavery' is possible.

With regard to Roman slavery the greatest challenge initially lies in identifying the remains of slaves in order to then ask questions about this group and how far their lives might have differed from those of others at this time. In this respect it may be difficult to differentiate the burials of slaves from those of people who were free but simply poor, in towns and cities. A further problem suggested with regard to urban slaves in more wealthy households is that they may have been cremated, bringing further challenges in obtaining information from their skeletons.[25] Perhaps the least ambiguous skeletal evidence found in recent years for Roman slavery was unearthed in 2014 in Saintes, south-western France. Here a cemetery dating from the first to the second century AD and containing over 100 individuals revealed repeated examples of people buried in pairs or larger multiples, very few with grave goods. Most strikingly, a group of five individuals were found wearing heavy iron shackles. Four adults each had a heavy iron ring around one of their ankles which would have been hot-riveted into place when it was put on. One of these individuals also had a similar ring around his neck, whilst the fifth individual, a child, had a smaller shackle around her/his wrist.[26] This cemetery differs in style from more usual Roman cemeteries and may have been used specifically for the burial of slaves. It may also be relevant that the site was just 250m from the town's large amphitheatre and an alternative suggestion is that some or all of those buried there might have died in the arena. Forcing unarmed individuals, usually slaves, to fight against armed opponents was another common practice in gladiatorial shows and analysis of these burials continues at the time of writing to try to resolve the question of these people's origins and living conditions and the circumstances of their deaths. However, rather than being an isolated example, the individuals from Saintes are in fact just the latest addition to a series of chained individuals from various parts of the Empire, including other examples from Gaul, Raetia (modern Switzerland), Germany and Spain. These in turn exist against a background of more than a hundred examples of various kinds of manacles, fetters and gang chains found particularly in the northern and western provinces. Three individuals of Roman date at Icklingham in Suffolk were found to have thickening of the lower arm bones (radius and ulna) or the tibia and fibula on one leg, suggesting them to have worn shackles for extended periods. Lastly, the find of an individual with fetters attached to his legs in a collapsed Roman-period quarry at Pellenz in the Rhineland is stark evidence for enslaved people in industrial contexts living and dying in chains, whatever postmodern historical discussions might say in arguing that we just don't know how slaves were treated.[27]

A more direct feature on the skeleton that may signal the ill-treatment of slaves can be seen in an unusual form of injury noted on several individuals that were also from Roman Gaul. The site of Vaison la Romaine (south-east France) has been interpreted specifically as a slave cemetery. Here a male individual was found with a significant healed fracture to his right scapula (shoulder blade).[28] Scapular fractures are rarely seen in modern emergency departments as this bone is very well protected by the muscles of the back and shoulder and it would take a significant impact to cause it to break. It is possible the man fell from a height landing on his shoulder blade although this would be unlikely to occur without also causing injuries to other bones. To fracture the other scapula as well would be even more unlikely to occur by accident. In this respect it is therefore even harder to explain two male individuals from a further cemetery at Îlot de Boucheries (Somme) who each had healed fractures to both scapulae, resulting from multiple impacts. A further example was found at Lisieux (Normandy) where again a mature adult male was excavated with healed comminuted fractures (this involves the bone being broken into several pieces) to both scapulae. These multiple examples of the same pattern of injury, consistent with repeated impacts across the back simply can't be explained by any obvious form of accident. Instead, a more convincing explanation suggested by Joel Blondiaux and colleagues is that these fractures were produced through deliberate beatings. In support they cite the comments of an eighteenth-century surgeon, Pierre Joseph Desault, who noted such injuries as being caused by severe blows across the back in his own time when such treatment was still in common use as a punishment. Whilst discipline in the Roman army was certainly tough, it simply wouldn't make sense to inflict such a potentially debilitating injury on a man who might be required to fight and so it seems unlikely that these could be military punishments. It is more plausible therefore that these injuries quite literally represent the 'impact' of civilization inscribed on the bodies of enslaved individuals.

The ongoing excavation at Winterbourne Kingston, Dorset, mentioned in the previous chapter, has revealed a landscape that changed from a native system of fields, stock enclosures and roundhouses to one of buildings in the Roman style with tiled rooves and rectangular layouts and a small villa-type residence with multiple rooms and painted plaster on the walls. This latter phase of the site also revealed sixty-two burials of babies and children aged under two, commonly within or close to the Roman-style buildings. The deaths of young children should come as no surprise during this period and the burial of infants under house floors, rather than in formal cemeteries where older individuals were interred was standard Roman practice. However, the find of so many in a small area does beg the question of whose babies these were? If the landscape had now become 'Romanized' it is quite plausible to suggest that the labour relations of those working the land had also changed. Someone wealthy enough to own even a small villa-type residence is likely to have also owned slaves. Such people are likely to have had hard lives and less than ideal diets and this group may well have experienced even higher rates of infant mortality than the norm for this time. In this respect these little burials may represent a particularly subtle form of the material remains of slavery that would be easy to miss as faint traces of the 'structural violence' inherent in Roman society.

The saying that 'you only find what you look for' commonly holds true in archaeology and even more so for the study of human remains. The examples I have discussed here show that human skeletons may hold more potential than any other line of material evidence for investigating the character of ancient slavery. Such investigations have been conducted very successfully with the remains of more recent slaves from the Americas where such studies have revealed a consistent picture across large numbers of people, throughout different regions where slavery was practised on an industrial scale. At present the study of the physical remains of ancient slaves is not so well developed, but shows clear potential for the future. As mentioned previously, written sources simply don't allow us to come to solid conclusions as to how slaves were 'normally' treated (although I suspect there was a lot more bad than good). The skeletal examples here are similar in that they allow us to conclude that 'some' slaves were ill-treated 'some' of the time but don't permit us to put any figures on such observations. As more examples are highlighted in future the numbers of recognized slave burials are likely to grow and so there is good reason to be optimistic (if that is the right word) as this is an area where human osteology is arguably in a better position than any other field to answer such questions reliably.

Hearth and Home: Domestic and Urban Violence

The rise of larger urban settlements with associated large cemeteries in the Roman period allows us for the first time to gain some insights into patterns of violence that might occur in daily life, as opposed to dramatic contexts such as battles or fights between armed warriors. Despite the high visibility of young adult males in a wide variety of studies of violence (including this one) the groups that are frequently most at risk of becoming victims of violence, whilst at the same time given the least attention, are those who are most vulnerable, particularly the very old and very young. A stark example of the latter can be seen in the skeleton of a child aged between two and three, from a large Roman period cemetery at Dakleh Oasis in Egypt.[29] This child had a shocking range of injuries to her or his skeleton including fractures to the left humerus, right clavicle, ribs on both sides of the chest, right and left pelvic bones and bones of the feet. In addition the child displayed new bone formation consistent with physical trauma on other bones throughout the skeleton. It was not possible that these injuries had been received in a single terrible incident such as being trampled by a horse or falling from a height as the various fractures were in different stages of healing indicating they must have occurred at different times. Some of these injuries, particularly rib fractures and the fractured clavicle, rarely occur accidentally in children. Taken together these injuries would be diagnosed today as consistent with severe physical abuse. Such cases are rarely observed archaeologically, although this may have more to do with poor survival of children's bones and misdiagnosis rather than necessarily indicating that child abuse was less common in the past. The team that analysed the Dakleh child, led by Tosha Dupras of University of Central Florida, noted that Egyptian texts indicate that children were regarded as very precious and appear to have generally been brought up in a relatively gentle manner. This differed from Roman notions that children should be treated in a strict manner with frequent physical punishment to toughen them up. But even if Roman ideas had permeated into Egypt at this time, the treatment of this child was clearly abnormal even by Roman standards. No other children from the cemetery exhibit such injuries and the authors are quite justified in noting this as the earliest example of physical child abuse recognized in the archaeological record. At the other end of what anthropologists call the 'life course' Rebecca Gowland of Durham University discusses two examples of older adult females from Roman Britain with injuries consistent with assaults (one to the frontal bone and the other to the face and neck) that would today raise concerns of elder abuse.[30] This latter kind of violence has only recently been recognized in our own society and may again have previously been missed in archaeological samples simply because people would take the view that healed injuries in an elderly person could have occurred at any time in their life with a presumption that such trauma most likely occurred during that person's younger days.

A further type of violence that becomes apparent during the Roman period involves a similar pattern to the type of injuries that might be seen in a modern (British) town on a Saturday night. In studying trauma among individuals from the Romano-British settlement at Poundbury, Dorset the late Philip Walker noticed a high prevalence of healed broken noses among adult males.[31] Some 16 per cent of those whose crania had the nasal bones preserved had such fractures, which as mentioned in Chapter 2 are rarely incurred by accident and more usually caused in assaults and contact sports. However, these individuals lacked any sign of weapon injuries. Boxing was certainly a popular sport among the Romans, who had inherited it from the Greeks where it had been an Olympic sport since the seventh century BC (Fig. 9.6). This version of boxing was a more damaging and bloody affair than its modern counterpart with participants wearing gloves designed to increase, rather than decrease, the risk of injury. Whilst the Greek gloves had been made of rough leather likely to catch the skin and cause cuts, the Roman version, the *caestus*, involved thick padding that reached far up the arm, with the fists both weighted and possibly studded with metal spikes.[32] Rather than indicating the injured individuals at Poundbury to have been boxers as such, these fractures may rather indicate a general popularity of the sport either as a leisure activity or as a means of settling disputes as would later become the norm in eighteenth and nineteenth-century Britain (see Chapter 12).

Ultimately Roman society and that of the Empire it acquired were created, maintained and powered through violence and brutality, both real and threatened. Of course Rome was neither the first nor the only civilization in the ancient world. However, the consideration of Rome as an example does illustrate a number of important points with regard to the rise of civilized and particularly urbanized ways of living that are either absent in earlier societies or at least inaccessible to modern investigations. In trying to get at the past some people are always more visible than others in written sources. Consideration of human remains has the potential to redress this imbalance. However, the nature of the Roman burial record is such that the greater proportion of signs of violence that might have been recorded in the skeletons of those who suffered it is beyond our reach. The Roman soldiers whose remains we have access to tend to be those who came home to live out a peaceful retirement and so were in a position to have a funeral inscription carved about them. Those who died on active service are largely lost to us. Where slaves have

Figure 9.6. (Top left) A male individual from Roman Poundbury Dorset with a healed nasal fracture (broken nose) consistent with a blow from to the right side of the face. (Top right) Boxers depicted in a mosaic, wearing *caesti* (Roman boxing gloves). (Bottom) The 'Boxer of the Quirinal' bronze sculpture discovered in Rome in 1885, apparently a veteran of multiple fights, denoted by his broken nose and cauliflower ear. (Photographs: Jean-Pol Grandmont; Acélan)

been identified in burials these have tended to be those who enjoyed the best conditions or even gained their freedom and again received the privilege of a funeral monument informing us of their identity in life. Remains of people who represent the less fortunate majority of slaves are only just beginning to be recognized, along with physical evidence for the ways they were treated.

The changes of moving to an urban way of living that came for many during the Roman period might offer an opportunity to investigate acts of violence against groups that were close to invisible in many previous historical and archaeological studies, particularly the oldest and youngest in society. Again, the examples presented here have shown what is possible and illustrate the kind of future directions such studies might take.

Arguably the strongest theme to emerge in considering violence in this period is the use of such acts as a systematic means of control. The innovation of violence as performance in gladiatorial fights is a particularly cynical example of such, serving both to occupy and entertain the masses, whilst sending a message that they were being provided for by those in power at least in one respect. The use of violent public punishments by the state was similarly theatrical and served in a way as a kind of large-scale version of the Roman household where children, slaves and anyone else thought to need it were kept in line by the head of the house through physical punishment or the threat of it. On a still larger scale, the provinces of the Empire were similarly controlled by the threat of violent repercussions should they fail to comply with the regime. Perhaps the most intriguing aspect offered by human remains from this period is that they provide an opportunity to test the overall strength of the available evidence in that here we have a huge, complex and well-documented state entity, that covered a vast geographic area and maintained itself for centuries while affecting the lives of millions. Surely then, skeletal evidence for the frequency and nature of Roman violence should be abundantly obvious. A question that may be intriguing to consider then is if we were to forget written sources as if they didn't exist, how apparent would Roman violence be? If a society where violence was so ingrained turns up relatively little skeletal evidence for such (for the reasons discussed above) this would have important connotations for less well-documented periods, as it would imply that an absence (or at least a low level) of evidence cannot necessarily be taken to mean that violence wasn't very prevalent. Moreover, where we have prehistoric periods for which violence appears quite frequent, such as the Neolithic, it may be that even then the skeletal evidence produces a picture that underestimates what was really happening. As in so many other areas of study, with regard to violence Roman society is therefore not only of interest in itself, but also offers a yardstick against which the evidence for other times and places can be measured.

Chapter 10

'The Judgement of God': Violence in Early Medieval England

In the years after the fall of Rome in the West, almost nothing worked properly any more. Local government structures collapsed, taking Roman law and administration with them. Taxation ceased to exist along with the public amenities it had paid to maintain such as roads and water supplies. The armies of the provinces melted away as their pay evaporated, along with the security they provided. The only institution that continued to function was the Church, although this was confined to southern Europe with the northern and western parts of the former empire now turning away from Christianity in favour of other beliefs. This vacuum left a situation where new powers could emerge as people were obliged to find new ways of providing for their own safety and well-being. In the absence of a state able to dispense judgement from above, the structure that people turned to for security and justice in the first instance was the family. Any group or individual who felt they had been wronged would call upon those linked to them either by blood, marriage or other local ties to assist them in seeking vengeance. In principle, then, anyone considering theft, murder or any other antisocial act should therefore think twice unless they were prepared to deal with all the adult male members of the victim's extended family and friends coming to exact vengeance and feeling righteously entitled to do so. Over time this custom, known as a 'blood feud', came to be generally accepted as the legitimate way to obtain justice and rather than resulting in society falling into violent chaos, a complex series of agreed rules and conventions grew up governing the way such vendettas could be pursued. In particular it was expected that the aggrieved party would publicly announce to their neighbours that they were in pursuit of justice before any action could be taken. This practice functioned to allow an opportunity for the two parties to make peace, for example through the payment of compensation. This practice in turn came to be regulated by the establishment of agreed levels of payment determined by the gravity of an offence or the status of a murdered individual. This latter point was important in that it allowed the dead person's relatives to demand an amount that was generally regarded as fair and honourable, without being seen as haggling for the highest price.[1] Whilst there are sufficient mentions in early English literature to make it clear that blood feuds were certainly not uncommon, at the same time this generally-agreed set of rules for engaging in such disputes is likely also to have served to deter individuals from the sorts of behaviour that might provoke such a situation in the first place. This latter effect has been referred to by scholars of the period as 'peace in the feud'.

A Fate Worse than Death: Anglo-Saxon Executions

As Rome declined in the West, increasing numbers of largely Germanic migrants from continental Europe, still popularly referred to as 'Anglo-Saxon' peoples (although this term is now less favoured among some academics), settled in the parts of the former Roman province of Britannia that would later come to be referred to as England. Over the following centuries emerging political entities gradually began to form and assert control over newly-defined territories. One sign of such growing authority from above is the gradual assumption of control over the custom of the blood feud in written law codes, with such practice eventually coming under the ultimate judgement of the rulers of the newly-emerging Saxon kingdoms. Such assumption of responsibility for justice by newly-forming state powers also shows itself in the archaeological record in the appearance of formal execution cemeteries, separate from the burial grounds used for the general population. The principal expert on Anglo-Saxon execution cemeteries is Andrew Reynolds of University College London, who identified a number of characteristic features by which they can be distinguished.[2] These features include randomly-orientated burials, rather than graves running in similar directions as is common in standard cemeteries, and also bodies in unusual positions such as lying prone (face down). Such burial grounds also display an unusual profile in terms of who is buried there, dominated by young adult males lacking grave goods, as well as having signs of trauma to the skeleton and particularly decapitations. Lastly, the siting of such cemeteries is unusual. They are commonly located away from settlements, on the boundaries of territories. Such siting may have fulfilled two functions: firstly, such burials were therefore symbolically pushed as far away from the general population as possible without trespassing into another territory. Secondly, such boundaries were also commonly defined by the course of roads and trackways and siting them nearby would ensure the greatest number of people came in sight of such cemeteries which could then act as a warning against similar lawbreaking. For example, the excavation of Bran Ditch, a Saxon-period land boundary defined by a 5km long earthen bank and ditch in Cambridgeshire in the 1920s, revealed the burials of around sixty decapitated adult males.[3] The excavator at the time, Cyril Fox, thought these must be victims of a battle or massacre, but the site has more recently been reassessed as an execution cemetery with the land boundary defining its limits and location. Lastly, those burying people following execution appear to have often made efforts to then further punish them beyond the grave by selecting places of burial believed to have supernatural qualities. Execution burials in this period often occur as secondary burials dug into the tops or sides of existing earthen mounds that would have already been ancient at the time. In addition to excluding people from a Christian burial as the principle of consecrated ground was now recognized, what we now know to have been Bronze Age or Neolithic barrows were believed in this (Early Medieval) period to be haunted by monsters or evil spirits that might then torment the executed person's soul after death.[4] Given their prominence in the landscape, prehistoric monuments were often themselves used as markers to define the limits of territorial boundaries and so in some cases the placement of execution victims at such sites is likely to have fulfilled the two objectives simultaneously. This may be the case for a decapitated man excavated from within the monument at Stonehenge in 1923, originally thought to be of Neolithic or perhaps Roman date but who has more recently been dated to the seventh century AD.[5] The man had been decapitated most probably with a sword, with the blow coming from behind and also clipping his mandible (lower jaw). Chemical analysis of his tooth enamel showed him to be of likely fairly local origin somewhere in central southern England. Stonehenge lay at the centre of three administrative territories known as 'hundreds',[6] while it is interesting that a possible explanation for the name of the monument '*Stan Hengen*' (literally 'Stone Gallows' in Old English[7]), may suggest the site was interpreted in this time as having always been a place of execution.

A further example of a cemetery that fits Andrew Reynolds' criteria very precisely was excavated in the late 1960s at Walkington Wold in East Yorkshire but not recognized for what it was until recently. Here at least thirteen individuals were buried on the periphery of a Bronze Age round barrow in a variety of positions and orientations, ten of whom had clearly been decapitated, with the remainder too badly preserved to tell. In the absence of scientific dating they were originally assumed to be possible execution victims or the victims of a battle or massacre during the immediate post-Roman period, however recent radiocarbon dates have placed these burials firmly in the Anglo-Saxon period. The cemetery also fits Reynolds' conditions in being sited on a territorial boundary. Re-analysis of the skeletal remains, principally by Jo Buckberry of Bradford University has further refined the information available regarding this group and how they were treated in death.[8] Eleven individuals were clearly male with the remaining two assessed as probably male, all were younger than 45 with at least five under 25. Two individuals displayed multiple flat slices to the backs of their heads indicating they were decapitated from behind, but also suggesting they might have been struggling as there were repeated blows to different points on the skull. Two individuals appear to have had their throats cut from the front indicated by cutmarks produced by a fine, sharp blade on the front of their cervical (neck) vertebrae. None had signs of weapon injuries to other parts of the skeleton and the radiocarbon dates obtained span several centuries, indicating the cemetery must have been used only occasionally over a lengthy period, rather than all the bodies having been deposited after a single dramatic episode such as a battle.[9] Eight of the eleven decapitated heads were only represented by the cranium with the mandible (lower jaw) absent. This was suggested by Jo Buckberry to indicate the heads had been displayed for some time before burial, during which time the mandible and neck vertebrae had fallen away as the soft tissues decomposed. This suggestion was bolstered by the find of a large post hole at the top of the barrow which may have been the site of some sort of structure for displaying the severed heads. A final point of interest was the observation of signs of biological stress in these skeletons indicating poor diets and perhaps suggesting these individuals to be from the lower end of the social scale. Such a social position might have influenced their fate, either in putting them in a position of feeling a need to commit crime in order to survive or of being more likely to be found guilty and to receive such a severe sentence when accused.

'The Woeful Inroads of Heathen Men': The Vikings in Britain

The Early Medieval period in England has come down to us since the time of the earliest English historians as the age of the Saxons, although it should be remembered that during the later part of this period a high proportion of new additions to the language, culture and also people that arrived in Britain came from Scandinavia. Between the ninth and tenth century the focus of Norse attention on Britain shifted from simply raiding to taking control of territory, with much of northern and eastern England coming under Viking administration in the territory known as the Danelaw. The now old-fashioned stereotype of the 'Vikings' as bloodthirsty raiders interested in nothing more than theft and destruction has come in for a lot of criticism in recent years, and rightly so as such a view ignored all manner of achievements and innovations in commerce, technology and exploration by the peoples of Scandinavia. However, it should equally be remembered that the 'Danes' (as the incumbent population referred to all Scandinavians) did not gain control of York and other important English settlements by simply 'trading' their way in – sharp objects and unpleasant behaviour had a lot more to do with it. Furthermore, the establishment of peace by the treaty between Alfred, King of

The Man from Maiden Castle: A Contradiction in (Burial) Terms?

The notion that 'context is everything' is a well-worn saying among archaeologists, and carries a lot of value in making the point that the interpretations we draw from objects and structures uncovered during excavation depend a great deal on their location relative to other aspects of the evidence. When objects are removed from their context without proper recording, for example by (irresponsible) metal detectorists[10] this often causes considerable frustration among archaeologists as it ultimately means that many further questions regarding that particular find can never be answered. Conversely, in instances where the context is recorded but mistakes are made, any further interpretations of the respective evidence may be considerably skewed. This is what happened when Sir Mortimer Wheeler's excavation of Maiden Castle hillfort in the 1930s explored an earlier feature of the site, dating from long before the Iron Age.[11] Running across what would later become the site of the hillfort is a 546m-long earthen bank dating from the Neolithic that probably served as some sort of territorial boundary. Wheeler's excavation uncovered a human burial at the eastern end of this feature, which he interpreted to date from the time the mound (usually referred to as the 'bank barrow') was constructed. Here the skeleton of a man assessed to be aged 25–35 had apparently been severely mutilated around the time of his death, with numerous sharp force injuries to his limbs, face and head (Figs 10.1 and 10.2). The body was then dismembered with the limbs and head removed before all the respective body parts were buried together in the side of the mound.

Wheeler's thoughts were later elaborated on in 1954 when Stuart Piggott,[12] the leading expert at the time on the Neolithic, went on to interpret the mutilated man as a victim of cannibalism. This opinion then stood for a further seventeen years until Don Brothwell, one of the first of a new breed of specifically trained archaeological osteologists re-examined the man's bones and made some important observations to the contrary. Most importantly Brothwell noted that the cuts made into the bones were narrow, regular and straight, with flat surfaces at the margins. These linear chops and slices could not have been made by the broad, irregular edges of the stone axes possessed by Neolithic people. Instead such wounds could only have been made by metal weapons and in particular one or more sharp,

Figure 10.1. Locations of sharp-force trauma observed on the skeleton of the man buried in the bank barrow at Maiden Castle. Here at least twenty-nine points of damage inflicted with a sharp, heavy blade are visible, comprising at least forty-one separate blows. This man suffered at least five wounds to the head and also sustained wounds to the forearms consistent with defensive injuries. Damage to two of his lumbar vertebrae indicates he was also stabbed in the abdomen. It would appear that after being incapacitated by these wounds he was then decapitated and the rest of his body extensively dismembered including severing his arms at the elbow and legs at the knee and ankle, in addition to chopping through his left thigh below the hip. The damage to his right humerus and left femur indicate at least six blows to sever each limb. There may have been further wounds to parts of the skeleton where poor preservation makes them more difficult to identify conclusively – particularly on the ribs and spine – and so the number illustrated here very likely underestimates the true figure.

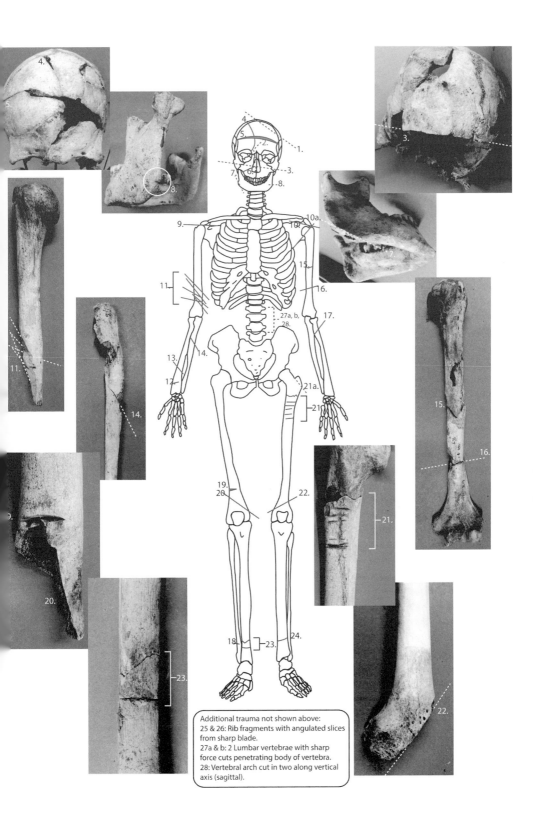

Additional trauma not shown above:
25 & 26: Rib fragments with angulated slices from sharp blade.
27a & b: 2 Lumbar vertebrae with sharp force cuts penetrating body of vertebra.
28: Vertebral arch cut in two along vertical axis (sagittal).

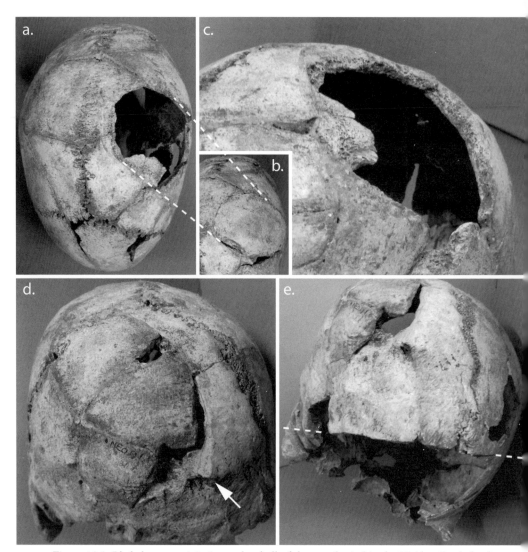

Figure 10.2. Bladed-weapon injuries to the skull of the man buried in the Maiden Castle bank barrow: (a–c) a blow to the top of his head sliced an oval window through the skull vault, for which the severed section of bone (b) must have remained attached by his scalp as it was still present in the grave; (d) a slice into the back of the skull runs in a vertical direction possibly having been delivered when the man was lying on the ground; (e) a flat plane slice across the base of the skull is one of three apparent attempts at decapitation – two further attempts are indicated by damage to the back of his mandible (lower jaw).

thin-bladed implements, most consistent with a sword. The man must therefore have lived at a more recent date. To test this assertion a means of further inquiry that hadn't been available to Wheeler or Piggott but which was in use by the time of Brothwell's re-examination was radiocarbon dating. A sample of bone sent for analysis revealed that the man had in fact died at some time around AD 635 (more recently recalculated as falling between AD 578–892). This re-evaluation has since raised further questions regarding the nature of this man's death and burial. The placement of his mutilated corpse in the ancient mound crossing the hillfort is suggestive of an execution victim, similar to those at Walkington Wold and this is how he has generally been interpreted in recent years. However, the wounds to his face and head (which would have been fatal) are more consistent with combat injuries than with a controlled judicial killing, as are the apparent defensive injuries to his forearm. Other injuries to his limbs and trunk are also more suggestive of a frenzied assault than an execution. A possible explanation for this apparent contradiction may lie in stepping back from the common assumption that all executions – or rather judicial killings – would necessarily have involved bound or otherwise restrained prisoners being killed in a controlled and specific manner such as decapitation. A means for dispensing justice where the accused was given an opportunity to defend themselves in a very literal sense but which hasn't been considered before is indeed known from this period – 'Trial by Combat'.

The custom of 'Trial by Battle', familiar to modern eyes as a well-used storyline in period films and television, was in fact a widely-used and legally-recognized means of deciding the fate of an accused man throughout Europe during the High Middle Ages,[13] although its origins were much earlier and the practice is first mentioned as early as AD 502. The practice was certainly in use in England from Norman times and although it is not mentioned directly by Saxon sources, such 'absence of evidence' can't necessarily be taken as 'evidence of absence' before 1066. It is certainly interesting that the poem Beowulf refers to the title character fighting the monster Grendel in circumstances where steps are taken to ensure the combatants fight on an equal footing in order to allow 'the judgement of God' to decide the outcome.[14] Also the poetic account of the battle of Maldon fought in Essex in AD 991 uses the same words when the Saxon leader Byrhtnoth offers terms on which to fight an invading party of Vikings, again implying that the concept was widely recognized in England at this time. If the man from Maiden Castle was indeed a victim of Trial by Combat he would constitute the earliest example of such identified from Britain. For now this remains purely a suggestion, although it is one that is more consistent with the evidence than previous ideas and if I am right would correct the apparent contradiction between the manner of this man's death and his treatment at burial.

Wessex, and the Danish leader Guthrum in AD 886 that gave legal status to the Danelaw, provided only a brief respite in the conflict between Danes and Saxons which would continue until 1066.

Throughout this time sporadic periods of raiding continued around the southern and western English coast, which may be the context for a dramatic event revealed near Weymouth in 2009. During the excavation and recording of archaeological features set to be destroyed by the construction of a new road providing access to the venue for the sailing events of the 2012 Olympic Games, came the unexpected find of a mass burial in a pit comprising around fifty decapitated skeletons.[15] The irregularly-shaped pit measured approximately 7m across and was identified as a quarry pit dating from Roman times, with the human remains initially thought to be of most likely similar date. This suggestion was taken up enthusiastically by the popular press in describing a 'war grave' containing native Britons who had fallen victim to 'the brutal invasion of the Roman legions',[16] particularly as the site was within view of Maiden Castle, with Mortimer Wheeler's story of the Roman assault on the fort still refusing to lie down. In fact there were between forty-seven and fifty-two individuals buried in the pit, some of which were damaged during the initial discovery by mechanical digger, making analysis (led by Louise Loe of Oxford Archaeology) more difficult. All were assessed as male or probably male with the majority being younger adults and only two individuals aged over 45. The skulls had been placed together as a pile of heads on the southern side of the pit whilst the bodies had been thrown haphazardly on top of one another at the centre (Fig. 10.3). Although clearly buried in a single event, the bodies lacked any associated objects by which they might be dated. Three radiocarbon dates obtained from the skeletons gave a range for the date of these individuals' deaths between AD 970 and 1025. Rather than being local lads, later analysis of the elements making up these men's tooth enamel revealed them to have originated in a colder region most consistent with various different parts of Scandinavia.[17] Correspondingly the Weymouth 'Celtic tribesmen' were retitled in the press as the 'Weymouth Vikings'.[18]

The men showed profuse signs of trauma (Fig. 10.4), mostly to the head and neck with most exhibiting signs of more than one blow with a sharp, heavy implement and one man having been struck at least seven times. These blows were all struck from behind and seem aimed at decapitation, although the wide variety of locations – from the top of the head to the scapula (shoulder blade) suggest the men may have been struggling hard. Five skulls also had incised cuts that had come from the front which were more consistent with combat wounds. These cuts hadn't penetrated the skull and were probably not fatal. In addition, twenty-seven out of forty individuals that were sufficiently well preserved to analyse had unhealed sharp force injuries to other parts of the skeleton. Of these most had more than one wound up to a maximum of seven (with seventy-six wounds noted across the twenty-seven men). Ten of these were injuries to the clavicle (collar bone) that may have been inflicted when the men were decapitated. Most of the other bones affected were those of the forearms, wrists and hands. These latter injuries are of a kind commonly seen

Figure 10.3. View of the mass burial pit discovered near Weymouth in 2012 containing the remains of around fifty individuals, whose decapitated skulls can be seen piled together in the background. (© Oxford Archaeology)

Figure 10.4. The skull of one of the 'Weymouth Vikings' with an oval-shaped slice cut through the bone with a sharp, heavy blade. (Copyright Oxford Archaeology).

in modern forensic cases where individuals instinctively try to defend themselves from an armed assailant by putting their arms up to block blows aimed at the head or upper body. When such defensive moves result in injury to the arms from a blunt weapon the victim may sustain a parry fracture as mentioned in previous chapters. In the case of the Weymouth mass burial the defensive injuries had been inflicted most likely with swords which had cut into the forearm bones and in some cases cut through the hand bones severing fingers.[19]

The meticulous analysis conducted on the 'Weymouth Vikings' has provided a wealth of highly detailed information but also leaves a number of questions unanswered. Perhaps the most likely explanation for these men's killings is that they were indeed a raiding party who had presumably fallen foul of the locals and had been taken up to the Ridgeway, a local territorial boundary, to be summarily executed. Such a story would explain the combat-related and defensive injuries, as these men would therefore represent those who were subdued and taken alive during such an encounter rather than killed in the fighting. The overall profile of this group, made up principally of well-built young men with a small number of older men who were presumably in charge, would also be consistent with the crew of a ship of this period. Other possibilities have been suggested such as the men being a group of foreign mercenaries employed to fight in a local conflict at this time. They might also have been immigrants living locally who had been killed in the events known as the St Brice's Day Massacre, when King Aethelred ordered the killing of all 'Danish' men living in England in the year 1002. This latter suggestion is a bit more problematic, however, firstly in that the age profile of the group doesn't fit a randomly-selected sample of the general population who happened to be of Scandinavian origin, and secondly as there are disagreements among historians regarding exactly which people this edict was referring to.

As for the rather 'messy' and uncontrolled manner in which the men were executed, a possible clue to exactly how this was done is given in the *Jomsvikingasaga*, a saga written in Iceland during the thirteenth century recounting the story of a group of eleventh-century Viking mercenaries who had by that time passed into legend. In AD 986 the Jomsvikings were defeated fighting for the Danes in a failed invasion of Norway. The saga recounts the fate of some of those who were captured by the forces of Hakon Sigurdsson, the ruler of Norway:

> Then the Jarl had Vagn and his men led up on land, and their hands were tied behind their backs, and they were bound with one rope, one at the other's side, not loosely ... it is said that Thorkel Leira was appointed to behead them all. First they talked to the Jomsvikings, and asked whether they were as hardy men as was said; but it is not told that the Jomsvikings gave them any answer. It is next stated that some sorely wounded men were untied from the rope; Skopti Kark and other thralls had hold of it and guarded them. When they were untied the thralls twisted sticks in their hair; first three wounded men were led forward in that way, and Thorkel went to them and cut off each head; ... The fourth Nuui was led out of the rope, and a stick twisted in his hair, and he was led to where Thorkel beheaded them; he was much wounded ...[20]

This picture of wounded men, subdued after a fight, being led to execution shortly afterwards with their hair used to pull the head into a position where they could be beheaded is certainly of interest in relation to the Weymouth mass burial. A further point of interest is the fact that the Weymouth men were all beheaded with a sword, as contrary to popular belief only the richest in society could have afforded such a weapon at this time. The mention in the *Jomsvikingasaga* of a single prominent individual being appointed as executioner while men of lower rank held the captives in position would therefore also fit the evidence as seen at Weymouth. A final intriguing piece of information has more recently become available as analytical work on the skeletons has continued. Further chemical analysis of the men's tooth enamel has in fact shown that rather than Norway, Denmark or Sweden, a number of the men appear to have actually originated in what is now Poland.[21] The precise location of Jomsborg – the point of origin of the Jomsvikings – is unknown, although it is generally agreed to have been somewhere on the southern coast of the Baltic Sea, perhaps near the mouth of the river Oder which forms the modern border between Poland and Germany. Perhaps then the Weymouth Vikings were in fact mercenaries after all.

Further north, at Repton in Derbyshire, is a site that can be more conclusively linked to historically known events, specifically the overwintering of the Viking 'Great Army' led by Ivar the Boneless and his brother Halfdan in AD 873–4. This coalition force drawn from various parts of Scandinavia, named in the Anglo-Saxon Chronicle as the 'Great Heathen Army' landed in the year 865 with the intention of conquering territory from the four Saxon kingdoms of England and holding on to it, rather than simply raiding the countryside and going home. In the year they occupied Repton the Norsemen seized the monastic church there, more for its strategic than symbolic importance as it was built on high ground with opportunity to control an important river crossing. The church building became part of a D-shaped defended enclosure built by the Vikings. Various burials that were then interred around the monastery building contained objects of Scandinavian origin and one in particular had clear evidence of a very violent end. Here a man aged between 35–45 had been buried with a sword at his side and wearing a small silver Thor's hammer amulet. A boar's tusk had been placed close to the groin area whilst the humerus of a raven or jackdaw had been placed between his legs, probably as a symbol of Odin. The man had suffered a penetrating injury most likely from a sword through his eye socket, which would have been fatal as the weapon then entered the brain. In addition to slicing injuries to his arm he also suffered deep wounds to his abdomen indicated by cuts to the front of his vertebrae in the lumbar region. Lastly there was a significant blade injury across the top of his left femur which would have severed or at least severely damaged his genitals. This been suggested to explain the placement of the boar's tusk to serve as a replacement in the afterlife. Certainly this man's fate would appear to indicate that the Mercian defenders of the monastery didn't go down without a fight.

A more ambiguous burial feature at Repton was a large mound sited over the burial of a presumably significant individual argued by the excavators (Martin Biddle and Birthe Kjølbye-Biddle) to be Ivar the Boneless himself, who is alleged to have died in AD 873. The mound overlying this central burial contained the disarticulated bones of at least 264 individuals. The excavators considered the possibility that these might be the bones of other members of the Great Army, but this now seems unlikely for several reasons. Firstly, the bones lack signs of violence, but they also lack parts of the skeleton, with very few small bones such as those of the hands and feet present.

This pattern is usually seen when previous burials are disturbed and bones are moved and redeposited elsewhere. Around a fifth of the bones present are those of women, whilst most conclusively, radiocarbon dates obtained are grouped around two periods, the late seventh to early eighth century and the later ninth century.[22] It seems much more likely that these are simply bones of previous burials which were disturbed when the Great Army were digging their defensive ditch around the church. Cemeteries often fill up in phases so that burials of a given date occupy particular areas of a churchyard and this is most likely what happened at Repton where the Viking defences cut across particular phases of the cemetery at different points. Quite what placing these bones in the mound meant to the Vikings remains open to debate, for example the souls of the deceased might then be believed to be bound in service to the dead Viking Leader in the afterlife. On the other hand the reburial of these bones might have more to do with superstitious fear at having disturbed the dead and functioned instead to placate them and dissuade their souls from troubling the living.

Returning to the time of King Aethelred (the Unready) who ruled at the turn of the eleventh century, the find of up to thirty-seven bodies, with severe trauma buried together in a mass grave at St John's College, Oxford[23] in 2008 may be more likely candidates for victims of the St Brice's Day Massacre than the Weymouth Vikings. These bodies were again heaped on top of each other in a chaotic manner, with the rather familiar profile of all being male and for the most part younger adults (mostly 16–25 or 26–35). All had multiple un-healed bladed-weapon injuries, whilst several of the skeletons had signs of charring indicating exposure to burning. There were no grave goods, suggesting the men had been stripped at least of anything of value and the bodies had been dumped in a ditch that had once surrounded a henge monument from Neolithic times, therefore fitting the pattern of execution burials. Radio-carbon results from the bones indicate a date somewhere in the late tenth or early eleventh century.[24] In addition to their unusual deaths this group of young men would also have been distinctive in life. They were physically robust and taller than the average male for the time. They had also eaten a different diet from that generally seen in the region as indicated by chemical analysis of their tooth enamel. These men had enjoyed a diet rich in marine fish – difficult to get in tenth-century Oxford, but much more consistent with the results seen in Scandinavian populations. A royal charter citing repairs to St Frideswide's church in Oxford following the massacre, which took place in 1002, refers to a group of Danes having barricaded themselves inside. Unable to dislodge them the besiegers set fire to the church and it can reasonably be assumed that things didn't end well for those inside. Given the signs of burn-ing on some of the skeletons it would seem these apparent Scandinavians are certainly strong contenders for having been victims of the massacre. A further point of distinction is that the group also had many healed wounds between them, leading to the suggestion that they may have been professional soldiers. This latter point has prompted the suggestion that they were more likely a raiding party than a random group of civilians,[25] but as noted earlier the precise meaning of the edict calling for the killing of all Danes is unclear. It may also be the case that a group of fighting men who happened to be in the town at the time would indeed stand a better chance than the average individual of making a stand against the townsfolk and successfully defending a rapidly-fortified position, with only the destruction of the church by fire managing to displace them. On this basis the St John's College 'Vikings' are certainly a strong candidate for being a group that fell foul of this Medieval act of ethnic cleansing.

'The (Occasional?) Groans of the Britons'[26]

Taken together the above examples of executions, trial by combat, Viking raids and ethnic cleansing paint a rather dramatic picture that threatens to take us back to the sort of grim view of the Early Medieval Period that characterized school history books in the 1950s or before, when this time was referred to as the 'Dark Ages'. Once again it should be remembered however, that for the most part life would generally have been tranquil and mundane with little sign of such tribulations. As with other periods covered in this book, various examples are known of individuals with injuries consistent with violence from otherwise 'standard' burial grounds. For example, a Middle Saxon period graveyard at Cherry Hinton near Cambridge excavated in 1999 was found to contain a dozen individuals with weapon injuries, such as a man probably in his forties with three unhealed sword cuts to the head and one cut to the upper back.[27] These traumatized skeletons were distributed randomly throughout the graveyard and would appear to have been buried at different times as the churchyard filled up. Other examples include two individuals from Buckland near Dover, one of who had a large D-shaped slice taken out of his skull vault presumably with a sword, which would have been fatal. The other had a depressed, elongated channel gouged out of his skull, measuring 78×10mm at its widest point.[28] This had clearly been inflicted with a wider, heavier edged weapon, most probably an axe, although surprisingly the victim had survived for some time as the edges of the wound were rounded and well healed.

Whilst the existence of human skeletons with such trauma clearly tells us something about the nature of violence in a given time it also leaves the unanswered question of how representative such evidence is? Small numbers of individuals with shocking injuries don't in themselves tell us how frequent such acts might have been and so we are no wiser as to whether violence and conflict were common occurrences, or in fact very unusual events in most people's lives. Attempting to consider all the excavated Early Medieval burials from Europe (or even just England) could easily fill a book the size of this one and would warrant a great deal more space than the current chapter could offer. However, one technique for getting around such an issue is by sampling, i.e. considering a random section of the total number of human remains available to us in order to draw inferences about this overall 'population'. With regard to the Early Medieval period, a study aimed at addressing such a question by looking at a sample of human remains from south-western Germany by Jochen Weber and Alfred Czarnetzki (respectively a neurosurgeon and an anthropologist) produced interesting results.[29] Here 304 adult individuals were selected at random from a wider sample of over a thousand burials from four sites in a region approximating to modern Bavaria. Among this sample dating from the sixth to the eighth century, thirty-three people (just under 11 per cent) were found to have head injuries consistent with blows from weapons. Eight of these (just over a quarter) showed no signs of healing, all of which were straight-edged wounds consistent with bladed weapons. The other three-quarters lived for a while at least, to tell the tale of how they had been injured with a mix of blunt and sharp force injuries showing rounded edges where the bone had remodelled during the healing process. Some individuals had more than one head injury, so there were in fact forty-five injuries in total, two-thirds of which were located on the left side of the head, consistent with face-to-face assaults by right-handed assailants. Three individuals also showed signs of surgical treatment in the form of circular sections of bone that had been cut away at the location of the injury. As suggested for the Bronze Age examples mentioned in Chapter 7, such an operation appears to have been a practical (and effective) means of treating head injuries in the past and shouldn't just be dismissed simply as a piece of ritual or magic engaged in by people who lacked modern understanding. This region of Germany was occupied in this period by the people known as the Alemanni. On one hand then this study would appear to show that violence was a frequent occurrence over time among this group, but of course this then raises a further question of the extent to which the Alemanni are representative of groups living in other parts of the continent. There are obviously limits to how far any such comparisons can be taken, but as part of a larger population of peoples occupying north-west Europe and sharing features of a broad Germanic language and culture, the picture provided by the Alemanni can reasonably be suggested to give us a general picture of the situation among other Germanic peoples across this region, including those who had crossed the North Sea to settle in Britain. Further west in Ireland over 140 Early Medieval cemeteries have so far been excavated, with weapon injuries found on burials among approximately 13 per cent of such burial grounds.[30] Again this would suggest that the swords, shields and other martial equipment that commonly occur in graves during this period were not simply for show and it is likely that few people would go through life without seeing such items used in anger.

Chapter 11

'The True Son of Gentle Blood': The High Middle Ages to the Renaissance

The period that stretched from the High Middle Ages to the Renaissance[1] in Europe is a time characterized by increasing formality and an ever-growing obsession with accepted etiquette. Society became increasingly hierarchical and organized by more complex social structures as time wore on. The idea of an agreed set of formalized rules governing all aspects of behaviour even extended into the conduct of conflict, both between factions and individuals. This is not to say that life became gentler on the wider stage, as a further defining feature of Medieval Europe was endemic warfare, both across the continent and exported to the eastern Mediterranean and the Holy Lands of the Levant. Violence during this period is frequently seen as the preserve of an elite class of mounted martial artists (knights), ostensibly affording each other a specific set of courtesies in the process according to a formalized set of accepted rules (chivalry). In this regard the period is characterized by apparent contradictions, however, in that according to their own rhetoric this purportedly belligerent warrior class went to considerable lengths not to kill each other. A knight, realizing defeat was imminent, had the option to yield and give himself up for ransom, whilst the degree and quality of armour worn by the upper classes meant that a well-armoured man could be reasonably secure in facing a much larger number of unarmoured opponents.[2] Written and artistic sources concerning the subject of war are abundant from this time, constituting the most common non-religious subject matter for such. However, such sources also come with limitations in that written documents concentrate almost exclusively on the upper class, whilst artistic representations depict the common soldiery only as bit-part players – the supporting cast in the background behind the supposedly important actors, the nobility. Meanwhile a further group of actors is all but invisible in such sources, the group who were at greatest risk during times of war were non-combatants as the principal objective in many acts of war were to despoil an enemy's lands and kill the peasants that farmed them. Here then the study of human remains offers an opportunity to develop a different and more representative picture of the nature of Medieval warfare, particularly as it was experienced by the majority of participants, the common people, whilst also perhaps clarifying some of the apparent contradictions in the world view of those at the top of society.

'Great Tumult and Clash of Arms':[3] Medieval Conflict and Evidence from the Skeleton

Given the frequent nature of war in the Medieval period it is actually rather surprising that relatively few examples of Medieval battle casualties have so far been identified from their skeletal remains. A partial reason for this may be that large-scale open battles were actually less frequent in Medieval warfare than is commonly believed. Instead, the majority of operations by Medieval fighting forces focused on raiding the countryside and laying siege to settlements and fortresses. Those killed in such actions may have commonly been buried in churchyards, rather than battlefield mass graves, and so may be dispersed and effectively hidden among the general populations contained within Medieval cemeteries. In this regard it is worth noting that weapon injuries – often occurring in small numbers – are certainly not infrequent among Medieval graveyard assemblages, where they are otherwise difficult to interpret. Multiple individuals with weapon injuries, placed in a single collective grave, are easily recognized as the likely victims of a single event, such as a battle or massacre – as illustrated elsewhere throughout this book. However, in cases where those killed in such an occurrence were buried separately, it may still be possible to make suggestions as to whether the injured individuals likely died in one or more related episodes. An example of the latter is provided by a dozen burials dating from the same phase at the Medieval cemetery of St Andrew's, Fishergate, York. Here twelve adult males were found to display various weapon-related injuries including blade wounds and projectile injuries caused by arrows or crossbow bolts. Eight of these men were buried in pairs, with such double graves absent from the rest of the cemetery. Seven of the twelve had arrow or crossbow injuries, whilst several also had healed weapon injuries indicating previous involvement in violent incidents and suggesting these men were professional fighters who had seen action before. The twelve weapon-injured men were all buried in a part of the cemetery dating from the late eleventh century and have been suggested by Chris Daniell of York Archaeological Trust[4] to have likely died in a single event. The city of York, as with England in general, had a turbulent history in the later eleventh century and there is no shortage of possible events to which these men's deaths might be attributed. Daniell suggested the nearby Battle of

Fulford[5] which took place in 1066 shortly before the Battles of Stamford Bridge and Hastings in the same year. This is certainly possible, although other events following the Norman Conquest may be equally likely candidates, such as the 'Harrying of the North' where William I's forces are variously alleged to have carried out systematic destruction of land, property and people in parts of northern England and specifically Yorkshire in order to put down resistance that sprang up after the conquest.[6]

Arguably the most important and influential investigation of Medieval weapon injuries undertaken to date was conducted during the late 1990s by a team from Bradford University following a chance discovery during building works near the Yorkshire village of Towton.[7] Unlike the Fishergate burials and unusually for this period, this find comprised a group of at least sixty-one individuals[8] buried together in a communal grave pit, dated archaeologically to the late fifteenth century. Damage to the skulls interpreted as weapon injuries was apparent from the outset, whilst analysis of the assemblage showed all the individuals recovered to be male, with the majority aged between 20 and 45, and so clearly differing from the more varied pattern that would be expected if this were a plague burial. More detailed examination of the remains following careful reconstruction of the skulls revealed copious signs of trauma consistent with brutal assaults throughout the whole assemblage. It was clear that the grave related to a battle event for which an obvious candidate presented itself in the Battle of Towton, known to have been fought nearby on 29 March 1461. This event was one of the largest engagements that took place during the decades-long struggle for the English throne between the noble houses of Lancaster and York, that has since become known as the Wars of the Roses.[9] In this regard the Towton mass grave presented an unprecedented opportunity. Here was a chance for the first time to apply modern methods to investigate aspects of a named Medieval English battle directly through the remains of some of those who participated, rather than through the incomplete, biased and ultimately untestable claims surviving in what those living at the time had chosen to write down.

Very few objects were recovered from the grave, suggesting those buried within had been stripped at least of anything of value before they were buried. This might indicate that they had been buried by the enemy rather than those on their own side, but such suggestions are not easy to test and rely on assumptions about how we think Medieval people 'might' have behaved. However, the most striking aspect of the Towton assemblage was simply the sheer number of wounds these men had suffered. The Bradford team were able to sufficiently reconstruct twenty-eight of the skulls for detailed analysis, twenty-seven of which had unhealed weapon injuries. In total a staggering 113 wounds were apparent with the injured crania displaying between one and thirteen separate injuries, averaging to 4.2 each. These had been inflicted with a variety of implements including sharp and blunt weapons as well as a number of penetrating wounds to the vault of the skull caused by a further assortment of different-shaped objects. These included square punctures of differing sizes, as well as rounded holes and one that had been caused by an object with a diamond-shaped profile. The former are likely to have been caused by a mixture of differing spiked weapons such as poleaxes, warhammers and so on, as well as some projectiles including the different kinds of arrowhead in use at this time. whilst the diamond-shaped wound may have most likely been produced by a sword tip. The brutal assaults that caused these wounds were brought further into focus in that the majority of skulls displayed damage caused by more than one weapon type. The Towton men had been hacked and clubbed to death by multiple opponents, with many of the puncture wounds in particular probably representing a *coup de grâce* as they lay incapacitated on the ground. Such an image is a far cry from the romantic image of Medieval combat as a courteous affair governed by ideals of fair treatment and chivalry. However, this may again underline the point that written sources tend to concern themselves only with the upper classes whilst remaining silent in regard to the rest of society.

The patterning of the injuries at Towton also provided an opportunity to ask questions about the type of protective gear these men might have been wearing and the relationship between offensive and defensive technology at the time. By the time of the Wars of the Roses the equipment in use by armies represented the result of a centuries-long arms race in which weapons were continually refined and modified in order to keep pace with improvements in armour. The full suits of plate armour that had emerged by the fifteenth century provided considerable protection from both cutting and clubbing weapons, whilst also incorporating clever design features that functioned to deflect arrows. In response, the swords of the period had become sharply tapered in order to deliver more effective thrusts that would take advantage of any gaps in armour, where cutting blows would be likely ineffective. This time is also characterized by a proliferation of diverse polearms as well as composite weapons designed to deliver a combination of crushing and penetrating damage.[10] In this respect the diversity of flanged maces, spiked poleaxes, halberds and warhammers in use by this time can be seen effectively as Medieval 'tin openers', designed primarily to punch through the metal plates now covering the best protected protagonists. Arrows too had undergone improvements with square-profiled armour-piercing heads incorporating four cutting edges able to penetrate even the best armour if the angle of impact was right. As well as head injuries, the Towton mass grave group also displayed injuries to other parts of the body, particularly the forearms and hands indicating these areas lacked armour. However, injuries to the chest region were conspicuously absent, suggesting the men's bodies were better protected. Some individuals had healed weapon injuries, most notably a healed sword cut to the face of one of the oldest men, aged 46–50. Given that these men appeared to be partly armoured and that some had seen combat before, it seems likely that whilst not of knightly rank they were professional soldiers, as opposed to peasant levies drafted in to swell the ranks on a temporary basis.

A further clue to these men's identity may be found in their physical characteristics. When compared with other skeletal samples that have been studied, the Towton men were physically undistinguished from other Medieval males except as regards the bones of the arms and shoulders. Here the Towton men exhibited larger than average proportions that indicate strenuous use of both arms from an early age. However, this over development had also occurred asymmetrically – the left and right arm were affected differently. Here the upper arm and shoulder were more developed on the right side, whilst the elbow region was more developed on the left. Christopher Knüsel[11] has pointed out that two-handed weapons of this period such as the larger late Medieval swords or the various polearms in use (halberds, poleaxes and similar) simply wouldn't have this effect. However, a good candidate that could very well produce such unequal changes is the powerful longbow, which would produce exactly the sort of stresses on the right shoulder in drawing the string, and the left elbow in steadying the bowstave, that would produce the changes seen in the Towton group. The suggestion that these men were archers would also fit the implied level of armour they were equipped with as to use a bow effectively the arms would need to be unencumbered and the vision unobstructed which may explain these men's apparent lack of head protection. Lastly, a particular anomaly in the skeleton further supports this suggestion in that three individuals (9.2 per cent) had the same developmental abnormality in the scapulae (shoulder blades). This condition known as *Os acromiale* occurs when considerable stress is repeatedly put across an individual's upper back at an early age, preventing one of the later developing parts of the scapula from fusing to the rest of the bone. The technique of using the upper back muscles to draw a bow as much as the arms, along with training to use the longbow from as young as six is well attested in Medieval England and the same skeletal defect was also famously observed in individuals suggested to be archers among the crew of the sunken Tudor warship the *Mary Rose*.[12] Archers were of course a standard component of any Medieval army, whose principal function came in the earlier phase of engagement to 'soften up' the enemy before close combat was joined. In this case it would appear a company of archers had later been engaged at close quarters and had come off worse.

A site which bears similarities to Towton was discovered two years earlier near the town of Naestved, on the island of Zealand, Denmark. A sandy ridge known locally as 'Sandbjerget' (Sand Hill) had been the location of several graves discovered in the nineteenth century containing multiple burials, one of which was claimed to contain over thirty skeletons with damage interpreted as weapon injuries. In 1994 a further grave was uncovered containing a large number of skeletons, lying in all directions and in haphazard positions. Sandy soils are notoriously bad for bone preservation and the condition of the remains was very variable, meaning that some were easier to analyse than others. The overall number of individuals originally buried there was difficult to assess, but was estimated to be around sixty. Where sex could be determined all were male, with at least half under 30 but some older men (aged 40–50) also present. The bodies lacked any associated objects or clothing fittings (buckles etc.), suggesting as at Towton that they had been stripped of anything of value before burial. It was clear that between them these men had suffered a great many injuries at or close to the time of their deaths, although the precise number of wounds was difficult to assess due to the poorly preserved and fragmented nature of many bones. The original investigator, Pia Bennike of the University of Copenhagen, noted 185 injuries, 122 to the skull with a further 63 recognized on other parts of the skeleton,[13] although one of my own students, Alexandra Boucherie,[14] has recently re-examined these remains microscopically and revised this figure upwards to a total of 201. All of these were consistent with bladed weapons, most likely swords, although again this picture was complicated by the fact that blunt injuries are more difficult to spot in poorly-preserved bones that have suffered a lot of breakage in the ground. In particular the ribs, spines and pelvic bones were often very fragmented and so the possibility of these individuals having also suffered blunt-force trauma remains an open question.

The presence of so much trauma to the skull would suggest these men lacked head protection. Most skulls displayed at least one injury, with many exhibiting more, up to a maximum of nine separate head wounds. A further point of interest regarding the way these injuries were distributed was that they were spread roughly equally between the left and right side of the head, whilst a large proportion had been struck from behind (Fig. 11.1). As mentioned variously throughout the preceding chapters, whilst individual head injuries sustained in face-to-face combat can occur anywhere on the skull, when they are considered as a group such wounds tend to cluster on the left side of the face and frontal part of the skull vault. The pattern at Sandbjerget therefore implies some other circumstance in which many of these injuries were inflicted rather than one-off 'fair fights' between two combatants. Given the high proportion of blows from behind it seems likely that many were

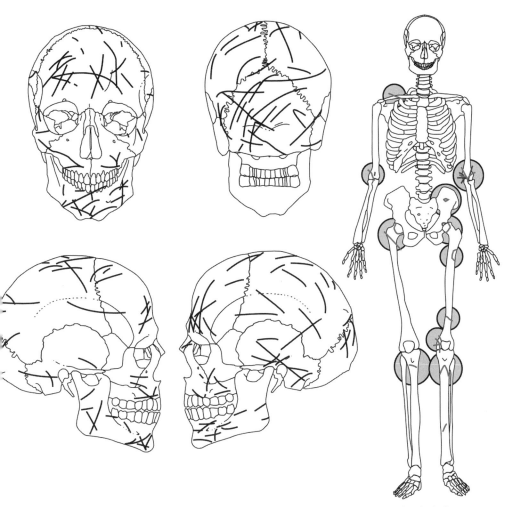

Figure 11.1. The pattern of combined injuries observed amongst the sixty or so individuals from the mass grave at Sandbjerget, Denmark.

struck against men who were running away and so as at Towton, at least a proportion of those in the Sandbjerget mass grave may have been killed in a rout. The large numbers of multiple injuries struck from different directions would be consistent with those individuals being attacked by multiple assailants, again suggesting a grim picture where an initial strike might leave the victim incapacitated after which they were surrounded and finished off by those pursuing them. Another possibility that should be considered is that the assailants could have been mounted. One of the key battlefield functions of cavalry was to pursue routed opponents to ensure they couldn't regroup and return to the fighting. Cavalry armed with swords would firstly be most likely to aim for the head of an opponent on foot and also would likely strike either from behind or from either side as they caught up with the fleeing men, with forehand or back-handed swings equally likely depending upon the position of the target relative to the rider. This latter possibility could explain the equal distribution of right and left-sided head injuries apparent and whilst some of the men at Sandbjerget may have gone down fighting, it appears likely that others had realized this was not their day and were attempting to flee for their lives.

Bones from the grave were radiocarbon dated[15] to between AD 1300 and 1350 which would place them amidst a period of civil war in Denmark, which lasted over a century from the death of King Valdemar Sejr in 1241 until peace was finally imposed by King Valdemar Atterdag in 1367. This time was a period of repeated civil strife during which clashes between opposing factions and localized raiding of settlements occurred frequently, many instances of which may not be mentioned in any surviving source. In consequence it may never be possible to attribute the Sandbjerget mass grave to a named historical event, although one possibility suggested by Pia Bennike took place in 1344 when Naestved was besieged by Valdemar Atterdag. A subsequent question would be whether these men were professional soldiers or local people who had banded together or been mustered by their local lord for their collective defence? The apparent lack of helmets might suggest the latter, along with the absence of healed injuries suggesting that unlike the men buried at Towton these individuals had not seen action before and so their 'day jobs' may have been very different.

'Off the Radar': Seeing what isn't there …

When trying to make sense of archaeological material it is always important to think not just about what the evidence includes but equally what is missing from it. When a 'site' is investigated the project director has to decide where to set the limits of the area to be uncovered. Excavation trenches have to start and end somewhere and can only ever provide a window on to a small part of a landscape from which we might then hope to make inferences about a wider area. Similarly, with human remains we can only ever recover a sample of the population who actually lived in a given area during a particular period. Some will have moved away and been buried elsewhere, some graves may have been cut through and damaged by later graves, some may have been damaged by ploughing or building work and finally only part of a burial ground might fall within the area designated for excavation. In this respect the 'sample' we might have to examine is in fact a 'sample of a sample of a sample' (etc.) of the actual past population.[16] Mass graves relating to past battles as found at Towton and Sandbjerget are subject to a further selection issue that has parallels with a question faced in a much more recent conflict. The Second World War saw all manner of innovations regarding the way wars are fought, the best-known of which tend to be new technologies that then went on to change the world in other ways such as radar, the V2 rocket, the atomic bomb and the digital computer. A less well-known but equally far-reaching innovation at this time was the use of teams of mathematicians, particularly by the US and British governments, to help make better strategic decisions, giving birth to a field of inquiry now known as Operational Research. Such teams often arrived at conclusions that seemed quite counter-intuitive, as the academics involved tended to start by questioning the basic assumptions surrounding a given problem. One example of such was a question given to Abraham Wald, an Austro-Hungarian statistician who had emigrated to the USA to escape anti-Semitic persecution by the Nazis. In order to reduce the numbers of aircraft being shot down on bombing missions it was intended to fit the planes with additional armour. However, to do so would increase the planes' weight, reducing manoeuvrability and increasing fuel consumption, so only selected parts of an aircraft could be reinforced in this way. Wald was therefore asked to advise on which areas of a plane to strengthen in order to maximize the chances of the aircraft surviving contact with the enemy. When Wald began collating data on the location of bullet holes in planes that had returned from bombing missions it was assumed that he was doing so in order to determine where they were most likely to be shot. He therefore provoked a degree of surprise when he advised that the areas that should be reinforced were the sections on which he had observed the least damage. Wald had in fact realized that the planes he was gathering data from were a 'biased sample' in that the group that was available for him to observe only included planes that had survived. When they were shot they had been hit in areas that didn't prevent the aircraft from making it home. The sections of plane where bullet holes appeared to be less common were in fact critical points where the planes couldn't afford to be damaged, those that had been shot in these areas simply never came back.[17] Returning to those killed in Medieval battles, a point that should be remembered when interpreting such assemblages is that they are effectively the same as Wald's sample of bombers in reverse. Those buried in such graves are the people whose armour failed them, whilst those who were better protected survived to be buried elsewhere (hopefully) many years later.

Dad's Army 1361? The Battle of Visby

A group of burials that raises just such issues was uncovered during the early decades of the twentieth century outside the walls of the Medieval city of Visby on the Swedish Island of Gottland. Here a total of five mass burials were discovered at various times. The first was destroyed in 1811 during building work when human bones thought to have battle wounds were uncovered. However, a century later three of the four remaining graves were excavated, with two smaller scale excavations in 1905 and 1912 then followed by a larger project spanning three years (1928–30) directed by the Swedish Medieval archaeologist Bengt Thordemann.[18] These projects were significant undertakings due to the large numbers buried in these features. In total Thordemann estimated the three excavated graves to have possibly contained 1,185 individuals, with the number rising to over 1,500 if the grave destroyed in 1811 and the unexcavated fifth grave contained similar numbers relative to the size of the pits. Unlike at Towton and Sandbjerget the Visby graves contained a large quantity of objects, particularly in the form of fragments of armour that were easily dated by their style and which together placed the events surrounding the burials in the mid-fourteenth century. The Visby graves are associated more conclusively with Valdemar Atterdag (the Danish king who may have been responsible for the mass grave at Sandbjerget), as the city was assaulted by an invading Danish army in the summer of 1361 in one of the best-known episodes of Scandinavian Medieval history. Having been initially defeated shortly after the Danes landed, a defending force made up mainly of local peasants and the male citizens of Visby made a stand in what may have seemed a strongly defensive position outside the city walls. Very little is known about the course of the battle except that the civilian defenders were decisively defeated with contemporary claims that around 2,000 were killed.

A written source from the time describes the defenders as 'unarmed and unaccustomed to battle', although Thordemann pointed out that unarmed in this sense is likely to have simply meant poorly equipped. He concluded that the mass graves principally contained the bodies of the civilian defenders, as much of the armour recovered was antiquated and obsolete by the fourteenth century, suggesting an image of old equipment that hadn't seen service for many years being 'hastily patched up and donned'. Unlike the mass grave at Towton many of those buried at Visby were still wearing their armour, with 185 skulls still wearing chainmail coifs (Fig. 11.2). However, this may perhaps have related more to the state of the bodies at the time they were buried than any particular respect for the dead. Following the fall of the city it is likely there were few able-bodied male citizens available to bury those killed in the fighting and given their numbers the bodies may have lain unburied for some time in the summer heat, therefore being in an advanced state of decay and decidedly unpleasant to handle by the time they were placed in the burial pits. The skeletons were examined by Bo Ingelmark, an anatomist from Uppsala University (Sweden) who found a significant proportion of those buried to be of dubious fitness to fight. Whilst a sizeable proportion were older adult males, he also noted various chronic pathological conditions among some of these men that would have limited their physical abilities. These include four cases of curvature of the spine due to long-standing tuberculosis, various badly-healed fractures and copious arthritic changes as well as other conditions that would place a fighting man beyond active service. Again a picture of civilians defending their homes is suggested, where all able bodied men and a good number who would not be classed as able-bodied by modern standards participated in the Gottlanders' last stand.[19]

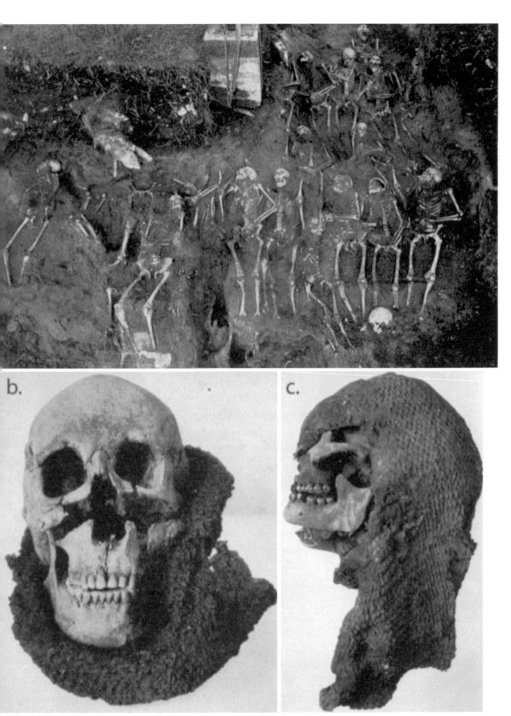

Figure 11.2 (a) One of the three mass graves excavated by Bengt Thordeman outside the Medieval city walls of Visby, on the Swedish Island of Gotland. (b and c) The skulls of two of the excavated individuals, still wearing their chainmail coifs, the damage across the face of individual (b) was attributed by Ingelmark as a single blade injury.

Ingelmark recognized widespread signs of weapon injury, most common of which were sharp-force injuries, although he was unable to determine whether the 456 examples he observed were caused by swords or other weapons such as axes. These cuts varied in severity from scratches on the bone surface to cuts that sliced cleanly through limbs. Examples of the latter included a severed foot, a femur sliced in two and one individual in whom both lower legs had been severed with a single blow. The greatest number of sword cuts noted were seen on the tibia and this may reflect a deliberate tactic of aiming at the (unarmoured) lower legs, causing opponents to drop to the ground where they could then be finished off. Ingelmark also noted 125 cases of head injury which he interpreted as caused by arrows, although many of these may in fact have been the sorts of puncture wounds observed at Towton as having been inflicted by a greater variety of penetrating weapons. In fact almost all of the injuries Ingelmark recorded were either wounds to the head or to the long bones of the limbs. Whilst the Battle of Visby was exactly 100 years earlier than Towton, the antiquated armour found among those killed there dated from even earlier when effective armour for the arms and legs was much less developed, whilst many appeared to have lacked head protection. Had a Medieval Abraham Wald been present to count them it is likely that the distribution of injuries seen among those who survived was considerably different from the pattern among those in the mass grave, and he would have quickly arrived at the conclusion that further developments in armour should concentrate on guarding the limbs and the importance of helmets[20] rather than reinforcing the areas already protected.

Keep Calm and Demand Trial by Combat

As with other periods, it shouldn't be assumed that all signs of violence on Medieval skeletons relate to episodes of conflict between warring factions. Returning to the cemetery at St Andrew's, Fishergate in York, mentioned earlier in the current chapter, in addition to the dozen individuals probably killed in a single event in the eleventh century, further burials of adult males with weapon injuries continued to be interred over the following centuries. This group of 'High Medieval' burials differed from the eleventh-century group in several respects. Rather than clustered around a particular date these seventeen further weapon injured-men spanned dates throughout the twelfth century running up to the late thirteenth or early fourteenth. They were buried singly, rather than in double graves as seen among the earlier group, and lacked projectile injuries with all but one injured by hand-to-hand weapons rather than arrows or crossbow bolts. Despite having died at widely-dispersed intervals, these men display intriguing similarities regarding the manner of their deaths. Most had multiple injuries with up to six wounds to the face and head, but also to other body areas including sword cuts to the ribs, spine, scapulae (shoulder blades) and bones of the legs. Two individuals also had blade injuries to their neck vertebrae consistent with attempts at decapitation. One of these men was also buried with his head to the east, the opposite orientation to the standard Christian burial position which places the head to the west, ready to face Jerusalem at the Day of Judgement. Taken together this combination of decapitation and unusual burial orientation might suggest this man to be an executed criminal. However, a further unusual aspect of this High Medieval group with weapon injuries is that they were buried in prominent locations inside the church. These parts of the church building (including the Chapter House, Nave and Tower Crossing) were normally reserved for prominent individuals of high standing within the community and certainly not where a convicted criminal could expect to be laid to rest.

In discussing the group Chris Daniell[21] has suggested several possible explanations for these unusual burials. These include the possibility that some form of long-running feud had taken place in which the rich patrons of the church had been involved, with the injured men representing those who had come off badly in repeated confrontations over time. On one hand this is arguably possible, although it would take quite a bit of special pleading to link all seventeen slain individuals to a single long-running dispute lasting up to two centuries and for which there is no written record. Daniell's second suggestion was that the church might have functioned as a Medieval version of a specialist trauma centre offering dedicated help to those with battle injuries. Again, whilst this is plausible on one hand, the severity of many of these men's injuries would have placed them clearly beyond medical help well before they could have been brought to the church as they would have died within minutes of receiving their wounds. Daniell's third suggestion may be the most plausible – that these individuals had in fact been killed in Trials by Combat. This explanation would account for the general features of these burials much more convincingly. The multiple injuries these men had suffered were on the one hand consistent with combat wounds, but on the other were considerably in excess of what was needed to kill an opponent in battle. The repeated sword blows to different parts of the body suggest firstly that feelings were running high between the combatants whilst also imply an audience of some kind witnessing the event. The mutilation and decapitations, along with the unusual orientation in the grave, are indeed more like a judicial punishment but the burial in prestigious parts of the church would be consistent with trial by battle in that these were presumably high-born individuals who had chosen this fate as even if they lost it would permit them to die with honour rather than undergo the ignominy of public execution. The

The Man from Hulton Abbey

The Middle Ages are well known as a time when state-administered justice was commonly very public and at times very cruel. Possibly the most striking physical evidence recognized to date for the brutal and inhumane nature of some Medieval punishments was brought to wider attention in 2006 with the analysis of the fragmented bones of a man originally uncovered in the 1970s during the excavation of a relatively minor Cistercian monastery in Staffordshire (Hulton Abbey). These skeletal remains had previously been recognized to display damage inflicted with sharp implements that was assumed to indicate death in battle, but careful re-analysis by Mary Lewis of Reading University[22] has since revealed a very different picture. The man was assessed as a mature adult, although less could be said about him than might be expected due to an unusual pattern of preservation in terms of which bones were present. All the bones of the hands and feet were missing, along with the sternum (breastbone), left radius, the greater part of the left femur and the skull, while the ribs were very fragmented. Few archaeological skeletons are perfectly preserved and when bones have not survived or are missed by those excavating them it is usually the smaller bones (especially of the hands and feet) that are absent. The Hulton Abbey skeleton was therefore rather odd in that the missing bones were a mixture of smaller and larger, more robust parts of the skeleton that imply something else was going on in addition to the normal processes of decay. Lewis' detailed examination revealed numerous chops and incisions into the man's bones which were quite inconsistent with the kinds of injuries normally associated with armed combat (Fig. 11.3). The third cervical (neck) vertebra had been sliced through and the man had been decapitated with cuts in three different planes, indicating this had taken more than one attempt. Further down the neck there was a pointed section of damage to the seventh neck vertebra suggesting he had been stabbed in the throat. A similar defect in his second lumbar vertebra (the lower back) was consistent with the man also being stabbed in the abdomen. Other damage to the spine was particularly unusual in that the central part of his spine had been vertically cut through in two places, whilst the first lumbar vertebra had been cut in the opposite plane, horizontally across the body. Together these cuts would have the effect of dividing the body into quarters. Other cuts to the bones of the shoulder and hip joints indicated further dismemberment of the body, whilst cuts across the forearm bones indicated that the man's hands had in fact been severed. Several of the cutmarks indicate the use of a fine sharp blade, whilst the overall character of this systematic dismemberment implies careful and arguably skilled work rather than any sort of frenzied attack. A possibility worth considering is that this treatment had been carried out after the man's death, perhaps to render his body easier to transport for burial if he had died a long distance from his intended resting place. Such treatments are documented where the bodies of nobles killed in battle were dismembered and boiled with selected parts, particularly the heart, being preserved and brought back to their relatives.[23] In the case from Hulton Abbey, Mary Lewis has argued that this seems unlikely as it would not explain the

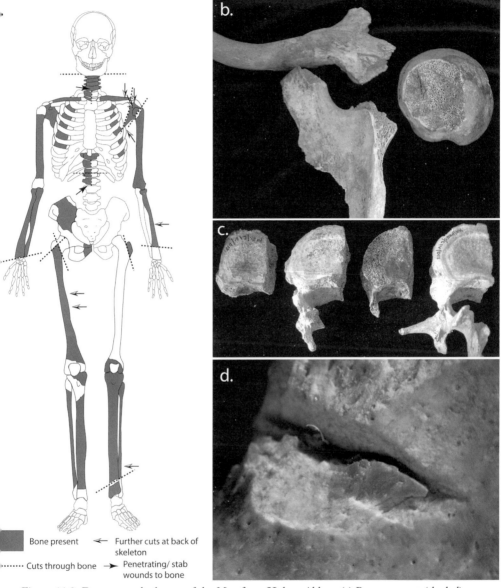

Figure 11.3. Damage to the bones of the Man from Hulton Abbey. (a) Bones present (shaded) plus locations of sharp-force trauma. (b) Bones of the left shoulder with cuts to the clavicle, scapula and head of the humerus. (c) Vertebrae from the central part of the spine, these have been systematically sawn through in a manner normally seen in animal butchery. (d) Close-up of blade wound to the left clavicle. (Photographs courtesy of Mary Lewis)

cuts splitting the individual bones of his spine in half which would be entirely unnecessary if all that was intended was to break the body down into more portable sections.

Instead then, it would seem that this man had been subject to a highly ritualized form of killing which Lewis has pointed out closely resembles written accounts of the punishments recorded for treason in Medieval England. The form of execution popularly known as being 'hanged, drawn and quartered' should really be termed 'drawn, hanged and quartered' as the first part refers to being drawn (or rather dragged) through the streets to the gallows tied behind a horse. By the late thirteen century this treatment was elaborated on the order of Edward I in specific cases of 'high treason' – plotting the death of the king – to involve only partially hanging or strangling the victim, who was then taken down from the gallows and disembowelled with their intestines burned in front of them. The condemned individual was then beheaded and their body cut into quarters to be dispatched to prominent locations throughout the country for display as a warning to others. Medieval justice was often a highly theatrical affair and like much of life in the period involved a high degree of symbolism. In this case the message intended was that the crime of high treason was so heinous as to warrant being 'killed' multiple times, with each form of 'death' relating to a different aspect of the crime. Edward I is commonly seen through modern eyes as a particularly ruthless king. His invasions of Wales and Scotland, which were followed by the imposition of heavy tax burdens, prompted several rebellions.[24] These uprisings then provoked vigorous responses from the English with the leaders becoming some of the best-known victims to be made examples by this particularly inhuman punishment in order to discourage further resistance, including the Welsh prince Dafyd ap Gruffudd in 1283 and the Scottish patriot William Wallace in 1305.

The most important point which the bones of the man from Hulton Abbey illustrate is that such treatments really were carried out as described and are not the product of the biases of Medieval authors or exaggeration by Hollywood screenwriters. A question this then raises with regard to this particular individual is who was this man? Lewis makes a convincing argument that the most likely candidate is Sir Hugh Despenser the Younger, an initially minor nobleman who climbed steadily through the social ranks through a combination of marriage, political intrigue and treachery and a close friendship, rumoured to be a sexual relationship, with King Edward II. Following the collapse of Edward's regime when the King was forced to abdicate by his wife Queen Isabella and her ally Roger Mortimer, both the younger Despenser and his father were brought to trial in 1326. The elder Hugh Despenser was hanged at Bristol whilst his son was hanged, drawn and quartered at Hereford while Mortimer and Isabella watched (Fig. 11.4). The man from Hulton Abbey is the right age, Despenser was around his late thirties when he died, whilst radiocarbon dating places his death most likely in the thirteenth to fourteenth centuries.[25] Hulton Abbey was located on land owned by Hugh Audley, Despenser's brother-in-law, whilst further support was provided in an account of

Figure 11.4. The execution of Hugh Despenser the Younger, from a manuscript of Froissart's *Chronicles of the Hundred Years War*. (Bibliotheque Nationale de France, MS Fr. 2643, folio 11r)

Despenser's wife being permitted to recover some of his bones for burial at the family estate at Tewkesbury Abbey. Interestingly the parts she is said to have had returned to her were his head, thigh bone and parts of his spine which Mary Lewis has noted were 'the very bones that are missing (from the Hulton Abbey skeleton)'.[26]

apparent contradictions in the treatment of these men would also appear similar to the pattern of injuries and 'execution' style burial of the Early Medieval burial at Maiden Castle suggested to be a victim of trial by battle (see Chapter 10). Chris Daniell has also noted that by the later Middle Ages such treatment of accused individuals was only offered to aristocratic individuals, rather than free-born commoners as in earlier times, which would again explain the prominent positions of their burials in parts of the church usually reserved for the 'great and the good'. A further point of interest regarding these men is that unlike the eleventh-century burials with weapon injuries thought to have been killed in a single event, the later group did not exhibit healed injuries from earlier combats. This may suggest that this latter group were not seasoned veterans or professional fighters, which raises the question of whether such lack of experience may have been an important factor in the outcome of the combats that killed them.

The era of the High to Late Middle Ages is characterized by a wealth of written and artistic evidence that provides greater depth and clarity to our understanding of this time than any previous period. In this respect it is reasonable to ask whether the evidence provided by human skeletons really tells us anything we didn't already know about Medieval violence? The current chapter has shown that in fact direct examination of the remains of those literally at the sharp end of such hostilities can not only demonstrate the accuracy of written sources that might otherwise be questioned, but also provide entirely new information on events and participants which were never recorded. The severity of many of the wounds apparent in the human remains excavated at Towton, Visby and Sandbjerget underline the highly effective nature of the weapons of the period. The weapons in use at the time of Towton in particular represent the high point of millennia of development of both hand-to-hand and (mechanical) missile technologies as well as protective gear to resist them. The treatments meted out to fallen individuals differ starkly from the chivalrous ideals of fair treatment and giving quarter to vanquished foes. As to what this means, the brutal injuries inflicted by multiple attackers on the men from the Towton mass grave could be taken as evidence that the 'courteous' treatment of defeated enemies only ever existed among the knightly class. A few years ago this is where this argument might have ended, but the discovery in 2012 of the skeleton of a man in his mid-thirties with a deformed spine buried beneath what was by then a car park but which had once been a central location at the site of Greyfriars Friary Church in Leicester, has since added further detail to what is known about the way wars were conducted at this time. A great deal has been written elsewhere regarding the bones of the man now identified as Richard III, the last English King to die in battle (killed at Bosworth, 22 August 1485),[27] but irrespective of any other questions this find might answer, the injuries apparent on this man's bones make it clear that high birth gave no exemption from the sorts of treatment suffered by the common folk at Towton and Sandbjerget. Eleven separate injuries had left signs in Richard's skeleton, nine of which were to his face and head, delivered with different weapons, again consistent with multiple attackers.[28] A series of slicing injuries to the skull were delivered with one or more sharp, heavy-bladed weapons, whilst a penetrating injury to the skull base may have been inflicted either with a sword tip, or the spike atop a composite weapon such as a poleaxe or halberd. Richard also had a combination of slicing and penetrating wounds to his head and face with a further stab wound incising one of his ribs consistent with one or more thin, sharp blades too delicate to be swords and more consistent with daggers. The head injuries indicate that Richard was not wearing a helmet at the time they were received. Whilst this could have been knocked or pulled off, the full plate armour he would have worn would have protected him from the stab wound to his chest and this was interpreted by the investigating team from Leicester University as evidence that some of the wounds were likely delivered after death with the body having been stripped at least of its armour. The final injury noted was a deep penetrating stab wound apparent on the pelvic bones indicating Richard had been stabbed in the right buttock with a thin dagger-like blade: again this would have been impossible while his armour was in place.

On the one hand the fact that Richard III's remains demonstrate similar treatment to that received by the men excavated at Towton, in terms of devastating wounds inflicted by multiple individuals, raises the possibility that such behaviour should be seen as representative of Medieval warfare in general. On the other hand, however, this conflict came very late, quite literally at the close of the Medieval period and was also a protracted civil war in which a great many personal enmities and local vendettas had developed. For example, an ongoing feud existed between the Percys and the Nevilles,[29] two prominent northern English families who were both present at Towton, where it is also claimed that a specific order of 'no quarter' was given – i.e. that no prisoners were to be taken.[30] The treatment given to Richard's body, which appears to have been stabbed by multiple individuals after he had died (slung naked across a horse according to near-contemporary sources[31]) implies a thoroughly hated enemy. Whilst the devastating wounds seen on the dead of Sandjerget and Visby are no less brutal, they do seem to have been more practical in terms of simply cutting down enemies who had the tenacity to resist an invading force intent on plunder, rather than characterized by the bitterness implied at Towton and in the skeleton from Greyfriars. In this respect the treatment given to King Richard's body after he had been killed in battle may have more in common with the examples of violent treatment of offenders apparent in the suggested Trial by Combat victims at Fishergate and the mutilated man from Hulton Abbey. In regard to these examples it would appear that violence had not only developed in terms of the technology it was inflicted with but also as regards how it was used ideologically. Here it would seem that the point at which later Medieval society really 'turned up the volume' in dealing out violent treatment was when it was carried out in front of an audience in the service of the state. The dismemberment of the apparently noble individuals buried at prominent points in St Andrew's Church, the excessive treatment of the man identified as Hugh Despenser the Younger and the deliberate desecration of Richard III's corpse, all demonstrate that the body had become a kind of battle ground in itself with violence now very much a political tool to be used by those in power to literally cut people out of history.

Chapter 12

The Shock of the New:
The Changing Face of Violence

The massed conflicts engaged in by increasingly professionalized standing armies that have characterized wars between nation states over the last five centuries need no introduction. However, until quite recently few contributions had been made to the understanding of such conflicts by the study of human remains. In fact the study of events of any kind that took place during recent centuries using archaeological evidence is still a relatively new concept. This is illustrated by a debate that took place at the time when the journal *Medieval Archaeology* was first published in 1957. One suggested name for the journal was simply *Post Roman Archaeology* as at that time all archaeological interest in anything after the Romans stopped with the Medieval period, beyond which study of the past was regarded solely as the domain of historians. More recent decades have seen a considerable amount of 'catching up' in this area with changes in research questions and also the way archaeology is managed in Britain leading to an ever growing number of 'post-Medieval' digs. One result of this change is that the remains of people who lived through the last five centuries have been encountered in ever-growing numbers with attendant insights into all manner of aspects of health, living conditions and events they experienced, some of which involved acts of hostility varying from violence between individuals up to the level of wars between states.

Up Close and Personal: Violence at Close Quarters

The advances in firearms technology that occurred throughout the early modern period[1] transformed the conduct of warfare. The kind of massed battles that took place during the Middle Ages have often been characterized as not unlike a rugby scrum, with limited potential for strategic manoeuvre once the two sides had engaged in close combat. The relative quality of armour and weapons, the extent of prior fighting experience and sheer weight of numbers then became the greatest deciding factors. The shift to the co-ordinated use of muskets by massed ranks of professional infantry, fighting at a distance, brought a new emphasis on formalized manoeuvring, where the side with the most perceptive officers, the most coherent command structure and the best-disciplined troops was now at a considerable advantage. The importance of weapons intended for use at close quarters then gradually diminished over time. This period saw a simultaneous decline in the relevance of cavalry, with the inability of Napoleon's repeated massed cavalry charges to break the British infantry squares at Waterloo perhaps the most prominent sign that the days of mounted troops as a significant battlefield force were ending. Although bayonets evolved steadily from the seventeenth century onwards and remain part of the infantryman's equipment today, their actual use had become comparatively rare by the later eighteenth century as hand-to-hand fighting declined in importance.[2] Where bayonets were employed their usefulness rested largely on their psychological effect in causing an enemy force to panic and retreat at the sight of a massed charge with such weapons fixed, rather than on their actual potential to inflict wounds. In reality the bayonet was often a weapon of last resort, or one suited to unusual circumstances where the formal tactics of massed line engagements weren't possible.

An example of the latter was investigated by a team overseen by Megan Brickley[3] from McMaster University, Canada in a project focusing on the War of 1812, fought between Britain and the USA between 1812 and 1814. The Battle of Stoney Creek took place in southern Ontario where around 700 British infantry mounted a surprise attack on a considerably larger US force, in the hours before dawn on 6 June 1813. According to contemporary accounts casualties on both sides were relatively low. However, the element of surprise and confusion inflicted on the invaders coupled with the capture of the American cannons and their two most senior officers prompted the Americans to retreat, resulting in a considerable strategic victory for the British. The majority of the dead were buried in a mass grave close to the site of the attack. In 1998–9 the grave was rediscovered and a large quantity of disarticulated and fragmented bones were recovered.[4] A dozen years later these bones were brought out from the monument in which they had been placed, for analysis by the McMaster team to coincide with the bicentenary of the conflict. The assemblage was comprised of 2,701 bone fragments assessed to be from a minimum of twenty-four individuals. Amongst the various observations that emerged from this project were repeated examples of apparent sharp-force injuries to fragments of bone. Thirty-eight rib fragments and six from other parts of the skeleton, including a fibula, displayed nicks and notches that might have been caused by edged weapons. To investigate these further, Professor Brickley and colleagues ran a series of experiments using replicas of the kinds of edged weapons in use by the two sides during the War of 1812. The type of bayonets of the period were effectively an offset, socketed spike with a tri-angular profile, whilst officers carried swords.

The 1796 model British officer's sword had developed from the slender small-swords carried by eighteenth-century gentlemen for self-defence in civilian settings. Whilst these fencing swords might work well against a single opponent who was similarly armed, many field officers found them insufficient for the decidedly ungentlemanly task of hand-to-hand fighting in battlefield conditions when it occurred, and of limited use against cavalry. Consequently, many chose to equip themselves with tools that were more suited to the job by purchasing cavalry sabres.[5] These heavy blades, designed for chopping rather than thrusting, were considerably more robust and felt to be of more use in a mass engagement. The habit of soldiers to modify or replace the equipment they are given as standard issue is as old as regular armies and when such a change becomes too widespread, army authorities are eventually obliged to decide whether to ban the respective non-regulation kit or give in and simply adopt it as standard. In this case the British army opted for the latter with the introduction of the 1803 model infantry officer's sabre, which was effectively a modified version of the cavalry sabres of the time.

Returning to the Stoney Creek assemblage, the experiments conducted by Brickley and colleagues used a combination of deer and lamb long bones to simulate the bones of the human lower leg, with pigs' ribs used to investigate the possible cuts seen on human ribs. The remains had been disturbed whilst buried and possibly hit by agricultural implements such as spades and ploughshares which might account for some of the damage observed. The experimental results suggested that fourteen of the thirty-eight rib fragments had likely been damaged by sharp implements around the time of the individuals' deaths, with the profile of the cuts into the edges of the bone most resembling that of the socket bayonet. A deep v-shaped cut on the fibula fragment didn't fit this profile but rather resembled cuts made on the animal limb bones with a replica cavalry sabre, which sliced through the tibia and cut into the fibula of the test sample. These results fitted well with written accounts of the battle which cite the use of bayonets by both sides. The battle took place in the dark, in confused and chaotic circumstances where neither side was organized into formal battle lines. In this respect it is unsurprising that swords and bayonets were brought into play, as the orderly musket fire that normally characterized engagements of this period was simply not possible with no organized ranks of soldiers to fire at – or to fire from.

'The Whites of Their Eyes': Powder and Shot

There is a common perception that pre-modern firearms were rather ineffective, and in several regards such opinions are well based in fact. The earliest handguns had a tendency to explode and injure the person using them, matchlock guns carried the inherent health and safety risk of trying to manipulate a

The Waddon Skull: A Mystery (Partly) Solved?

Whilst careful study of skeletal remains can provide sometimes quite detailed information regarding the occurrence of acts of violence in the past, such analyses commonly give rise to as many questions as they answer. The 'Waddon Skull' is a human cranium that has been in the care of Dorset County Museum, Dorchester, since some time in the mid-nineteenth century. The cranium lacks the mandible (lower jaw) and has no teeth in place, but is otherwise very well preserved and shows no signs of ever having been buried. The features of the 'skull' indicate a young adult male. Most strikingly the skull displays multiple sharp-force injuries with no signs of healing. These cuts are well defined, with sharp margins and flat, polished surfaces indicating the bone had the properties that would be expected in a living person when the cuts were made (Fig. 12.1). Whilst the precise cause of death cannot be assessed with certainty from skeletal remains, and we cannot know whether there were injuries elsewhere on the body, the man certainly didn't survive these wounds. In fact the cranium has six wounds, consistent with having been struck with a thin, straight, sharp-bladed implement, most likely a sword. Three of these injuries cut through the full thickness of the skull vault, whilst the remainder occurred at oblique angles, causing slivers of bone to break away from the outer layer of solid bone only. Three of these wounds intersect with each other. Where this occurs it is possible to tell the order in which they were inflicted as when a cut or fracture intersects with an existing break in the bone it will either stop at that point, or deviate in its course slightly, indicating that the other injury must have happened first. Four wounds were struck to the top of the man's head, with a further two to the back of his skull.

It is always possible to make more than one suggestion regarding the mechanism by which an injury was inflicted and I am always wary of reconstructions that claim an assault could only have happened in one particular circumstance. For example, a blow to the left side of the face might most likely indicate a face-to-face opponent using their right hand, but could alternatively have been inflicted by a mounted assailant with a back-handed swing from beside the victim's left. In the case of the Waddon Skull a possible set of circumstances is suggested by the positioning of the wounds. Five of the strokes to the head are roughly parallel to each other, running diagonally from left to right across the top of the head, with the sixth angled about 30 degrees closer to the mid-line of the skull. These suggest the attacker to have struck repeatedly from a single position to the victim's left. Rather than standing opposite, facing the victim, the position of the injuries on the top of the head suggest the attacker to have been striking from above. A possible explanation for this is that the victim might have fallen to his knees at the time these head wounds were inflicted, having already received injuries elsewhere on the body which we cannot now detect. These terrible wounds to the head would have likely then caused the victim to slump forwards after losing consciousness, which may explain the final two sword cuts to the very back of the head.

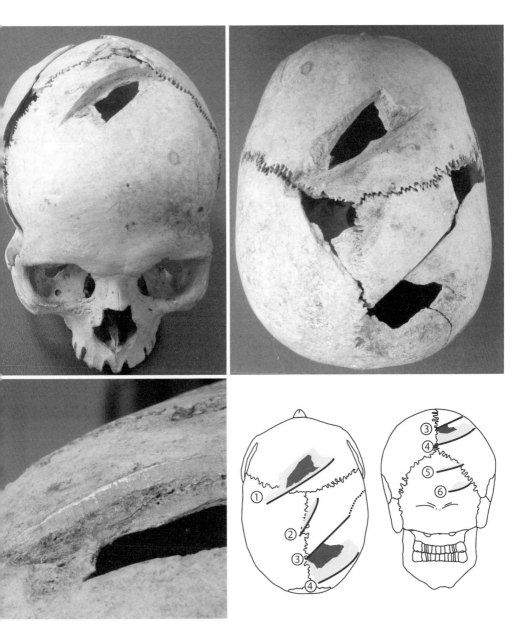

Figure 12.1. The Waddon House cranium, displaying six sword cuts. These blade wounds are roughly parallel and appear to have been inflicted sequentially as this man collapsed forwards.

In the case of most archaeological examples of violence, this point is where this rather grim account would end, with an idea of a shocking assault having occurred but no further information available to us to try to make sense of it. However, in the case of the Waddon Skull some interesting details have survived in local folklore that may shed at least a little light on who this man may have been. The Waddon Skull is in fact one of two 'skulls', or rather crania, now curated at the County

Museum, both of which have similar stories attached. The two crania are claimed to have been kept in the houses of two wealthy South Dorset families,[6] each has a similar story attached that they are the skull of a 'black servant' who returned from the West Indies with the master of the house, and lastly both were alleged to scream if removed from their respective resting places. Ignoring this latter part of these stories, it would appear that some time in the past a single thread had become mixed up between the two, although whether these stories contain any truth about either 'skull' is unknown. The stories differ in that the individual represented by the Waddon Skull was claimed to have been killed by his employer, who mistook him for an intruder when the servant came into his room at night. The multiple deep sword cuts to the man's head are consistent with a sustained and frenzied attack. The story that this was prompted by confusing a household member for a burglar has echoes of a recent celebrity trial that suggest a modern jury would be unlikely to believe it. Whatever the actual motivation for this man's killing, some interesting points have emerged from a recent re-analysis of the skull conducted by Alistair Byford-Bates.[7] Firstly when measurements taken from the skull were run through a piece of software designed to assess the ancestral population from which an individual originates,[8] the result obtained indicated surprisingly that the skull's measurements were most similar to populations from southern Africa. Secondly, a radiocarbon date obtained from a sample of the bone dated this man to the latter half of the seventeenth century.[9] A last point of interest in relation to the story is that Azariah Pinney, the owner of Bettiscombe Manor, near Beaminster, Dorset, during the period covered by the radiocarbon result, was convicted of treason for taking part in the Monmouth Rebellion and sentenced to death at Dorchester in 1685. However, Mr Pinney appears to have had friends at court who arranged for his sentence to be commuted to a period of transportation to the West Indies. After a few years' labour on a sugar plantation Azariah appears to have gained his freedom and gone on to purchase a plantation of his own, along with a number of slaves, before later returning to Britain.[10] Given this seemingly unlikely convergence of circumstances, whereby the owner of one of the houses to which the stories of the skulls are attached had indeed been to the West Indies and acquired servants of African ancestry, with one of the skulls now in the County Museum returning both a radiocarbon date consistent with the story and also indicating African ancestry, it would seem that the legend attached to one of the skulls might have some basis in truth after all. However, the precise truth as to why this man suffered such a violent death will probably always remain an open question.

container of gunpowder in one hand and a piece of burning string in the other, wheel-lock guns were so expensive that only the richest could afford them, whilst flintlocks often simply failed to go off. The invention of percussion caps improved this situation although the problem of progressive 'fouling' as the inside of the barrel became caked with unburned powder persisted, whilst early breech-loading rifles such as the Martini-Henry (made famous in accounts of the Anglo-Zulu wars) were prone to fail due to rapid overheating with continued use. Further to this before the introduction of rifling, small arms and artillery lacked both range and accuracy. The Brown Bess musket, the staple small arm of the British army throughout the eighteenth century, had an effective range of just 75 yards (46m), whilst its more accurate contemporary – the Baker Rifle of Waterloo fame – became inaccurate at ranges greater than 100 yards (91m).[11] When considered together with their slow rate of fire in comparison to the bows and arrows that muskets replaced, all these limitations raise the question of why such weapons were ever adopted at all?

The answer to this question lies in their effectiveness when a target was actually struck. Examples of bullet wounds recognized in human skeletons dating from the seventeenth to the nineteenth century tend to involve discrete rounded holes in the skull, confirmed to be bullet entry wounds by the kind of 'internal bevelling' and possibly also 'radiating fractures' described in Chapter 2 (Fig. 12.2). Such ballistic injuries to other parts of the skeleton have rarely been identified to date in archaeological remains. However, this is more likely due to such wounds being less characteristic in other parts of the skeleton and consequently much less likely to be recognized as a gunshot wound. For example, a musket ball smashing through ribs and spine might well produce a high level of fragmentation in these areas, but to distinguish such damage from post-mortem breakage in the ground might then be very challenging and so may well be missed if such bones were excavated centuries later.

When asking questions as to what patterns of damage a particular mechanism of injury might cause in the skeleton, anthropologists have several options open to them. The first of these is modern medical literature published by clinical doctors treating such injuries in living patients. In principle

Figure 12.2. Gunshot wound in cranial bone (the left parietal) of a male individual from the cemetery of St Augustine the Less, Bristol. This burial was not precisely dated, but may be from the seventeenth century. This rounded defect, with a secondary fracture radiating from the point of impact and a bevelled margin on the interior surface, also illustrates the large calibre of black-powder firearms.

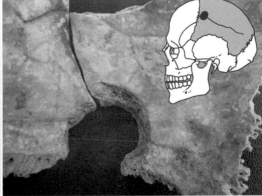

such material might sound like a highly useful prospect, but the reality is often different. When writing books and articles on traumatic injuries the doctors involved are aiming at an audience of other doctors whose sole intention is to save the life and limb of the patient. Such articles on gunshot wounds or similar catastrophic injuries tend to assume the diagnosis is fairly obvious and instead concentrate on how best to treat the patient rather than how to spot the problem. When a patient arrives in an emergency department bleeding profusely from a 9mm hole in their skull or abdomen there is no need to directly examine their bones in order to find the injury. Instead a more useful avenue is offered by published accounts of less-fortunate victims of violence in the form of modern forensic cases. Books and articles of this kind are commonly very helpful for those analysing the remains of past people as they are based on 'known' occurrences where we have a generally secure idea of what has happened to the victim. Where such works cover events that still occur in the modern world, such as stabbings or blows from a blunt object, such forensic pathological literature can be very useful. However, should an anthropologist wish to ask questions concerning a means of injury that is difficult to observe in the modern world such as the effects of weapons that went out of use centuries ago, modern forensic cases have less to offer. In such instances the best option available to the anthropologist is to 'recreate' such injuries so they can be observed directly, through experimentation.

On one hand the idea of setting up experiments to test the effects of obsolete weapons that haven't seen use in living memory sounds relatively straightforward. One simply obtains a suitably authentic working replica of the weapon to be tested and then shoots/swings it (etc.) at a relevant target. However, this then raises the question of what constitutes a 'relevant target'? The question under investigation looks at the 'wounding potential' of a given weapon when used against human beings. Consequently, any experimental target needs to be reasonably similar to the aspect of the human body being tested. In the case of the long bones of the limbs, various animal bones work well as substitutes for human arm and leg bones as illustrated by the Stoney Creek project. Replicating other parts of the human body can present more of a challenge. Having run various experiments of this kind in the past, I have been faced with this question on a number of occasions. Black-powder firearms are among the weapon types my students and I have been involved in testing, initially to investigate the kind of head injuries they could cause. As discussed in Chapter 5, areas of flat bone in larger animals can work really quite well as substitutes for the human cranium and so these were used in the initial stages of this project. Shooting cattle scapulae (shoulder blades), in this case with a replica 1861 black-powder carbine, worked well for exploring the overall size and shape of the bullet holes produced. However, a further effect seen in gunshot wounds to the head is the kind of complex skull fractures (radiating and concentric fractures) that form away from the point of impact (see Chapter 2). Whilst such fracture patterns are caused by modern high-velocity rifle bullets which travel faster than the speed of sound, propelled by tremendous energies, there has been a degree of debate as to whether the same kinds of damage would be caused by old-fashioned black-powder weapons where the projectile is propelled considerably more slowly. When such fractures are caused they occur essentially because the skull is a (more or less) closed sphere, filled with fluid and soft tissues. When a bullet is suddenly propelled into this space a vast amount of kinetic energy is released along with it, which causes a shockwave to travel outwards through the contents of the skull. With nowhere to go within this confined cavity, this rapid release of energy causes the skull to crack, producing the additional fractures. The issue this raises for anyone wishing to run such an experiment is that simply simulating the bone is not enough. Shooting a clean, dry animal skull for example simply won't produce the same pattern of breakage, as the brain, blood vessels and associated fluids are not there for the bullet's energy to travel through.

The answer to this problem might seem to be to simply shoot 'fleshed' animal heads. However, apart from any ethical questions this might raise, this option then leads to the question of which species of animal to use? Due to our large brains no other mammal species has a skull shaped quite like ours. The skulls of four-legged animals are really quite different in terms of both shape and strength, for example pig skulls are around three times the thickness of human skulls at the front of the head, and so any patterns of breakage couldn't be directly compared to gunshots in human skulls. Instead an option that has become available in recent years is a form of 'synthetic bone' made of a brittle type of plastic with similar strength and thickness to human bone. Originally invented for training orthopaedic surgeons (to avoid the need to practice on living patients) this material has more recently been found useful in simulating the skull for ballistic tests. Here, by using simple spheres of the synthetic bone as substitute skulls, every target is the same and so any differences in the damage produced by different weapons must be a product of differences in the bullet type and velocity etc. As for then adding synthetic 'brains' to such targets, again a handy 'off-the-shelf' product exists in the form of specially formulated 'ballistic gelatine', this is gelatine constituted to have the same density as human soft tissue. This material is used as the standard substitute for soft tissue in tests of firearms and behaves very similarly in terms of the way the energy from a bullet travels through it to form permanent and temporary cavities (see Chapter 2).

Having previously experimented with firing modern high-velocity hunting rifles at these kind of synthetic 'skulls' we were expecting the black-powder musket to cause damage that was similar, but less dramatic. But in fact the opposite was true. The effect of the 1861 replica was truly devastating, not only punching larger bullet holes through the simulated bone but also causing very extensive fracturing that literally blew the spheres apart.[12] The amount of damage caused to soft tissues and the extensive area affected would be equally catastrophic for anyone struck in the chest or abdomen by such a projectile. A similarly shocking pattern of damage was produced when this gun was fired at cattle long bones which are both thicker and stronger than human limb bones (Fig. 12.3). On seeing the extent of the damage produced it was clear as to why so many accounts of casualties in the early modern period refer to those injured as either being beyond medical help or as inevitably losing limbs. A large component of the destructive power of these weapons lies simply in the form of projectile they were firing. Modern bullets tend to be considerably smaller and lighter than those of earlier times, commonly weighing less than 10 grams, whereas black-powder musket balls commonly weighed up to 30 grams. The balls fired by black-powder weapons also differed from more complex modern constructions in being simple balls (or later cones) of solid lead. Such lumps of soft lead are highly prone to deforming when they strike a target, and especially if they strike a hard object such as bone. Consequently, the amount of damage wrought upon soft tissues as such bullets travel through is even greater. Coupled with the ability of musket balls to penetrate armour,[13] rendering such gear rapidly obsolete, and the fact that a new recruit could be taught to load and fire a musket within weeks, it is in fact entirely understandable why firearms were adopted in such large measure. The issue of limited accuracy was overcome by having large numbers of men firing synchronized volleys in the same general direction, although even if these weapons had been more accurate the clouds of smoke they produced often rendered the targets impossible to see. Whilst the muskets of the seventeenth to the nineteenth centuries were superseded by weapons that had fewer limitations, the ability to inflict damage when a target was actually hit wasn't one of them. In fact, having seen the destruction they can produce, if I was unlucky enough to be struck by a bullet I would rather be shot with a modern gun than with a black-powder firearm.

Figure 12.3. Exploring black-powder technology. (a) Replica 1861 carbine, shown here strapped to a cradle for experimental use at fixed angles. (b) Minié balls: these large solid lead projectiles came into general use from the 1850s and were designed to expand and grip the rifling, giving better stability and greater velocity. (c) 'Forensic' spheres made of brittle plastic designed to simulate the human skull. (d and e) Bullet holes produced in spheres filled with gelatin, displaying similar qualities to cranial gunshot wounds in real bone. (f) A cattle tibia shot during the experiments, the devastating damage done to this large, solid bone indicates the catastrophic level of damage such firearms would inflict on the thinner, lighter limb bones of a human.

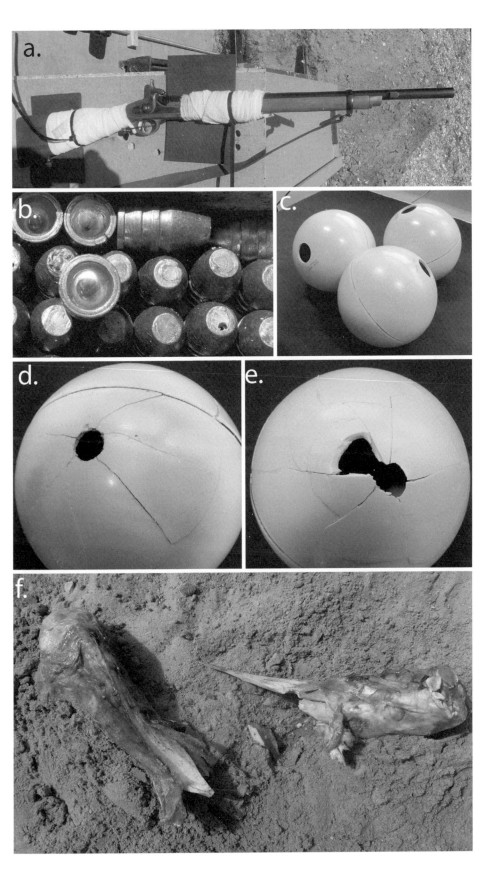

'Here I leave my Second Leg and the Forty-Second Foot': The Effects of Artillery

A further type of ballistic injury of which even fewer examples in skeletal remains are known is the damage wrought by pre-modern artillery. Whilst the principle developments in gunpowder artillery between the fourteenth and seventeenth centuries were focused on the use of cannon as siege weapons and in naval warfare, large guns were also used directly against soldiers in the field from the beginning of this period.[14] Sources of information regarding the effects of such weapons on human targets are almost exclusively confined to contemporary written accounts. Mentions of traumatic amputations where individuals had whole limbs taken off or were even decapitated by cannonballs appear repeatedly among such sources, such as the account of Sergeant Talbot of the Light Brigade (17th Lancers) who 'had his head carried clean off by a round shot' while his 'headless body kept the saddle ... the lance firmly gripped under the right arm'[15] or the fictional 'Ben Battle' from the poem by Thomas Hood (1799–1845) from which this section's title is taken, for whom a 'cannonball took off his legs, so he laid down his arms'.[16] The usual issues that affect written evidence apply and the extent to which such accounts are accurate has remained unclear. Of course a cannonball would do a great deal of damage to a limb, but whether it would sever it entirely has remained debatable. A rare example among museum collections of human bone known to have been injured in this way is curated at the National Museum of Health and Medicine in Maryland. US Major General Dan Sickles was hit in the right lower leg by a 12lb cannonball at the Battle of Gettysburg (July 1863). Sickles was mounted at the time but surprisingly his horse, although distressed, appears not to have been injured.[17] Sickles received prompt surgical attention and his shattered leg was amputated just above the knee. He recovered well from the operation, shortly after which he donated his leg to the then Army Medical Museum (after which he visited it once a year). Sickles' shattered tibia and fibula remain on display, with the larger fragments wired together in their normal anatomical position. The tibia had been completely smashed and consists of eight or so fragments large enough to wire together, with much of the mid portion of the shaft missing, presumably having been broken into many finer fragments too small to reconstruct (Fig. 12.4). However, all the fracture margins in the surviving bone are straight-edged, linear breaks running at diagonal angles spiralling around the shaft of the bone as would be expected in an injury sustained during life. Such a pattern differs markedly from the jagged-edged, crumbling breaks straight across the shaft, often at right angles that are commonly seen in bones that have broken in the ground due to soil pressure and other physical forces

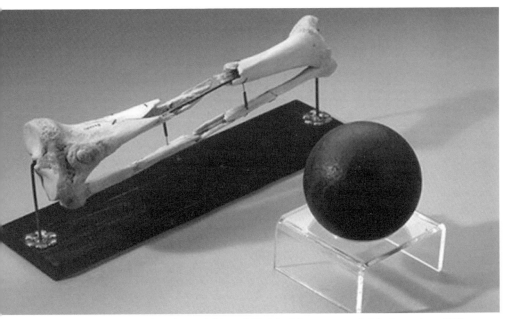

Figure 12.4. The shattered long bones (tibia and fibula) of the amputated right lower leg of US General Dan Sickles, who was struck by a cannonball on 2 July 1863. (Courtesy of the National Museum of Health and Medicine, Silver Spring, Md)

during burial. If Sickles' limb, or that of another casualty who had been similarly injured, was encountered by excavators it should in principle therefore be possible to recognize this extensive pattern of breakage and to conclude that it must have been caused by a tremendous impact to living bone rather than deterioration under the ground or damage occurring after excavation. In modern times a road traffic collision could certainly cause such extensive damage, but in a nineteenth-century battlefield context the prime suspect would be an artillery round.

A second example which illustrates the catastrophic effects of pre-modern artillery on individuals, incidentally curated by the same museum as Sickles' leg, is the skull of a US infantryman who was less fortunate. Whilst standard cannon shot were undoubtedly devastating to individual soldiers, their impact was limited in that a solid cannonball would only kill or injure those directly in its path. Given the time needed to load and fire, in addition to the costs of ammunition, such use of artillery directly against enemy personnel rather than for smashing through ships' hulls or battering down fortress walls was simply inefficient, whilst artillery crews faced with a mass of enemy infantry or cavalry at close quarters would soon be overwhelmed. Since at least the sixteenth century gunners had known that cannon could be packed with small stones, nails or pieces of scrap metal, which would spray outwards from the barrel, effectively turning the cannon into a giant shotgun and a far more effective anti-personnel weapon. From the seventeenth century such ordnance became standardized with mass-produced case shot (also known as canister rounds) consisting of a metal cylinder packed with smaller projectile balls, with the later addition of a cloth bag containing a powder charge attached at one end. Canister rounds were effective at killing infantry at distances of up to 400 yards, a considerably greater range than pre-rifled small arms, with the ammunition dispersing outwards by around 30 feet per 100 yards.[18] In the face of such armaments it required considerable bravery to mount a charge against massed artillery, in which success could not be guaranteed.

Such an assault was attempted on the night of 18 July 1863 when US soldiers charged the strongly-defended Confederate artillery emplacement known as Battery Wagner on Morris Island, South Carolina. This extremely courageous action was unsuccessful, the battery was never taken, although the besieged Confederates abandoned it a few weeks later. Of around 600 men that charged the defences 256 never returned. In 1876 a skull belonging to a man of African ancestry was found near the Confederate positions, most likely from a soldier of the 54th Massachusetts Volunteer Infantry, a unit made up of free African-Americans who famously led the attack. The man's skull bears a large roughly circular opening on the right side, a little way behind the eye socket (Fig. 12.5). This wound is surrounded by secondary and tertiary (radiating and concentric) fractures consistent with having been caused by a large round object travelling with considerable energy. Opposite and in line with this defect on the left side of the skull is a slightly larger and more irregularly shaped wound where the projectile causing it had exited. The soldier was dead before he knew anything had hit him. From the size of the entrance wound (1.18in) Stephen W. Hill, a medical doctor who examined the skull more recently has assessed the man to have been killed by a canister ball from a 12lb field howitzer, two of which were present at Battery Wagner.[19] These guns fired canister rounds packed with 1.17in balls made of iron, from which a rusted fragment was embedded inside the skull.

As with trauma caused by archaic muskets, relatively little is known regarding the effects on the body of pre-modern artillery. For perhaps obvious reasons however, this is an area for which experimentation is even more challenging, although this didn't stop one of my students whose project I oversaw in 2014. After many setbacks largely relating to 'health and safety issues' and problems with obtaining the necessary permissions for live-firing obsolete ordnance, my student Liesbeth Massagé succeeded in enlisting the help of staff at the Royal Armouries National Collection of Artillery at Fort Nelson in Hampshire. In addition to surviving guns from past centuries, the collection also includes several modern replica artillery pieces including a working replica sixteenth-century iron cannon, firing 3lb solid shot. Whilst this had been tested before in live firing for public displays, the gun had understandably not been previously fired at a flesh-and-bone target. In this instance a

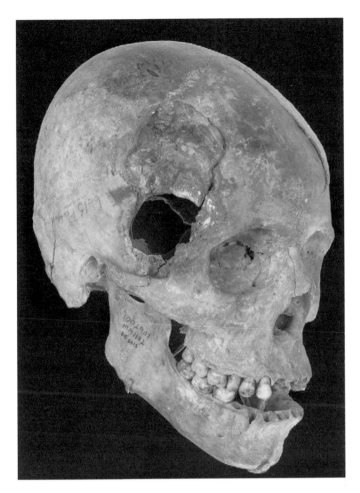

Figure 12.5. Top: Skull of an adult male, likely to have been from the 54th Massachusetts Volunteer Infantry, which lost 256 men attempting to storm a Confederate artillery battery on Morris Island, S. Carolina, in July 1863. The circular 'through and through' injury that killed this man is consistent in size with a canister ball from a 12lb field howitzer. Bottom: Canister round with cutaway illustrating balls packed inside. (Images courtesy of the National Museum of Health and Medicine, Silver Spring, Md)

simple replica such as the synthetic bone spheres used in our musket experiments would not be sufficient to answer the question of how a solid cannonball might affect the body and a more complex target was required. Here the cannon was fired at freshly-killed deer carcasses, acquired as deer were being locally culled (i.e. these animals had been shot already – no deer were harmed for these experiments). The barrel lacked rifling and so the ball exited the gun in a somewhat irregular trajectory and it took a number of attempts to perfect hitting the suspended carcasses even at close range (10m and 15m). This is unsurprising of course as such weapons were never designed to be aimed at individuals but rather closely-packed ranks of troops or objects as large as a ship.

Once we succeeded in striking the target, however, the effects were shocking. Our first successful hit smashed through the deer's ribcage and exited the other side, producing a very large wound with the ball continuing until it embedded itself deep in the earthen bank of the fort (an ideal test location as it is a structure built to withstand far larger cannon shot). The carcasses were examined by CT scanning in order to establish the overall pattern of damage, and this revealed that the ball had not only smashed its way through the bones it had come into contact with, but had also damaged parts of the skeleton it hadn't even touched. It was clear at the time of the experiment that a shock-wave effect had occurred similar to that discussed above in relation to gunshot wounds but on a much larger scale. In this case the majority of the chest and abdominal contents, lungs, gastrointestinal tract and so on, had been blown out of the exit wound and were left hanging out of the body (I have spared the reader photographs of this). In light of this devastating damage it was clear that the indirect fractures visible on the CT scan images had resulted from the same tremendous release of energy through the body cavity, snapping bones that were outside the path taken by the cannonball. Further shots to subsequent carcasses confirmed that this was not a freak occurrence and it was clear that such an artillery shot striking an individual would invariably pass directly through whatever part of the body (and likely the bodies of any others standing behind) that it struck (Fig. 12.6). These results underline and give support to further written accounts such as that of the death of Colonel Chester of the Bengal Army, who was disembowelled when a cannonball struck him and his horse during the Indian Mutiny of 1857. One of his

Figure 12.6. Experimentation with a replica sixteenth-century cannon, firing 3lb solid shot.[20] The middle images show some of the effects on the deer carcasses used as proxies for human targets, with a through-and-through injury to the chest region and a traumatic amputation at the hip. The lower image shows a 3D reconstruction from CT scan data illustrating the extent of damage to the skeleton wrought by the cannon shot (NB: no deer were harmed for these experiments).

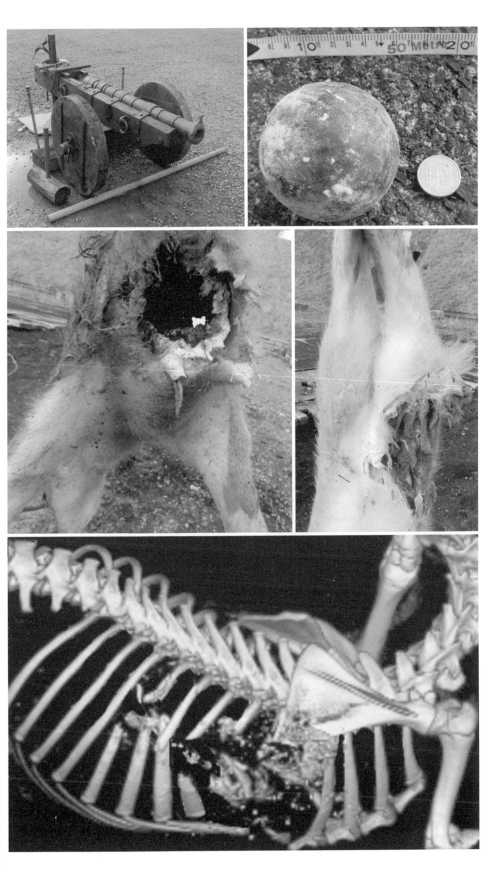

officers, Richard Barter wrote 'how he could speak at all was a puzzle to me for the whole of his stomach lay beside him on the ground as if it had been scooped out of his back, and yet I heard afterwards that he lived a quarter of an hour'.[21] Our final experimental shot struck one of the carcasses at the hip joint, effectively severing the whole leg which remained attached to the body only by a piece of skin. Given that the replica used in this experiment, a three-pounder, was among the smallest artillery pieces in use in recent centuries it would seem there is no reason to doubt the accuracy of contemporary accounts of the damage such pieces did. If anything, many accounts are probably considerably sanitised as the true details were felt too awful to present to the public back at home.

Urban and Domestic Violence

A category of violence that has likely always been with us on one hand but which is likely to have increased with the dawn of the modern age on the other, is acts of aggression committed by individuals against members of their own communities. The great migration of people from the countryside to towns and cities that began and gathered pace in early industrial Britain and continues to play out in the wider world today, occurred ultimately as the promise of regular paid work and housing which might be poor by modern standards but which was often considerably better than that available in the countryside were attractive prospects. However, the pressures exerted on the rapidly growing populations of urban centres also brought new problems of their own. The stresses and difficulties of urban living in eighteenth and nineteenth-century towns and cities are familiar subjects to modern eyes from a wide range of historical and literary accounts. In recent years a further category of evidence has contributed to this picture in the form of the remains of the people who lived through this period.

Up until the 1980s the vast majority of archaeological excavations that took place in Britain were conducted purely as research projects, commonly by university departments and local societies with few sites investigated dating from later than the Middle Ages. The minority of digs that were conducted within towns generally focused on questions regarding the earlier development of settlements such as Medieval Winchester or Roman London. The redevelopment of many British towns and cities between the 1950s and 1970s wrought a great deal of destruction on both the standing and buried remains of urban centres that had survived for centuries in towns such as Worcester and Leicester, with relatively few of what used to be called 'Rescue digs' mounted by volunteers to try and save any of it. But from 1990 the tide turned as British archaeology underwent a quiet revolution with the inclusion of archaeology within the planning laws. From this point onwards building developers were required to fund the costs of excavation of any significant site that stood to be destroyed in the process of development. This change led not only to the formation of large numbers of commercial excavation companies ready to conduct such work, but also to a shift in the emphasis of archaeology in Britain. With the majority of excavations now driven by the building industry the proportion of archaeological sites excavated in towns and cities shifted accordingly. A further shift that accompanied this was a growing number of cemetery excavations. From London to Birmingham to Manchester, commercial pressures on building land resulted in the redevelopment of large numbers of disused burial grounds leading to the excavation of a skeletal population never before seen in such numbers. For the first time the remains of thousands of individuals who lived between the beginning of the Industrial Revolution and the end of the Victorian Age became available for scientific study. The majority of such work has focused on the disease loads borne by such populations, the diets and living conditions they experienced and the differences between rich and poor at this time. However, another aspect of urban life that has been brought to light in this way is evidence for physical assaults.

The church of St Martin's in the Bull Ring stands in the commercial and previously the industrial centre of Birmingham. As part of a major city redevelopment in 2001 the churchyard and the burials it contained were excavated with a view to later reburying them following a period of study. The spaces occupied by the dead in eighteenth and nineteenth-century urban centres tended to be even more densely populated than those occupied by the living, as churchyards that had once served small country parishes were required to accommodate greatly-increased populations with high rates of mortality from diseases associated with overcrowding and poor diets. St Martin's was no exception with 857 burials recovered from an excavated area of around just 150m². Analysis of these remains, most of which dated from between 1750 and 1850, led to a variety of insights regarding health and living conditions.[22] There was also a range of healed injuries that the city's inhabitants had acquired during their lives, most of which likely related to working conditions and occupational risks. However, some were more likely the result of violent altercations.[23]

Of 352 adult skeletons examined in detail 24 had healed fractures consistent with incidents of violence. These included five fractured nasal bones ('broken noses'), two fractured mandibles (the lower jaw), four blunt injuries and one healed sword cut to the vault of the skull and eighteen fractured metacarpals (the bones that make up the back/palm of the hand). In total these twenty-four individuals made up 6.81 per cent of the overall sample, meaning that one person in every fourteen had a violence-related injury

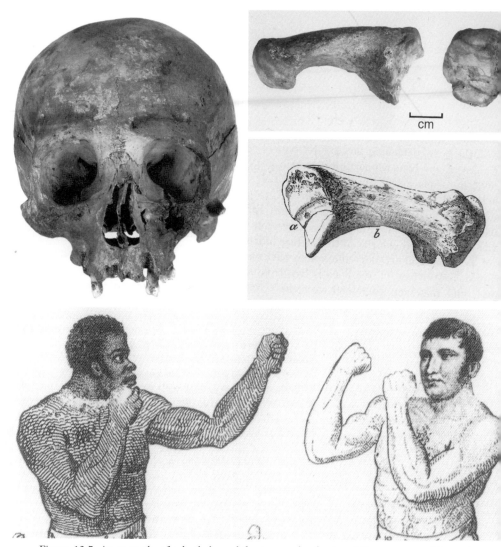

Figure 12.7. An example of a healed nasal fracture and a fractured first metacarpal from the churchyard of St Martin's in the Bull Ring, Birmingham. Both these injuries are consistent with fist-fighting in a style characteristic to boxing, which became the accepted way for men to settle disputes following the rise in popularity of the sport. (bottom image) Contemporary depiction of a boxing match that took place in 1810 between Tom Cribb (right) and Tom Molineaux (left). (Photographs by permission of Birmingham Archaeology)

apparent in their skeleton (Fig. 12.7). Injuries to the vault of the skull have been dealt with at length earlier in this book. Nasal fractures, as mentioned earlier (see Chapter 2), are most commonly caused through deliberate blows to the face, whilst studies of fractures to the mandible show between 50 per cent and 79 per cent to be caused through violence.[24] Among patients attending modern Accident and Emergency departments fractured metacarpals are usually caused in one of two ways, either through a direct blow to the bone such as from a heavy object falling onto the hand or, much more commonly, through the individual striking a solid object (such as a wall or another person) with a clenched fist. This type of injury is therefore associated specifically with punching and is often referred to as a 'boxer's fracture', it is also perhaps unsurprising that such fractures are most commonly seen amongst young adult males. The violence-related injuries at St Martin's were distributed very unequally between the sexes with males making up twenty-two of the twenty-four affected individuals, an even greater imbalance than among modern people. However, as these were healed fractures it wasn't possible to be sure at what point in their lives these injuries had occurred and so whether these breaks were sustained when these people were young, or later in life wasn't clear.

The population of Georgian and Victorian Birmingham is not alone in displaying such injuries. In studying two early twentieth-century skeletal collections from the USA the anthropologist Phillip Walker had previously noticed a high number of nasal fractures.[25] However, when looking at other nineteenth and twentieth-century remains Walker found such injuries to be less common, although other signs of violence were certainly present. To explain this difference Walker suggested that fist-fighting might only have come to prominence as the accepted 'manly' way for males to settle disputes relatively recently. The collections he studied with high numbers of broken noses were from the East Coast of the USA, whilst those without such injuries were from the west of the country. Walker suggested this change might relate to the growing popularity of boxing which took root first in the eastern cities of the US, before it became popular nationally. In this respect he suggested that although there was clearly no shortage of violence in the American West (evidenced by blunt injuries and gunshot wounds) the Hollywood image of the 'fist-fighting cowboy' would appear to be a modern myth. In Britain boxing became popular earlier than in the US, with bare-knuckle fights patronised by prominent members of the aristocracy from the mid-eighteenth century. By the nineteenth century boxing had replaced earlier forms of combat sports that had been popular in Britain such as cudgel-fighting or fighting with quarter staves. Broken noses and 'boxer's fractures' are rare among Medieval populations, whilst Walker also pointed out that if the broken noses he noted were from accidents such as falls then we should see higher rates of them among very mobile groups such as prehistoric hunter-gatherers, but this just isn't the case. These examples therefore underline the important points that firstly acts of violence are not just a 'practical' or a 'biological' action, but rather they are 'culturally specific' i.e. they are heavily influenced by what is considered acceptable and legitimate within a given society. In this case for example, it is likely that the inhabitants of early twentieth-century New York or Victorian London would have found it 'culturally unacceptable' to hit below the belt. Secondly the appearance of such fighting styles coinciding with the rise of boxing also shows that violence is not static within a given society, the concept of what is 'acceptable' can change over time.

Returning to Birmingham, a further point of interest was the distribution of injuries by social class. Whilst the majority of burials at St Martin's were in simple graves dug into the earth, representing the poorer classes, others were interred in expensive brick-lined shafts and vaults, often in costly lead-lined coffins marking them out as wealthier members of society. This division between rich and poor allowed for a range of interesting comparisons, including the relative numbers of injuries among these two groups. When we compared the fracture rates, those buried in earth cut graves had sustained greater numbers of injuries during their lives, 34 per cent of 'poor' people had healed fractures compared to 17 per cent of the better-off individuals. This was suggestive of a picture where the working classes were subject to greater risks of accidents in their working lives. However, this pattern did not apply to violence-related injuries which affected each group at almost exactly the same rate (8 per cent). It would seem then that the notion of resolving disputes through fisticuffs was not confined to the 'lower orders' but rather extended at least to the middle class as well. Birmingham also seems not to have been unusual in this period as similar rates of both broken noses and boxer's fractures have been found among other eighteenth and nineteenth-century cemetery samples from urban settings.[26] However, such levels of violence-related injuries have yet to be seen amongst rural cemeteries from this time, suggesting the pressures of city life may indeed have played a strong part.

Lastly, whilst the majority of signs of violence at St Martin's were present in males, the two women with probable violent injuries, a fractured jaw and a fractured metacarpal, raise interesting questions. As mentioned previously, skeletal trauma generally tells us only who was a victim of violence, whilst leaving us to draw our own conclusions about the perpetrator. How these two women sustained their injuries remains unknown, although other injuries amongst this cemetery that are less specific to particular causes raise further questions. None of the wealthier women had fractured ribs, as opposed to six women from the earth-cut graves.[27] Among these, one individual had five separate rib fractures. Perhaps these occurred in one or more accidents, although such an argument is more difficult to make for a further individual excavated from the cemetery of St Brides, Farringdon Street London. In addition to a broken nose and fractured radius, this woman aged between 35 and 49 had multiple fractures affecting at least ten of her ribs. Some ribs were fractured in up to three places and most ominously were in different stages of healing at the time this woman died.[28] These injuries must have been received at different times and therefore fit a picture of domestic abuse more convincingly than being explicable as the result of any terrible industrial accident. This underlines the point that many other signs of violence in skeletal remains may be either too subtle or too ambiguous to define a clear cause. Blows to the face and injuries to the perpetrators hands are the 'public' signs of violence that we can detect from a society in which such acts were generally accepted between men. However, it is a sobering thought that at the same time many crimes of violence against other members of society that were hidden while the victims were alive, probably remain elusive to anthropologists even when the evidence is preserved in bone long after their deaths.

The period spanning the time from the Middle Ages up to the last century saw the pace of human social change accelerate like never before. As with previous chapters, I have once again settled on particular examples to illustrate a bigger picture that is emerging from the study of human remains from across this period. In some respects the types of injuries people have chosen to inflict on each other have never changed, with trauma caused through hand-to-hand fighting and direct interpersonal assaults still apparent as in any preceding time. Of course we are well aware that at the same time new technologies arose and were progressively refined, aimed at killing ever greater numbers of people at ever greater distances than anything seen before. The evidence such innovations might leave on the human skeleton has only recently become a focus for attention amongst anthropologists with regard to how we might recognize damage to bones caused by lead shot and iron cannonballs. Now that such signatures are becoming better defined, the potential for the remains of those killed in battle to add to our understanding of conflicts in this period is now set to be explored as a previously-neglected component in the still relatively new field of Conflict Archaeology. At the same time that we are now positioned to observe the literal impacts of the wars that built the modern world at the level of individual human beings, the excavation of urban cemeteries that spanned the industrialization of towns and cities allows a more direct view of the effects on human behaviour of the 'pressure cooker' of overcrowding, poor housing and stressful working conditions than was previously possible. Such observations are not just of interest in their own right, but rather as part of the wider consequences of a set of socio-economic conditions that might now have been effectively ended in developed countries but which are still very much in existence elsewhere in the world.

Conclusion

The views of the past that we can piece together from archaeological evidence are far from perfect. They are often fraught with vagueness, inconsistency and missing pieces. The pictures painted by human remains are no exception to this and we are faced with the position of only ever encountering a tiny fraction of any past population through their preserved bones. The interpretations I have presented throughout this book have been made up at the level of individual injuries as represented by breaks, dents and scratches in cases where people didn't survive their wounds and patches of smoothed-over, healed bone in those that did. When viewed individually these examples are often difficult to make sense of and tell us little that is concrete about the time from which they date. However, when considered together in light of what is known from other lines of evidence, these damaged and altered fragments of bone converge in mutual support of each other and develop a voice of their own as a highly important, and arguably the most important single strand of evidence for the existence and nature of hostilities in the past.

In regard to the periods considered here the remains of people who suffered at the hands of others discussed in the preceding chapters not only paint vivid, and often disturbing pictures of the acts human beings have been prepared to perpetrate against each other to achieve their aims, but also reveal important insights regarding the nature of the periods from which they are drawn, and in some cases the nature of human beings in general. The observation that violence both between individuals and groups appears to have occurred frequently, both among our direct ancestors and our evolutionary cousins, is particularly important. The notion of a peaceful prehistory as might be attached to the suggestions of Rousseau is just not sustainable. Acts of violence, including the use of weapons, are in fact older than human beings and certainly older than anatomically-modern humans like ourselves. Secondly, contrary to recent debates, the phenomenon of war as it has existed in recent millennia is unlikely to have appeared fully formed at any single point in time, either recently or far off in the deep past. Such polarized views are a pair of red herrings. The different components of social, economic and biological conditions that have given rise to the kinds of organized, group conflict we call war appeared at very different times over a period spanning millions of years from before humans and chimpanzees diverged as separate species to the time of the development of agriculture. War therefore developed in a series of incremental steps, rather than a sudden explosion of a new kind of behaviour.

Through the increasingly complex social developments that came on the heels of agriculture, acts of violence acquired new kinds of symbolism going into the Bronze Age, becoming almost a kind of language or writing in themselves, used to send particularly strong and presumably unambiguous messages. This point underlines the notion that acts of violence are far from simply practical actions but rather are channelled and given form by the values and expectations of the society in which they are carried out. If violence is conducted in the 'wrong' way then the wrong message will be sent, with all manner of potential consequences for the perpetrator. The evidence apparent for Iron Age hostilities demonstrates a growth in the size of the groups engaging in violence and increasingly suggests a picture of ongoing warfare that has resurrected the notion of warlike times in pre-Roman Europe that had until recently been dismissed. With such a pattern, smaller tribal groups or polities will inevitably become progressively swallowed up to become part of larger entities until something approaching states begin to appear. In this respect violence takes on an albeit unconscious role as an important driver of human social development in itself, which underlines that such behaviour is indeed worth studying after all, rather than simply being dismissed as an unfortunate but ultimately irrelevant aspect of the past that we would rather not think about. Of course none of this is to say that life in any part of prehistory (or any later period for that matter) was always violent all of the time, most people's lives have likely been relatively peaceful and mundane most of the time throughout any given period. Instead it is simply that a version of the past that leaves violence out is just not convincing as a rounded picture of life during a given time.

The skeletal evidence from the Roman period, which was previously rather neglected in the face of the vast wealth of other material surviving from the time, illustrates the extent to which the rise of civilization and the power of the state rested firmly on violence, firstly in taking and maintaining territory, but also on a smaller level in terms of violence, or the threat of it, being a strong component of the glue that held society together. This was particularly the case regarding the subjugation of the 10 per cent of the population (slaves) which powered the 'civilized' world. These latter people have been almost invisible to archaeologists up to now and arguably represent a particular area where further study of human remains has potential to fill a crucial gap which no other evidence can. The stresses and strains that characterize the world of post-Roman Europe and Britain in particular manifested themselves in a variety of violent forms from raiding, to interstate warfare, with violence or the threat of it used repeatedly to try and hold the initially fragile threads of society together. The signs of violence apparent from the High and Later Middle Ages expose the inherent contradictions that increasingly ran through a society which claimed that the upper classes position by right of birth was well deserved as they exposed themselves to risk in protecting the weak. However, in reality the opposite was largely the case with the lower orders at far greater risk of violence from the upper classes than vice-versa. This time is also characterized as one where violence came increasingly to be used in acts of theatre designed to shore up the social order and to tell the stories those in power wanted to be believed. The final chapter has demonstrated how skeletal studies of violence between the Early Modern period and the end of the nineteenth century, which have lagged behind until recently, are now rapidly catching up. This is a period in particular where continued attention to human remains now has great potential to literally flesh out our knowledge of events which are misrepresented or simply neglected by written sources.

I have chosen to bring the coverage of the current book to a close with the nineteenth century, but this is not because of a lack of material which could be included in a subsequent chapter. Recent years have seen varied applications of first archaeological and now anthropological techniques to evidence recovered from conflicts of the twentieth century, with the Great War of 1914–18 receiving particular attention. With regard to this war and also others that came after such as the Spanish Civil War, the attention given to human remains that have been recovered has been aimed at answering very different questions from those applied to earlier periods. Rather than trying to further our understanding of such conflicts as an aim in itself, such investigations have instead been more akin to modern forensic work in aiming to identify the remains of individuals who were denied the formal burials they would otherwise have had. Such work is quite rightly concerned with bringing closure to families who previously regarded their relatives as lost forever, rather than being conducted in order to answer any wider academic question. Investigations of the remains of those killed in more recent events such as the Rwandan genocide or the atrocities committed during the Balkan wars of the 1990s have been carried out with similarly important objectives, the latter also leading to important contributions to several international criminal trials. In consequence I have resisted the temptation to include a twentieth-century chapter, although such a piece will undoubtedly become easier to write in the future as more work is conducted aimed at investigating the events themselves.

Perhaps most importantly, a further category of injury wrought by advancing technology which will be of increasing importance to studies of the evidence left by conflict in the future is trauma to the body caused by explosions. By design weapons that cause explosive blasts are intended to kill or injure multiple individuals and the growing use of both standard and improvised explosive ordnance has meant that more people are injured or killed in modern wars by blast trauma than by bullets.[1] As to how damage to the skeleton wrought by explosions might be recognized, this situation has until very recently been similar to that described for musket balls and cannon in the last chapter, where the only material published covered the medical care of such injuries, rather than how they might be recognized in bone. Efforts have recently been underway to rectify this situation with the work of Marie-Christine Dussault[2] aimed specifically at recognizing blast injuries to the skeleton. Such studies are likely to be of (regrettably) increasing value in the future.

I said in the Introduction that this book comes at an exciting time for this subject. In fact the wider subject of biological anthropology has undergone a similarly exciting time over recent years. Studies of past disease in particular have undergone a transition from considering individual case studies to much larger studies comparing the prevalence and effects of particular diseases across and between populations and also over long periods of time. The study of past violence has now passed the threshold of a similar change with studies beginning to appear that combine the sorts of individual cases and assemblage level investigations presented in this book to form much larger samples that can be used to ask bigger questions about the nature and trajectory of conflict over time. The 2011 book *The Better Angels of our Nature* by the psychologist Stephen Pinker has received a great deal of attention for vigorously claiming that violence amongst human beings has actually been declining for some time and will continue to do so in the future. Pinker's case is well argued and I am strongly inclined to agree with it. He makes good use of historical data, in so far as they are available, to demonstrate that whatever the modern media might tell us to think, the overall proportion of human beings killed in conflict has been in steady decline for centuries. The reasons he suggests for this vary from the rule of law, to the rise of commerce (and more lately globalization) and even the rise of popular literature increasing general levels of empathy. Pinker's work falters however in that prior to about AD 1500 historical data on the numbers killed in wars become increasingly fuzzy and unreliable and his case rests on ever greater levels of conjecture. This is not to say that I think Pinker has got it wrong, but rather that another source of evidence offers a far more useful basis upon which to reach such conclusions – human remains.

The examples given throughout the current book are just that – selected examples used to illustrate the character of the evidence we have for particular periods. For some periods I have cited all or most of the evidence we have such as the Palaeolithic, whilst for others such an all-encompassing approach would have prevented this book from ever being finished. For some periods, such as the Neolithic, we are able to be fairly confident about the overall numbers of individuals showing signs of violence in their skeletons, whilst for others such as the eighteenth century further work is still needed to get to this point. The Neolithic is of particular interest with regard to this thought, however, as the proportions of injured individuals are so high, with repeated studies from throughout Europe consistently finding around 10 per cent of Neolithic people to display a violence-related injury in their bones. Most of these are head injuries with the rest of the skeletons poorly preserved and soft tissue of course absent, and so once again the point is worth making that this figure undoubtedly underestimates the true prevalence. As similar combined studies assessing such prevalences for other periods appear in the years to come, I suspect the rates seen for the Neolithic will not be surpassed and that this period at the dawn of agriculture in fact represents the high-water mark of human violence. Even with the millions killed in the conflicts of the last century (each an individual tragedy) the First and Second World Wars saw the deaths of just 1.4 per cent and 3 per cent of the world's population respectively. The average person during prehistory was far more likely to die at the hands of another human being than at any time since. This is a good note to end on, as although taken together the 'mortal wounds' considered throughout this book might be seen as painting a grim and rather depressing picture of human nature, we certainly have no reason to regard such a picture as unchanging.

Notes

Introduction

1. Various recent publications on this topic have tended to agonize at length over how to define 'violence'. For the purposes of the current book it should simply be taken to mean 'the deliberate infliction of physical harm upon one or more human beings by one or more others'.
2. In fact Rousseau never used the phrase 'Noble Savage', although it has come erroneously to be most closely associated with him. The term originated in a play by John Dryden, *The Conquest of Grenada* (1672), spoken by a Spanish Muslim, and was later to be associated with ideas expressed by a range of writers who were critical of Hobbes including Anthony Ashley-Cooper, the 3rd Earl of Shaftesbury (1671–1713).
3. Hobbes (1651) *Leviathan* Ch. 13. The full quote is that life in the earliest times was characterized as having 'No arts; no letters; no society; and which is worst of all, continual fear, and danger of violent death: and the life of man, solitary, poor, nasty, brutish and short.'
4. Dates are given as BC and AD with use of the former purely on conventional grounds (BCE could equally be substituted). Where radiocarbon dates are given these are listed as years 'cal BC' to denote that this is the calibrated date – i.e. as close as possible to the actual date, rather than an uncalibrated, raw radiocarbon result.
5. For a useful discussion of the varied roles of women in war from prehistory to the present see Grant de Pauw (2000).

Chapter 1. 'I See Dead People': The Human Body as Archaeology

1. Wolff (1892).
2. White *et al.* (2011), 27.
3. Spindler (2013).
4. Schmidt and Symes (2008).
5. Properly called the innominate bones or *os coxae*.
6. Byers (2010).
7. Buikstra and Ubelaker (1994).
8. Ancestry is the more correct anthropological term for what is still commonly referred to as 'race'. In fact the concept of race is a survival from before the twentieth century, incorporating both cultural and biological characteristics that simply does not stand up to scrutiny. Humans do not divide into discrete biological sub-groups: we are a single inter-related species that varies continuously across the world. Instead then, anthropologists use the term 'ancestry' to denote biological (genetic) variation/relatedness and 'ethnicity' to refer to cultural issues and groupings.
9. For further reading some excellent introductory texts covering skeletal pathology are provided by Mays (2010); Ortner (2003); Roberts (2009); Roberts and Manchester (2010); and Waldron (2008).

10. Derry (1913).
11. Wood *et al.* (1992).
12. Thurnam and Davis were themselves applying ideas drawn from earlier researchers particularly the American physician and anatomist Samuel Morton (1799–1851) who has been much criticized for dividing human beings into racial hierarchies based on differences he claimed to have observed in brain size from measuring the internal volume of skulls.
13. Keeley (1996).

Chapter 2. The Fragile Body: Recognizing Injuries to the Skeleton

1. For further explanation of the biomechanics of bone fracturing see Wescott (2013).
2. Each time a person takes a step the force exerted through the hip joint is around three times the person's bodyweight (minus the weight of the respective leg). In fast walking this figure increases to seven times bodyweight (Mullins and Skinner (2007), 164).
3. Redrawn after Fenton *et al.* (2005).
4. First described by the French surgeon René Le Fort (1869–1951) in 1901. Le Fort established that there were three general patterns to midfacial fractures through experimenting by inflicting blunt impacts on the heads of cadavers.
5. Redrawn after Hochban (1997).
6. Brickley and Smith (2006).
7. Bach *et al.* (2001); Brink *et al.* (1998); Kjaerulff *et al.* (1989); Reijnders and Ceelen (2014).
8. Reichs (1998); Wolfe-Steadman (2008); Wedel and Galloway (2013).
9. (a) Winterbourne Kingston, Late Iron Age; (b) skull of one of the Dorset Ridgeway 'Vikings'; (c and d) Danebury, Late Iron Age.
10. See Oakeshott (2000), Chapter 6
12. Fiorato *et al.* (2000), 180.
13. For a detailed account of the events and processes involved in significant head injuries see Bauer and Kuhn (1997).
14. Mild, moderate and severe injuries are also characterized by relative Glasgow Coma Scale (GCS) scores (13–15, 3–12 and 3–8 respectively) (Dennis (2009)). The GCS is a widely-used system for assessing impairment of consciousness and neurological functioning in response to defined stimuli. See: www.glasgowcomascale.org for an explanation of this system.
15. Saoût *et al.* (2011).
16. Boylston (2000), 360 cites forces of between 400 and 935 psi as being needed to induce living human bone covered with soft tissue to fracture, whereas dry bone will break under as little as 40psi.
16. Bill (1862); Also see Smith *et al.* (2007) for further discussion of the proportion of arrow wounds likely to affect bone.

Chapter 3. The Earliest Times: Violence in the Deep Past

1. This situation has recently become more complicated by the discovery of a further species of extinct human, who have been given the name 'Denisovans', currently known only from hand and foot bone fragments and two teeth found in a cave in Denisova in Siberia from which DNA has been extracted that is neither modern human nor Neanderthal. It would appear that the Denisovans also interbred with Neanderthals as well as with another as-yet unidentified lineage of humans whose bones have yet to be discovered (Krause *et al.* (2010)).
2. Coalitionary violence among chimpanzees is in fact more complex and varied than described here and takes several forms from simple incursions into a neighbouring group's

territory, to ambushes of individuals and even silent surprise attacks nicknamed 'commando raids'. See Wrangham (1999) for a more comprehensive account.

3. Prüfer *et al.* (2012).
4. Plummer *et al.* (2009).
5. Wilkins *et al.* (2012).
6. Kingdon *et al.* (2013), 240–244.
7. The fossil gelada bones at Olorgesaillie and Olduvai were those *Theropithecus oswaldi*, one of several extinct gelada species. *T.oswaldi* are regarded as having a common ancestor with modern geladas rather than being ancestral to them, see Shipman *et al.* (1981); Jolly (1972); and Leakey (1993).
8. Various opinions have been put forward as to which species of earlier human is present at *la Sima de Los Huesos* based partly on differing opinions on the date of the assemblage. In 2012 the bones were argued by Chris Stringer to be most likely to be an early form of Neanderthals however analysis of DNA from the bones (Callaway (2013)) shows closer affinities to the Denisovans. It may be that the assemblage represents a third group that could have later interbred with both species.
9. Sala *et al.* (2015).
10. Indriati and Antón (2010).
11. Wu *et al.* (2011).
12. The collection of bone fragments discovered at Feldhoffer Cave in the Neander Valley, Germany, in 1856 was the first find to be recognized as the remains of an earlier form of human dating from the time of the last Ice Age. Earlier finds at Engis, Belgium (1829) and Forbes Quarry, Gibraltar (1848) were not realized to be part of the same species until years later. The Gibraltar skull was recognized as that of a Neanderthal when it was examined by Charles Darwin in 1864, whilst the Engis find was not recognized until 1936.
13. Higham *et al.* (2014).
14. For a more detailed introduction to Neanderthal anatomy see Conroy (2005).
15. The most recent evidence for personal ornamentation among Neanderthals involves the talons and feathers of raptor type birds (Romandini *et al.* (2014), Radovčić *et al.* (2015)), which has influenced the 'Feathered Neanderthal' reconstruction shown in Figure 3.4.
16. Although whether Neanderthals were truly cold-adapted remains a subject of ongoing debate (for example see Noback *et al.* (2016)).
17. Berger and Trinkaus (1995).
18. This is to say that the Neanderthal remains at Krapina cannot have been deposited as articulated bodies but instead made their way into the cave deposits as individual bones. Possible explanations for this include the bones being transferred from a primary location elsewhere where bodies had either been exposed on the ground, subject to primary burial or defleshed and dismembered manually, deposition by scavenging animals, that the rock shelter was the site of a Palaeolithic massacre and/or that the bones represent the material residue of cannibalism.
19. Hutton Estabrook and Frayer (2013).
20. Roper (1969); Keith (1928) and Dart (1953) – all cited in Hutton Estabrook and Frayer (2013).
21. Berger and Trinkaus (1995); Underdown (2006).
22. Kremer *et al.* (2008).
23. Zollikoffer *et al.* (2002).
24. Churchill *et al.* (2009).
25. The *aorta* and *vena cava*.

26. Churchill *et al.* (2009).
27. The notion that Neanderthals were incapable of producing or using thrown projectiles has long been the accepted view in palaeoanthropology, although suggestions have recently been made that this may not always have been the case (Hardy *et al.* (2013)). It should also be noted that Neanderthal technology need not have been static throughout their existence and may have been developing towards greater complexity at the time they became extinct.
28. Trinkaus and Zimmermann (1982).
29. For a detailed account of the changing ways in which Neanderthals have been portrayed over time see Drell (2000).
30. Berger and Trinkaus (1995).
31. Trinkaus (2012) – this article also restates Trinkaus' position to clarify a number of points where people have since misunderstood or misquoted his previous study (Berger and Trinkaus (1995)).
32. There is currently no securely dated evidence for modern *Homo sapiens* in Europe before ~45,000 years BP (Benazzi *et al.* (2011)).
33. Churchill *et al.* (2009).
34. Shea (2003).
35. Green *et al.* (2010); Sankararaman *et al.* (2012).

Chapter 4. Rolling Back the Temporal Frontier: Modern Humans and the Origins of War?

1. A recent re-dating programme by Higham *et al.* (2014) has dated the disappearance of the Neanderthals to no later than 39,260 years cal BP. Until recently the generally-accepted view was that Neanderthals had hung on for possibly as much as 10,000 years after this date. It is of further interest that this updated view brings the demise of the Neanderthals even closer to the appearance of modern *Homo sapiens* in Europe (see Chapter 4, note 32). There is a possible (but somewhat pedantic) caveat in relation to this point with regard to the fossils excavated in 2003 on the Pacific island of Flores (Brown *et al.* (2004)) about which debate continues as to whether these represent a newly-discovered species of hominin that was still in existence until relatively recently or whether these finds were simply a population of small modern humans. On balance it seems the former is actually more likely, although the original Flores skeleton has recently been redated to around 60,000 years ago thus predating the demise of the Neanderthals (Culotta (2016)) although this is ultimately of no consequence with regard to the spread of modern humans into western Asia and Europe and what role this played in the Neanderthals' demise.
2. See Chapter 3, notes 1 and 8.
3. Tattersall (2009).
4. Hoffecker (2009); Tattersall (2009).
5. Mithen (1998).
6. Wild *et al.* (2005).
7. Teschler-Nicola (2006); NB Maria Teschler-Nicola is well experienced in the recognition and interpretation of prehistoric weapon injuries having conducted extensive analysis on the assemblage from the Neolithic massacre site at Asparn Schletz (Teschler-Nicola (2012) – see Chapter 5).
8. Robb and Harris (2013), p. 38.
9. The Qafzeh and Skhul populations were once thought to be transitional between Neanderthals and modern humans, but they have more recently been regarded simply as a more archaic form of early modern human although it is also possible they represent a separate

extinct population that was later superceded by modern humans spreading out of Africa in a later radiation.

10. McCown and Keith (1939), 281.

11. A further issue relating to trauma recognition in the Palaeolithic is the frequently poor state of preservation which presents a particular challenge to distinguishing genuine injuries from damage which occurred long after death, even more so than is usual for archaeological bone. Notably, an example of such in the form of an injury to the left frontal bone was identified on a female individual from the Cro Magnon rock shelter at Les Eyzies in south western France (Brennan (1991), cited by Guilaine and Zammit (2001), 49). These individuals were the first anatomically-modern humans from the Upper Palaeolithic to be recognized archaeologically when they were discovered in 1868. They remain among the earliest modern humans known in north-west Europe dating from 40,000–45,000 years ago, with Cro Magnon previously used for many years as the popular name for anatomically-modern humans. The apparent injury is slit-like, being elliptical and tapered at each end rather than a rounded depression and so might appear to have been caused with a sharp implement, most likely a hafted spear similar to the injuries noted on the St Cesaire Neanderthal and the older man from Sunghir. However, opinion is divided on this issue and it has alternatively been claimed that this defect was in fact caused by a workman's pick in 1868 (Bahn and Vertut (1997), 214). Similarly, what had previously been interpreted as a spear injury piercing the left femoral head and ilium (pelvis) of one of the Skhul individuals (McCown and Keith (1939)) has more recently been identified as damage caused at the time of excavation – again by a pickaxe (Churchill *et al.* (2009)). These examples further iterate the value of re-examining old samples as not only can re-analysis identify evidence that was initially missed, but also inaccurate observations can be rectified. Given the early date of excavation of many of the best known early human fossils, often by less careful standards than today, such re-consideration is highly desirable.

12. Each of these beads has been estimated to take at least 45 minutes to make, meaning that in total the beads covering the Sunghir 1 burial must have taken between 2,000 and 3,000 hours of labour to produce (Trinkaus and Buzhilova (2012)).

13. Trinkaus and Buzhilova (2012) The Sunghir burials have been dated to between *c.*24,000 and *c.*32,000 years cal BP.

14. The 2009 investigators (Trinkaus and Buzhilova (2012)) point out that the object could also have been a flint knife, although this is less likely given the generally small and utilitarian nature of hand-held blades at this time.

15. Guilaine and Zammit (2005), 50; Begouen *et al.* (1922).

16. Lillie (2004); Danilenko (1955).

17. It is not generally possible to determine the sex of children and younger adults from their skeleton as the sexually dimorphic features – those that are expressed differently between the sexes – are not sufficiently developed which was the case for Qafzeh 11.

18. Coqueugniot *et al.* (2014).

19. Dastugue (1981).

20. Coqueugniot *et al.* (2014) assessed the cranial capacity of Qafzeh 11 to be that of a 4–6 year old child and concludes that the injury therefore must have occurred before this age.

21. Coqueugniot (2014).

22. Bechachi *et al.* (1997).

23. The point was lodged in the lateral face of the right ilium between the superior and inferior anterior iliac spines.

24. Dastugue and Lumley (1976) cited in Bechachi *et al.* (1997).

25. Marean, C. (2015) 'The most invasive species of all', *Scientific American* 313 (2), 22–9. Also for a more detailed version of the material on which this article is based see: Brown *et al.* (2012); Marean (2014).
26. Brown (1964).
27. Pinker (2011); Livingstone Smith (2007).
28. Fry (2007); Ferguson (2013).
29. Allen (2015a).
30. Le Blanc (2015).
31. Roscoe (2015).
32. Allen (2015b); Pardoe (2015).
33. Pardoe (2015).
34. Kelly (2000).
35. Wendorf (1968).
36. Friedman (2014).
37. Holliday (2013).
38. Allen (2015a).
39. Le Blanc (2015).

Chapter 5. Out from the Cold: Mesolithic Hostilities?

1. The LGM was between approximately 26,500 and 19,000–20,000 years ago (Clark *et al.* (2009)). Following this the climate underwent a series of fluctuations over the next 10,000 or so years within which warmer, wetter and colder, drier periods are discernible before stabilizing around 11,600 years ago within a much smaller range. The climactic conditions we are familiar with today, have been constant since then, although new shifts driven by human actions are now changing the picture again (Mithen (2003)).
2. The observation that the development of early human societies could be broadly divided into three 'ages' (Stone, Bronze and Iron) was first developed on a scientific basis by the Danish antiquarian Christian Jürgensen Thomsen during the 1820s. This three age system was later elaborated to four ages with John Lubbock's proposal of an 'old' and 'new' Stone Age (Palaeolithic and Neolithic) in his 1865 work *Prehistoric Times*. Seven years later Hodder Westropp suggested a third Stone Age division which he entitled the Mesolithic, although the precise dates and features of this period were initially rather poorly defined. This latter point may explain why Westropp's suggestion met with varying degrees of opposition and it was several decades before it was generally accepted. In so far as the term remains useful it functions as a continuing shorthand for post-glacial/Holocene peoples subsisting by foraging/hunting and gathering. In this respect the term can only denote a period on a local/regional basis as peoples in some regions continued to live 'Mesolithic' ways of life thousands of years after domesticated crops and animals had been adopted in other regions (see Jones (2008), 6–7).
3. Kristian Pedersen cited in Spinney (2008).
4. Péquart *et al.* (1937); Cap-Jédikian (2010).
5. McIntosh (2006), 282.
6. Meiklejohn *et al.* (2005).
7. Cap-Jédikian (2010); 'Sépulture de Teviec Global' by Didier Descouens. Licensed under CC BY-SA 4.0 via Commons – https://commons.wikimedia.org/wiki/File:S per centC3 per centA9pulture_de_Teviec_Global.jpg#/media/File:S per centC3 per centA9pulture_de_Teviec_Global.jpg

8. Although surprising progress has been made in this area, principally by a team led by Vince Gaffney (now of Bradford University) who carried out the impressive task of mapping 23,000 square kilometres of the sunken landscape of Doggerland below the North Sea using seismic survey data originally obtained for geological prospection by the oil industry (see Gaffney *et al.* (2007)).

9. Mithen (2003).

10. Thorpe (2000).

11. Jones (2004), 16.

12. The use of the terms Mesolithic and Neolithic here further illustrate the difficulties of using technological stages as shorthand for chronological periods which in fact overlap. In reality there were no 'Mesolithic' or 'Neolithic' people, but rather simply people pursuing activities which tend to be labelled as characteristic of each period.

13. Papathanasiou (2012).

14. Smits and van der Plicht (2009).

15. Schulting (2013).

16. Péquart *et al.* (1937).

17. Cap-Jédikian (2010).

18. Jackes (2004), Cunha *et al.* (2004).

19. Mithen (2003).

20. Larsson (1993).

21. Frayer (1997), 183.

22. Brinch Petersen *et al.* (1993).

23. Karsten and Knarrström (2003).

24. Roksandic *et al.* (2006).

25. Roksandic *et al.* (2006) present their results and interpretations of assemblages from the right side of the Danube whilst also giving a concise summary of injury frequencies on the opposite side at Schela Cladovei.

26. Not every proposed example has been included on this map, for example I am sceptical about the well-known allegedly infected head injury on the skeleton known as Cheddar Man from Gough's Cave, Somerset, England (Tratman (1975)) which looks more like water erosion in a cave environment to me.

27. Sources for sites shown on map (Fig. 5.2): 1. Newell *et al.* (1979); 2. Newell *et al.* (1979); 3. Jankauskas (2012); 4. Papathanasiou (2012); 5. Brinch Petersen *et al.* (1993); 6. Smits and van der Plicht (2009); 7. Frayer (1997); 8. Newell *et al.* (1979); 9. Roksandic *et al.* (2006); 10. Newell *et al.* (1979); 11. Jackes (2004), Cunha *et al.* (2004); 12. Frayer (1997), Orschiedt (2004); 13. Roksandic *et al.* (2006); 14. Larsson (1993), Mithen (2003); 15. Newell *et al.* (1979); 16. Karsten and Knarrström (2003); 17. Péquart *et al.* (1937); 18. Schulting (2013); 19. Newell *et al.* (1979); 20. Newell *et al.* (1979); 21. Roksandic *et al.* (2006).

28. Judd (2008).

29. Schmidt (1913).

30. Orschiedt (2005).

31. Frayer (1997).

32. Orschiedt (2005).

33. Frayer (1997).

34. Lahr *et al.* (2016).

35. The additional find of the bones of an unborn foetus in the abdomen of one of the females raises the number present to twenty-nine individuals.

36. Champlain's Battle with the Iroquois. This version of image from Parkman (1885).

37. Robb (2008).
38. Otterbein (1979).
39. Baugh (2011).
40. Fenimore-Cooper (1824).
41. Baugh (2011), 261.
42. Hutton Estabrook (2014).

Chapter 6. 'The Children of Cain': Conflict in the Neolithic

1. Sir John Lubbock (1834–1913) differentiated the 'New Stone Age' or Neolithic (Trigger (2006)) on the basis of the appearance of polished stone axes, replacing the chipped and flaked versions of earlier periods. These were produced by abrading stone axe blanks over many working hours by polishing them with sandstones. This not only has the effect of making them aesthetically pleasing but also less susceptible to breakage in use as the grinding away of edges and corners removed points of stress where the axe might shatter. Debate continues as to relative importance of function and practicality as opposed to attractiveness in relation to why such items came to replace earlier lithic technology.
2. Keeley (1996).
3. Carman (2013).
4. Castleden (1987).
5. The skull from Clachaig on the Isle of Arran was recovered from a long stone cairn covered by a turf mound excavated by T. Bryce in 1900. The mound contained disarticulated and broken bones which Bryce assessed to be from at least nine people of various ages and both sexes (Bryce (1902)).
6. Due to the poor general level of preservation of Neolithic skeletal remains which are commonly highly fragmented and with many bones absent (Smith and Brickley (2009)), it simply isn't possible to arrive at meaningful proportions of injuries to other parts of the body.
7. Office for National Statistics (2016) (available at: http://www.ons.gov.uk/ons/taxonomy/index.html?nscl=Crime+and+Justice).
8. See Schulting and Fibiger (2012) for a comprehensive compilation of evidence for violence in Neolithic Europe.
9. Smith and Brickley (2009), 49–51.
10. Chenal *et al.* (2015).
11. Wild *et al.* (2004).
12. Teschler-Nicola (2012).
13. Wahl and Trautmann (2012).
14. Meyer *et al.* (2015).
15. Mercer (1999).
16. Schulting R., speaking at a conference on *Neolithic Violence in a European Perspective* (Oxford University, March 2008).
17. Gamble *et al.* (2014), 196.
18. Such as the views espoused by Fry (2007).
19. Ridley (1993).
20. Teschler-Nicola (2012); Wahl and Trautmann (2012); Meyer *et al.* (2015).
21. Haas (1999).
22. Bonsall *et al.* (2002).
23. Mercer (1999).
24. Gamble *et al.* (2014).

25. Sherratt (1990).
26. Livy, *History of Rome*.
27. Barb (1972) makes a convincing case for the Old Testament reference to Cain killing his brother with 'the jawbone of an ass' being a reference to an early agricultural tool whereby animal lower jaws with teeth still *in situ* used for harvesting grain came to be replaced first by setting flint blades in the bone where the teeth had been and then by copying the form of the bone in wood to produce a composite wooden and stone artefact. He further argues a range of references to similar primitive weapons used by Samson, Hercules and various other Classical and Near Eastern heroes and deities to be part of a single tradition across the region where such a tool is symbolic of an earlier age with such myths serving variously to explain the origins of society as it then existed.

Chapter 7. Cutting-Edge Technology: Violence in Bronze Age Europe

1. This time was also preceded by a period where life essentially followed the same patterns as those of the final part of the Neolithic but where small quantities of metal had come into use and circulation mainly in the form of copper artefacts. Perhaps the best-known example of such is the copper-headed axe carried by the Ice Man, the mummified body of a man who died high in the Alps (Spindler (1994)) radiocarbon dated to have died between 3359 and 3105 BC (calibrated date, 95 per cent C.I.). Smaller numbers of gold items are also known from this period, generally referred to as the Chalcolithic (or 'Copper Stone Age') for which the acknowledgement of a British version of this period has recently grown in acceptance.
2. Harding (2000).
3. Kristiansen and Suchowska-Ducke (2015) give a detailed and comprehensive account of the physical and social reach of trade and exchange networks across Bronze Age Europe using the movement and distribution of swords as an example.
4. Sherratt (1993).
5. Of course whether this is really true is open to debate. For example, the transition to the leaf-shaped arrowheads of the Early Neolithic or the barbed and tanged versions that appeared at the close of the Neolithic have long been speculated specifically to have been weapons of war rather than simply hunting gear put to occasional alternative uses in targeting other people. The concept of a 'material culture of violence' appearing during the Bronze Age, as this is the time when helmets and shields first appeared, is also open to question. Shields made of wood and hide would not survive in most archaeological contexts, whilst there are ethnohistoric accounts of various pre-industrial peoples employing armour made similarly of organic materials (Jones (2004); Allen and Jones (2014) – cover illus.). The idea that the bronze shields that are known from the second millennium BC, such as the well-known Wittenham shield (Needham (1979)), were a completely new innovation rather than a new development on a pre-existing artefact seems particularly untenable. It is likely that the idea of material objects dedicated to violence only appearing after the development of metallurgy has more to do with the vagaries of different aspects of the archaeological record and the way people have chosen to interpret it than reality. But notwithstanding these points, it remains true that the production and circulation of weapons and armour as prestige items was a genuine phenomenon that gathered pace throughout the Bronze Age and whether these were the 'first' items manufactured specifically for conflict is really a moot point.
6. For a comprehensive synthesis of the wider evidence for Bronze Age warfare across Europe see Osgood *et al.* (2010).

7. Robb (1997).
8. Coles (1962).
9. Whilst this point remains essentially correct (there are greater numbers of single burials in Bronze Age contexts and greater proportions of Early Neolithic burials occur multiply), recent studies have shown that the situation is in fact more complicated with single graves occurring during the Neolithic and a broad range of differing burial practices known from throughout the Bronze Age (Brück (2008)). The latter have been noted to include both complete and incomplete bodies, articulated limbs, isolated skulls/crania and multiple as well as single individuals. It now seems likely that a range of different treatments of the dead were practised at different times and places throughout the Bronze Age including cremation, excarnation/exposure, the retention of ancestral bones (*ibid.*) and even mummification (Booth *et al.* (2015); Smith *et al.* (2016)).
10. For examples see: Gilchrist (1999); Lewis (2006); Crawford and Shepherd (2007); Cave and Oxenham (2014); Smith *et al.* (2015).
11. Shepherd and Bruce (1987).
12. The skeletons from Pitdrichie produced radiocarbon ranges of 1780 ($\pm$60) cal BC and 1745 ($\pm$95) cal BC.
13. Shepherd and Bruce (1987) cite various further examples of male Beaker burials with both healed and unhealed injuries. Whilst some of these may derive from accidents, others are clearly violence-related including bladed-weapon injuries, a purportedly severed humerus and defence wounds such as parry fractures.
14. Needham *et al.* (forthcoming).
15. Using stature data from sixty-one Bronze Age males Roberts and Cox (2003), p. 86, arrived at a range of 167–177cm, with a mean of 172cm (5ft 7.7in).
16. See Mays (2010), Chapter 10 for an introduction to bone stable isotope analysis.
17. McKinley (2016).
18. '... About 60 to 80 per cent of the difference in height between individuals is determined by genetic factors, whereas 20 to 40 per cent can be attributed to environmental effects, mainly nutrition' (Lai (2006)).
19. Rundin (1996); Sainero (2003).
20. Barclay and Halpin (1999), 140–1. Interestingly, a further individual excavated at Barrow Hills during earlier fieldwork in the 1940s was described as having three arrowheads in the fill immediately above the skeleton (Williams (1948)). The excavators assumed these to be grave goods and were puzzled by the fact that the arrowheads were not placed together and so thought they had been added at different times. In fact it may be that these points arrived 'in' rather than 'with' the body and may have caused this man's death.
21. See Smith *et al.* (2007, 2011) for further detail.
22. Murphy *et al.* (2003); the arrowhead had in fact been visible on the initial radiographs taken closer to the time of the Ice Man's discovery, although it was understandably not recognized at the time, as this aspect of the respective image wasn't particularly clear and formed only a small part of a great wealth of observations greeting the analysts.
23. Fernández-Crespo (2015).
24. A radiocarbon result obtained from this skeleton dated it to 2170 BC ($\pm$110) (Evans *et al.* (1984)).
25. Evans *et al.* (1984).
26. Keeley (1996), 102.
27. St Sebastian purportedly died around AD 288 having been sentenced to death by the Emperor Diocletian. Despite being repeatedly shot with arrows Sebastian recovered, only

to be later executed by being clubbed to death. There are no contemporary mentions of him and the extent to which the story is based on a real individual is unknown. The earliest written source dates from the fifth century AD – see Barker (2007) for a detailed exploration of the ways he has been depicted and interpreted over time.

28. McKinley *et al.* (2013).
29. See Arnott *et al.* (2003).
30. For example see Novak and Knüsel (1997).
31. Common suggestions regarding the reasons for conducting trepanations include the treatment of headaches and epilepsy in addition to the possibility that such procedures were carried out for entirely ritual reasons rather than being a prehistoric version of medical treatment as we would now define it (see Arnott *et al.* (2003)).
32. The earliest securely dated example is from the Mesolithic site of Vasilyevka II in Ukraine, dated by radiocarbon to 7300–6220 BC (Lillie (2003)).
33. Piggott (1940); Roberts and McKinley (2003); Bennike (2003); Moghaddama *et al.* (2015).
34. McKinley (forthcoming).
35. Jiménez-Brobeil *et al.* (2012).
36. Fyllingen (2003).
37. Signs of biological stress noted at Sund (Fyllingen (2003)) include Harris Lines (lines of arrested and recommenced growth visible on X-ray in the children's long bones) and linear enamel hypoplasia (again lines of interrupted growth visible in tooth enamel). Both conditions are general signs of physiological stress and occur most commonly when children are either severely ill or malnourished. Cribra Orbitalia is areas of porosity which develop in the roofs of the orbits (eye sockets) as the body recycles bone mineral at times of stress – this condition is sometimes, but not exclusively associated with dietary deficiencies including anaemia and scurvy. Lastly, three of the children had marked signs of rickets (Vitamin D deficiency) likely to be caused by a lack of calcium in their diet. Taken together these conditions suggest a general picture of inadequate dietary intake, possibly coupled with illness.
38. Osgood (2005, 2006); Osgood *et al.* (2010).
39. The ages of the Tormarton individuals were assessed as mid-late 30s, mid 20s, mid-late 20s, early 30s, with the last individual aged perhaps in his early teens (Osgood (2005), 14), the salient point however is that these ages are inconsistent with simultaneous natural deaths.
40. Osgood (2006).
41. Smith *et al.* (in press).
42. Brinker *et al.* (2013); Flohr *et al.* (2015).
43. Schulting and Bradley (2013).
44. Finkelstein (2002).

Chapter 8. Out of the Shadows: The End of Prehistory

1. Attempts were made by various scholars writing at different times to arrive at a specific date for the Creation based on literal reading of the Bible. The best-known of these today is Archbishop James Ussher's chronology published in 1701 which placed the first day of Creation on Sunday, 23 October 4004 BC.
2. For example, the famous antiquary and prolific barrow digger Richard Colt Hoare stated that Britain was likely to have been populated for perhaps 'a thousand years before Christ' (Hoare (1812), 12).
3. As with other archaeological periods, the dates accepted for the beginning and end of the 'Iron Age' vary by geographical region. Iron working was first developed in western Asia around 1300 BC and reached eastern Europe by *c.*1100 BC. This new technology then

spread westwards and northwards over the course of the next five centuries. For the British Isles iron working is generally accepted as first appearing around 800–750 BC, with the respective 'period' running up to the Roman conquest of AD 43. This period is also commonly subdivided into an Early (750–600 BC), Middle (600–400 BC) and Late Iron Age from 400 BC onwards, with some authors going a step further in identifying a Latest Iron Age from *c.*50 BC to AD 100 (Cunliffe (2005), 652).

4. James (1999), 33, also see the remainder of this text for a comprehensive deconstruction of the view of the Celts as a distinct and coherent pan-European people, whose surviving descendants supposedly now occupy the western Atlantic fringe of Europe from Scotland to Brittany. The construction of modern 'Celtic' identities in Britain in particular has more to do with the political currents of the eighteenth and nineteenth centuries and the emergence of nation states at this time than with any historic or prehistoric reality.

5. Cunliffe (2013), 235–49; by applying statistical techniques used to identify evolutionary relationships between biological species, several studies of Indo-European languages have come to similar conclusions regarding their development from a single language which originated somewhere in Asia on the western fringes of Europe and began to diverge sometime around 6500 BC (with a large margin of error). It appears likely then that this may have been the original language spoken by Neolithic farmers as they radiated into Europe.

6. Cunliffe (2013), 309; this text also gives a clear and useful general overview of the means by which La Téne metalwork and presumably other associated aspects of culture appear to have spread northwards and westwards across the continent.

7. Strabo, *Geographica*, IV, 4:2.

8. Cunliffe (2013), 311.

9. Heath (2009), 136.

10. King (2013); this study found 11/435 individuals (2.5 per cent) at Wetwang Slack and 10/100 or so individuals from six sites in Hampshire (10 per cent) to have weapon injuries.

11. Dent (1983).

12. Heath (2009), 136.

13. Schulting and Bradley (2013).

14. Bournemouth University summer training excavation, directors Miles Russell and Paul Cheetham, North Down near Winterbourne Kingston, Dorset, ongoing since 2009. At the time of writing the Latest Iron Age phase of this site is discussed in an interim report (Russell *et al.* (2014)) with further publications to follow in due course.

15. Brittain *et al.* (2014).

16. Redfern (2009); also King (2013) notes two individuals from Wetwang Slack (Yorks) with small healed depressed fractures that may be sling stone injuries.

17. Boulestin (2014).

18. There are persistent problems with terms when evidence relating to the head is discussed, even among trained osteologists. For correctness the term 'skull' should only be used to mean the cranium and mandible together. Where the mandible is lacking, only the term 'cranium' should be used. Where the skull is accompanied by vertebrae of the neck there is in fact a technical term to describe such finds which in French are referred to by the elegant-sounding 'extrémité céphalique', although many English speakers are not yet familiar with discussing the 'cephalic extremity' as an indicator of decapitation.

19. Diodorus Siculus, *Bibliotheca Historica*, V.29.

20. Redfern (2011).

21. Armitt *et al.* (2011).

22. Cunliffe (2011), 149–56.
23. McKinley (1997).
24. Keeley (1996), 102, and plate 2; also Meggitt (1977), 24.
25. Although it should be borne in mind that many 'Iron Age' hillforts started life as simpler enclosures in the Late Bronze Age.
26. Wheeler (1943).
27. See Armitt (2007) for a balanced discussion of the arguments for and against a martial interpretation of hillforts.
28. Waddington *et al.* (2012).
29. Pickstone and Mortimer (2012).
30. Hencken (1938).
31. Western and Hurst (2013).
32. Cunliffe (2011).
33. Gresham (1939).
34. Wheeler (1943).
35. Sharples (1991).
36. Redfern (2011).
37. Redfern and Chamberlain (2011).
38. Mike Bishop (pers. comm); also Bishop and Coulston (2006), 89: this reference notes that ballista bolt heads are one of the most common finds associated with Roman artillery. These square-sectioned projectiles are confirmed as such by the find of a complete example from Dura Europos with wooden shaft and flights intact. The alleged ballista bolt from Maiden Castle was also found in a context interpreted as pre-Roman by Sharples (1991), 124–5.
39. Jones (2004), 2–9; it should also be noted that such fortifications were regarded by European observers as both practical and necessary in function, with descriptions of horrific massacres being visited on communities sheltering within should the defences be overrun.
40. Clearly all manner of other activities went on at hillforts as well, including the production and trading of artefacts, storage of crops, corralling of livestock and no doubt various ritual/religious activities. The most elaborate hillforts, with their multivallate defences and complex entrances, must indeed also have served as statements of power and prestige (it's hard to see how they could not). But like Medieval castles, which functioned as local hubs for a range of symbolic, administrative and economic functions, as well as serving to make grand statements about their owners, hillforts are still most convincingly interpreted as being primarily intended for defence. Moreover, where hillforts seems to have been centres of specialized activities such as horse rearing as at Bury Hill (Hants), metalworking as at Hod Hill (Dorset) or Continental trade as at Hengistbury Head (Hants), the enclosing defences were presumably needed to protect the high-value commodities being produced and/or exchanged within. Such roles as centres of production and defence are therefore not mutually exclusive but rather the opposite. Without high-value resources at risk of being raided the defences wouldn't be needed, without security the production or storage of such commodities wouldn't be possible.
41. Ardagna *et al.* (2005).
42. Such pit burials are relatively common on southern British sites of the Late Iron Age, at Winterbourne Kingston the pit burials, probably dating from the second to first centuries BC were later succeeded by burials in formally-dug graves likely dating from *c.*50 BC to *c.*AD 100.

43. Cunliffe (2011), 146.
44. Armitt *et al.* (2011).
45. Aldhouse-Green (2015).
46. Schulting and Bradley (2013).
47. www.sciencenordic.com (2012); also www.museumskanderborg.dk – this project is still ongoing at the time of writing with published sources of a more academic nature currently awaited.
48. Jones (2004), 62–3.

Chapter 9. Imperial Anger: Violence under Roman Rule

1. The author most commonly credited with the invention of this term is Bordieu (1977) who was commenting from a social science perspective on the nature and function of education as a means through which society and particularly social inequalities are reproduced and maintained across time. Studies applying such theory to Roman society have focused on themes such as marriage and sexual relations (Harper (2011), 281–325), education and the role of oratory (Corbeill (2006)) and the structure of Roman households (Razavi (2013)).
2. See Haglund and Sorg (1997) for a comprehensive account of a broad range of taphonomic (post-mortem) processes which act to progressively degrade an unburied body after death until effectively no trace remains.
3. Sheldon (2001) gives a useful summary of the background to the disaster as well as the underlying causes for both the revolt and the Romans' failure to see it coming. Also Rost and Wilbers-Rost (2010) give a more detailed account of the earthworks and artefactual finds.
4. James (2011).
5. Suetonius X.4.
6. Kenyon (1953).
7. Maull (in Kenyon (1953)) cites various Roman examples of the decapitation both of conquered enemies and previously subjugated peoples who had rebelled against Roman rule.
8. Lethbridge (1936).
9. Dodwell (2004).
10. Matthews (1981).
11. It is popularly believed that Emperor Constantine outlawed crucifixion sometime in the late 330s or early 340s AD, although there is no contemporary source for this and the truth of this claim remains debatable. Various examples of crucifixion or essentially similar practices where people have been suspended in a fixed position and left until dead have been documented in recent times, in contexts including the Second World War where such treatment was inflicted on prisoners by the Japanese (Bourke (2006), 34–5) and the Syrian conflict in 2014, alleged to have been carried out by members of Daesh/Isis (BBC News, 8 May 2014). None of which have offered the chance for modern medical observations regarding the precise way in which such treatment results in death.
12. Maslen and Mitchell (2006).
13. Regan *et al.* (2013).
14. Josephus, *The Jewish War* V.449.
15. Appian, *The Civil Wars* 120.
16. For example Bergeron (2012) attempts to come to an arguably over-specific conclusion regarding Jesus' cause of death, basing his study on the assumption that the gospel accounts are 'historically accurate' (although he fails to elaborate as to why he thinks this) with

various assumptions then taken as fact, such as the statement that Jesus died at precisely 3.00pm.

17. '*Crudelissimum taeterrimumque supplicium*' Cicero, *In Verrem* 2.5.165; here the word *taeter-rimumque* derives from a term relating to ashes or cinders meaning literally 'blackened' but is usually translated in this context as 'disgraceful', 'disgusting' or 'offensive'. It should be noted that in this instance Cicero was criticizing the use of crucifixion against a Roman citizen rather than condemning the practice *per se*.

18. Kanz and Grossschmidt (2006).

19. Grant (2000), 13–19.

20. See Caffell and Holst (2012) for a detailed and comprehensive report on the human remains from this cemetery, also Hunter-Mann (2015) for a general account of the excavation. Details of the stable isotope analyses are published in Müldner (2011).

21. Redfern and Bonney (2014).

22. The ancient historian Niall McKeown (2007) presents a well-argued and elegant analysis of the way different interpretations can be drawn from the same evidence with regard to both written sources in general and slavery in particular.

23. McKeown (2007) estimates that between 200 BC and AD 200 between 5 and 10 per cent of the 50 million to 100 million inhabitants of the Roman Empire may have been slaves.

24. Examples include: Rathbun (1987), De la Cova (2011) and Coruccini *et al.* (1982), for further osteological studies of New World slave populations see past issues of *American Journal of Physical Anthropology* and *International Journal of Osteoarchaeology*.

25. Ubelaker and Rife (2011).

26. Méténier (2014).

27. Thompson (1993) gives a lengthy and detailed account of the known examples of Iron Age and Roman slave chains and shackles. The concentration of such in the northern and western provinces has been argued to indicate the role of the military in capturing slaves for transport back eastwards to Rome and the core of the Empire but nothing more (McKeown (2007)), but Thompson further suggests it indicates the use of chains in the daily control of agricultural slaves in the western provinces.

28. Blondiaux *et al.* (2012): these authors note that scapular fractures are rare today comprising only 3–5 per cent of all shoulder girdle fractures and just 1 per cent of all fractures. Bilateral scapular fractures (especially in the absence of injuries to other bones) are almost never seen in modern populations, let alone examples where there are multiple fractures to each scapula from separate impacts.

29. Wheeler *et al.* (2013).

30. Gowland (2015).

31. Walker (1997).

32. Poliakoff (1995), 73–6.

Chapter 10. 'The Judgement of God': Violence in Early Medieval England

1. Hyams (2001) gives a helpful account of the gradual incorporation of the principles of blood feud into law and its influence on the development of the early English legal system.

2. Reynolds (1997).

3. Lethbridge and Palmer (1929); also Historic England Heritage List Entry: 1410907 (https://historicengland.org.uk).

4. Semple (1998).

5. Pitts *et al.* (2002).
6. In this case a 'hundred' boundary – an Anglo-Saxon administrative unit based on the idea of the amount of land able to support a hundred armed men to serve in times of conflict.
7. Chippindale (1994).
8. Buckberry (2008).
9. Three radiocarbon results were obtained from human bone from the Walkington Wold cemetery. These were 640–775 cal AD; 775–980 cal AD and 900–1030 cal AD (95 per cent C.I.) (Buckberry (2008)).
10. Note that not all metal detectorists are irresponsible thieves looking to make money by selling their finds on Ebay. Many finds of crucial national and international importance would be unknown without the efforts (as well as the honesty and integrity) of metal detectorists of the more scrupulous kind.
11. Wheeler (1943).
12. Piggott (1954), 47–8.
13. Elema (2012).
14. Bloomfield (1969) considers both Beowulf and the Battle of Maldon with regard to possible allusions to Trial by Combat existing in pre-Norman England.
15. Loe *et al.* (2014).
16. *Daily Mail*, 11 June 2009.
17. Chenery *et al.* (2014).
18. *Daily Mail*, 12 March 2010.
19. See Loe *et al.* (2014) for a detailed technical account of the injuries noted on the human remains from the Ridgeway Hill mass burial.
20. The *Jomsvikingasaga* as translated by Paul du Chaillu, cited in Lethbridge and Palmer (1929).
21. Loe (2016).
22. Biddle, M. and Kjølbye-Biddle, B. (1992, 2001); also Richards (2003).
23. Pollard *et al.* (2012).
24. Here C^{14} results that indicate dates around half a century before the massacre may in fact need to be modified by the 'marine reservoir effect' as if the men had a strong marine component to their diet they will have been ingesting 'old' carbon which would make their radiocarbon dates seem older than they really were and so a date around the turn of the eleventh century may in fact be more correct (Pollard *et al.* (2012)).
25. Pollard *et al.* (2012).
26. 'The Groans of the Britons' is the term used by the sixth-century author Gildas that has come to refer to the complaints of the British appealing to Rome for assistance against the raids of the northern barbarians (the Picts and Scots) in the fifth century AD.
27. Patrick (2006).
28. Anderson (1996).
29. Weber and Czarnetzki (2001).
30. Geber (2015).

Chapter 11. 'The True Son of Gentle Blood': The High Middle Ages to the Renaissance

1. The term 'High Middle Ages' is generally taken to refer to the period between *c.*AD 1000 and 1300, with the European Renaissance then occurring from *c.*1300 to *c.*1600, although as is common with widespread periods of social change these dates vary geographically. In

England the Medieval period is commonly agreed to have ended and the Renaissance begun with the cessation of the Wars of the Roses in 1485.

2. Keen (1984), 219–24.
3. From Galbert of Bruges (Chapter 28).
4. Daniell (2001).
5. The Battle of Fulford took place on 20 September 1066 somewhere close to the village of Fulford, 3 miles south of York. Here a hastily-assembled force led by Edwin and Morcar, the Earls of Mercia and Northumbria was defeated by a larger army of the combined forces of the Norwegian King, Harald Hardrada, and the rebel Earl Tostig (brother of the English King Harold Godwinsson). After agreeing terms with the city, where the Norwegians agreed not to sack York providing the city surrendered, the invaders then withdrew east to Stamford Bridge, where they were surprised and defeated a week later following King Harold's famous lightning march from London. The Battle of Fulford has previously been dismissed as of limited importance and is sometimes referred to as the 'Forgotten Battle of 1066', but in fact it likely contributed significantly to the overall losses suffered by the English in the Autumn of that year that were a major factor in Harold's defeat at Hastings. Jones (2011) gives a comprehensive account of the written sources relating to Fulford along with a detailed report of recent archaeological work to define the location of the battle.
6. Rex (2004), 87–106.
7. The excavation, analysis and interpretation of the Towton mass grave are described in exemplary detail in Fiorato *et al.* (2000).
8. The building contractors who initially discovered the Towton mass grave counted twenty-three skulls among the remains they had had exhumed, which were then reburied in nearby Saxton churchyard. Following a rescue excavation conducted by WYAS and Bradford University remains from at least thirty-eight further individuals were recovered giving an overall minimum number of sixty-one (Fiorato *et al.* (2000)).
9. The origin of the term 'Wars of the Roses' is generally attributed to Sir Walter Scott who introduced it in his 1829 novel *Anne of Geierstein*. Certainly the term would not have been recognized by those living in England during the fifteenth century, most of whom would also not have recognized that they were living through a civil war (Grummit (2013), p. xii).
10. Oakeshott's (2000) work – originally published in 1964 – remains one of the most useful accounts of the variety and development of later Medieval weapons and armour.
11. Knüsel (2000).
12. Stirland (2005), 118–30.
13. Bennike (2006).
14. Boucherie (2015); Boucherie *et al.* (forthcoming).
15. Bennike (2006).
16. Waldron (2007), Ch. 2.
17. In fact this is a slightly simplified account of Wald's work which looked at the specific probability of aircraft surviving being shot at particular points with particular types of ammunition. For a mathematically-grounded discussion of Wald's work see Mangel and Samaniego (1984) published after Wald's original memoranda to the Strategical Research Group in which he was employed were declassified. For the original work on aircraft vulnerability see Wald (1980).
18. Thordemann (1939).
19. Thordemann suggested that some of the armour found at Visby was of a style dating back to the Viking period. This point is debatable although much of the armour worn by the presumed defenders was certainly antiquated by 1361 which does raise the question of how

they came to be wearing it? Thordemann implies a picture of the citizens of Visby taking their grandfathers' armour out of chests of family heirlooms and hurriedly pressing it back into service. Perhaps this was correct in some cases, although the similarities in much of the armour suggest it might have been issued from some sort of central store. Perhaps the local lord had released armour that had lain in storage since an earlier time, for the general defence of the city. Alternatively perhaps a local city watch or militia existed whose equipment was overdue to be updated. Again the fact that the mass graves contain only those whose armour failed them should also be borne in mind – if other defenders had more up-to-date protection this might have kept them alive and so their armour is not available for modern investigators to study.

20. Although the open basinet helmets worn at this time would have been less unpleasant to remove from a decomposing body and so more of the Visby men may have had helmets during the battle than was apparent at excavation. However, the high number of severe head injuries apparent does indicate that a good proportion of the defenders lacked head protection sufficient to keep them alive.
21. Daniell (2001).
22. Lewis (2008).
23. Mafart *et al.* (2004).
24. Prestwich (1997), 202–32 and 469–516.
25. AMS dating of bone from the man from Hulton Abbey returned the result of AD 1215–85 (68 per cent C.I.) and AD 1050–1385 (95 per cent C.I.) (Lewis (2008)).
26. Lewis (2008).
27. Appleby *et al.* (2015); Buckley *et al.* (2013); Greyfriars Research Team (2015); Mitchell *et al.* (2013).
28. Appleby *et al.* (2015).
29. Grummit (2013).
30. The claim of an order of 'no quarter' at Towton originates in a short fragment of text 'Hearne's fragment' which stretches to just 305 words and was written several decades after the battle. On one hand this source is difficult to verify although it is certainly plausible given the bitter nature of this ongoing conflict.
31. Polydore Vergil (XXV) writing in the early 1500s, specifically mentions Richard's body being slung across a horse, whilst a range of near-contemporary sources agree that his body was subject to all manner of physical insults after death.

Chapter 12. The Shock of the New: The Changing Face of Violence

1. Once again the limits of this period are open to debate, the term 'Early Modern Period' is here used to refer to the period between *c.*AD 1500 and *c.*AD 1800.
2. Holmes (2001), 209, although this point is more specific to Europe and North America; actions by European armies in other world regions where styles of warfare were different could involve greater degrees of close combat – such as the Indian Mutiny of 1857–9.
3. Lockau *et al.* (2013, 2016).
4. Bones in the Stoney Creek grave had been disturbed and damaged in the ground by agricultural activity, the grave was initially discovered in 1889 by Allen Smith who was ploughing his father's field and recognized the uniforms and insignia of British and American troops. The site, thereafter known as Smith's Knoll, is also believed to be the site of the American guns which the British captured (Carstens and Sandford (2011), 82).
5. This trend occurred principally among the sections of regiments most likely to engage the enemy at close quarters, the grenadier companies, riflemen and light infantry.

6. The two skulls are claimed to have been kept at Bettiscombe Manor, near Beaminster and Waddon House, near Weymouth, the two locations are about 20 miles apart.

7. Byford-Bates (2012).

8. CRANID6 (Wright (2010)).

9. 1640–60 Cal AD at 68 per cent C.I., 1630–70 Cal AD at 95 per cent C.I.

10. Udal (1910).

11. These ranges are frequently quoted by modern authors and occasionally questioned, although modern tests in controlled circumstances are difficult to conduct due to variations in the quality of manufacture of musket parts, the consistency of gunpowder and the lead composition and shape of musket balls in the past. However both contemporary accounts of battlefield experiences (such as that of the often-quoted Colonel George Hanger (1816)) and various experiments conducted when such weapons were in use, generally agree on the poor accuracy of black-powder firearms even at ranges of less than 100 yards (Holmes (2001), 198). Of course the ultimate indicator of the effectiveness of these weapons must be the range at which they were actually employed. If the muskets of the period could have been reliably used at greater distances there would have been no need for armies to close to within 100 yards of each other before firing. In fact during the early parts of the American Civil War a great many casualties were caused through the continued use of Napoleonic tactics by commanders who failed to take account of improvements in the range and accuracy of both small arms and artillery (Keegan (2011), 133).

12. Smith *et al.* (2015).

13. Roberts *et al.* (2008) describe experiments investigating the capabilities of the eighteenth-century Brown Bess musket which further confirm the catastrophic effects of being shot by such weapons as well as demonstrating their armour-piercing capabilities.

14. For example there are various references to the use of cannon in field battles during the Hundred Years War, the first of such by Edward III at Crécy (1346), although the sources are vague and the precise details of this development remain rather nebulous (Neillands (1990), 62). Two fragments of a cannon barrel along with a composite lead and iron cannonball of a size consistent with use against people rather than fortifications have also been found on the Towton battlefield (Sutherland (2011)).

15. Source: Pte. Thomas Wightman, 17th Lancers, cited in Adkin (2000), 161.

16. From the poem *Faithless Nelly Gray* by Thomas Hood (1799–1845) (source: Seaver (1907)).

17. In relation to Sickles' injury it is worth noting that the range at which a target is struck is of obvious importance. Sickles was hit from a distance of approximately 1,200 feet; had he been struck at closer range his horse might have been less fortunate.

18. Bull (2004), 56.

19. Hill (2014).

20. Full experiment detailed in Massagé (2014) with a related journal article in preparation.

21. Barter, R. (1984), 14.

22. See Brickley and Buteux (2006) for the full account of this project.

23. See Brickley and Smith (2006) for a more detailed treatment of the violence-related injuries among the St Martin's Church sample.

24. Brickley and Smith (2006).

25. Walker (1997).

26. Such as St Peter's Church Wolverhampton (Adams and Colls (2007)), Red Cross Way in Southwark, London (Brickley *et al.* (1999)) and St Brides Lower Cemetery, Farringdon Street London (Museum of London: archive.museumoflondon.org.uk).

27. Brickley (2006).
28. Museum of London (available at: archive.museumoflondon.org.uk).

Conclusion

1. For example, between October 2001 and August 2009 US forces in Iraq and Afghanistan suffered 25,353 casualties (with a 10 per cent mortality rate) from explosive devices as opposed to 4,102 casualties (albeit with a higher mortality rate of 20 per cent) from small-arms fire. Source: *New York Times* (19 August 2009).
2. Dussault (2013); Dussault *et al.* (2014, 2016).

Bibliography

Adams, J., and Colls, K. (2007) *"Out of darkness, cometh light": Life and Death in Nineteenth Century Wolverhampton: Excavation of the Overflow Burial Ground of St Peter's Collegiate Church, Wolverhampton, 2001–2002.* BAR 442, Oxford: Archaeopress.

Adkin, M. (2000) *The Charge: The Real Reason why the Light Brigade was Lost* London: Pimlico.

Aldhouse-Green, M. (2015) *Bog Bodies Uncovered: Solving Europe's Ancient Mystery* London: Thames and Hudson.

Allen, M.W. (2015a) "Hunter gatherer conflict: the last bastion of the pacified past?" in: Allen, M.W. and Jones, T.L. (eds) *Violence and Warfare among Hunter Gatherers* Walnut Creek (CA): Left Coast Press, 15–25.

Allen, M.W. (2015b) "Hunter gatherer violence and warfare in Australia" in: Allen, M.W. and Jones, T.L. (eds) *Violence and Warfare among Hunter Gatherers* Walnut Creek (CA): Left Coast Press, 97–111.

Anderson, T. (1996) "Cranial weapon injuries from Anglo Saxon Dover" *International Journal of Osteoarchaeology* 6, 10–14.

Appian *The Civil Wars* (transl. J. Carter) London: Penguin (1996).

Appleby, J., Rutty, G., Hainsworth, S., Woosnam-Savage, R., Morgan, B., Brough, A., Earp, R., Robinson, C., King, T., Morris, M. and Buckley, R. (2015) "Perimortem trauma in King Richard III: a skeletal analysis" *The Lancet* 385, 253–259.

Ardagna, Y., Richier, A., Vernet, G. and Dutour, O. (2005) "A case of beheading dating from the Celtic period (La Téne B, Sarlie've-Grande Halle, France)" *International Journal of Osteoarchaeology* 15, 73–76.

Armitt, I. (2007) "Hillforts at war: from Maiden Castle to Taniwaha Pa" *Proceedings of the Prehistoric Society* 73, 25–37.

Armitt, I., Schulting, S., Knüsel, C., and Shepherd, I. (2011) "Death, decapitation and display? the Bronze and Iron Age human remains from the Sculptor's Cave, Covesea, North-east Scotland" *Proceedings of the Prehistoric Society* 77, 251–278.

Arnott, R., Finger, S. and Smith, C. (eds) (2003) *Trepanation: History, Discovery, Theory* Lisse: Swets & Zeitlinger.

Bach, T., Dierks, E.J., Ueeck, B.A. and Potter, B.F. (2001) "Maxillofacial injuries Associated with domestic violence" *Journal of Oral and Maxillofacial Surgery* 59, 1277–1283.

Bahn, P. and Vertut, J. (1997) *Journey Through the Ice Age* Berkeley: University of California.

Barb, A.A. (1972) "Cain's murder-weapon and Samson's jawbone of an ass" *Journal of the Warburg and Courtauld Institutes* 35, 386–389.

Barclay, A. and Halpin, C. (1999) *Excavations at Barrow Hills, Radley, Oxfordshire: Volume 1 The Neolithic and Bronze Age Monument Complex* Thames Valley Landscape Series 11. Oxford: Oxford University.

Barker, S. (2007) "The Making of a Plague Saint: Saint Sebastian's imagery and cult before the Counter-Reformation" in: Mormando, F. and Worcester, T. (ed.) *Piety and Plague: from Byzantium to the Baroque* Kirksville (MO): Truman University Press, 90–130.

Barter, R. (1984) *The Siege of Delhi: Mutiny Memories of an Old Officer* London: The Folio Society.

Bauer, B. L. and Kuhn, T.J. (eds) *Severe Head injuries: Pathology, Diagnosis and Treatment* London: Springer, 76–81.

Baugh, D. (2011) *The Global Seven Years War 1754–1763* London: Longman.

Bayle, P., Coquerelle, M., Condemi, S., Ronchitelli, A., Harvati, K. and Weber, G.W. (2011) "Early dispersal of modern humans in Europe and implications for Neanderthal behaviour", *Nature* 479, 525–579.

Bechachi, L., Fabbri, P.F. and Malegni, F. (1997) "An arrow-caused lesion in a Late Upper Palaeolithic human pelvis", *Current Anthropology* 38, 135–140.

Begouen, H., Cugulières, and Miquel, H. (1922) "Vertebra humaine traversée par une lame en quartzite" *Revue Anthropologique* 32, 230–232.

Bennazzi, S., Douka, K., Fornai, C., Bauer, C.C., Kullmer, O., Svoboda, J., Pap, I., Mallegni, F. (2011) "Early dispersal of modern humans in Europe and implications for Neanderthal behaviour" *Nature* 479, 525–579.

Bennike, P. (2003) "Ancient trepanations and differential diagnoses: a re-evaluation of skeletal remains from Denmark" in: Arnott, R., Finger, S. and Smith, C. (eds) *Trepanation: History, Discovery, Theory* Lisse: Swets & Zeitlinger, 95–115.

Bennike, P. (2006) "Rebellion, combat and massacre: a Medieval mass grave at Sandbjerget near Naestved in Denmark" in: Otto, T., Thrane, H. and Vandkilde, H. (eds) *Warfare and Society: Archaeological and Social Anthropological Perspectives* Aarhus: Aarhus University, 305–318.

Berger, T.D.E. and E. Trinkaus (1995) "Patterns of trauma among the Neanderthals" *Journal of Archaeological Science* 22, 841–852.

Bergeron, J.W. (2012) "The crucifixion of Jesus: review of hypothesized mechanisms of death and implications of shock and trauma-induced coagulopathy" *Journal of Forensic and Legal Medicine* 19, 113—116.

Biddle, M. and Kjølbye-Biddle, B. (1992) "Repton and the Vikings" *Antiquity* 66, 36–51.

Biddle, M. and Kjølbye-Biddle, B. (2001) "Repton and the 'Great Heathen Army', 873–4" in Graham-Campbell, J., Hall, R., Jesch, J. and Parsons, D. (eds) *Vikings and the Danelaw: Selected Papers from the Proceedings of the Thirteenth Viking Congress* Oxford: Oxbow Books, 45–96.

Bill, J.H. (1862) "Notes on arrow wounds" *American Journal of the Medical Sciences* 44, 365–387.

Bishop, M. C. and Coulston, J.C.N. (2006) *Roman Military Equipment from the Punic Wars to the Fall of Rome* Oxford: Oxford University.

Blondiaux, J., Fontainea, C., Demondiona, X., Flipoa, R., Colarda, T., Mitchell, P.D., Buzong, M. and Walker, P. (2012) "Bilateral fractures of the scapula: Possible archeological examples of beatings from Europe, Africa and America" *International Journal of Paleopathology* 2, 223–230.

Bloomfield, M.W. (1969) "Beowulf, Byrhtnoth, and the judgment of God: trial by combat in Anglo-Saxon England" *Speculum* 44, 545–559.

Bonsall, C., Macklin, M., Anderson, D. and Payton, R. (2002) "Climate change and the adoption of agriculture in north-west Europe" *European Journal of Archaeology* 5, 9–23.

Booth, T.J. Chamberlain, A.T. Parker Pearson, M. (2015) "Mummification in Bronze Age Britain" *Antiquity* 89, 1155–1173.

Boucherie, A. (2015) *Wounded to the bone: traumata analysis in Danish Medieval mass grave* (unpublished MSc thesis) Bournemouth University.

Boucherie, A., Jørkov, M. and Smith, M.J. (forthcoming) "Wounded to the bone: digital microscopic analysis of traumata in a Medieval mass grave assemblage (Sandbjerget, Denmark, AD 1300–1350)" submitted to: *International Journal of Palaeopathology*.

Boulestin B. (2014) "Des têtes-trophées gauloises sur le site de l'immeuble des Services fiscaux à Angoulême?" *Bulletins et Mémoires de la Société archéologique et historique de la Charente*, 170, 32–36.

Bourdieu, P. (1977) "Cultural Reproduction and Social Reproduction" in: Karabel, J. and Halsey, A. H. (eds) *Power and Ideology in Education* Oxford: Oxford University.

Bourke, R. (2006) *Prisoners of the Japanese: Literary Imagination and the Prisoner of War Experience* St. Lucia, Queensland: University of Queensland Press.

Boylston, A. (2000) "Evidence for weapon related trauma in British archaeological samples" in: Cox, M. and Mays S. (eds) *Human Osteology in Archaeology and Forensic Science* Greenwich Medical Media, London, 357–380.

Brennan, M. (1991) *Health and Disease in the Middle and Upper Palaeolithic of South-western France: A Bioarchaeological Study* Unpublished PhD thesis, New York University.

Brickley, M. (2006) "Rib Fractures in the archaeological record: a useful source of sociocultural information?" *International Journal of Osteoarchaeology* 16, 61–75.

Brickley, M.B. and Buteux, S. (2006) *St. Martin's Uncovered: Investigations in the Churchyard of St. Martin's-in-the-Bull-Ring, Birmingham, 2001* Oxford: Oxbow.

Brickley, M.B., Miles, A., and Stainer, H. (1999) *The Cross Bones burial ground, Redcross Way Southwark, London : Archaeological excavations (1991–1998) for the London Underground Limited Jubilee Line Extension Project* London: Museum of London Archaeology Service and Jubilee Line Extension Project.

Brickley, M.B. and Smith, M.J. (2006) "Culturally Determined Patterns of Violence: Biological Anthropological Investigations at a Historic Urban Cemetery" *American Anthropologist* 108, 163–177.

Brinch Petersen, E., Alexandersen, V. and Meiklejohn, C. (1993) "Vedbaek, Graven Midt i Byen" *Nationalmuseets Arbejdsmark* 61–69.

Brink, O., Vesterby, A. and Jensen, J. (1998) "Pattern of Injuries due to Interpersonal Violence" *Injury* 29, 705–709.

Brinker, U., Flohr, S., Piek, J. and Orschiedt, J. (2013) "Human remains from a Bronze Age site in the Tollense Valley: victims of a battle?" in: Knüsel, C., Smith, M.J. (eds) *The Routledge Handbook of the Bioarchaeology of Human Conflict* London: Routledge, 146–160.

Brittain, M., Sharples, N. and Evans, C. (2014) "Excavations at Ham Hill, Stoke Sub Hamdon, 2013" *Proceedings of the Somerset Archaeology and Natural History Society* 156, 125–128.

Brown, J. (1964) "The evolution of diversity in avian territorial systems" *The Wilson Bulletin* 76, 160–169.

Brown, K.S., Marean, C.W., Jacobs, Z., Schoville, B.J., Oestmo, S., Fisher, E.C., Bernatchez, J., Karkanas, P. and Matthews, T. (2012) "An early and enduring advanced technology originating 71,000 years ago in South Africa" *Nature* 491, 590–593.

Brown, P., Sutkina, T., Morwood, Soejono, R.P., Jatniko and Saptomo, E.W. (2004) "A new small-bodied hominin from the Late Pleistocene of Flores, Indonesia" *Nature*, 431, 1055–1061.

Brück, J. (2008) "Prospects and potential in the archaeology of Bronze Age Britain" *Bronze Age Review* 1, 23–33.

Bryce, T.H. (1902) "Note on prehistoric human remains found in the Island of Arran" *Journal of the Anthropological Institute of Great Britain and Ireland* 32, 398–406.

Buckberry, J. (2008) "Off with their heads: the Anglo Saxon cemetery at Walkington Wold, East Yorkshire" in: Murphy, E.M. (ed.) *Deviant Burial in the Archaeological Record* Oxford: Oxbow, 148–168.

Buckley, R., Morris, M., Appleby, J., King, T., O'Sullivan, D. and Foxhall, L. (2013) "'The king in the car park': new light on the death and burial of Richard III in the Grey Friars church, Leicester, in 1485" *Antiquity* 87, 519–538.

Buikstra, J. and Ubelaker, H. (1994) *Standards for Data Collection from Human Skeletal Remains* Fayetteville: Arkansas Archaeological Survey.

Bull, S. (2004) *Encyclopaedia of Military Technology and Innovation* London: Greenwood Press.

Byers, S.N. (2010) *Introduction to Forensic Anthropology* Upper Saddle River, NJ: Pearson Higher Education.

Byford-Bates, A. (2012) *The Waddon Skull* unpublished MSc dissertation, Bournemouth University.

Caffell, A. and Holst, M. (2012) *Osteological Analysis 3 and 6 Driffield Terrace York North Yorkshire* York: York Archaeological Trust.

Callaway, E. (2013) "Hominin DNA baffles experts" *Nature* 504, 16–17.

Cap-Jédikian, G. (2010) "La Préhistoire au Muséum aujourd'hui: le cas Téviec" in: Bon F., Dubois S., Labails M.-D (eds) *Le Muséum de Toulouse et l'Invention de la Préhistoire* Toulouse: Éditions du Muséum de Toulouse, 205–212.

Carman J. (2013) *Archeologies of Conflict* London: Bloomsbury Academic.

Carstens, P.R. and Sanford, P.L (2011) *Searching for the Forgotten War -1812* Dartford: XLibris Corporation.

Castleden, R. (1987) *The Stonehenge People: An Exploration of Life in Neolithic Britain 4700–2000 BC* London: Routledge.

Cave, C., and Oxenham, M. (2014) "Identification of the archaeological 'invisible elderly': An approach illustrated with an Anglo-Saxon example" *International Journal of Osteoarchaeology* 26, 163–175.

Chenal, F., Perrin, B., Barrand-Emam, H. and Boulestin, B. (2015) "A farewell to arms: a deposit of human limbs and bodies at Bergheim, France, c.4000 BC." *Antiquity* 348, 1313–1330.

Chennery, C., Evans, J., Score, D., Boyle, A. and Chenery, S. (2014) "A boat load of Vikings?" *Journal of the North Atlantic* 7, 43–53.

Chippindale, C. (1994) *Stonehenge Complete* London: Thames and Hudson.

Churchill, S.E., Franciscus, R.G., McKean-Peraza, H.A., Daniel, J.A. and Warren, B.R. (2009) "Shanidar 3 Neandertal rib puncture wound and Paleolithic weaponry" *Journal of Human Evolution* 57, 163–178.

Clark, P.U., Dyke, A.S., Shakun, J.D., Carlson, A.E., Clark, J., Wohlfarth, B., Mitrovica, J.X., Hostetler, S.W. and McCabe, A.M. (2009) "The Last Glacial Maximum" *Science* 325, 710–714.

Coles, J.M. (1962) "European Bronze Age shields" *Proceedings of the Prehistoric Society* 28, 156–190.

Conroy, G.C. (2005) *Reconstructing Human Origins* London: W.W. Norton & Co.

Coqeugniot, H., Dutour, O., Arensburg, B., Duday, H., Vandermeersch, B. and Tillier, A. (2014) "Earliest cranio-encephalic trauma from the Levantine Middle Palaeolithic: 3D re-appraisal of the Qafzeh 11 skull, consequences of paediatric damage on individual life condition and social care" PLoS ONE 9, e102822. doi:10.1371/journal.pone.0102822.

Corbeill, A. (2006) "Rhetorical education and social reproduction in the Republic and early Empire" in Dominik, W. (ed.) *A Companion to Roman Rhetoric* Chichester: Wiley.

Corruccini, R., Handler, J., Mutaw, R. and Lange, F. (1982) "Osteology of a slave burial population from Barbados, West Indies" *American Journal of Physical Anthropology* 59, 443–459.

Crawford, S., and Shepherd, G. (eds) (2007) *Children, Childhood and Society* IAA Interdisciplinary Series Vol. I. B.A.R. International Series 1696. Oxford: Archaeopress.

Culotta, E. (2016) "Tiny jaw reveals dawn of the Hobbit" *Science* available from: http://www.sciencemag.org/news/2016/06.

Cunha, E., Umbelino, C. and Cardoso, F. (2004) "About violent interactions in the Mesolithic: The absence of evidence from the Portuguese shell middens" in: Roksandic, M. (ed.) *Violent Interactions in the Mesolithic: Evidence and Meaning* British Archaeological Reports, International Series, 1237, Oxford: Archaeopress, 41–46.

Cunliffe, B. (2005) *Iron Age Communities in Britain: an Account of England, Scotland and Wales from the seventh century BC until the Roman Conquest* London: Routledge.

Cunliffe, B. (2011) *Danebury Hillfort* Stroud: The History Press.

Cunliffe, B. (2013) *Britain Begins* Oxford: Oxford University.

Daniell, C. (2001) "Battle and Trial: Weapon injury burials of St Andrew's Church, Fishergate, York: Notes and News" *Medieval Archaeology*, 45, 220–226.

Danilenko V.N. (1955) "Voloshkij epipaleoliticheskj mogil'nik" *Sovetskaja Etnografija* 3, 56–61.

Dart, R. (1953) "The predatory transition from ape to man" *International Anthropological and Linguistic Review* 1, 201–208.

Dastugue, J. (1981) "Pièces pathologiques de la nécropole moustérienne de Qafzeh" *Paléorient* 7, 135–140.

Dastugue, J. and De Lumley, M.A. (1976) "Les maladies des hommes prehistoriques du Paleolithique et du Mesolithique" in: *La Prehistoire Francaise, Vol. I* Paris: Editions du Centre National de la Recherche Scientifique, 612–622.

De la Cova, C. (2011) "Race, health and disease in 19th century born males" *American Journal of Physical Anthropology* 144, 526–537.

Dennis, K.C. (2009) "Current Perspectives on Traumatic Brain Injury" *Access Audiology* 8, available from: http://www.asha.org/aud/articles/currentTBI.htm (accessed June 2015).

Dent, J.S. (1983) "Weapons, wounds and war in the Iron Age" *Archaeological Journal* 140, 120–128.

Derry, D.E. (1913) "A case of hydrocephalus in an Egyptian of the Roman period" *Journal of Anatomy and Physiology* 48, 436–458.

Diodorus Siculus *Bibliotheca Historica* Loeb Classical Library, Vol. III (transl. C.H. Oldfather) Harvard (MA): Harvard University (1939).

Dodwell, N. (2004) "Human remains" in: Alexander, M., Dodwell, N. and Evans, C. "A Roman Cemetery in Jesus Lane, Cambridge" *Proceedings of the Cambridge Archaeological Society* 93, 67–94.

Drell, J.R.R. (2000) "Neanderthals: a history of interpretation" *Oxford Journal of Archaeology* 19, 1–24.

Dussault, M.C. (2013) *Blast Injury to the Human Skeleton: Recognition, Identification and Differentiation using Morphological and Statistical Approaches* PhD Thesis. Bournemouth University.

Dussault, M., Smith, M.J. and Osselton, D. (2014) "Blast injury and the human skeleton: An important emerging aspect of conflict related trauma" *Journal of Forensic Sciences* 59, 606–612.

Dussault, M.C., Smith, M.J. and Hanson, I. (2016) "Evaluation of trauma patterns in blast injuries using multiple correspondence analysis" *Forensic Science International* 267, 66–72.

Elema, A. (2012) "Trial by battle in France and England" Unpublished PhD Thesis, University of Toronto.

Evans, J. (1984) "Stonehenge: the environment in the late Neolithic and Early Bronze Age and a Beaker burial" *Wiltshire Archaeological Magazine* 78, 7–30.

Fenimore-Cooper, J. (1824) *The Last of the Mohicans* Ware (Herts): Wordsworth Classics (this edition 1992).

Fenton, T., Stefan, V.H., Wood, L.A. and Sauer, N.J. (2005) "Symmetrical fracturing of the skull from midline contact gunshot wounds: reconstruction of individual death histories from skeletonized human remains" *Journal of Forensic Sciences* 50, 1–12.

Ferguson, B. (2013) "Pinker's list: exaggerating prehistoric war mortality" in: Fry, D.P. (ed.) *War, Peace and Human Nature: The Convergence of Evolutionary and Cultural Views* Oxford: Oxford University.

Fernández-Crespo, T. (2015) "An arrowhead injury in a Late Neolithic/Early Chalcolithic human cuneiform from the Rockshelter of La Peña de Marañón (Navarre, Spain)" *International Journal of Osteoarchaeology* (early view online: DOI: 10.1002/oa.2513).

Finkelstein, I. (2002) "The Philistines in the Bible: A Late-Monarchic perspective" *Journal for the Study of the Old Testament* 27, 131–167.

Fiorato V., Boylston A., and Knüsel C. (eds) (2000) *Blood Red Roses* Oxbow Books: Oxford.

Flohr, S., Brinker, U., Schramm, A., Kierdorf, U., Staud, A., Piek, J.Jantzen, D., Hauenstein, K. and Orschiedt, J. (2015) "Flint arrowhead embedded in a human humerus from the Bronze Age site in the Tollense valley, Germany – A high-resolution micro-CT study to distinguish antemortem from perimortem projectile trauma to bone" *International Journal of Paleopathology* 9, 76–81.

Frayer, D.W. (1997) "Ofnet: evidence for a Mesolithic massacre" in Martin, D.L. and Frayer, D.W. (eds) *Troubled Times: Violence and Warfare in the Past* Amsterdam: Gordon and Breach, 181–216.

Friedman, R. (2014) "Violence and climate change in prehistoric Egypt and Sudan" *British Museum Blog* available from: http://blog.britishmuseum.org/tag/jebel-sahaba/ (Accessed July 2015).

Fry, D.P. (2007) *Beyond War: the Human Potential for Peace* Oxford: Oxford University Press.

Fyllingen, H. (2003) "Society and Violence in the Early Bronze Age: An analysis of human skeletons from Nord-Trøndelag, Norway" *Norwegian Archaeological Review* 36, 27–43.

Galbert of Bruges *The Murder of Charles the Good* (transl. James Bruce Ross) New York: Columbia University Press (1953).

Gaffney, V., Thompson, K. and Fitch, S. (2007) *Mapping Doggerland: The Mesolithic Landscapes of the Southern North Sea* Oxford: Archaeopress.

Gamble, C., Gowlett, J. and Dunbar, R. (2014) *Thinking Big: How the Evolution of Social Life Shaped the Human Mind* London: Thames and Hudson.

Geber, J. (2015) "Comparative study of perimortem weapon trauma in two Early Medieval skeletal populations (AD 400–1200) from Ireland" *International Journal of Osteoarchaeology* 25, 253–264.

Gilchrist, C. (1999) *Contesting the Past: Gender and Archaeology* London: Routledge.

Gowland, R.L. (2015) "Elder abuse: evaluating the potentials and problems of diagnosis in the archaeological record" *International Journal of Osteoarchaeology* (online prior to print; DOI: 10.1002/oa.2442).

Grant, M. (2000) *Gladiators: The Bloody Truth* London: Penguin.

Grant de Pauw, L. (2000) *Battle Cries and Lullabies: Women in War from Prehistory to the Present* Oklahoma City: University of Oklahoma Press.

Green, R., Krause, J, *et al.* (2010) "A Draft Sequence of the Neanderthal Genome" *Science* 328, 710–722.

Gresham, C.A. (1939) "Spetisbury Rings, Dorset" *Archaeological Journal* 96, 114–131.

Greyfriars Research Team (2015) *The Bones of a King: Richard III Rediscovered* London: Wiley-Blackwell.

Grummit, D. (2013) *A Short History of the Wars of the Roses* London: I.B.Tauris.

Guilaine, J. and Zammit, J. (2001) *The Origins of War: Violence in Prehistory* (English version 2005) Oxford: Blackwell.

Haas, J. (1999) "The origins of war and ethnic violence" in Carman, J. and Harding, A. (eds) *Ancient Warfare: Archaeological Perspectives* Stroud: Sutton Publishing, 11–24.

Haglund, W. and Sorg, M. (eds) (1997) *Forensic Taphonomy: the Postmortem Fate of Human Remains* London: CRC Press.

Hanger, G. (1816) *Colonel George Hanger's Advice to all Sportsmen, Farmers, and Gamekeepers* London: JJ Stockdale.

Harding, A. (2000) *European Societies in the Bronze Age* Cambridge: Cambridge University.

Hardy, B.L., Moncel, M-H., Daujeard, C., Fernandes, F., Béarez, P., Desclaux, E., Chacon Navarro, M.G., Puaud, S. and Gallotti, R. (2013) "Impossible Neanderthals? Making string, throwing projectiles and catching small game during Marine Isotope Stage 4 (Abri du Maras, France)" *Quaternary Science Reviews* 82, 23–40.

Harper, K. (2011) *Slavery in the Late Roman World, AD 275–425* Cambridge: Cambridge University.

Heath, J. (2009) *Warfare in Prehistoric Britain* Stroud: Amberley.

Hencken, T. (1938) "The excavation of the Iron Age camp on Bredon Hill" *Archaeological Journal* 95, 1–111.

Higham, T., Douka, K., Wood, R., Bronk Ramsey, C., Brock, F., Basell, L. *et al.* (2014) "The timing and spatiotemporal patterning of Neanderthal disappearance" *Nature* 512, 306–309.

Hill, S.W. (2014) "Effects of canister shot in the Civil War: skull of a soldier of the 54th Massachusetts Volunteers" *Military Medicine* 179, 1171–1172.

Hoare, R.C. (1812) *The Ancient History of Wiltshire Vol. 1* London: Miller (Reprinted 1975) Wakefield: E.P. Publishing.

Hobbes, T. (1651) *Leviathan* Cambridge: Cambridge University (this edition pub. 1996).

Hochban, W. (1997) "Panfacial fractures" in: Bauer, B. L. and Kuhn, T.J. (eds) *Severe Head injuries: Pathology, Diagnosis and Treatment* London: Springer, 76–81.

Hoffecker, J.F. (2009) "The spread of modern humans in Europe" *Proceedings of the National Academy of Sciences* 106, 16,040–16,045.

Holliday, T.W. (2013) "Population affinities of the Jebel Sahaba skeletal sample: limb proportion evidence" *International Journal of Osteoarchaeology* (earlyview online) doi: 10.1002/oa.2315.

Holmes, R. (2001) *Redcoat: The British Soldier in the Age of Horse and Musket* London: Harper Collins.

Hunter-Mann, K. (2015) *Driffield Terrace Web Report* York: York Archaeological Trust, available from: http://www.yorkarchaeology.co.uk/resources/finding-the-future/gladiators-2/

Hutton Estabrook, V. (2014) Violence and warfare in the European Palaeolithic and Mesolithic" in: Allen, M.W. and Jones, T.L. (eds) *Violence and Warfare among Hunter Gatherers* Walnut Creek (CA): Left Coast Press, 49–69.

Hyams, P. (2001) "Feud and the State in Late Anglo-Saxon England" *Journal of British Studies* 40, 1–43.

Indriati, E. and Antón, S.C. (2010) "The calvaria of Sangiran 38, Sendangbusik, Sangiran Dome, Java" *Homo* 61, 225–243.

Jackes, M. (2004) "Osteological evidence for Mesolithic and Neolithic Violence: problems of interpretation" in: Roksandic, M. (ed.) *Violent Interactions in the Mesolithic: Evidence and Meaning* British Archaeological Reports, International Series, 1237, Oxford: Archaeopress, 23–39.

James, S. (2011) "Stratagems, combat, and "chemical warfare" in the siege mines of Dura-Europos *American Journal of Archaeology* 115, 69–101.

Jankauskas, R. (2012) "Violence in the Stone Age from an eastern Baltic perspective" in: Schulting, R. and Fibiger, L. (eds) *Sticks, Stones and Broken Bones: Neolithic Violence in a European Perspective* Oxford: Oxford University, 35–50.

Jiménez-Brobeil, S.A., Roca, M.G., Laffranchi, Z., Nájera, T. and Molina, F. (2012) "Violence in the central Iberian Peninsula during the Bronze Age: a possible prehistoric homicide" *International Journal of Osteoarchaeology* 24: 649–659.

Jolly, C. (1972) "The classification and natural history of Theropithecus (Simopithecus) baboons of the African Plio-Pleistocene" *Bulletin of the British Museum, Natural History (Geology)* 22, 4–123.

Jones, A. (2008) *Prehistoric Europe: Theory and Practice* Chichester: Wiley-Blackwell.

Jones, C. (2011) *Finding Fulford: the Search for the First Battle of 1066* WPS www.writerprintshop.com.

Jones, D.E. (2004) *Native North American Armor, Shields, and Fortifications* Austin (TX): University of Texas.

Josephus *The Jewish War* (transl. G.A. Williamson) London: Penguin (1981).

Judd, M. (2008) "The parry problem" *Journal of Archaeological Science* 35, 1658–1666.

Kanz, F. and Grossschmidt, K. (2006) "Head injuries of Roman gladiators" *Forensic Science International* 160, 207–216.

Karsten, P. and Knarrström, B. (2003) "Tågerup: Fifteen hundred years of Mesolithic occupation in western Scania, Sweden: a preliminary view" *European Journal of Archaeology* 4, 165–174.

Keegan, J. (2010) *The American Civil War* London: Vintage.

Keeley, L.H (1996) *War Before Civilization: the Myth of the Peaceful Savage* Oxford: Oxford University.

Keen, M. (1984) *Chivalry* New Haven (CT): Yale University Press.

Keith, A. (1928) *The Antiquity of Man*. Philadelphia: Lippincott.

Kelly, R. (2000) *Warless Societies and the Origin of War* Ann Arbor (MI): University of Michigan.

Kenyon. K.M. (1953) "Excavations at Sutton Walls, Herefordshire, 1948–1951" *Archaeological Journal* 110, 1–87.

King, S. (2013) "Socialized violence: contextualizing violence through mortuary behaviour in Iron Age Britain" in: Knüsel, C., Smith, M.J. (eds) *The Routledge Handbook of the Bioarchaeology of Human Conflict* London: Routledge, 185–200.

Kingdon, J., Happold, D., Buttynski, M., Hoffmann, M., Happold, M. and Kalina, J. (eds) (2013) *Mammals of Africa, Volume II: Primates*. London: Bloomsbury.

Kjaerulff, H., Jacobsen, J., Aalund, O., Albrektsen, S.B., Breiting, V.B., Danielsen, L., Helweg-Larsen, K., Staugaard, H., Thomsen J.L. (1989) "Injuries due to deliberate violence in areas of Denmark. III. Lesions" *Forensic Science International* 41, 169–180.

Knüsel, C. (2000) "Activity-related skeletal change" in: Fiorato V., Boylston A. and Knüsel C. (eds) *Blood Red Roses* Oxbow Books: Oxford, 103–118.

Krause, J., Fu, Q., Good, J., Bence, V., Shunkov, M., Derevianko, A., and Pääbo, S. (2010), "The complete mitochondrial DNA genome of an unknown hominin from southern Siberia" *Nature* 464, 894–897.

Kremer, C., Racette, S., Dionne, C., and Sauvageau, A. (2008) "Discrimination of falls and blows in blunt head trauma: systematic study of the hat brim line rule in relation to skull fractures" *Journal of Forensic Sciences* 53, 716–719.

Kristiansen, K. and Suchowska-Ducke, P. (2015) "Connected histories: the dynamics of Bronze Age interaction and trade 1500–1100 BC" *Proceedings of the Prehistoric Society* 81, 361–392.

Lahr, M.M., Rivera, F., Power, R.K., Mounier, A., Copsey, B. (*et al.*) and Foley, R. (2016) "Inter-group violence among early holocene hunter-gatherers of West Turkana, Kenya" *Nature* 529, 394–398.

Lai, C-Q. (2006) "How much of human height is genetic and how much is due to nutrition?" *Scientific American* available from: http://www.scientificamerican.com/article/how-much-of-human-height/ (accessed Feb 2016).

Larsson, L. (1993) "The Skateholm Project: Late Mesolithic coastal settlement in Southern Sweden" in: Bogucki, P. (ed.) *Case Studies in European Prehistory* London: CRC, 31–62.

Leakey, M.G. (1993) "The evolution of Theropithecus in the Turkana basin" in: Jablonski, N. (ed.) *Theropithecus: the Rise and Fall of a Primate Genus* Cambridge: Cambridge University, 85–124.

Le Blanc, S.A. (2015) "Forager warfare and our evolutionary past" in: Allen, M.W. and Jones, T.L. (eds) *Violence and Warfare among Hunter Gatherers* Walnut Creek (CA): Left Coast Press, 26–46.

Lethbridge, T. (1936) "Further excavations in the Early Iron Age and Romano-British cemetery at Guilden Morden" *Proceedings of the Cambridge Antiquarian Society* 36, 109–120.

Lethbridge, T. and Palmer, W. (1929) "Excavations in the Cambridgeshire Dykes. Vi. Bran Ditch. Second Report" *Proceedings of the Cambridge Antiquarian Society* 30, 78–93.

Lewis, M. (2006) *The Bioarchaeology of Children: Perspectives from Biological and Forensic Anthropology* Cambridge: Cambridge University.

Lewis, M. (2008) "A traitor's death? The identity of a drawn, hanged and quartered man from Hulton Abbey, Staffordshire" *Antiquity* 82, 113–124.

Lillie, M. (2003) "Cranial surgery: the Epipalaeolithic to Neolithic populations of Ukraine" in: Arnott, R., Finger, S. and Smith, C. (eds) *Trepanation: History, Discovery, Theory* Lisse: Swets & Zeitlinger, 175–188.

Lillie, M. (2004) "Fighting for your life? Violence at the Late Glacial to Holocene transition in Ukraine" in: Roksandic, M. (ed.) *Violent Interactions in the Mesolithic: Evidence and Meaning* British Archaeological Reports, International Series, 1237, Oxford: Archaeopress, 89–97.

Livingstone-Smith, D. (2007) *The Most Dangerous Animal: Human Nature and the Origins of War* New York: St. Martin's Griffin.

Lockau, L., Dragomir, A.-M., Gilmour, R., Mant, M., Brickley, M. (2013) "Bioarchaeological investigation of sharp force injuries to the ribs and lower leg from the Battle of Stoney Creek in the War of 1812" *Anthropological Science* 121, 217–227.

Lockau, L., Gilmour, R., Menard, J-P, Balakrishnan, N., Dragomir, A-M., Mant, M., Watamaniuk, L. and Brickley, M.B. (2016) ""Buck and Ball': Identification and interpretation of buckshot injuries to the pelvis from the War of 1812" *Journal of Archaeological Science: Reports* 6, 424–433.

Loe, L. (2016) "Application of Scientific Techniques in Commercial Archaeology" spoken presentation: *Human Remains in Commercial Archaeology: Legal, Ethical and Curatorial Considerations* Historic England Heritage Practice Programme, Bristol.

Loe, L., Boyle, A., Webb, H. and Score, D. (2014) *Given to the Ground: A Viking Age Mass Grave on Ridgeway Hill, Dorset* Oxford: Dorset Natural History and Archaeology Society Monograph Series 22.

Mafart, B., Pelletier, J-P. and Fixot, M. (2004) "Post-mortem ablation of the heart: a Medieval funerary practice. a case observed at the cemetery of Ganagobie Priory in the French Department of Alpes De Haute Provence" *International Journal of Osteoarchaeology* 14, 67–73.

Mangel, M. and Samaniego, F. (1984) "Abraham Wald's work on aircraft survivability" *Journal of the American Statistical Association* 386, 259–267.

Marean, C. (2014) "The origins and significance of coastal resource use in Africa and Western Eurasia" *Journal of Human Evolution* 77, 17–40.

Maslen, M.W. and Mitchell, P.D. (2006) "Medical theories on the cause of death in crucifixion" *Journal of the Royal Society of Medicine* 99, 185–188.

Massagé, L. (2014) *Hit or Miss; an Experimental Approach towards Identifying Cannon-related Trauma in Skeletal Remains* unpublished MSc dissertation, Bournemouth University.

Matthews, C.L. (1981) "A Romano-British inhumation cemetery at Dunstable" *Bedfordshire Archaeological Journal* 15, 1–74.

Mays, S. (2010) *The Archaeology of Human Bones* London: Routledge.

McCown, T.D. and Keith, A. (1939) *The Stone Age of Mount Carmel, Vol. II* Oxford: Clarendon University Press.

McIntosh, J. (2006) *Handbook to Life in Prehistoric Europe* Oxford: Oxford University.

McKinley, J. (1997) *Sovell Down, Gussage-All Saints, Dorset: Human Bone Report* Salisbury: Wessex Archaeology (Unpublished).

McKinley, J. (2016) "Human Bone and Mortuary Deposits" in: Powell, A. and Barclay, A. (ed.) *Between and beyond the monuments: prehistoric activity on the downlands south-east of Amesbury* Salisbury: Wessex Archaeology Monograph.

McKinley, J., Schuster, J. and Millard, A. (2013) "Dead sea connections? A Bronze Age and Iron Age ritual site on the Isle of Thanet" in: Koch, J. and Cunliffe, B. (eds) *Celtic from the West 2: Rethinking the Bronze Age and the Arrival of Indo-European in Atlantic Europe* Oxford: Oxbow, 157–184.

McKeown, N. (2007) *The Invention of Ancient Slavery* London: Bristol Classical Press.

Meggitt, M. (1977) *Blood is Their Argument: Warfare Amongst the Mae Enga Tribesman of the New Guinea Highlands* Palo Alto (CA): Mayfield.

Meiklejohn, C., Merrett D.C., Nolan, R.W. Richards, M.P. and Mellars P.A. 2005. Spatial relationships, dating and taphonomy of the human bone from the Mesolithic site of Cnoc Coig, Oronsay, Argyll, Scotland *Proceedings of the Prehistoric Society* 71, 85–105.

Melton, N., Montgomery, J., Knüsel, C., Batt, C., Needham, S., Parker Pearson, M., Sheridan, A., Heron, C., Horsley, T., Schmidt, A., Evans, A., Carter, E., Edwards, H., Hargreaves, M., Janaway, R., Lynnerup, N., Northover, P., O'Connor, S., Ogden, A., Taylor, T., Wastling, V. and Wilson, A. (2009) "Gristhorpe Man: an Early Bronze Age log-coffin burial scientifically defined" *Antiquity* 84, 796–815.

Melton, N., Montgomery, J. and Knüsel, C. (eds) (2013) *Gristhorpe Man: a Life and Death in the Bronze Age* Oxford: Oxbow.

Mercer, R. (1999) "The origins of warfare in the British Isles" in: Carman, J. and Harding, A. (eds) *Ancient Warfare* Stroud: Sutton Publishing, 143–156.

Méténier, F. (2014) *Une Nécropole Antique dans le Quartier Périphérique Occidental de la Ville de Saintes: Plusieurs Individus Entravés, Dont un Enfant* Viennes, Poitou Charentes: INRAP.

Meyer, C., Lohr, C., Gronenborn, D. and Alt, K. (2015) "The massacre at Schöneck-Kilianstädten reveals new insights into collective violence in Early Neolithic central Europe" *Proceedings of the National Academy of Sciences* 112, 11,217–11,222.

Mitchell, P., Hui-Yuan, Y., Appleby, J. and Buckley, R. (2013) "The intestinal parasites of King Richard III" *The Lancet* 382, 888.

Mithen, S. (1998) *The Prehistory of the Mind: a Search for the Origins of Art, Science and Religion* London: Orion.

Mithen, S. (2003) *After the Ice: A Global Human History 20,000–5000BC* London: Phoenix.

Moghaddama, N., Mailler-Burcha, S., Karab, L., Kanzd, F., Jackowskib, C. and Löscha, S. (2015) "Survival after trepanation – Early cranial surgery from Late Iron Age Switzerland" *International Journal of Osteoarchaeology* 11, 56–65.

Müldner, G. (2011) "The 'Headless Romans': Multi-isotope investigations of an unusual burial ground from Roman Britain" *Journal of Archaeological Science* 38, 280–290.

Mullins M. and Skinner J. (2007) "Biomechanics and joint replacement of the hip" in: Ramachandaran, M. (ed.) *Basic Orthopaedic Sciences: The Stanmore Guide* London: Hodder Arnold, 164–169.

Murphy, W., zur Nedden, D., Gostner, P., Knapp, R., Recheis, W. and Seidler, H. (2003) "The Iceman: Discovery and Imaging" *Radiology* 226, 614–629.

Museum Skanderborg "Alken Enge – The mass grave at Lake Mossø" available from: http://www.museumskanderborg.dk/Alken_Enge-English_version-1070.aspx (accessed March 2016).

Needham, S., Kenny, J., Cole, G., Montgomery, J., Jay, M., Davis, M. and Marshall, P. (forthcoming) "Death by combat at the dawn of the Bronze Age? Profiling the dagger-grave from Racton, West Sussex" *Antiquaries Journal*.

Neillands, R. (1990) *The Hundred Years War* London: Routledge.

Noback, M.L., Samo, E., van Leeuwen, C., Lynnerup, N. and Harvati, K. (2016) "Paranasal sinuses: A problematic proxy for climate adaptation in Neanderthals" *Journal of Human Evolution* 97, 176–179.

Novak, S. and Knüsel, C. (1997) "Comment on Mallegni and Valassina's secondary bone changes to a cranium trepanation in a Neolithic Man discovered at Trasano, South Italy" *International Journal of Osteoarchaeology* 7, 555–557.

Oakeshott, E. (2000) *European Weapons and Armour* Woodbridge: The Boydell Press.

Orschiedt, J. (2005) "The head burials from Ofnet cave: an example of warlike conflict in the Mesolithic" in: Parker Pearson, M. and Thorpe, I.J.N. (eds) *Warfare, Violence and Slavery in Prehistory: Proceedings of a Prehistoric Society conference at Sheffield University* British Archaeological Reports, International Series 1374, Oxford: Archaeopress, 67–73.

Ortner, D. (2003) *Identification of Pathological Conditions in Human Skeletal Remains* London: Academic Press.

Osgood, R. (2005) *The Unknown Warrior* Stroud: Sutton Publishing.

Osgood, R. (2006) "The dead of Tormarton: Bronze Age combat victims?" in: Otto, T., Thrane, H. and Vandkilde, H. (eds) *Warfare and Society: Archaeological and Social Anthropological Perspectives* Aarhus: Aarhus University Press, 331–340.

Osgood, R., Monks, S. and Toms, J. (2010) *Bronze Age Warfare* Stroud: The History Press.

Otterbein, K.F. (1979) "Huron vs. Iroquois: A Case Study in Inter-Tribal Warfare" *Ethnohistory*, 26, 141–152.

Papathanasiou, A. (2012) "Evidence of trauma in Neolithic Greece" in: Schulting, R. and Fibiger, L. (eds) *Sticks, Stones and Broken Bones: Neolithic Violence in a European Perspective* Oxford: Oxford University, 249–263.

Pardoe, C. (2015) "Conflict and territoriality in Aboriginal Australia: evidence from biology and ethnography" in: Allen, M.W. and Jones, T.L. (eds) *Violence and Warfare among Hunter Gatherers* Walnut Creek (CA): Left Coast Press, 112–132.

Parkman, F. (1885) *Historic Handbook of the Northern Tour. Lakes George and Champlain; Niagara; Montreal; Quebec* Boston: Little, Brown and Co.

Patrick, P. (2006) "Approaches to violent death: a case study from Early Medieval Cambridge" *International Journal of Osteoarchaeology* 16, 347–354.

Péquart, M., Péquart, St-J., Boule, M. and Vallois, H. (1937) *Téviec. Station-nécropole Mésolithique du Morbihan* Archives de l'Institut de Paléontologie Humaine. Mémoire 18, Paris: Masson et Cie.

Pickstone, R. and Mortimer M. *et al.* (2012) "War Ditches, Cherry Hinton: Revisiting an Iron Age Hillfort" *Proceedings of the Cambridge Antiquarian Society*, 101, 31–61.

Piggott, S. (1940) "A trepanned skull of the Beaker Period from Dorset and the practice of trepanning in Prehistoric Europe" *Proceedings of the Prehistoric Society* 6, 112–132.

Piggott, S. (1954) *Neolithic Cultures of the British Isles: A Study of the Stone-using Agricultural Communities of Britain in the Second Millennium BC* Cambridge: Cambridge University.

Pinker, S.A. (2011) *The Better Angels of our Nature: a History of Violence and Humanity* London: Penguin Books.

Pitts, M., Bayliss, A., McKinley, J., Boylston, A., Budd, P., Evans, J., Chenery, C., Reynolds, A. and Semple, S.J. (2002) "An Anglo-Saxon decapitation and burial at Stonehenge" *Wiltshire Archaeological and Natural History Magazine* 95, 131–146.

Plummer, T.W., Ditchfield, P.W., Bishop, L.C., Kingston, J.D., Ferraro, J.V., Brown, D.R., Hertzel, F. and Potts, R. (2009) "Oldest evidence of toolmaking hominins in a grassland-dominated ecosystem" *PLoS ONE* 4: e7199.

Poliakoff, M.B. (1995) *Combat Sports in the Ancient World: Competition, Violence and Culture* New Haven: Yale University.

Pollard, A., Ditchfield, P., Piva, E., Wallis, S., Falys, C. and Ford, S. (2012) "'Sprouting like cockle amongst the wheat': the St Brice's Day Massacre and the isotopic analysis of human bones from St John's College, Oxford" *Oxford Journal of Archaeology* 31, 83–102.

Polydore Vergil (1555 version) *Anglica Historia* (transl. D.F. Sutton) Irvine: University of California (2005).

Prestwich, M. (1997) *Edward I* London: Yale University Press.

Prüfer, K., Munsch, M., Hellmann, I. *et al.* (2012) "The bonobo genome compared with the chimpanzee and human genomes" *Science* 486, 527–531.

Radovčić, D., Oros Sršen, A., Radovčić, J. and Frayer, D.W. (2015) "Evidence for Neanderthal jewelry: modified white-tailed eagle claws at Krapina" *PLoS One*, 10, e0119802. doi:10.1371/journal.pone.0119802.

Rathbun, T. (1987) "Health and Disease at a South Carolina Plantation: 1840–1870" *American Journal of Physical Anthropology* 74, 239–253.

Razavi, S. (2013) "Households, Families, and Social Reproduction" in: Waylen, G., Celis, K., Kantola, J. and Weldon, S. (ed.) *The Oxford Handbook of Gender* Politics Oxford: Oxford University, 289–312.

Redfern, R.C. (2009) "Does cranial trauma provide evidence for projectile weaponry in Late Iron Age Dorset?" *Oxford Journal of Archaeology* 28, 399–424.

Redfern, R.C. (2011) "A re-appraisal of the evidence for violence in the Late Iron Age human remains from Maiden Castle hillfort, Dorset, England" *Proceedings of the Prehistoric Society* 77, 111–138.

Redfern, R.C. and Bonney, H. (2014) "Headhunting and amphitheatre combat in Roman London, England: new evidence from the Walbrook Valley" *Journal of Archaeological Science* 43, 214–226.

Redfern, R.C. and Chamberlain, A.T. (2011) "A demographic analysis of Maiden Castle hillfort: evidence for conflict in the late Iron Age and early Roman period" *American Journal of Palaeopathology* 1, 68–73.

Regan, J.R., Shahlaie, K. and Watson, J.C. (2013) "Crucifixion and median neuropathy" *Brain and Behavior* 3, 243–248.

Reijnders, U. and Ceelen, M. (2014) "7208 Victims of domestic and public violence; an exploratory study based on the reports of assaulted individuals reporting to the police" *Journal of Forensic and Legal Medicine*, 24, 18–23.

Rex, P. (2004) *The English Resistance: The Underground War Against the Normans* Stroud: Tempus.

Reynolds, A. (1997) "The definition and ideology of Anglo Saxon execution sites and cemeteries" in: De Boe, G. and Verhaege, F. (eds) *Death and Burial in Medieval* Europe Zellick: I.A.P. Rapporten, 33–41.

Richards, J.D. (2003) "Pagans and Christians at the frontier: Viking burial in the Danelaw" in: Carver, M. (ed.) *The Cross Goes North: Processes of Conversion in Northern Europe, AD 300–1300* York: York Medieval Press, 383–395.

Ridley, M. (1993) *The Red Queen: Sex and the Evolution of Human Nature* London: Penguin.

Robb, J. (1997) "Violence and gender in early Italy" in: Martin, D.L. and Frayer, D.W. (eds) *Troubled Times: Violence and Warfare in the Past* Amsterdam: Gordon and Breach, 111–144.

Robb, J. (2008) "Meaningless violence and the lived body: the Huron-Jesuit collision of world orders" in: Borić, D. and Robb, J. (eds) *Past Bodies: Body-Centred Research in Archaeology* Oxford: Oxbow, 89–99.

Robb, J. and Harris, O. (2013) *The Body in History: Europe from the Palaeolithic to the Future* Cambridge: Cambridge University.

Roberts, C. (2009) *Human Remains in Archaeology: a Handbook* York: CBA.

Roberts, C. and Cox, M. (2003) *Health and Disease in Britain* Stroud: Sutton Publishing.

Roberts C. and Manchester M. (2010) *The Archaeology of Disease* Stroud: The History Press.

Roberts, C. and McKinley, J. (2003) "Review of trepanations in British antiquity focusing on funerary context to explain their occurrence" in: Arnott, R., Finger, S. and Smith, C. (eds) *Trepanation: History, Discovery, Theory* Lisse: Swets & Zeitlinger, 55–78.

Roberts, N., Brown, J., Hammett, B. and Kingston, P. (2008) "A detailed study of the effectiveness and capabilities of 18th century musketry on the battlefield" in: Pollard, T. and Banks, I. (eds) *Bastions and Barbed Wire: Studies in the Archaeology of Conflict* Leiden: Koninklijke Brill, 1–22.

Roksandic, M., Djurić, M., Rakoč, Z. and Seguin, K. (2006) "Interpersonal Violence at Lepenski Vir Mesolithic/Neolithic Complex of the Iron Gates Gorge (Serbia-Romania)" *American Journal of Physical Anthropology* 129, 339–348.

Romandini, M., Peresani, M., Laroulandie, V., Metz, L., Pastoors, A., Vaquero, M. and Slimak, L. (2014) "Convergent evidence of eagle talons used by late Neanderthals in Europe: a further assessment on symbolism" *PloS One* 9, e101278.

Roper, M. (1969) "A survey of the evidence for intrahuman killing in the Pleistocene" *Current Anthropology* 10, 427–459.

Roscoe, P. (2015) "Foragers and war in contact-era New Guinea" in: Allen, M.W. and Jones, T.L. (eds) *Violence and Warfare among Hunter Gatherers* Walnut Creek (CA): Left Coast Press, 223–240.

Rost, A. and Wilbers-Rost, S. (2010) "Weapons at the battlefield of Kalkriese" *Gladius* 30, 117–136.

Rundin, J. (1996) "A Politics of Eating: Feasting in Early Greek Society" *American Journal of Philology* 117, 179–215.

Russell, M., Cheetham, P., Evans, D., Hambleton, E., Hewitt, I., Manley, H. and Smith, M. (2014) "The Durotriges Project, Phase One: An Interim Statement" *Proceedings of the Dorset Natural History & Archaeological Society* 135, 217–221.

Sala, N., Arsuaga, J.L., Pantoja-Pérez, A., Pablos, A., Martínez, I., Quam, R.M., Gómez-Olivencia, A., María Bermúdez de Castro, J. and Carbonell, E. (2015) "Lethal Interpersonal Violence in the Middle Pleistocene" *PLoS One* 10(5): e0126589.

Sainero, R. (2003) "The Greek influence on primitive Irish literature" *Brazilian Journal of Irish Studies* 5, 99–104.

Sankararaman, S., Patterson, N., Li, H., Pääbo, S. and Reich, D. (2012) "The Date of Interbreeding between Neanderthals and Modern Humans" *PLoSOne* 8, 1–9.

Saoût, V., Gambart, G., Leguay, D., Ferrapie, A.-L., Launay, C. and Richard, I. (2011) "Aggressive behavior after traumatic brain injury" *Annals of Physical and Rehabilitation Medicine* 54, 259–269.

ScienceNordic (2012) "An entire army sacrificed in a bog" available from: www.sciencenordic.com (accessed March 2016).

Schmidt, R.R. (1913) *Die Altsteinzeitlichen Schädelgraber der Ofnet und der Bestattungsritus der Divialzeit* Stuttgart: E. Schweizerbartsche.

Schmidt, C.W. and Symes, S.A. (2008) *The Analysis of Burned Human Remains* London: Elsevier.

Schulting, R. (2013) "'Tilbury Man': A Mesolithic Skeleton from the Lower Thames" *Proceedings of the Prehistoric Society* 79, 19–37.

Schulting, R. and Bradley, R. (2013) "'Of human remains and weapons in the neighbourhood of London': New AMS ^{14}C dates on Thames 'River Skulls' and their European context" *Archaeological Journal* 170, 130–177.

Schulting, R. and Fibiger, L. (eds) (2012) *Sticks, Stones and Broken Bones: Neolithic Violence in a European Perspective* Oxford: Oxford University.

Seaver, R. (1907) *Faithless Nelly Gray, a Pathetic Ballad Written by Thomas Hood* New York: Houghton Mifflin and Company.

Semple, S. (1998) "A fear of the past: the place of the prehistoric burial mound in the ideology of middle and later Anglo-Saxon England" *World Archaeology* 30, 109–126.

Sharples, N. (1991) *Maiden Castle. Excavations and Field Survey 1985–6* London: English Heritage

Shea, J.J. (2003) "Neandertals, competition, and the origin of modern human behaviour in the Levant" *Evolutionary Anthropology* 12, 173–187.

Sheldon, R.M. (2001) "Slaughter in the forest: Roman intelligence mistakes in Germany" *Small Wars & Insurgencies* 12, 1–38.

Shepherd, I. and Bruce, M. (1987) "Two beaker cists at Keabog, Pitdrichie, near Drumlithie, Kincardine and Deeside" *Proceedings of the Society of Antiquaries of Scotland* 117, 33–40.

Sherratt, E.S. (1990) "'Reading the texts': archaeology and the Homeric question" *Antiquity* 64, 807–824.

Shipman, P., Bosler, W. and Lee-Davis, K. (1981) "Butchering of giant geladas at an Acheulian site" *Current Anthropology* 22, 257–268.

Smith, M.J., Allen, M.J., Delbarre, G., Booth, T., Cheetham, P., Bailey, L., O'Malley, F., Parker Pearson· M. and Green, M. (2016) "Holding on to the past: southern British evidence for mummification and retention of the dead in the Chalcolithic and Bronze Age" *Journal of Archaeological Science Reports: Funerary Taphonomy Issue*.

Smith, M.J., Atkin, A. and Cutler, C. (in press) "An age old problem? Estimating the impact of dementia on past human populations" *Journal of Aging and Health*.

Smith, M.J. and Brickley, M.B. (2009) *People of the Long Barrows: Life, Death and Burial in the Earlier Neolithic* Stroud: The History Press.

Smith, M.J., Brickley, M.B. and Leach S.L. (2007) "Experimental evidence for lithic projectile injuries: Improving recognition of an under-recognised phenomenon" *Journal of Archaeological Science* 34, 540–553.

Smith, M.J., Brickley, M.B. and Leach, S. (2011) "A shot in the dark: interpreting evidence for prehistoric conflict". in: Saville, A. (ed.) *Flint and Stone in the Neolithic Period* Oxford: Oxbow Books.

Smith. M.J., James, S., Pover, T., Ball, N., Barnetson, V., Foster, B., Guy, C., Rickman, J. and Walton, V. (2015) "Fantastic Plastic? Experimental evaluation of polyurethane bone substitutes as proxies for human bone in trauma simulations" *Legal Medicine* 17, 427–435.

Smits, E. and van der Plicht, J. (2009) "Mesolithic and Neolithic human remains in the Netherlands: physical anthropological and stable isotope investigations" *Journal of Archaeology in the Low Countries* 5, 55–85.

Spindler, K. (2013) *The Man in the Ice* London: Phoenix.

Spinney, L. (2008) "Archaeology: The lost world" *Nature* 454, 151–153.

Stirland, A. (2005) *The Men of the Mary Rose: Raising the Dead* Stroud: The History Press.

Strabo *Geographica* Books III-V, Loeb Classical Library, Vol. II (transl. H. Jones) Harvard (MA): Harvard University (1923).

Stringer, C. (2012) "The status of *Homo heidelbergensis* (Schoetensack 1908)" *Evolutionary Anthropology* 21, 101–107.

Suetonius *The Twelve Caesars* (transl. R. Graves) London: Penguin (1989).

Sutherland, T. (2011) 'Guns at Towton' *Battlefield, The Magazine of the Battlefields Trust* 16, 13.

Tattersall, I. (2009) "Human origins: Out of Africa" *Proceedings of the National Academy of Sciences* 106, 16,018–16,021.

Teschler-Nicola, M. (ed.) (2006) *Early Modern Humans at the Moravian Gate: The Mladeč Caves and their Remains* New York: Springer.

Teschler-Nicola, M. (2012) "The Early Neolithic site Asparn/Schletz (Lower Austria): anthropological evidence of interpersonal violence" in: Schulting, R. and Fibiger, L. (eds) *Sticks, Stones and Broken Bones: Neolithic Violence in a European Perspective* Oxford: Oxford University.

Thompson, H. (1993) "Iron Age and Roman slave shackles" *Archaeological Journal* 150, 57–168.

Thordemann, B. (1939) *Armour from the Battle of Wisby, 1361* Stockholm: Almqvist and Wiksell.

Thorpe, I.J.N. (2000) "Fighting and feuding in Neolithic and Bronze Age Britain and Ireland" in: Otto, T., Thrane, H. and Vandkilde, H. (eds) *Warfare and Society: Archaeological and Social Anthropological Perspectives* Aarhus: Aarhus University Press, 141–165.

Tratman, E.K. (1975) "Problems of the 'Cheddar Man', Gough's Cave Somerset" *Proceedings of the University of Bristol Spelaeological Society* 14, 7–23.

Trigger, B. (2006) *A History of Archaeological Thought* Cambridge: Cambridge University.

Trinkaus, E. (2012) "Neanderthals, early modern humans, and rodeo riders" *Journal of Archaeological Science* 39, 3691–3693.

Trinkaus, E. and Buzhilova, A.P. (2012) "The death and burial of Sunghir 1" *International Journal of Osteoarchaeology* 22, 655–666.

Trinkaus, E. and Zimmerman, M. (1982) "Trauma among the Shanidar Neandertals" *American Journal of Physical Anthropology* 57, 61–76.

Ubelaker, D. and Rife, J. (2011) "Skeletal Analysis and Mortuary Practicein an Early Roman Chamber Tomb at Kenchreai, Greece" *International Journal of Ostearchaeology* 21, 1–18.

Udal, J. S. (1910) "The story of the Bettiscombe skull" *Proceedings of the Dorset Natural History and Archaeological Society* 31, 176–203.

Underdown, S. (2006) "A comparative approach to understanding Neanderthal trauma" *Periodicum Biologorum* 108, 485–493.

Waddington, C., Beswick, P., Brightman, J., Bronk Ramsey, C., Burn, A., Cook, G., Elliot, L., Gidney, L., Haddow, S., Hammon, A., Harrison, K., Mapplethorpe, K., Marshall, P., Meadows, J., Smalley, R., Thornton, A. and Longstone Local History Group (2012) "Excavations at Fin Cop, Derbyshire: An Iron Age Hillfort in Conflict?" *Archaeological Journal* 169, 159–236.

Wahl, J. and Trautmann, I. (2012) "The Neolithic massacre at Talheim: a pivotal find in conflict archaeology" in: Schulting, R. and Fibiger, L. (eds) *Sticks, Stones and Broken Bones: Neolithic Violence in a European Perspective* Oxford: Oxford University, 77–100.

Wald, A. (1980) *A Reprint of "A Method of Estimating Plane Vulnerability Based on Damage of Survivors"* Alexandria (VA): Center for Naval Analyses, VA Operations Evaluation Group.

Waldron, T. (2007) *Palaeoepidemiology: the Measure of Disease in the Human Past* London: Routledge.

Waldron, T. (2008) *Palaeopathology* Cambridge: Cambridge University.

Walker, P. (1997) "Wife beating, boxing and broken noses: skeletal evidence for the cultural patterning of violence" in: Martin, D.L. and Frayer, D.W. (eds) *Troubled Times: Violence and Warfare in the Past* Amsterdam: Gordon and Breach, 145–179.

Weber, J. and Czarnetzki, A. (2001) "Brief Communication: Neurotraumatological aspects of head injuries resulting from sharp and blunt force in the Early Medieval period of southwestern Germany" *American Journal of Physical Anthropology* 114, 352–356.

Wedel, V. L., and Galloway, A. (2013) *Broken Bones: Anthropological Analysis of Blunt Force Trauma* Springfield (IL): Charles C Thomas Publisher.

Wendorf, F. (1968) "Site 117: A Nubian final Paleolithic graveyard near Jebel Sahaba, Sudan" *The Prehistory of Nubia (Volume Two)*, Wendorf, F. (ed.) Dallas: Southern Methodist University Press, 954–995.

Wescott, D.J. (2013) "Biomechanics of bone trauma" in: Siegel, J.A. and Saukko, P.J. (eds) *Encyclopaedia of Forensic Sciences* Waltham (MA): Academic Press, 83–88.

Western, G. and Hurst, D. (2013) "Soft heads: Evidence of sexualized warfare during the Late Iron Age from Kemerton Camp, Bredon Hill" in: Knüsel, C., Smith, M.J. (eds) *The Routledge Handbook of the Bioarchaeology of Human Conflict* London: Routledge, 161–184.

Wheeler, R.E.M. (1943) *Maiden Castle, Dorset* Oxford: Research Report for the Committee of the Society of Antiquaries of London.

Wheeler, S., Williams, L., Beauchesne, B., and Dupras, T. (2013) "Shattered lives and broken childhoods: evidence of physical child abuse in ancient Egypt" *International Journal of Palaeopathology* 3, 71–82.

White, T.D., Black, M.T. and Folkens, P. (2011) *Human* Osteology Amsterdam: Elsevier Academic Press, 27.

Wild, E.M., Teschler-Nicola, M., Kutschera, W., Steier, P., Trinkaus, E. and Wanek, W. (2005) "Direct dating of Early Upper Palaeolithic human remains from Mladeč" *Nature* 435, 332–335.

Wild, E.M., Stadler, P., Häußer, A., Kutschera, W., Steier, P., Teschler-Nicola, M., Wahl, J. and Windl, H. (2004) "Neolithic massacres: local skirmishes or general warfare in Europe?" *Radiocarbon* 46, 377–385.

Wilkins, J., Schoville, B.J., Brown, K.S. and Chazan, M. (2012) "Evidence for Early Hafted Hunting Technology" *Science* 338, 942–946.

Williams, A. (1948) "Excavations in Barrow Hills Field, Radley, Berkshire, 1944" *Oxonensia* 13, 1–17.

Wolfe-Steadman, D. (2008) *Hard Evidence: Case Studies in Forensic Anthropology* London: Routledge.

Wolff, J. (1892) *Das Gesetz der Transformation der Knochen* Berlin: August Hirschwald.

Wood, J.W., Milner, J.R., Harpending, H.C. and Weiss, K.M. (1992) "The Osteological Paradox" *Current Anthropology* 33, 343–370.

Wrangham, R. W. (1999) "Evolution of Coalitionary Killing" *Yearbook of Physical Anthropology* 42, 1–30.

Wright, R. (2010) *Guide to Using the CRANID6 Programs CR6aIND: For Linear and Nearest Neighbours Discriminant Analysis* available at time of writing from: http://osteoware.si.edu/forum/osteoware-communityannouncements/cranid-richard-wright-0.

Wu, X.J., Schepartz, L.A., Liu, W. and Trinkaus, E. (2011) "Antemortem trauma and survival in the late Middle Pleistocene human cranium from Maba, South China" *Proceedings of the National Academy of Sciences* 108, 19558–19562.

Zollikoffer, C., Ponce de León, M.S., Vandermeersch, B. and Lévêque, F. (2002) "Evidence for interpersonal violence in the St. Césaire Neanderthal" *Proceedings of the National Academy of Sciences* 99, 6444–6448.

Index

Accidental injuries 17, 19, 26, 37, 39, 46, 242
Acklam 134
Aethelred, King 195, 197
Alemanni 199–200
Alfred, King of Wessex 187–191
Alken Enge 154
American Civil War 232–4
Amputation 38, 95–96, 232
Anglo-Saxon *see* Medieval – early
Antemortem trauma (definition) *see* Timing of injuries
Archaeology (development of) 9–11, 12, 45–6, 86–7, 103, 107–9, 129–32, 238–9
Armour 107, 162, 201, 204, 209–12, 218, 219, 230
Asparn Schletz 96–9, 101
Atapuerca 35–6
Australia 61–2

Barrow Hills 113
Battlefield archaeology ix, 140
Bavaria 199
Beaker 106–7, 110–13, 132
Belas Knap 90
Bergheim 95
Bevelling (internal/external) 23, 34, 36, 90–3, 119, 227
Bill, J.H. 30
Biological profiling (of skeletal remains)
    age-at-death estimation 6–7
    ancestry 7, 64, 130, 173, 226, 234
    sex determination 6
    stature estimation 7, 112–13
Biomechanics 13–15
Bipedalism 13, 31
Birmingham 239–42
Blood feud 184–5
Blunt force injuries *see* Trauma, blunt force
Bog bodies 153–4
Bone
    fracture mechanics 12–30, 232
    mechanical properties 3, 12–17
    structure
        gross 1–4, 13,

microscopic 1–4, 13–14, 25
survival (archaeological) 4–6, 7, 8, 9, 29–30, 84, 137, 206–8, 232–3
taphonomic damage 4, 19, 33, 34
    root etching 20
    scavenging (vertebrate) 4, 5, 33, 96, 154, 159, 165
Bonobo 32–3
Boxgrove 34
Boxing/fistfighting 17, 174, 181–3, 239–42
Brain injury *see* Head injuries/TBI
Bran Ditch 185
Bronze Age xiii, 65, 85, 105–28, 133, 245
Buckland 198
Burial practices 5, 37–8, 45, 52, 54, 69–70, 77, 86–7, 93, 95, 96, 109, 126, 134, 139, 166
Burton Fleming 135
Buttressing (skeletal) 15

Cannibalism 12, 102, 188
Cannon *see* Weapons – artillery
Care/compassion – evidence of 43–5
Carn Brea 98
Causewayed Enclosure 98
Cavalry *see* Horses
Celts 10, 129–34, 141, 192
Champlain, Samuel de 81–2, 102
Champions 127
Cherry Hinton 198
Child abuse 57, 60, 180
Children *see* Sub-adult remains
Chimpanzee 31–3, 36, 60, 65
Chivalry 201, 204, 218
Chopmarks 22
Clachaig 89
Clades Variana 159–60
Cliff's End Farm 118
Computerized tomography 15, 40, 56, 74, 236–7
Conflict Archaeology ix, 243
Cremation/Cremated/Burned bone 5, 87, 110, 116, 118, 146, 177, 197
Crickley Hill 98–9
Crucifixion 167–70

CT Scanning *see* Computerised tomography
Cutmarks 19–22, 33, 80, 95, 144, 155, 187, 214–17, 223

Dakleh Oasis 180
Danebury 136, 147, 153
Danelaw 187–91
Dating xiii
Decapitation 79–80, 95, 135–40, 151, 165, 166, 174, 185–7, 188–96, 213, 214–17, 232
Defensive injuries 15, 38, 64, 74, 77, 112, 122, 188–91, 193, 204
Denmark/Danes 206–12, *see also* Vikings
Despenser, Hugh 216
Dinnington 89
Disarticulation 5
Disease *see* Pathology (skeletal)
DNA 32–3, 48–9
Dolní Věstonice 53, 56
Domestic violence 56–7, 180, 238–43
Driffield Terrace 173–5
Dunstable 166
Dura Europos 160–3

Edward I/Edward II 216
Environmental evidence 101–2
Elder abuse 180–1
Ephesus 171–3
Ethnography/ethnohistory 60–3, 72, 81–2, 150
Excavation damage 20, 29–30
Exchange *see* Trade
Execution 117–18, 126, 139, 151, 165, 167–70, 185–7, 188–91, 192–6, 213, 214–17
Experimentation 42, 90–3, 109, 159, 222–3, 228–31, 234–8
Explosions *see* Trauma, blast injuries

Falls *see* Accidental injuries
Farming 15, 72–73, 77–8, 95, 100–1, 105
Feizor Nick Cave 93, 114–15
Fin Cop 141–4
First World War (1914–18) – *see* Great War
Fiskerton 134, 136
Fistfighting *see* Boxing/fistfighting
Flint *see* Stone
Forensics 18–19
Fortifications ix
  Neolithic 96–9, 101
  Bronze Age 121–2
  Iron Age 132, 136–51
  Roman 160–3
  Medieval (early) 196
  Medieval (high–late) 202

Fossil record 31, 33, 35–49
Fracture healing/healed injuries 25–9, 36, 40, 43–5, 77, 88–93, 110–13, 119–20, 121, 171, 174, 198–9, 202, 239–41
Fracture types
  Bennett's 174, 239–42
  boxer's 239–42
  Colles' 17, 121
  comminuted 90
  concentric (tertiary) 17, 24, 30, 73, 229–31, 234
  cranial *see* Skull/cranium
  depressed 19, 23, 24, 35, 36, 38, 39–40, 48, 53, 73, 74, 75, 88–93, 119–20, 239–42
  facial 15, 43
  fibular 17
  Le Fort 15, 30
  nasal 15, 17, 110, 112, 175, 181, 239–42
  parry 15, 38, 64, 74, 77
  radiating (secondary) 19, 24, 73, 229–31, 234
  rib 17, 113, 170, 174, 180, 242–3
  scapular 23, 34, 178–9
  secondary *see* radiating fracture
  skull/cranium (general) 17, 19, 23, 24, 26–8
  stellate *see* radiating fracture
  tertiary *see* concentric fracture
  see also Bone (fracture mechanics)
Franchthi Cave 73
Free riding 98
Fulford, Battle of 202–3
Funerary treatment *see* Burial practices

Gelada 34–5
Genetics *see* DNA
Glaciation 36, 69, 71
Gladiator/Gladiatorial shows 171–5
Gongehusvej 75
Grave goods 86, 90, 106–7, 177, 197
Great War (1914–1918) 246
Gristhorpe Man 112–13
Grosser Ofnet Cave 79–80, 96, 99–100
Grotte dei Fanciuli 57
Guilden Morden 166

Haemothorax *see* Pneumothorax
Ham Hill 135
Hambledon Hill 98, 101
Hardinxveld-de-Bruin 73
Hard-wiring (for group aggression) 32–3
Harrying of the North 203
Hat Brim Line 39, 120
Head injuries *see* Trauma
Healed injuries (to bone) *see* Fracture healing
Helmets 107–8, 132

Henriksholm/Bøgebakkken   74
Herding   85, 100–1, 106
Hillfort *see* Fortifications – Iron Age
Hobbes, Thomas   xi, 8–11, 32, 46, 104
Homo erectus   35–6
Horses   106, 133, 207–8
Hulton Abbey   214–217
Human nature   ix, xi, 248
Hunter-gatherers   15, 49, 60, 69–84, 85
Hunting   33–5, 37, 46, 48, 50–2, 55, 65–6, 71, 96, 99–101
Huron   81–2
Hyperprosociality   58–9

Ice Age *see* Glaciation
Ice Man   4, 115–16
Îlot de Boucheries   178
Inequality   100, 106–10, 177, 201–2, 242
Infection, of wounds   25, 26, 38, 57, 77, 88, 113, 119–20
Intracranial pressure (ICP) *see* Head injuries/TBI
Intraspecific killing   31–3
Ireland   200
Iron Age   127, 129–56, 245
Iron Gates Gorge   75
Iroquois   81–2
Ivar the Boneless   196–7

Java   36
Jebel Sahaba   63–5
Jesus Lane   166
Jomsborg   196
Juveniles *see* Sub-adult remains

Kalkriese   160
Keeley, Lawrence   11, 86
Kemmerton Camp   146–7
Knight   201
Krapina   38

La Téne   130–1
Le Fort, René   16
Lisieux   178
Littleton Drew   91
London   175
Long barrow   5, 11, 86, 89–91, 93, 95, 99–101, 186
Long Wittenham   135
Lubbock, John   85

Maiden Castle   98, 135, 136, 141, 147–50, 188–91
Malnutrition *see* Stress (biological)
Mary Rose   205

Massacre   64, 79–80, 83, 96–8, 99–100, 123, 146, 195, 197
Mass burial   79–80, 96–9, 125–6, 141–7, 154–6, 159–60, 160–3, 163–5, 177, 191–6, 197–8, 202, 203–5, 206–8, 209–12, 222
Material culture (of violence)   107–9
Medieval period (general)   22, 40, 91, 127, 221, 241
   Early   184–200, 246
   High–Late   201–20, 246
Mesolithic   xiii, 65, 69–84, 96, 99, 102, 105
Metallurgy (general)   86, 105–9, 133
Microscopy   20, 42, 53, 64, 93, 114, 206
Mladeč Caves   52–3
Montfort-sur-Lizier   54
Monuments (prehistoric)   86–7
Motilla del Azuer   121
Muge Valley   74
Mummification *see* Soft tissue preservation

'Nasty, brutish and short'   xi
Nataruk   83–84
Navarre   116
Neanderthals   31, 37–49
Neolithic   xiii, 5, 65, 72–3, 75, 77–8, 85–104, 105–6, 108, 109, 119, 188, 245, 248
Nether Swell   95
New bone   25–8,38
New Guinea   61
Noble Savage   xi, 37–49

Ofnet Cave *see* Grosser Ofnet Cave
Olduvai   35
Olorgesaillie   34–5
Orkney   89–90
Os Acromiale   205
Osteological paradox   9
Overkill   117
Oxford   197

Pacified past   11, 86
Palaeolithic   22, 73
   Lower   33, 34, 36
   Middle   37–49
   Upper   48–9, 50–68
Pastoralism *see* herding
Pathology (skeletal)   7–8, 9, 12
Penetrative Injuries *see* Trauma – penetrative injuries
Perimortem trauma (definition) *see* Timing of injuries
Pinker, Stephen   247
Pitdrichie   110–12
Pleistocene   36

Pneumothorax/haemothorax   42, 122
Polygamy/Polygyny   100
Post-Medieval Period   23, 221–43, 246
Postmortem damage (to bone)   12, 29–30
Poundbury   181
Primates   31–5
Punching *see* Boxing/fistfighting, *see also* Fracture
    types, boxer's fracture
Pygmy Chimpanzee *see* Bonobo

Qafzeh   53, 56

Race *see* Biological profiling, ancestry
Racton Man   112
Repton   196–7
Raiding   32, 49, 61, 64, 81–2, 98, 100–1, 103,
    187–96, 202
Richard III   218–20
Ritual killing/wounding   12, 97, 116–18, 126–8,
    139, 151–4, 214–17
Rock art   108, 127
Rodmarton   90
Roman Empire   10, 22, 104, 133, 141, 157–83,
    184–5, 192, 245
Rousseau, Jean-Jacques   xi, 8–11, 32, 46, 104, 244
Royal Armouries   23, 234–6

Sangiran   38
Sacrifice, human *see* Ritual killing
Saintes   177–8
Sandbjerget   206–8, 218–19
San Teodoro   57
Sarliéve-Grande-Halle   151
Scavenging (vertebrate) *see* Bone, taphonomy of
Schöneck-Kilianstädten   97–8
Sculptor's Cave   136, 153
Sedentism   78, 85
Shanidar   40–5
Sharp-force injuries *see* Trauma, sharp-force
    injuries
Shields   107–8, 132, 154, 162, 200
Sickles, General Dan   232–3
Skateholm   74
Skhul   53, 56
Slaves/slavery   152, 153, 171, 175–80, 245
Sling/slingstone *see* Weapons
Social substitutability   63, 66, 80, 98–9
Social reproduction   157–8
Soft tissue injury (where bone is unaffected)   30,
    88, 93, 112
Soft tissue preservation   4, 6, 153–4
Sovell Down   137–40
Spetisbury   147

Stable isotope analysis   113, 174, 186, 192, 195,
    197
Standlake   132
Stature *see* Biological profiling
St. Andrews, Fishergate   202–3, 212–18
St. Brice's Day Massacre   195, 197
St. Bride's   242
St. Césaire   40
St. John's College   197–8
St. Martin's-in-the-Bull Ring   239–42
Stepped trajectory model (of development of war)
    65–7, 244–5
Stone Age *see* Palaeolithic; Mesolithic; Neolithic
Stone implements
    arrowheads   54, 57, 64, 73, 74, 75, 83, 88, 90–3,
        96, 97–8, 102, 113–17, 125
    axe   40, 79–80, 88, 90, 93, 96, 97
    spear   34, 40, 42–3, 51, 61, 96
    tools   33, 50–1, 54, 70, 85, 95, 96
Stonehenge Archer   117–18, 186
Stoney Creek, Battle of   222–3
Strain (in relation to bone) *see* Stress/strain
Stress/strain (in relation to bone)   13
Stress (biological – malnutrition etc.)   123, 177,
    187
Structural violence   158, 176
Sub-adult remains   6–7, 56, 60, 79, 83, 90, 95,
    96–8, 101, 118, 121, 123, 143, 146, 163, 173,
    177, 179, 180
Subperiosteal new bone *see* New bone
Sund   122–3
Sunghir   53–4
Surgery   119–20
Sutton Walls   163–5

Tågerup   75
Talheim   97–9, 101
Taphonomy *see* Bone, taphonomy of
Temporal frontier   65–8
Temporary cavitation   24, 229–31, 236–7
Téviec   70, 73
Thames (river)   126, 132, 154
Thurnam, John   10
Tilbury Man   73
Timing of injuries   29–30
Toldnes   123
Tollense Valley   125–7
Tormarton   123–5
Torture   97
Towton, Battle of   23, 203–9, 212, 218–19
Trade   10, 106–7, 131–3
Trampling   19

Trauma (skeletal)
  ballistic injuries   23–5, 26, 30, 42–3, 54, 57, 64, 73, 74, 83, 88, 90–3, 202, 204–5, 212
  blast injuries   247
  blunt-force injuries   19, 25, 38–40, 43–5, 53, 62, 73, 74, 75, 83, 88–93, 97, 113, 121–2, 126, 135, 146, 148, 154, 171–2, 199, 204
  facial   15–16, 17
  general   12–30
  hacking   22, 146, 214
  head injuries (general)/TBI   17–18, 24, 26–8, 39, 43–5, 56, 88, 119–20, 206
  penetrative injuries   22–3, 24, 26, 34, 36, 90–3, 122, 123–4, 135, 148, 154, 165, 171–2, 196, 204, 212, 219
  projectile injuries *see* ballistic injuries
  sharp-force injuries   19–22, 40, 42, 110–113, 118, 121–2, 123, 126, 134, 139, 146, 148, 154, 165, 171, 174, 188–91, 192–6, 198–9, 202, 204, 206–8, 212–18, 219, 222–3, 224–6, 239
  stab wounds *see* penetrative injuries
  Traumatic Brain Injury (TBI) *see* Head injuries
Trepanation   119–20, 199
Trial by Battle/Combat   188–91, 212–18
Trophy-taking   80, 82–3, 95–6, 102, 135–40, 175
Twentieth Century   246–8

Upper Palaeolithic Revolution   51–2, 66
Urban violence   181–3, 238–43

Vaison la Romaine   178
Varian Disaster *see Clades Variana*
Vikings   187–98
Visby, Battle of   209–12, 218–19
Voloshkoe   54

Waddon Skull   224–6
Wagner, Battery/Fort   234
Wald, Abraham   208–9, 212
Walkington Wold   186–7
War
  definitions of   62–3

origins of   32–3, 36, 48, 57–68, 98–104, 107–9, 244–5
War Ditches   144–6
War of 1812   222–3
Wars of the Roses   23, 203–5
Wealth *see* Inequality
Weapons   ix, 33, 86, 95, 107, 244
  arrows/archery   23–4, 30, 54, 57, 64, 73, 74, 75, 83, 88, 90–3, 97–8, 102, 106, 113–17, 125, 202, 204–5, 212
  artillery   149, 151, 222, 232–8
  axe   22, 79–80, 88, 90, 96, 97, 116, 122, 198, 212
  ballista bolt   149
  bayonet   22, 222–3
  bow   23–4
  club   35, 38, 39–40, 73, 90, 96, 97, 122
  dagger   106, 112, 122, 134, 219
  firearms   23–4, 221, 223–31
  lance *see* spear
  mace   22, 204
  polearm (various)   204–5, 219
  sling/slingstones   23, 90, 96, 147
  spear   22, 33, 37, 40, 42–3, 51, 54, 61, 112, 122, 123–4, 135, 147, 148, 149, 172
  sword   23, 95, 107, 108, 118, 123, 132, 134, 136, 147, 154, 162, 186, 188–91, 192–6, 198, 200, 204, 206–8, 212, 219, 224–6, 239
West Ridge   113
West Tump   91
Wetwang Slack   135
Weymouth   191–6
Wheeler, Sir Mortimer   141, 147–9, 188, 192
Windeby   153
Winterbourne Kingston   133, 135, 151–2, 179
Woven bone *see* New bone
Written sources   ix, 103–4, 127, 129–30, 134, 158, 167–70, 176, 181, 185, 191, 195, 201, 203–4, 218, 219, 232, 246
Wolff, Julius *see* Wolff's Law
Wolff's Law   1

York   173–5, 202–3